Digital Presences of Organizations

SCIENCES

Computer Science, Field Directors –
Valérie Berthé and Jean-Charles Pomerol

Digital Documentation, Subject Head – Fabrice Papy

Digital Presences of Organizations

Coordinated by
Nathalie Pinède
Luc Massou
Patrick Mpondo-Dicka

ISTE

WILEY

First published 2024 in Great Britain and the United States by ISTE Ltd and John Wiley & Sons, Inc.

ISTE Ltd
27-37 St George's Road
London SW19 4EU
UK

www.iste.co.uk

John Wiley & Sons, Inc.
111 River Street
Hoboken, NJ 07030
USA

www.wiley.com

Library of Congress Control Number: 2023938465

British Library Cataloguing-in-Publication Data
A CIP record for this book is available from the British Library
ISBN 978-1-78945-104-7

ERC code:
PE6 Computer Science and Informatics
PE6_10 Web and information systems, database systems, information retrieval and digital libraries, data fusion
SH3 The Social World, Diversity, Population
SH3_13 Digital social research

Contents

Foreword

Peter Stockinger
INALCO, Plidam, Paris, France

It gives me particular pleasure to introduce this collection of texts entitled *Digital Presences of Organizations*. As its scientific publishers, Nathalie Pinède, Luc Massou and Patrick Mpondo-Dicka rightly point out the digital challenge is without a doubt one of the major issues in the communication of today's organizations.

We should bear in mind that one of the distinctive elements of the communication of organizations – compared to other communication ecosystems – is the fact that it is built around an institutional actor called an "organization" which, in order to deliver on its missions, has to build and maintain (beneficial) relationships with a greater or lesser diversity of collective and individual actors. The social organization in the sense of a collective institutional actor constitutes a very particular kind of social actor. This type of social actor is characterized by the coming together of a group of individuals who occupy specific functions in order to achieve common (and pre-defined) objectives. Typical examples of an institutional actor are companies, local authorities, associations and NGOs (non-governmental organizations), political organizations, educational and research establishments or heritage institutions such as museums, archives and libraries.

A social organization is an actor in its own right whose voice cannot be reduced either to the voice of one individual actor who is a member of it or to all the combined voices of the actors who constitute it. As an actor in its own right, a social organization finds itself faced with missions and tasks that it must or is supposed to fulfill in a given social environment in which it spreads and evolves.

Digital Presences of Organizations,
coordinated by Nathalie Pinède, Luc Massou and Patrick Mpondo-Dicka.

One of the main issues which is revisited on a regular basis by almost all the experts in this field of specialized communication is that of creating, then maintaining and furthering, through the widest possible variety of activities and communication campaigns, a certain vision of a social organization (such as a company or a university), of its missions and activities, its service and products, the communities of actors with whom it maintains a relationship. In other words, the issue here is to maintain and (above all) to gain acceptance of a world of images that is used as a theatrical stage, as a simulation space for the world of life (personal, everyday, professional, etc.) in which the diversity of actors evolves and shapes itself into a community of stakeholders (agonistic or antagonistic) around a social organization.

This world of images (or of the imagination) can be closer to or further from the world of life, the world as it is lived by the actors involved; it can also break away from it and offer a more or less probable fictitious world. Nevertheless, this world of images (or of the imagination) is a world that offers a certain meaning, whose interest, so to speak, lies in the fact of being potentially able to serve as a benchmark for the diversity of actors involved in the maneuverings and service delivery of an organization (such as a company, a university or an association). To "make sense" actually means to have a value, a quality that responds to a need, an interest or a wish of the actors concerned. This is how we assess the intellectual, emotional, practical and utilitarian or even moral value of an object, a person, an activity, a place, etc.

As a shared meaning, the world of images (or of the imagination) that is built, disseminated and which gradually gains acceptance (with a greater or lesser number of clashes) through an organization's diverse activities and communication campaigns, becomes a *topos*, a common place that is shared by the diversity of actors with whom the social organization forms a community.

To become an epistemic landmark – and thus also to become a kind of norm, a maxim – it is not enough for the imaginary world constructed by and disseminated through the diverse activities and communication campaigns to be known and understood by the diversities of the actors concerned. It must also be accepted and thus (tacitly or explicitly) adopted by the actors concerned. Thus, the world of images or the imagination that the organization's communication activities are supposed to produce and maintain claims the status of a standard, the status of a culture, of a cultural framework offering a greater or smaller population of individuals an identity, values and also resources (cognitive and practical). Reference to a cultural framework such as this not only provides an identity (a "social face", as Erving Goffman says) to an individual (precisely by assigning them an actor's role) but also allows them to respond to a set of problems (which they can regard as having greater or lesser significance) that they encounter in their world of life.

"Claim" means in fact that the status of standard is not already established. It has to be acquired, often in the face of a diversity of voices that are pursuing objectives different from those that define the communication activities of an organization. It must also be acted upon by the interested parties themselves, in other words, by the actors who are the stakeholders. Sometimes these are the potential beneficiaries of a service announced by an organization, sometimes they are partners, sometimes they are groups of actors who can influence the very destiny of an organization, sometimes again there is a whole panoply of actors who wish to compete with the maneuverings of an organization or who, in one way or another, quite simply wish for its demise.

Finding a way through this diversity and this cacophony of voices, each having its own weight, its own audience, in order to win acceptance of a certain vision as a standard, as a cultural reference, is, as we know, a very arduous and difficult task. In any case, this is the great challenge of what in English we call *branding*, in the sense of a technique, or rather, a whole diversity of (communication) techniques for creating, for gaining acceptance of and maintaining – through the creation of many messages about an object, a particular field of expertise – an imaginary world in which, as we might say, the various actors involved gather together, "see each other", for the widest possible variety of reasons.

The process of creating these messages consists of various steps, among which we include those of their localization (in a given environment), their conceptual design, their expression and embodiment in the diverse formats, instruments and media devices, their dissemination and circulation, their appropriation and exploitation and, finally, their actual evaluation. The overall objective of all these steps is to produce important information, information that has a value for the actor or the community of actors concerned in the form of varied and multimodal messages, messages that can be appreciated, experienced and exploited using very diverse media techniques.

Understood as one of the constituent media of the communication ecosystem of organizations, the website in particular and the digital medium in general play here, of course, an absolutely decisive role. The contributions in this collection offer us a very rich panorama of this.

Introduction

Nathalie PINÈDE[1], Luc MASSOU[2] and Patrick MPONDO-DICKA[3]

[1] *MICA, Université Bordeaux Montaigne, Pessac, France*

[2] *Crem, Université de Lorraine, Metz, France*

[3] *LERASS, Université Toulouse 2 – Jean-Jaurès, France*

I.1. Websites and digital presences of organizations

This book concludes a trilogy devoted to the study of websites[1] and more generally of digital info-communicational devices from a number of perspectives (epistemological, methodological and pedagogical, in particular). This book is a result of a cycle of study days, initiated in 2015 by Patrick Mpondo-Dicka at the University of Toulouse 2 – Jean-Jaurès, around a somewhat provocative question: Is website analysis still relevant from an info-communicational point of view? The debates from this study day had then been considered sufficiently fascinating, relevant and topical for a small group of researchers (Luc Massou, Patrick Mpondo-Dicka, Nathalie Pinède, Sébastien Rouquette and Peter Stockinger) to take up this issue and give it life through a series of study days dedicated to the subject. Thus, four other days were organized between 2017 and 2021, each presenting one particular angle of questioning arising from this website "object": the websites of organizations at the heart of plural digital dynamics (Bordeaux Montaigne University, 2017), the website in the new ecosystems of multi-cultural and intercultural communication (National Institute of Oriental Languages and

1 A first collective book, *Site internet : audit et stratégie* (edited by Sébastien Rouquette), was published by Boeck in 2017. A second collective book, entitled *Analyzing Websites* (edited by Luc Massou, Patrick Mpondo-Dicka and Nathalie Pinède) was published by ISTE – Wiley in January 2024.

Civilizations, 2018), audience representations and the practices of Internet users (Clermont Auvergne University, 2019) and finally the communication of organizations and online storytelling (University of Lorraine, 2021).

This book, prefaced by Peter Stockinger, thus completes the showcasing of the main contributions that emerged from this cycle of five study days, and brings together 23 authors around one main hub, that of the communication of organizations (companies, communities, NGOs, etc.), in the light of websites and, more broadly, digital ecosystems orchestrating differentiated strategies, themselves inscribed in a heterogeneous and complex multicultural space.

The concept of "digital presence" for organizations, chosen as the generic title of this book, testifies to the extension of our consideration of organizational communication in digital environments. Merzeau (2014) emphasizes the intrinsically temporal character of online presence, as a "form of existence in a space". To this temporal dimension must be added a mode of existence, between representation and intervention (Rieder 2010). The digital presence of an organization is not confined to what it produces and controls in terms of discourse, rhetoric and narrative. By revealing a certain representation of its identity on the Web, it offers this up to be read but also to be rewritten, whether by its users, customers or by forms of algorithmic calculations of the traces produced by and around the organization. Therefore, if "institutions and organizations try to define themselves as stable entities with boundaries permitting a certain control of their image" (Le Béchec and Alloing 2016), this perimeter is constantly pushed back, redefined, its contours evolving all the time, the conditions of digital presence being constantly subjected to reinterpretation. Pélissier (2018) suggests defining the digital presence of an organization "as a system introduced into digital devices, formed from the traces of interactions between identity construction and reputation processing. […] The digital presence of an organization is thus evolutive, changing, corresponds to voluntary or involuntary traces and can be observed at least in part" (p. 112). We find in this definition the ingredients of the digital presence mentioned above, between dynamics, the construction of a mediated ethos and the unpredictable reuse of an interweaving of ephemeral and shifting traces. As a result, we cannot capture the totality of this digital presence and we are condemned to grasp only fragments, incomplete snapshots, inscribed in a given space-time.

If we return to our main topic, namely the role and legitimacy of websites through the prism of the digital presence of organizations, the website embodies one of the facets of the organization's online presence, relatively stable in the register of inscription, but also a springboard to other spaces and always (re)negotiable when put into operation and calculated. The various contributions in this book propose, although with no claims to be exhaustive or able to explore every dimension, various levels of reading of this digital presence of organizations, for example, by updating the links that are forged between anchorage and flow or between representation and intervention, mobilizing and re-examining the concept of media ethos, analyzing the narrative logics and the reappropriations that are made of them, etc. The whole thus contributes to setting out a multifaceted and multi-strategic vision of the digital presences of organizations.

This work is structured on three major thematic axes built around 12 chapters. In the first part, we will look at the different strategies (content, services, territorialization) identified in various organizational contexts with various audiences. In the second part, the focus will be more specifically on the cultural dimension of websites, raising the issue of a digital organizational communication that oscillates between local and global. Finally, in the third part, we will pay particular attention to the role of storytelling and narratives in organizations' online communication strategies.

I.2. Websites and organizational strategies

Between stability and dynamics, websites enroll organizations in a complex digital environment where their presence and their identity are constantly redrawn, according to practices, from being put into symbolic circulation but also from the logics of economic and technical development of the Web. This is highlighted by Mariannig Le Béchec through the concept of circulating entities, the symbolic signs transmitted by websites and put into circulation in a changing digital environment. This dynamic of transposition of signs, which the author describes as "agency", thus contributes to modeling digital territories, in which the major challenge faced by organizations will be to control the circulation of their brands.

This link that is forged between statics and dynamics around websites is also highlighted by Stela Raytcheva, Thierry Côme and Gilles Rouet, who apply it through their approach to strategies for stabilizing a company culture. They use a processual reading of corporate culture through discursive strategies that can be identified in the communication narratives produced by an organization (in this case Danone) on its institutional website and Facebook pages. This discursive analysis thus operates at two levels: identifying the company's values in the communication texts produced (static level) and analyzing the discursive sequencing and interweaving of the texts produced by the organization on social media (dynamic level). By adopting a dual perspective, semiotic and material, the communicational texts are analyzed in themselves but also at the heart of a set of interrelated texts from which a corporate culture is co-constructed in a performative and meaningful way.

Marion Rollandin for her part focuses on the representations made by companies on their websites, using the example of six manufacturers of photographic equipment. To do this, she mobilizes a semio-pragmatic analysis and the concept of media ethos to update the relationship between, on the one hand, media ethos and product promotion strategies and, on the other hand, media ethos and typology of target audiences, as read through websites. Although the organizations studied seek to produce a very positive media ethos while using the ploy of differentiation from their competitors, two factors of uncertainty remain: the risk of a mismatch between user perception of content and the communication's intentions, and the difficulty of mastering and controlling a media ethos subject to change, whether by the company itself or by forms of reappropriation and reinterpretation of this ethos in digital spaces such as social media, which brings us back to this question of the circulation of signs, mentioned previously by Mariannig Le Béchec.

Christelle Larguier and Sébastien Rouquette examined the role of websites (belonging to associations and profit-making organizations) aimed at caregivers, in particular reviewing in this context the initial question that led to the cycle of events about websites: Are they still relevant in terms of digital communication strategies relayed by social media? To answer this question, they use a mixed methodological framework (comparative analyses of traces of activity on websites and social media sites, and in-depth interviews), which reveals that websites offer communicational advantages for which social networks are no substitute.

Marcy Delsione Ovoundaga extends the study initiated by Christelle Larguier and Sébastien Rouquette by focusing on the communication of associations based on their discursive online strategies. The author draws on the example of two associations, La Chaîne de l'Espoir and Action Contre la Faim, and on the analysis of a corpus of Facebook posts and comments. His study highlights the use of these socio-digital platforms as a renewed space of expression for associations, in which social marketing strategies emerge, themselves drawing upon discursive online strategies highlighting the argumentative and empathic dimensions.

I.3. Websites and cultural dynamics

The second part of our book puts a particular focus on the cultural development of websites and the differentiated strategies that can be associated with them. For this, Alexander Frame and Will Noonan propose to revisit the concept of website localization, through the prism of the cultural dimension. Based on a review of the scientific and professional literature on the subject as well as discourses by professionals and practitioners in the sector, they give a critical reading of a certain number of approaches giving prominence to national cultures to foster an apprehension and implementation of localization as a communicational activity based on a "liquid" approach to cultures and identities and inscribed in a trans-creational paradigm. In this perspective, they open up three pedagogical axes to train specialists in cultural localization.

Cécile-Marie Martin explores the place of indigenous minorities on the Web, this being understood as a political, material, technological and cultural system largely dominated by representations, operationalization and governance by Western states. Having identified these barriers to access and to representation of minority indigenous communities on a Web space that is less open and universal than is portrayed in discourses, the author suggests a number of concrete paths that would lead to a better appropriation of Web as well as a reaffirmed digital presence of these communities.

Sandra Mellot, Thomas Hoang and Anaïs Theviot decode the cultural, political and rhetorical dimensions anchoring the online environmental communication of non-governmental organizations and new collectives. By deploying a multimodal semiotic analysis of a corpus of websites and video clips arising from the concept of ethos, the authors highlight registers of differentiated ethos (ethos of action, of will, of justice, of belief) and also the emergence of a new ecological homonoïa, marked with the stamp of urgency, between praise and blame. Websites and other media productions such as video clips provide here a form of stabilization of this collective positioning.

Finally, Géraud Ahouandjinou, Ornheilia Zounon, Agnès Badou and Ismène Kpédjo explore e-fundraising strategies in a context of pandemic emergency (Covid-19) as they were deployed in France between March and May 2020. To complete this study, conducted on the basis of a content analysis of fundraising campaigns collected from a corpus of NGO Web pages and Facebook, an exploratory questionnaire survey was conducted among Beninese representatives in order to collect the perceptions, sometimes ambivalent, of this fundraising for Africa in the context of COVID.

I.4. Communication of organizations and online storytelling

In the third part, we focus on the issue of storytelling in digital media and transmedia environments, particularly in relation to communication dynamics in organizations. Julien Falgas sets out to discuss and differentiate the three elements –

storytelling, narration and stories, a triad within which storytelling is situated as an act of communication. Based on this notional positioning, he mobilizes an approach inspired by Howard S. Becker breaking down the communication process into four stages constituting the "manufacturing of representations" to analyze Web pages published by a banking organization. Through this example, he shows the analytical potential of this approach to reveal the fabric of storytelling.

The last two chapters of this section focus on online storytelling in connection with TV series. Using a diachronic approach to emblematic media productions, Mélanie Bourdaa explores the development and diversification of narrative, transmedia (websites, apps, social media) and audience strategies through multiple entertainment experiences, whose nature in the context of targeted marketing campaigns can be ephemeral. The fan audience thus has to take on another role, that of preserving traces and records of these strategies and labile digital universes.

Frédéric Aubrun and Thomas Bihay, for their part, look at the series produced by the Netflix platform and examine how the fictional universe of these series is extended, reused in promotional strategies and diffracted on different media platforms. Using a reading grid inspired by three types of textures (explicit, implicit, zero) of fictional worlds, the authors analyze two Netflix series and show the reuse made of narrative sources in promotion strategies where the brand seems to be effaced in a logic of de-advertising that masks hyper-advertising where Netflix adopts a role of social influencer.

I.5. What next?

So here we are at the end of a cycle of events and questioning around a study object that is somewhat neglected today, the website. From these 7 years of reflections, what has emerged for us is that the website is still a living and legitimate object. But its place and role must now be debated, thought about and analyzed within complex digital ecosystems, oscillating between visibility and invisibility, articulated to intersecting communication issues related to the current (and future) socio-economic and socio-political challenges of organizations. This is what we will set out to do in a future cycle of scientific meetings and discussions on these objects.

I.6. References

Le Béchec, M. and Alloing, C. (2016). Les humanités numériques pour repenser les catégories d'analyse. *Revue française des sciences de l'information et de la communication*, 8 [Online]. Available at: http://journals.openedition.org/rfsic/1804.

Merzeau, L. (2014). Présence numérique : traces, éditorialisation, mémoire. In *Séminaire EHESS : Étudier les cultures du numérique : approches théoriques et empiriques*, Casilli, A. (ed.) [Online]. Available at: https://merzeau.net/traces-editorialisation-memoire/.

Pélissier, D. (2018). La présence numérique des organisations au regard de la marque employeur, le cas des banques françaises. *Commposite*, 20(1), 108–131.

Rieder, B. (2010). Pratiques informationnelles et analyse des traces numériques : de la représentation à l'intervention. *Études de communication*, 35(2), 91–104.

PART 1

Websites and Organizational Strategies

1

Websites and the Agency of Circulating Entities

Mariannig LE BÉCHEC
ELICO, Université Claude-Bernard Lyon 1, France

1.1. Introduction

Our everyday environment is made up of digital objects, and we frequently hear the expressions "digital environments" and "digital ecosystems" (Agostinelli and Koulayan 2016). These are linked to the issue of the digital transformation of organizations. Websites, on account of their potential to showcase the organization and its digital transformation, have been studied since the 2000s as markers of the digital transformation of organizations.

A website, from its namespace in the Web browser to the hyperlinks that point to or come from its online environment, provides a stage-set. The focus of our analysis in this chapter is on the possible links between websites and the elements that can circulate on them. How can a set of websites constitute a brand's digital territory (Le Béchec and Alloing 2016)? Beyond the interface accessible to Internet users or the notion of qualculation (Callon and Law 2005) available to the Web designer through audience analysis tools, we will focus here on brands in the symbolic sense that circulate between groups of websites.

In this chapter, the website is analyzed according to the organizational communication concept of symbolic processes that are interpreted as "info-communicational phenomena" (Bouillon et al. 2007) pertaining to the compositions of organizational digital identities.

Digital Presences of Organizations,
coordinated by Nathalie PINÈDE, Luc MASSOU and Patrick MPONDO-DICKA.

In a digital environment, the study of websites characterizes the symbolic processes operating on the Web according to a number of methods of analysis. The term "website" can refer to a static analysis method, often represented in semiotic analyses of websites. However, the Web's technical properties have created a dynamic environment according to network science. The collective work of Newman et al., *The Structure and Dynamics of Networks* (2006), and more specifically a chapter by Jon M. Kleinberg on navigation in small worlds enables us to think beyond a situated analysis in an inter-connected space. These methods will be included within the field of information and communication sciences through Web analysis manuals (for instance, Barats 2013).

In the course of our studies of websites, let us add that analyzing the signs found on websites also takes account of so-called propagation, imitation phenomena (Tarde 2001). Symbolic processes are replaced by symbolic dynamics that have changed in line with the evolution of digital ecosystems and their arrangement of digital content circulation.

The purpose of our analyses is therefore not to think without categories, obtaining responses in the collected data and their visualization in the form of website networks, but to question the strategies of the actors in the field, that is, the organizations, institutions, and so on that have a presence in a digital environment via their website. In this chapter, we will define circulating entities. They play a part in the symbolic dynamics and the info-communicational phenomena of organizational digital identities. But beyond the website from which they were sent, their circulation between websites allows us to qualify them as symbolic processes. According to our analyses and in a semio-pragmatic perspective, these circulating entities are signs, which we call transposable because they have the potential to represent a territory, a culture. They have the potential to become a brand on the Web and to aggregate websites, giving them a collective dynamic. We will therefore examine the topological analyses of the Web, which can help us to summarize the dynamics of these circulating entities (signs in a digital environment) and how their transposition, circulation and potential for action that we call agency enable us to define digital territories on the Web.

1.2. From website analysis to website network analysis

1.2.1. *The website as a defined and static semiotic entity*

The analysis of the composition of organizational digital identities works for limited bodies of websites with monographic analyses (Stockinger 2005; Rouquette 2009, 2017). The methods developed in monographic analyses describe a website as a static place, anchored in a territory. Thus, Stockinger (2005) compares the definition of a website to an institution in the sociological meaning of the term.

> The place occupied by a website thus resembles in many respects that which in sociological terminology is termed an institution, which responds in a standardized way to a set of problems encountered by a community of actors, an "instrument" to satisfy certain types of needs, interests or desires. (p. 24)

With directories and search engine result lists in the 2000s, methods were established to retrieve result lists by city and situate them on territorial maps. According to Duféal and Grasland (2003), each website is a territorial marker, in other words it contains a spatial and territorial meaning, in the sense that it "gives information about the places and activities most receptive to dissemination of Internet innovation" (p. 55). This method does not show any Web-related dynamics. It duplicates the role of a territorial institution on the Web, taking into account the history of the development of the Internet and observed uses. Thus, we deduce a change that may be a move into new cultural or economic models.

1.2.2. *A dynamic analysis of the arrangement of digital identities*

Pinède (2018) shows the value of conducting monographic or digital geographic analysis. She proposes studying the composition and arrangement of organizational digital identities based on data, actors, devices and representations. The author proposes modeling an organizational "self", from which three aspects arise: a staging of the self, a putting into use of the self and a process of evaluation of the self. This analysis leads her to question the data collection techniques specific to each aspect of organizations' digital identities (qualitative and quantitative approaches) as well as the analysis methods (always in the plural) necessary for the modeling of digital identities (Pinède 2018). The plurality of analyses, the complementarity of qualitative and quantitative analyses to refine our understanding of the potential to represent interconnected entities on the Web becomes essential in our methods, according to the author. We will not revisit qualitative analyses in this chapter, although we do subscribe to this approach in many other works.

To give a more detailed description of the organizational digital identity, the method of analyzing websites by scene places the website in scenarios, of navigation in particular, and helps us to understand the dynamics operated within a website through hypertext links. The method developed by Stockinger (2005) is already starting to take into account the semantic properties of websites. It thus becomes easy to continue the process to look at the semiotic properties of a website. Since lists of directory results could proliferate on the Web before 2010, the question is: Why do websites have sections where they cite other websites? What method enables us to analyze the practice of setting up a "digital social network" or affinity network composed of hypertext links to other websites? The methods for analyzing the connection between websites therefore use approaches developed in the sociological and economic theories of network analysis, in particular (Le Béchec 2016).

We add an additional theoretical input to semio-pragmatic analyses by using network analysis. These approaches arouse criticism in information and communication sciences (Bigot 2018) for their practice of bringing out realities constructed according to their own systems of writing. Network analysis also enables us to contribute to the observation through their heuristic quality of relational properties that cannot be accessed by a semiotic analysis of digital interfaces.

1.2.3. *The hybridization of semiotic analysis and website networks*

The sign, the act of union between signifier and signified, between percept and concept, is used in our work in the strict semiotic sense of organized representation. The interpretation of a sign arises from a memory phenomenon. The sign does not have only one value as a symbol whose meaning depends on a single actor, an elected political actor for example, who has the power to define it and lock its meaning. A sign, on the other hand, is easily identifiable by its prominence on a website. The same sign can be used by a set of websites which then allows us to define collectives with variable geometry by the repetition of the same sign on a set of websites. Understanding the potential of a sign, a meme, a gif to circulate, shows that the agency of these signs becomes decisive.

The agency of signs has a role in the three aspects defined by Pinède (2018): the staging of the self, the making use of the self and the process of evaluation of the self. A sign refers to an organization that circulates and has a role in all the Web metrics established by digital platforms.

What method are we to use? When we analyze data extracted from the Web and visualized in the form of networks (graphs), we base the analysis of "community" on visual patterns, that is, clusters calculated by algorithms (Le Béchec 2016). Data are extracted from the Web by non-stabilized digital humanities methods of scraping, crawling (Vinck 2016) employed at various times during a survey, which can therefore be subject to variations over time.

> Scraping, in other words the extraction of website content or metadata *via* a computer script; crawling: automated Web browsing to gather resources such as Web pages, images, videos, documents, etc., archive and index them; the retrieval of logs – event histories such as the consultation of Web pages, the opening of files or typed commands – on computer applications to study for instance the practices of users, human-machine interactions or the performance of a computer system. (Vinck 2016, p. 63)

The objective of methods of visualizing data extracted from the websites is easy to understand: it is to identify patterns. The objective of representing a category solely by the pattern of relationships, for example, has been criticized in network analysis, in particular the work on blockmodeling (1970s), and here we repeat the criticism of structural equivalence noted by Mercklé (2004).

> The blockmodel thus obtained constitutes a simplified representation of the structure of the relationships (present, or above all absent) between the various classes of structural equivalence: in other words, an image of the social structure obtained directly from the aggregation of relational data, without the prior imposition of any categories or attributes. (pp. 86–91)

The hybridization of semiotic analysis and network analysis in the study of websites allows us to minimize the risk of focusing only on statistical patterns by taking away the context. Similarly, the analysis of all the circulating entities on the Web for their semiotic properties and the study of their sender or receiver according to info-communication phenomena does not allow us to characterize even temporary collectives that form around the circulation of a sign, meme or gif. Combining the analysis of specific properties of signs on the Web by understanding how it remains attached to an organization and how it aggregates throughout the duration of our website analysis goes beyond the static analysis of digital organizational identities and the limits of a network analysis that ignores the properties of digital organizational identities.

1.3. The concept of digital territories of brands

1.3.1. *A conceptual framework to support hybrid analyses of websites*

How can the notion of territory be effective on the Web while this notion can easily be related to boundaries corresponding to a restricted space in the common sense? The problem is that the Web is not circumscribed. It allows entities to circulate according to algorithmic models, especially on platforms where the ability to symbolize, in other words to unify, is becoming obsolete; we can at best aggregate collectives over short periods of time. One of the basic principles of the Web is content circulation, since Expression Web 2.0 is based on a definition of user-generated content in a collaborative space (Bouquillion and Matthews 2010).

We have noted that, in the field of digital humanities, a researcher analyzing Web corpuses experiences problems in using concepts and their categories (Le Béchec and Alloing 2016). Terms such as "community" have been defined and are defined in environments and according to methods that are not commensurable in digital environments. One part of our work is to seek to better understand the conditions for establishing boundaries between "communities" in a digital environment. In our view, the practices of Internet users, the content produced and also the computational systems should be taken into consideration to interrogate the categories that are used in our analyses. The content produced by Internet users and the methods of appropriation must therefore be analyzed as relevant corpuses for the study of digital organizational identities.

Categories and attributes are still operative but digital media must lead us to rethink them, not from statistical models but from ethnographic and semiotic observations, so as not to project categories that presuppose strong and lasting relationships between individuals, as in the case of the term "community", when in fact the observed communities appear to exist only for the duration of the observation.

The analysis of the digital territory of brands is therefore based on an understanding of info-communication phenomena, which is the flow of information. The methods link the ethnographic analysis of online and offline audiences through the prism of the signs attached thereto. This approach raises the issue of informational authority (Alloing 2017) within "imagined communities", even though our observations may take place over much shorter durations than those studied by Anderson (1996) in his work.

Also, the word "transposition" highlights that we are moving from a physical territory to a territory on the Web, and that we lose stable landmarks (space-time) when analyzing websites or more generally digital media. The study of the circulation of signs has borrowed the idea of propagation and imitation from Gabriel Tarde's (2001) work. The author defines imitation as "elective and reflective" (Tarde 2001, p. 154), while propagation gives the prospect of an agency of the ideas, discourses and symbolic processes that accompany them.

The desire to leverage the notion of digital territories is not a given, and its usage is thus based on conceptual work.

> A digital territory of brands appears as a set of transposable signs, memorized by computational systems, which include algorithms, and are given added value by the reputational authority of Internet users who thus mark their attachment to a territory or an organization on the Web. (Le Béchec and Alloing 2016)

Analysis of the digital territories of brands carried out since 2006 takes into account the routine use (de Certeau 2010) of content producers who are neither institutional actors, nor economic actors, nor associative actors from the territories. But contrary to observations made prior to 2010 based on websites, digital platforms now organize these periods of routine usage where content is produced and circulates. The goal is not to objectify individuals who produce content on Web 2.0, given all the problems we have in identifying whether this content was produced by a human or a bot, nor the technique, as is frequently raised in public debate by critics of algorithms. Our methods do not allow us to analyze all the content circulating on the Web, although models derived from artificial intelligence or deep learning give us hope.

By focusing on the notion of brands, in the sense of markers, as symbolic landmarks in digital territories, we characterize natively digital content that has its own relationship to time, its own agency, defined here as its own potential for action.

1.3.2. *Are entities circulating on the Web always tied to a territory?*

What are territory markers on the Web? How do they multiply on the Web? And how can we identify them?

Boullier (2017) explains the concept of transposable sign as the "replication of circulating entities" and bases his third-generation social science theory partly on work related to the concept of the transposable sign (Le Béchec and Boullier 2014). This concept therefore becomes operative for the author, who associates with it "like, click, meme, timestamps, hashtags, connected objects" (Boullier 2018).

The analysis can be turned around. Scientific literature in English in the humanities and social sciences presents data and metadata that describe likes, clicks, memes, gif and hashtags on the basis of datafication (Dijck et al. 2018) performed by platforms, that is, a calculation of their replication. A semiotic analysis of triviality in the French literature (Jeanneret 2020) puts the focus on the semiotic qualities of these circulating entities, which are able to replicate themselves on the Web according to the layout of the platform. Their circulation does not automatically lead to territorialization, because these entities retain attachments with organizations that are present in the territories.

Work to identify the circulating entities linked to a territory shows that the meaning of the signs present on website interfaces is not locked. Their presence on a website does not only have a symbolic value. For example, a flag belonging to the "list of material and symbolic elements" of a nation (Thiesse 2001) could be interpreted in the context of a Web analysis with a regional dimension in France as a kind of statement, a strong political and symbolic act. Its materialization in the form of a linguistic icon potentially calls into question this power of unification of meanings and action that its presence implies. The circulation and transposition of signs produce a new version of what amounts to a territorial scale, of an organization on the Web. Taking the word "sign" in the strict semiotic sense of an organized representation, are all signs transferable on the Web; in other words, do they circulate easily on the Web?

How can the signs being studied be separated from all potential to become symbols? Balandier (2005) associates the development of a technicalization of social issues as a form of major disruption where symbols lose their potential to lead to action.

> This technicalization of social issues increases, in its expansion, the power of the sign and the fading of the symbol, which is weakened by being removed far away from its own areas. (p. 82)

Through repeated exposure on various websites, signs create a territorial and symbolic attachment to the website where it is used. "Territorial attachment" is considered "faire-faire" (Latour 2000, p. 204). The meanings of signs are shaped by organizations or Internet users who display them on websites. Signs are displayed on the Web and their meaning may vary according to the "territorial attachment" adopted by the user.

We have defined a scale to characterize the territorial attachment that a sign confers upon a website. The scale of territorial attachment determines the variation in meanings in a semio-pragmatic approach (Le Béchec 2016). The scale comprises five levels: statement, manipulation, convocation in the sense of presence, absence (Goody 2006, p. 17) and objection in the sense of rejection (p. 22). Each of the five levels is based on a literature analysis for their development and emphasizes that the presence of a sign on a website in 2007 does not override its meaning on another in 2021. Each of the contexts of use must be analyzed on a Web page to determine territorial attachment. What is the sender, what is the purpose of the act of communication, how has this sign been picked up on a set of websites connected to the Web page analyzed?

Figure 1.1. *Partial screenshot of Petit Navire's homepage*[1]*. For a color version of this figure, see www.iste.co.uk/pinede/digital.zip*

In Figure 1.1, no sign marks a territorial attachment of this brand located in the Brittany region, Petit Navire, whose website address is petitnavire.fr.

The only element that signifies a territorial attachment is the product traceability available via the *D'où vient mon poisson?* ("Where does my fish come from?") interface.

Figure 1.2. *Partial screenshot of bretagne.bzh's homepage*[2]*. For a color version of this figure, see www.iste.co.uk/pinede/digital.zip*

1 Available at: www.petitnavire.fr [Accessed September 30, 2021].

2 Available at: www.bretagne.bzh [Accessed September 30, 2021].

On the other hand, the homepage of Conseil Régional de Bretagne (Brittany Regional Council) (Figure 1.2) shows a more explicit territorial attachment right from the address bar, with a domain name in bretagne.bzh. The .bzh stands for Breizh, literally Brittany. The institution's logo uses the ermine, which appears on numerous coats of arms. Finally, the website is accessible in French, Breton and Gallo. We were involved in drawing up the application for the creation of .bzh and its currently usage does not take into account the history of these three letters that in former times were used to make a statement about the Breton language. We therefore conclude that the two websites do not leverage the same level of territorial attachment. On Région Bretagne's homepage, we can see various points where digital organizational identities are arranged on the basis of data, actors, devices and representations described by Pinède (2018).

1.3.3. *The agency of signs as an object of digital study*

The levels of meaning show that leverage for a cause is subject to variations in its presence or absence if the temporality of a sign or its agency is taken into account. Between the production context and the usage context of a sign, there are variations or changes in connotation as a function of the time of utterance and as a function of the sender. A transposable sign is therefore a sign that has the power both to remain attached to a territory, to an organization and to circulate on the Web, thus becoming capable of translating and reformulating a territory or a brand on the Web. This circulating element allows us to define collectives of Internet users with variable geometry. And the activity, or the agency of these signs (Hoskins 2006), becomes an object of digital study (Casemajor 2014).

Agency characterizes a symbolic process during which the production context of a sign differs from its usage context. The significative variable of signs over time goes beyond focusing on the production context of a website editor to take into account what actors do with it when it is appropriated on the Web. Moreover, its transposition on the Web, the presence of a flag for example, and its circulation from one website to another, from account to account on digital platforms keeps collectives together at variable scales and over increasingly ephemeral times. This idiosyncrasy of the Web as compared to the long durations of the territories defined by Fernand Braudel (1984) is a topic for study in the field of information and communication sciences.

In addition to Internet users, other economic and technical actors are involved in the creation and validation of signs in digital media. The signs thus have a meaning that varies over time and cannot be locked by one single actor. But the semio-diversity of the early websites is becoming increasingly standardized on digital platforms. Organizations must therefore compose their organizational identity from the choices available on a website and the iconic restrictions deployed by digital platforms using emojis and emoticons.

1.3.4. *Signs essential to the social world and variable significance on the Web*

An organization can no longer use a website to lock the meaning of the signs that hold brand value for it. The strategy therefore is to manage the elements that are circulating on the Web to guide the circulation of brands that define a territorial scale, a digital organizational identity on the Web.

> Through the concept of performative agency, Butler (2010) demonstrates that it is not the sender, an institution, but the discourse itself that has this potential for action. The notion of agency (Hoskins, 2006) underlines this discourse potential, of objects to detach themselves from their production context in order to circulate. (Le Béchec 2016)

These signs always refer to an entity, and it is in this sense that we call them "transposable" because they are able to adopt the properties of the medium that causes them to circulate. By not having the status of symbol, a sign in digital conventions acquires new meanings and does not have only an index value. The sign makes allusion in order to capture our attention and adopts the semiotic properties of platforms and other websites to multiply. Yves Jeanneret makes the same observation about the "triviality of cultural objects" (2020). Technical and mediated dimensions are present in this definition of triviality.

> As a "trivial" (translated, circulating, instrumentalized) category, the index essentially and correctly serves to combat the reduction of signs to conventional ("arbitrary") realities, as Saussurian linguistics, or rather its interpretation by structuralism, may suggest. (Jeanneret 2020, p. 40)

The question then becomes: how can signs mark degrees of territorial attachment according to their usage context in a digital medium and their appropriation context, that is, the way in which the sign is arranged, leveraged by the user and picked up by digital media?

1.3.5. *The notion of digital territories of brands as a framework for a hybrid analysis of circulating entities on an "affective Web"*

Digital objects also have the potential to affect us, from the point of view of attention and also "faire-faire".

> As Yves Citton (2008) points out, we must understand the rise of an economy of affects and focus on what there could be in these phenomena as modalities of influence, domination, control or setting in motion. (Allard et al. 2017)

Our analyses of the signs on Web 1.0 show a proliferation that cannot be classified, thus leaving the digital territory in a state of imagery that cannot be scoped in the imagination (Musso 2005). However, studies of meme virality have made it possible to establish typologies, common places consumed through opinion mining or conversation tracking techniques (Boullier and Lohard 2012). Because the signs that make up a Web interface or interactions on platforms (likes) have a reduced semio-diversity through the strategic choices of platform development and the universal character encoding system to which these signs belong. The aim is not to structure but to standardize in order to be able to measure more easily the affects employed. It is the platforms and their business model, and also Web standards, that define content circulation on digital media. Studying the "affective Web" (Alloing and Pierre 2017), sign circulation becomes an important element in understanding content circulation in the composition of the digital territories of brands.

This conceptual approach advances further in the context of the development of a platform Web and more specifically an affective Web (Alloing and Pierre 2017), in other words one based on affective and emotional work. As these two authors underline in their book, advertisers are faced with re-documentarization (Pedauque 2007) by users, who may attach brand emojis or emoticons to content, which alters the interpretation that can be made of it.

> Because these emojis/emoticons are "transposable signs" within a "circulating fiction". They link to the online presence of the organization, making reference to a symbolism that the brand cannot lock. Their circulation, which cannot be controlled, turns them into affects that have to be constantly measured and evaluated. (Alloing and Pierre 2017, p. 83)

It is important to stress this point; affective and emotional work is orchestrated by platforms (in the following example, Twitter) and the standardization consortium (Unicode). Developed by the Unicode Consortium, Unicode is a computing standard designed to enable the exchange of content in all languages, for any platform and any software, by assigning a name and a numerical identifier to a character.

> Unicode [...] has since 2010 provided key combinations on the keyboard to bring up emoticons and emojis. (Alloing and Pierre 2017, p. 83)

The Brittany region launched an operation in January 2021 on Twitter, with #emojiBZH and #GwennHaDu, to display the Brittany region's flag on an account profile or a message. The affective and emotional work mobilized as part of a political communication campaign leverages the re-postings of user accounts on a commercial platform such as Twitter, which mark territorial attachment by taking up this hashtag, and in replicating it leverage a political intention to influence the Unicode character coding standard. Sign circulation is no longer accomplished solely by the webpages and their hypertext links.

1.3.6. *Signs linked to brands*

One point should be clarified. The circulation of a sign leads it to acquire new meanings according to the appropriations made of it. Circulation is facilitated through the algorithms developed by the platforms. But websites remain spaces where signs are displayed and produced.

Platforms participate in their circulation according to their own commercial strategy. The work carried out for stance in the field of digital artifact studies (Casemajor 2014) underlines issues of ad hoc categories that are to be found in the analyses of websites or digital media.

And digital media, the platforms, produce value markers that go beyond the symbolic forms developed by organizations. They organize the meaning of signs according to their potential to orientate uses and users in their own digital environment (Le Béchec and Alloing 2018). Their organization of circulations is based on algorithms that are for the most part developed by platforms that seek to define their digital territory in order to arrange information flow outside the laws, standards and roles related to territories (Alloing and Le Béchec 2021). Their model can be defined as a computer program of relationships between units which makes it possible to create numerical indicators.

In order to feed their algorithms, platforms leverage user-generated content to refine their algorithm and their business model. They are now seeking to organize the circulation of this content with their own models of symbolic meanings (emoji, filter, etc.) and according to their own temporality, but often in connection with territorial events (elections, sporting events, etc.) transposed into a digital environment via websites.

1.4. Conclusion

In a digital environment of presence of the self, organizations leverage websites to define a stable and static landmark of a digital territory of brands. Their analysis shows that websites are a static semio-discursive space while also belonging to a digital environment that takes over dynamics linked to the Web and to its technical and commercial development. Info-communication phenomena are taken up in Web-specific strategies in the world of digital media.

The digital organizational identity must therefore go beyond self-presentation to determine what remains of the organization caught up in an environment that is complexified by connections made either by users or by the organizations themselves between websites and digital platforms. Strategies of economic development and control of symbolic processes will come up against strategies of definition of digital territories of brands that are sometimes hostile because the issue becomes control of brand circulation by organizations according to the arrangement applied to them by digital platforms.

In our analyses of the attachment of circulating entities to a territory, a scale of territorial attachment of signs present on the Web on five levels permits us to define the digital territories of brands. A memetic analysis does not seem to take into account these long durations of territories nor the inclusion of these signs in standards and conventions related to computing and the Web.

To conclude, we stress that all circulation on digital media, and more specifically on platforms, leverages content produced by websites that remain symbolic reservoirs, stable and even immutable points of centralization and reference.

1.5. References

Agostinelli, S. and Koulayan, N. (eds) (2016). *Les écosystèmes numériques : Intelligence collective, développement durable, interculturalité, transfert de connaissances*. Presses des Mines, Paris.

Allard, L., Alloing, C., Le Béchec, M., Pierre, J. (2017). Introduction. Les affects numériques. *Revue française des sciences de l'information et de la communication* [Online]. Available at: https://doi.org/10.4000/rfsic.2870.

Alloing, C. (2017). La réputation pour questionner l'autorité informationnelle : Vers une "autorité réputationnelle" ? *Quaderni*, 93(2), 33–41.

Alloing, C. and Le Béchec, M. (2021). La plateforme comme frontière. *Balisages*, 3 [Online]. Avalaible at: https://publications-prairial.fr/balisages/index.php?id=590.

Alloing, C. and Pierre, J. (2017). *Le Web affectif : Une économie numérique des émotions*. Ina Édition, Bry-sur-Marne.

Anderson, B. (1996). *L'imaginaire national : Réflexions sur l'origine et l'essor du nationalisme*. La Découverte, Paris.

Balandier, G. (2005). *Le grand dérangement*. Presses universitaires de France, Paris.

Barats, C. (ed.) (2013). *Manuel d'analyse du Web en sciences humaines et sociales*. Armand Colin, Paris.

Bigot, J.-É. (2018). Instruments, pratiques et enjeux d'une recherche numériquement équipée en sciences humaines et sociales. PhD Thesis, Université de technologie de Compiègne, Compiègne.

Bouillon, J.-L., Bourdin, S., Loneux, C. (2007). De la communication organisationnelle aux "approches communicationnelles" des organisations : Glissement paradigmatique et migrations conceptuelles. Communication et organisation. *Revue scientifique francophone en communication organisationnelle*, 31, 7–25.

Boullier, D. (2017). Pour des sciences sociales de troisième génération (SS3G). In *Big data et traçabilité numérique*, Menger, P.-M., Paye, S. (eds). Collège de France, Paris.

Boullier, D. and Lohard, A. (2012). *Opinion mining et sentiment analysis : Méthodes et outils*. OpenEdition Press, Marseille.

Bouquillion, P. and Matthews, J.T. (2010). *Le web collaboratif : Mutations des industries de la culture et de la communication*. Presses universitaires de Grenoble, Grenoble.

Braudel, F. (1984). *Écrits sur l'histoire*. Flammarion, Paris.

Butler, J. (2010). Performative agency. *Journal of Cultural Economy*, 3(2), 147–161.

Callon, M. and Law, J. (2005). On qualculation, agency, and otherness. *Environment and Planning D: Society and Space*, 23(5), 717–733.

Casemajor, N. (2014). Matérialisme numérique et trajectoires d'objets : Les artefacts numériques en circulation. *French Journal for Media Research*, 1 [Online]. Available at: https://frenchjournalformediaresearch.com:443/lodel-1.0/main/index.php?id=263.

de Certeau, M. (2010). *Arts de faire*. Gallimard, Paris.

Citton, Y. (2008). Esquisse d'une économie politique des affects. In *Spinoza et les sciences sociales : De la puissance de la multitude à l'économie des affects*, Citton, Y., Lordon, F. (eds). Amsterdam Editions, Le Kremlin-Bicêtre.

van Dijck, J., Poell, T., de Waal, M. (2018). *The Platform Society*. Oxford University Press, Oxford.

Duféal, M. and Grasland, L. (2003). La planification des réseaux à l'épreuve de la matérialité des TIC et de l'hétérogénéité des territoires. *Flux*, 54(4), 49–69.

Goody, J. (2006). *La peur des représentations. L'ambivalence à l'égard des images, du théâtre, de la fiction, des reliques et de la sexualité*. Découverte Poche, Paris.

Hoskins, J. (2006). Agency, biography and objects. In *Handbook of Material Culture*, Tilley, C., Keane, W., Kuechler, S., Rowlands, M., Spyer, P. (eds). SAGE, Thousand Oaks.

Jeanneret, Y. (2020). *The Trace Factory*. ISTE Ltd, London, and John Wiley & Sons, New York.

Latour, B. (2000). Factures/fractures. De la notion de réseau à celle d'attachement. In *Ce qui nous relie*, Micoud, A., Peroni, M. (eds). Editions de l'Aube, La Tour d'Aigues.

Le Béchec, M. (2016). Le territoire comme un graphe. Pratiques, formes, éthique. *Les Cahiers du numérique*, 12(4), 131–156.

Le Béchec, M. and Alloing, C. (2016). Les humanités numériques pour repenser les catégories d'analyse. Le cas du "territoire numérique de marques". *Revue française des sciences de l'information et de la communication*, 8 [Online]. Available at: http://journals.openedition.org/rfsic/1804.

Le Béchec, M. and Alloing, C. (2018). Les territoires numériques de marques pour repenser les cadres d'analyse du web. *Questions de communication*, 34, 7–20.

Le Béchec, M. and Boullier, D. (2014). Communautés imaginées et signes transposables sur un "web territorial". *Études de communication. Langages, information, médiations*, 42, 113–126.

Manovich, L. (2010). *Le langage des nouveaux médias*. Les Presses du réel, Dijon.

Mercklé, P. (2004). *Sociologie des réseaux sociaux*. La Découverte, Paris.

Musso, P., Ponthou, L., Seulliet, É. (2005). *Fabriquer le futur : L'imaginaire au service de l'innovation*. Village Mondial, Paris.

Newman, M.E.J., Barabasi, A.-L., Watts, D.J. (eds) (2006). *The Structure and Dynamics of Networks*. Princeton University Press, Princeton.

Pédauque, R.T. (2007). *La redocumentarisation du monde*. Cépaduès, Toulouse.

Pinède, N. (2018). Du site web aux identités numériques organisationnelles. *Questions de communication*, 34(2), 75–94.

Rouquette, S. (2009). *L'analyse des sites Internet. Une radiographie du cyberesp@ce*. De Boeck/Ina, Louvain-la-Neuve/Paris.

Rouquette, S. (ed.) (2017). *Site internet : Audit et stratégie*. De Boeck, Louvain-la Neuve.

Scroferneker, C.M.A. (2004). Qu'est-ce que la "Communication organisationnelle" dans un pays de contact ? *Sociétés*, 83(1), 79–88.

Stockinger, P. (2005). *Les sites Web : Conception, description et évaluation*. Hermès Science Lavoisier, Paris.

Tarde, G. (2001). *Les lois de l'imitation*. La Découverte, Paris.

Thiesse, A.-M. (2001). *La création des identités nationales : Europe XVIIIe-XXe siècle*. Éditions Points, Paris.

Vinck, D. (2016). *Humanités numériques : La culture face aux nouvelles technologies*. Éditions du Cavalier bleu, Paris.

2

Danone's "Did You Know?": Narrative Strategy and Identity Dialogue

Stela RAYTCHEVA, Thierry CÔME and Gilles ROUET
LAREQUOI, Université de Paris-Saclay, Guyancourt, France

2.1. Introduction

This chapter sets out to study strategies for stabilizing a corporate culture, focusing on the discursive strategy of the organizations (Silberzahn 2014) and in particular its performative effects in terms of the co-construction of a corporate culture and organizational identity.

The concept of corporate culture, borrowed from anthropological studies, has aroused great interest and, at the same time, disappointment. The "right" organizational culture (that drives innovation, agility and customer focus) is seen as an asset for the company. In this framework, a strong corporate culture results in the social body becoming self-regulating and self-monitoring. The role of the manager is no longer, among other things, to supervise, but to give a vision, a direction that is inspirational and that focuses on the energies of the workforce (Alvesson 2002). The "corporate culture" metaphor, assimilated to an asset, suggests that it can be managed, that it is a tool that can be improved, for instance by focusing on cultural values. But while companies may proclaim values, it is not enough to simply state

Digital Presences of Organizations,
coordinated by Nathalie PINÈDE, Luc MASSOU and Patrick MPONDO-DICKA.

them (Alvesson and Sveningsson 2008). To be sustainable, organizational values must be "acted out" in day-to-day life. It is in fact a collective construction (management, staff, etc.), even though some actors may possess and utilize a stronger symbolic capital than others.

From a semiotic point of view, access to a culture as a social object or as an object of study is not direct. Behaviors, speeches, symbols, etc., are constantly reinterpreted in order to become meaningful. These interpretations are certainly not always conscious and the social actor leverages reading habits which are themselves cultural (in the sense of collective co-constructions). This chapter proposes a dual analysis of the discursive work carried out through the organization's institutional communication: from a static point of view to identify the corporate values contained or presumed in the texts of communications; from a dynamic point of view, by following the succession and interdiscursivity of the texts on different digital media, to seek to identify the performative role of these texts in terms of stabilizing an organizational culture and identity[1]. Thus, our analysis forms part of an approach to the culture both as a structuring framework for constructing meaning and as performance, or, to employ the terms used by Taylor and Van Every (2000), as discourse and conversation.

A study of cultural processes based on discursive work on isolated texts risks leading to tautologies. A text presupposes a culture and at the same time reproduces it; it is both a product and an "agent". On the other hand, by adopting a process perspective, where each text is interpreted in a set of "contexts", it is possible to study the more or less successful stabilization through subtle nuances of an organizational culture. The process approach rejects a content approach to culture that often studied, as a given, an element of pre-existing context where each actor is assumed to be able (should be able) to adapt to it, under penalty of collective sanctions. In a content culture approach, values are given particular prominence in the case of supposed cultural changes decided by top management. Hence it is recommended to provide support for the staff. Thus, an organizational culture focuses the attention of researchers, primarily as a context and in periods of supposed cultural upheavals.

1 The concepts of culture and professional identity are separate. The differences are on the following axes: objectivity *versus* subjectivity, neutrality *versus* distinction, material effects *versus* symbolic effects, etc. We will not develop these aspects. When it comes to communication strategies, culture is likely to be seen by social actors as a resource for working on organizational identity.

The objective of this chapter is to study the actors' day-to-day, mundane work on upholding and transforming the culture. In this perspective, the actors are not regarded as cultural robots (in the sense of Garfinkel (2007)) but as participants (active or passive) in its co-construction. We propose to follow the discursive-cultural process underlying the narratives produced in Danone's corporate communication. The texts studied have been taken from the company's institutional website and Facebook page. A number of reasons led us to choose Danone as our field of study. The company is a pioneer of brand-based communication and not on products alone, using diverse and varied but always positive axes such as health, happiness, social relationships within the company, social and environmental responsibility. The company's directors, and in particular the Riboud family, while minority shareholders, embodied the company and identified with it, which enabled them to stay at the top for decades. Communication has been at the heart of this strategy for a long time: Antoine Riboud, by brandishing a Carambar during a TV show in 1989 to explain his business and his strategy and to justify his salary through the employment he creates, upturned the image of the serious boss, egoistical in the eyes of most French people, and played his part in, at the time, reconciling the Left with the company. This image of a social enterprise has become indissociable from Danone, as is clearly demonstrated by its recent adoption of the status of mission-driven company (the French status of *entreprise à mission*). All these aspects justify, in our view, the choice of Danone as a case study of the links between narrative strategy and identity dialogue.

The first section, devoted to the presentation of the theoretical and methodological framework, is followed by the corpus analysis that allows us to consider the process of discursive stabilization of Danone's culture or identity.

2.2. Culture, strategy and narratives

Organizational culture is a complex and multidimensional phenomenon that mobilizes actors in a variety of ways. This section looks at the use of this concept in the literature of management sciences and management, and at its treatment in the anthropological literature, especially in linguistic and semiotic anthropology, and presents the analysis methodology and the corpus used.

2.2.1. *Corporate cultures and management*

An organization, like any human group, can be analyzed from a cultural perspective, considering that it has a culture and/or that it is a culture (Alvesson

2002; Abdelwahed and Antit 2016). Corporate culture is a visible or non-visible manifestation of the organizational identity, which can be defined by a set of beliefs, values, standards and also of heroes, myths, codes, rites, taboos and practices (Cohendet and Diani 2003; Godelier 2006). This culture is common and shared, organizational (Pettigrew 1979; Bertrand 1991; Pohl and Battistelli 2019; Bruna 2021), but also operationalizable in the context of the implementation of the company's strategy, in particular (Chanal and Tannery 2005). Thus, culture is both resource and vector, subject to change (Godelier 2009) and to communication issues (Rouet 2018; Eyries 2021). It enables us to define and explain the basic organizational rules of the community constituted by the company and it communicates to its new members, actors or consumers, the right ways of thinking and acting, thus playing a role in their training and integration. Paraphrasing Barthes (1991), for whom there has never been any people without narrative, there is no organization that constructs and organizes itself without a culture and a history. Corporate culture is a construct and the story of its history is its main tool for dissemination and appropriation. As such, it cannot be ignored by the company's strategic summit. This point can also be seen as differentiating a company (public or private) from other forms of organization that do not necessarily implement an explicit strategic approach, often top-down, often leveraging an idealized and inspirational form of culture defined or adopted by a dominant coalition.

The corporate culture can be regarded as a foundation for the creation of discursive elements by at least one of the actors (dominant coalition) of the organization. It is then objectified, in the sense that it becomes the object of strategic thinking, an asset of the company in the same way as a brand, an image, a reputation, to which it is then linked. This management of the culture presupposes being in a position to give prominence to organizational values to advertise them and seek to illustrate some of them in the framework of "official" narratives. This public form implies a materialization, a textualization of the values and norms that have become official. Thus, once "en-textualized" (Silverstein and Urban 1996), certain aspects of the corporate culture are systematically invoked and leveraged and contribute to the justification and legitimization of strategic decisions by the stakeholders, giving meaning to organizational change (Kahane 2005). Culture can therefore be acted out, particularly to ensure a form of historical continuity between past, present and future. This continuity makes it possible to essentialize or reify the organization with its own characteristics, which can encourage its stakeholders to identify with it.

The corporate culture, or organizational culture, is obviously co-constructed in the framework of a permanent dialogue between subcultures that are differentiated and fragmented to a greater or lesser degree, but it can also be leveraged to try to impose a particular vision of the organization, without taking into account, for instance, conflicts of interest between stakeholders (Martin 1992). Corporate culture is very specific to an organization, but the values put forward by companies are often part of a "universal" cultural framework (responsibility, innovation, customer orientation, etc.).[2] Thus, it is intended to be differentiating but consensual. While it is less usual to promote corporate cultures "borrowed" from societal cultures (e.g. popular cultures), some brands can become symbols not only through the lifestyles with which they are associated, but also by the popular cultures where they are to be found, for example through cinema and other elements of everyday life (e.g. when a brand becomes a household name). Thus, corporate culture can be studied not only as an internal dialogue (between sub-cultures and fractions) but also as the result of a dialogue with professional, managerial and societal cultures, etc. But what does dialogue involve? First of all, a dialogue can only exist under certain conditions, specifically the creation of meaning, the temporal and interpretative aspects. Any phenomenon can be part of a form of dialog, but it must have sense or make sense, in order to be thus "enrolled" by virtue of one or more of its aspects in a thread of interactions. Moreover, in the context of a dialogue (or monologue), it is necessary to have some form of interpretant (in the sense of Peirce (1998)) becoming part of a chain of interpretants. Thus, many texts or narratives created by a company can be seen as being part of a dialog between the company and its stakeholders. In this form of dialogue (more or less monologic), the texts produced appear as answers to questions or to assumed or real comments from its audiences (Angermuller 2014).

2.2.2. *Narratives and strategies*

Historical narratives have an important role to play in constructing a corporate culture. In the first place, in relation to the continuity sought: the past is presented from the point of view of the present and renders the future accessible and understandable. This continuity is reassuring and facilitates identification centered on characteristics presented as enduring. The tense of the historical events is not necessarily the narrative tense. The narrative tense itself facilitates the reading of the past in the light of the present. Narratives are vectors of legitimation, using values and evaluations of events and actions of the actors in those narratives (Thevenet 2015). This is a common practice of large companies that, since the 2000s, have

2 To our knowledge, no company advertises values (or anti-values) such as discrimination, exploitation, manipulation and so on.

been telling their stories more and more. According to Jeanne Bordeau, 95% of large American companies and 60% of large French companies have a document in which their values are mentioned (Bordeau 2012). The events considered worthy of inclusion, the type of narrative and the narrative strategies make it possible to argue for the current and future functioning of the organization, to legitimize its structure, to promote its choices (Girard 2007). These values do not always need to be explained clearly; they are part of how the actors and events are defined.

Narratives do not take into account all the significant events in the life of a company, only those that lend themselves to the desired interpretation. Thus, the stories told by a company (storytelling) narrate a reconstructed history in line with the objectives set for it by the strategic summit. The choices made in favoring this or that event or this or that way of interpreting it reflect the positions taken by the coalitions at the top of the company. This is especially true of official narratives and press releases that promote the organization and avoid talking about critical situations. Narratives, because of their very structure which focuses on events and not processes, individual decision-makers more than groups are leveraged to also play a role in the evolution of the construction of the corporate culture, or its reconstruction. They thus tend to put the collective and continuous construction of the company culture in the background to showcase only a particular vision, updated and reconstructed. These narratives give meaning to the evolution of the company, certainly by giving it a place in history, but above all by showing both the durability of the values highlighted in the story (at each stage of the company's development, these values have always existed) and the fact that they were there ahead of the competition in order to better differentiate themselves. Moreover, these narratives do not analyze the true weight of the values set out in the company's value system at the various dates selected; they thus limit the possible interpretations to highlight only the progressive and positive side of the company. These simplified, even simplistic, narratives are easy to assimilate, largely based on nostalgia and the acceptability today of the values put forward, creating a positive link between generations of consumers and with the company, ever present. These narratives are thus shared the more easily by all the target groups they address since they encourage them to experience emotions that are common to all, but different at each of the selected stages in the story.

However, following Taylor and Van Every (2000), organizational discourse (culture) lives only through mundane conversations (everyday storytelling) that become meaningful through it, while at the same time shaping it in subtle ways. Nevertheless, every conversation is not an identical replica of the organizational culture, but a reinterpretation of it in the light of the context of the action. Thus, from a process perspective, every conversation is an opportunity both to uphold and transform the organizational culture. In other words, the stabilization of an organizational culture, always at risk of going off at a tangent, is accomplished through multiple performances (and counter-performances with regard to the intended objectives) of narratives which can be reproduced in various versions according to the media used and/or the relational contexts. While these different performances allow us to recognize the same event, the different versions can be regarded as so many interpretations that constitute a network of interrelated texts. Nevertheless, each new rendering has a material form that carries meaning and guides subsequent interpretations (Sleiman et al. 2020). Different audiences can have different readings of the same text. Consequently, each new rendering of a text can form part of a co-construction based on the readers' interpretations, taking into account the context as well as the material form and symbolic aspects of the text (Lehtonen 2000). One of the contextual elements that orients the material form and the relational modes between authors and audiences is the media used.

2.2.3. *Media and content*

It is clearly essential to consider what the media (in the sense of intermediation between company and audiences) represent. From a socio-material perspective, a medium has capacities, some (not all) of which can be leveraged by the actors who use them. Thus, the use of media is not defined by the medium itself or by the user alone, but by the joint action of both.

Structuring discourse *versus* mundane conversations: first, depending on the media used in social interactions, relational contexts can vary. We can make a schematic comparison between the institutional website and the social media leveraged by companies. The diversity of audiences can be very wide on institutional websites, particularly in terms of the objectives of website visitors. The institutional website is a shop window not only for customers, but also for investors, the media and numerous stakeholders. The presentation style is chosen so as to promote the company, enabling it to set out its stall, offering documentation and an overview of the company. Even though most institutional websites include a "News" section, the rest of the content is relatively stable, compared to content on other digital media. The aforementioned are public and accessible to all (without a subscription, an account, etc.).

Through interactivity, feedback and evaluation in the case of social media, the relationship between a company and its audiences is seen as being more horizontal. Social media can be compared to conversations, because the participant, whether active or not, can join in the thread of posts at any time, but without having to scroll back through the entire thread of conversations, which therefore seem to have a more ephemeral nature than the texts on institutional websites. This quality is not due to texts disappearing, but to their being submerged by other texts, on the one hand, and the uses made of them, on the other hand.

Hierarchical *versus* horizontal social interactions: although the texts on institutional websites are constructed in such a way as to promote the company, and often monologically, they are presented as informational texts, particularly for external audiences. However, the institutional website also makes the assumption that audiences do not know the company, its history, its products, its contact details, etc., without being off-putting for visitors who do know these elements.

The first uses of social media such as Facebook focused on interpersonal communication, with more or less frequent discussions with members of one's personal network (Bastard et al. 2017) who share information and photos, find things out, get involved in joint projects, etc. When companies make use of Facebook to communicate with their audiences, we can see a form of usage mimicry, but taking into account elements of marketing strategy, seeking to influence and managing images and reputation. Despite that, when reading institutional websites, the user has a certain autonomy in the use of hypertext and in navigation via the tree structure, but it nonetheless remains relatively passive. The texts and contents on these websites are not co-constructed directly between authors and audiences, whereas in social media the case is different. Even taking into account algorithms and their effects on content provision (Cardon 2019), Internet users can evaluate posts, post comments, give feedback, etc.

2.2.4. *Discourse and storytelling*

In order to study the strategies for stabilizing Danone's corporate culture, we propose to study the storytelling acts carried out in the various texts by studying not only the narration, but also the circulation or reinterpretations of certain narratives by others. The study of the stability of narrative structure from one narrative to another makes use of the narrative analysis of Daiute (2014) and Abbott (2014). The analysis of values introduced into a text involves identifying explicit or implicit values, which can be done by studying the way in which events and associated evaluations are categorized.

Studying the plot consists of identifying the positions of the various protagonists, the structure of the narrative, the temporal sequence and the cause–effect relationships assumed or made explicit in the narrative. Character analysis makes it possible to identify the social roles assigned (in relation to a social structure and not the plot structure) to the protagonists and the value attached to their actions, while a study of the tense of the narrative allows us to identify how the past is viewed and its relationship with the present and the future. The identification of meaning sets out to study the elements of the narrative picked out by the narrator that express their emotions and their relationship to the narrated event. Finally, a consideration of the narrator's position allows us to analyze their relationship with audiences. The analysis of these elements allows us to put them into perspective in the multitude of texts and media studied in order to identify those that are relatively stable, those that change, and also their consequences in terms of identification and of relationships between stakeholders.

While there are a number of approaches to narrative analysis (Kohler Riessman 2008), we have chosen to use a form of structural analysis applied to texts considered to be "performances" of a narrative. This is not a dialogical or performative analysis in the "classical" sense. In the case being studied, Danone, we focus on a form of "interposed" dialogue carried out by the various authors and not on audience participation in the construction of the narratives.

2.3. Danone: storytelling of a culture

This section puts forward an analysis of the telling of Danone's story, according to the institutional website[3], focusing solely on the "Our History" page, then on the intertextual narratives put on the company's Facebook page[4], with the "Did you know?" content. As a general rule, this heading is a rhetorical question about little-known but intriguing historical facts and anecdotes likely to attract the interest of audiences. Knowledge of these anecdotes can be part of a process of appropriation of a general or erudite culture. In particular, it is about knowing the historical origins of common phenomena in daily life, whose genesis may however be unknown.

These days there are many websites and books which bring together anecdotes in this way or which use the same heading, "Did you know?", taken from a much older editorial tradition that can be found in almanacs, particularly during the 19th century in France. In 2017, Facebook launched a "Do you know?" section, allowing Internet users to answer questions asked previously by other Internet users and which appear randomly.

---

3 Available at: www.danone.com/en/about-danone/ourhistory.html.

4 Available at: www.facebook.com/Danone/.

However, the use of this form of post is not leveraged by Danone, because the random aspect is not manageable. Danone takes up and uses the "Did you know?" concept on its Facebook page by giving a character of "general culture" to the information communicated under this banner.

After a presentation of three different retellings of Danone's history that have been put on its institutional website, we propose to follow the circulation of some of these narratives on the social media of Facebook in connection with the company's centenary.

2.3.1. *The history of Danone on its institutional website: textual analysis*

Danone's story is presented in an epic genre (Gabriel 2011). In the introductory paragraph, three elements are highlighted:

> Danone story as you know it today is above all an incredible human adventure that began at the beginning of the 20th century with encounters, adventures and convictions. This section looks back to Danone's history, the foundation on which we will continue to build and shape the future of our company.

"Danone story as you know it" thus presupposes another story, which is part of the audiences' cultural heritage. But the narrator assumes that while the facts may be known, their meaning needs to be made explicit in that it "is above all an incredible human adventure". Its constitutive elements are listed, "encounters, adventures, and convictions", inviting the audience to understand that these "adventures" are indeed constructed by humans and not by nature, technology or economics. The repetition of the term "adventure" brings to mind discoveries, courage, risk-taking, self-confidence. From the introductory paragraph, the tone is set. As in most company histories, the narrator adopts a monological style and seeks to impose a form of reading and values. The website offers three types of narration. In the first, a periodization of the story is put forward, in four stages, from the family business to the "mission-driven" global group, with one presentation on one single page and, for each period, a photo accompanying a text. In the second, a series of four videos is grouped under the title "Danone is a story of pioneers", referring again to the three elements of the opening paragraph: adventures, encounters and convictions. The fourth video is the celebration of the company's 100th anniversary by staff teams that one imagines are happy to work for a company like Danone. The third historical presentation is set out as 17 key dates presented with a short text accompanied by a photo and frequently complemented by a video. The series of dates is given via a scrolling menu.

Figure 2.1. *The "Did you know?" logo and "Our History" on the French website*[5]. *For a color version of this figure, see www.iste.co.uk/pinede/digital.zip*

5 Available at: www.danone.com/en/about-danone/ourhistory.html.

2.3.2. *Analysis of the key narrative of the Danone story*

In the first narrative, the key to the chosen periodization is the company's strategic development mode. During the first period, "1919, fresh milk & ferments", Isaac Carasso, the company founder, is then in Spain and becomes conscious of people's intestinal disorders and malnutrition. He launched a new product: yogurt. The narrative form connects an element of explanatory context to a decision, an action. The "then" connector creates a cause-and-effect link between these two elements. The product is defined as new, maintaining an ambiguity, because while the product may be new in Spain, yogurt has been around in the Balkans for centuries. The text stresses the link between health and innovation by emphasizing the founder's use of the scientific research of the Pasteur Institute, in particular of one of the researchers, a Nobel prize winner. The new product is distributed in pharmacies, which contributes to the coherence between convictions and actions. Three other key themes are flagged in these opening paragraphs: a simple and natural product, paternal love or the family symbol and leaders (Isaac and Daniel Carasso, his son) who devote their lives to their beliefs. The second period, "The 1930s, from pharmacies to the world", is introduced with the takeover of the company by Isaac Carasso's son. The world referred to here comprises the French market and then the American market. Success in the latter market is substantiated by adaptation to local specificities (brand name and adapting to tastes). The two world wars are leveraged in the narrative to highlight the context of adversity and the visionary spirit of the leaders. Here, we can note a break in the linear narrative strategy. "Did you know?" is presented as a form of diversion from the narrative to stress not only a fact that impacts Danone and its stakeholders, but also the entire world with a unique form of example (see Figure 2.1). The "Did you know" logo is used to mark out an event on the page whose importance goes beyond that of the company. This is the dual social and economic project expounded by Antoine Riboud in 1972.

Reverting to the linear discursive strategy, the story continues with Danone's development through internal and external growth: the Carasso family meets Antoine Riboud (then president of the BSN group), the founder of the dual social and economic project. This encounter is described as "a professional 'love at first sight'", which explains the implicit fusion of visions of the business leaders, thanks to the "entrepreneurial talent" of Antoine Riboud. Thus, the BSN-Danone merger is presented as being coherent from the point of view of the two groups' missions rather than through critical-size research objectives or synergies.

During the third period, "1990s, opening up to the world", succession within the Carasso family is continued with that of the Riboud family. Franck Riboud is expanding the geographical growth of the Danone Group toward the countries of Eastern Europe, Asia and Latin America. Finally, during the fourth period, "2000, holding the Carasso torch up high", Franck Riboud and, from 2017, Emmanuel Faber continue the mission "to bring health through food to as many people as possible". It is claimed that "our mission stands stronger than ever. It remains our anchor point to Danone's original values". The slogan "One Planet. One Health" reflects the development of "quality products made from natural ingredients, to protect the health of people and of our planet"[6] (see Table 2.1).

This text provides a fairly classic example of mythologization, the usual approach to industrial groups' use of historical elements. The point is to illustrate the leadership shown by the "great" men of the company, often the founders and CEOs. In adversity and in the general interest, while leveraging their entrepreneurial talent, these men are presented as the explanatory factor of the company's success and the affiliation of its stakeholders, which brings legitimacy without discussion. This narrative develops a monolithic vision of the organization where the potentially conflicting interests of its stakeholders are all unified toward that of the higher interest that surpasses them. This division into four episodes is unusual but can be justified by various motivations: facilitating reading, emphasizing the longevity and durability of the company (therefore its solidity), presenting a development that is simultaneously linear and punctuated by major changes related to strategic choices, showcasing the contributions of each family of entrepreneurs, serving as an underlying subplot for the other narratives. Myths allow us to construct and assert, in an accessible way, some of the emblematic values of an organizational culture.

According to the Danone Group's website[7], the official values of the organization are humanism, openness, proximity and enthusiasm. This first narrative of the group embodies the values of enthusiasm and/or humanism through the company's mission.

6 This phrase reflects a specific production context, that of the industrialization of the food sector. Indeed, it is mainly industrialized products that contain "unnatural" ingredients.

7 Available at: www.danone.com/impact/people-communities.html.

	1919–1930	1930–1990	1990–2000	2000–2020
Values	Helping the weak, leveraging science, paternal love, nature and simplicity, devoting oneself to a cause	Entrepreneurship, adapting to different markets, a social and economic project	Seeking growth Internationalization	Promoting health through food Tradition and continuity Simple, natural products
Plot	Spain, post-war, I. Carasso proposes to help people in need. Assisted by E. Metchnikoff (Nobel prize winner) and then by his son. A simple, healthy product	The son follows in his father's footsteps and surpasses him in expanding the business internationally. Another great entrepreneur, A. Riboud	F. Riboud continues the quest of Carasso and his father, A. Riboud	Through F. Riboud and E. Faber, Danone continues the founders' quest
Meaning	"New Product", "Nobel Prize" "health benefits", "after his son's Catalan nickname", "a simple product"	"He transforms", "Did you know?", a dual social and economic project, "professional love at first sight", "entrepreneurial talent"	"Further afield", "with F. Riboud"	"Health for as many people as possible" "One planet. One health", "quality products made from natural ingredients"
Characters	I. Carasso, a hero, father and entrepreneur D. Carasso, a hero and son Metchnicoff, a scientist	D. Carasso, a pioneer, a successful entrepreneur A. Riboud, a pioneer, a hero of "radical" change, entrepreneur	F. Riboud, a successful entrepreneur and "inventor of the Danone mission"	F. Riboud, social CEO E. Faber, social CEO Danone, a mission-driven group
Tense	Historical context, present tense. Continuity, dynamism, proximity to "the present"	Historical context, present tense. Future "quickly known", presupposes a realized projection.	Context in past, but present and future tense	Present context, present tense highlighting continuity with the past
Narrative	External narrator Monological narration, presupposing its "credibility" Focus: Danone Group	Narrator external to the story Form of monological narration Focus: Danone Group	External narrator Focus: Danone Group	External narrator Focus: Danone Group

Table 2.1. *Analytical summary of the periodization on the Danone institutional website*

2.3.3. *Analysis of the videos available on the institutional website*

The second form of narration consists of four short videos, available by scrolling along the page, which requires a specific action on the part of the Internet user. In these videos, the visuals, the musical background and the interviews with the "main actors" may reinforce the credibility of the narrative and the pathos, and are thus likely to reduce the likelihood of a critical form of reading. These narratives adopt both a linear and a thematic reading of the Danone story. The four topics are associated with the official values of the company and especially with the three elements that contributed to Danone's human adventure, according to the introductory paragraph. These videos embody and interpret the symbols of Danone and thus at least partially steer Internet users' reading (see Table 2.2).

The first narrative, "Danone is a story of pioneers", focuses on the period between 1910 and 1990. Here, we do indeed have adventures and enthusiasm, with the history of the Carasso family, introduced as the creator of the Danone brand. Isaac and Daniel Carasso are presented with a typical entrepreneurial profile, which involves courage, self-belief, perseverance, but also the ability to leverage only their own resources, to be visionary, to respond to the particular issues of their time. These pioneers are seen as being inspiring for employees, and through them, the company itself becomes a pioneer.

The second video, "Danone, a story of encounters", is about encounters and openness. Between 1910 and 2000, the meetings between the Danone heroes define not so much the significant events in Danone's history as the profiles and the strategies that each of Danone's four directors wished to develop: for Isaac Carasso, science for the benefit of nutrition, for Daniel Carasso, marketing to conquer new markets, for Daniel Carasso and Antoine Riboud, a merger between men and companies, the integration of economic and social objectives, and for Franck Riboud, addressing social issues through nutrition.

The video "Danone, a story of visions" is devoted to convictions and humanism, with a presentation of the history of the visions of Danone's leaders from 1910 to the present day. Danone thus offers an analysis framework of its strategies and its inspiring vision that goes beyond simple economic objectives and shapes its future environment. According to this narrative, the social dimension of Danone's vision has been reinforced over the years, with the exception of Daniel Carasso's vision which focuses more on brand development. This video aims to clearly define the organization and to suggest a link between visions and essential characteristics or the cultural paradigm.

	Danone is a story of pioneers	Danone is a story of encounters	Danone is a story of visions	Danone, 100 years with our teams
Values	Innovate and work for the health of all, healthy and simple product	Friendships Openness Passion	Follow your environmental and socio-environmental convictions	Diversity Collaboration
Plot	Carasso leaves the Balkans for Spain and combats malnutrition with a healthy, simple product. His son launches the business in France and then achieves his American dream. He follows the dream: to meet the needs of the population – the health of all	I. Carosso is inspired by Metchnikoff Encounter between D. Carasso and designer R. Loewy: Americanizing the brand Encounter of F. Riboud with Muhammad Yunus (Nobel Peace Prize) to combat child malnutrition in Bangladesh	Conviction of having a unique product with high added value Danone Project "One planet. One health" Isaac's visions on health, Daniel's vision on brands, Antoine's vision on social and environmental issues and Franck's vision on emerging countries	Empowering each employee to co-construct by fully embracing the food revolution
Meaning	"Pioneers", "shared dream", "American dream", "new meetings, new countries", "meeting the needs of the population and innovating for the health of all", "incredible intelligence and alertness"	"A story of encounters", "produce healthy and accessible food for children suffering from malnutrition", "social entrepreneurship", "you have to be free-spirited, iconoclastic, open, express this joy of living"	"The conviction of having a unique product with high added value", "a visionary discourse", "it is no longer the brands that make people, it is the people who make brands", "will win the food revolution"	"Co-constructing by fully embracing the food revolution"
Characters	Isaac and Daniel Carasso, pioneers	Partners: inventor-researcher; entrepreneur and designer; entrepreneur and "revolutionary" entrepreneur; entrepreneur and Nobel Peace Prize winner	The five leaders of the company	E. Faber and a number of colleagues involved in the Danone twin project
Tense	Present	Present	Present	Present and future
Narrative	External and proximity to the heroes through interviews	External but authenticity and internal perspective through interviews	External and authenticity	Multiple voices

Table 2.2. *Synthetic analysis of periodization taken from the videos*

Finally, the last video, "Danone, 100 years with our teams", focuses on proximity. This is about celebrating Danone's centenary, with a kind of "coda", a narrative with a happy ending. The years of adventures, encounters and convictions end in one great, happy company, with partners who represent various subsidiaries, brands, cultures and relevant geographical regions, all committed to the food revolution, all proud to belong to this visionary group.

We can observe that the first three videos represent three different interpretations (performances) of the main narrative. This is a form of composing the leader paragraph composed from elements of Danone's history. By personalizing, by humanizing the company, these narratives constructed to be empathetic stir up emotion and pride. These three narratives also represent a different narrative tense. The "pioneers" narrative is the shortest in the Danone story, but the individual stories are the longest: entire life stories. The encounters narrative traces a longer Danone story, but one that tells intertwined personal stories. Finally, the last video draws comparisons between the Danone story and the achievements in the lives of its leaders. In other words, the tenses of each individual narrative (video) orient and are influenced by the tense of the global narrative composed of the four videos.

As we can see, each new narration adds complexity to the story, adopts a slant, specifies varying narrative and social roles for the same actor. This complexity is not a limit or an inconsistency; on the contrary, it tends to make the protagonists complex and realistic. The narratives conduct a dialogue among themselves and help give probably more substance to the characters (always positive, of course, as is obligatory for this kind of institutional communication).

2.3.4. *Analysis of key dates*

The third form of narration is more detailed in terms of key dates, but more succinct in terms of text[8]. The narratives are not accessible at first glance, but call for proactiveness on the part of the user, who must open them one after another (but this can be done randomly).

Most of the texts are accompanied by a video that must be activated by the user. Thus, there are numerous reading possibilities with this system of cascading texts, which present evidence of the company's dynamism (see periodized synthesis in Table 2.3).

8 Available at: www.danone.com/en/about-danone/ourhistory.html. At the bottom of the page: dates scroll across laterally.

In these narratives, the episodes are more numerous, increasing in number toward the last 20 years of history. They are not divided up as in the initial narrative on the basis of the reign of the chief leaders, but rather on the basis of business events.

The speech is therefore more managerial and leverages growth prospects, brand portfolios, focus on core activities, strategy, etc. It shows the competence, rationality and ambitions of the directors through their results and their reasoning. This narrative (which consists of 17 episodes) is different from the main narrative, with a more economic and rational slant rather than social and emotional, at least for the period 1910–2000. The style is always positive, the events praiseworthy and the directors visionary, but what matters most is managing the brands, consolidating positions and becoming a global giant.

On the other hand, for the period 2000–2020, we can observe a new narrative bifurcation. It becomes strongly rooted in a perspective of health through food and then the food revolution. This shift in direction is not at odds with the previous period, but is presented as strategic consistency and reasoning. Instead of focusing on the directors, the discourse presents the brands. This decentralization transfers the humanism and leadership skills to the brands and ensures continuity, while at the same time reifying the organization.

On the Danone institutional website, we can thus identify three cycles of between 4 and 17 episodes, each made up of narratives. They are all of an epic, sometimes romantic genre (Gabriel 2011). Even the official narratives are complex and, despite being managed by the communication department, they appear multidimensional and allow multiple readings. This complexity allows the organization to affiliate heterogeneous audiences, but at the same time can in some cases be used as an argument for their opponents. It is also necessary for these audiences to be so persevering (as us) as to read every one of the texts relating to the history of Danone. We can observe a strategy in the periodization or rather serialization of the narratives. This helps to retain the interest and attention of the Internet user, not to frighten him/her off with a long text, to make the narrative dynamic, to put forward different forms of reading according to the mode of periodization, different presentations, to leave more room for maneuver to the Internet user, while ensuring the continuity of the essence of the organization.

The serialization postulates a double narrative: one within an episode and another for the series as a whole. In each episode, the heroic plot is reiterated and also expanded, from the individual to the group, from the man to cultural artifacts (brands, products), from socioeconomic issues to socioeconomic and environmental issues.

The multitude of superimposed episodes helps to reinforce and freeze the message, thus contributing, in our opinion, to a cultural stabilization, but without simplifying or reducing this culture. The serialization carried still further in the form of a conversational turn can also be observed on the company's Facebook page.

	First steps 1919–1978	Global ambitions 1979–1995	Toward health 1996–2013	Accelerated growth 2014–2016
Values	Offer products that meet market needs – differentiators Primary brand Dual social and economic project Synergy and critical size	Ongoing international growth through acquisitions Always going the extra mile	Continuity Strategic refocusing around sectors with high growth potential "Bringing health through food"	Corporate governance is important – social issues must be at the heart of brands Global change Confidence in brands
Plot	Progressive entrepreneur heroes Products: varying needs of markets Innovative and coherent strategies	The group takes off, thanks to the coherence of its strategies and brands	Group led by a rational strategist in continuity with his father's dual project	In continuity with his predecessor, E. Faber re-enforces the dual economic and social project
Meaning	Suffering of Spanish children "Popularizing a product whose benefits are recognized in the Balkans" "First pots in pharmacies" "Danone Brand" "BSN takes the lead" "Shatters the traditional concept of a business leader" "Moved by the ideals of May-68" "Professional love at first sight" "Giant of the agri-food industry"	"Looking toward Asia and Latin America" Change of sector, name, size, geography, strategy, but "we have still kept what we inherited" "The Star Child" "The story continues, offering new development opportunities for the group"	Mission "to bring health through food to as many as possible" "Enhanced portfolio" "Global leaders in infant and medical nutrition" "New pillar of growth and profitability" "New level of growth, profitability and expansion in emerging countries"	"Founded by moms" "By placing child malnutrition issues at the heart of its project, Happy Family is revolutionizing its sector" "Responsible and transparent in its practices, Happy Family is the first of our brands to join a global movement to change the way businesses operate" "Making both money and a difference"

	First Steps 1919-1978	Global ambitions 1979-1995	Towards health 1996-2013	Accelerated growth 2014-2016
Characters	I. and D. Carasso, A. Riboud, entrepreneurs and strategists, social fiber	A. Riboud, builder of a multinational business	F. Riboud, a visionary leader	E. Faber, leader of the food revolution Responsible brand
Tense	Text in present Videos: past tense, but indirect speech in the present	Text in present Videos in past, present tense for interviews with A. and F. Riboud	Text in present Videos in past and present tense for interviews with E. Faber and F. Riboud	Present and future
Narrative	External narrator, abstract, vision of the Danone Group Videos: D. Carasso and A. Riboud relate the thoughts of I. and D. Carasso	External narrator, abstract, vision of the Danone Group, Videos: A. and F. Riboud on their vision	External narrators in texts and videos. Interviews with E. Faber and F. Riboud on their strategic arguments	External narrators in texts and videos Excerpt from E. Faber's speech on Danone's commitment to becoming a mission-driven company
	Organizational changes 2017–2018		**Driving the food revolution 2019**	**Danone, a mission-driven company 2020**
Values	Responding to market trends Healthier and more responsible food Consolidating its market share The food revolution Leadership Economic growth and social and environmental progress		Tradition Simple product with simple goals: to improve health High quality products and natural ingredients Nourishing the health of the planet and of people	Being a pioneer A mission-driven company (*entreprise à mission*) Transparency and credibility
Plot	The group is changing in order to strengthen its social and environmental commitment, while at the same time consolidating its market share. The transparency of commitments is certified by external experts and a new slogan		The company has remained faithful to its history and its values	The company incorporates its dual project into its statutes and as an essential characteristic (of identity)

	Organizational changes 2017-2018	Driving the Food Revolution 2019	Danone, a mission-driven company 2020
Meaning	"Ideal partner", "global leader", "largest Public Benefit Corporation in the world", "our health and the health of the planet are interdependent", "healthier and more sustainable consumption habits", "one of the world's most influential food companies", "balancing economic growth with social and environmental progress", "supporting people's aspirations for healthier lives." "Positive impact on the entire value chain", "nourishing and protecting a planet, a health", "the end of large pyramidal multinational models", "inventing new organizations, closer to life, closer to reality"	"A hundred years ago" "Our mission today." "Highlights values going back to the first Danone yogurt" "Continue to develop high quality products made of natural ingredients in a way that nourishes both people and the planet"	"Becomes the first listed company to take this legal form", "eminent and qualified experts", "our progress"
Characters	F. Riboud, CEO and creator of Danone's mission E. Faber, CEO committing the group to the food revolution	Danone yogurt, emblematic of history and values "We" at Danone, committed staff	Danone, a mission-driven company Committee of eminent independent experts
Tense	Present and future	Present	Present and future
Narrative	In the text and videos, the narrator is sometimes external, marketing style, sometimes internal and speaks on behalf of the company (us), extract from a speech by E. Faber on behalf of the company (us)	Internal narrator (us), proximity, commitment	Internal narrator

Table 2.3. *Synthetic analysis of key dates on the Danone institutional website*

2.4. Danone's history and the use of the "Did you know?" insets on Facebook

This part is devoted to the study of the link between Danone's Facebook[9] page and the narratives on the institutional website. We study the texts related to or

9 Available at: www.facebook.com/Danone.

referring to Danone's centenary, in 2019, as well as the texts of the "Did you know?" insets of this year. A simple reading of these texts and an analysis of the situations enable us to highlight five periods relating to the study of the published posts. Each period is differentiated either by the themes developed, or by the mode of enunciation, or by both.

2.4.1. *From February 7 to April 18, 2019*

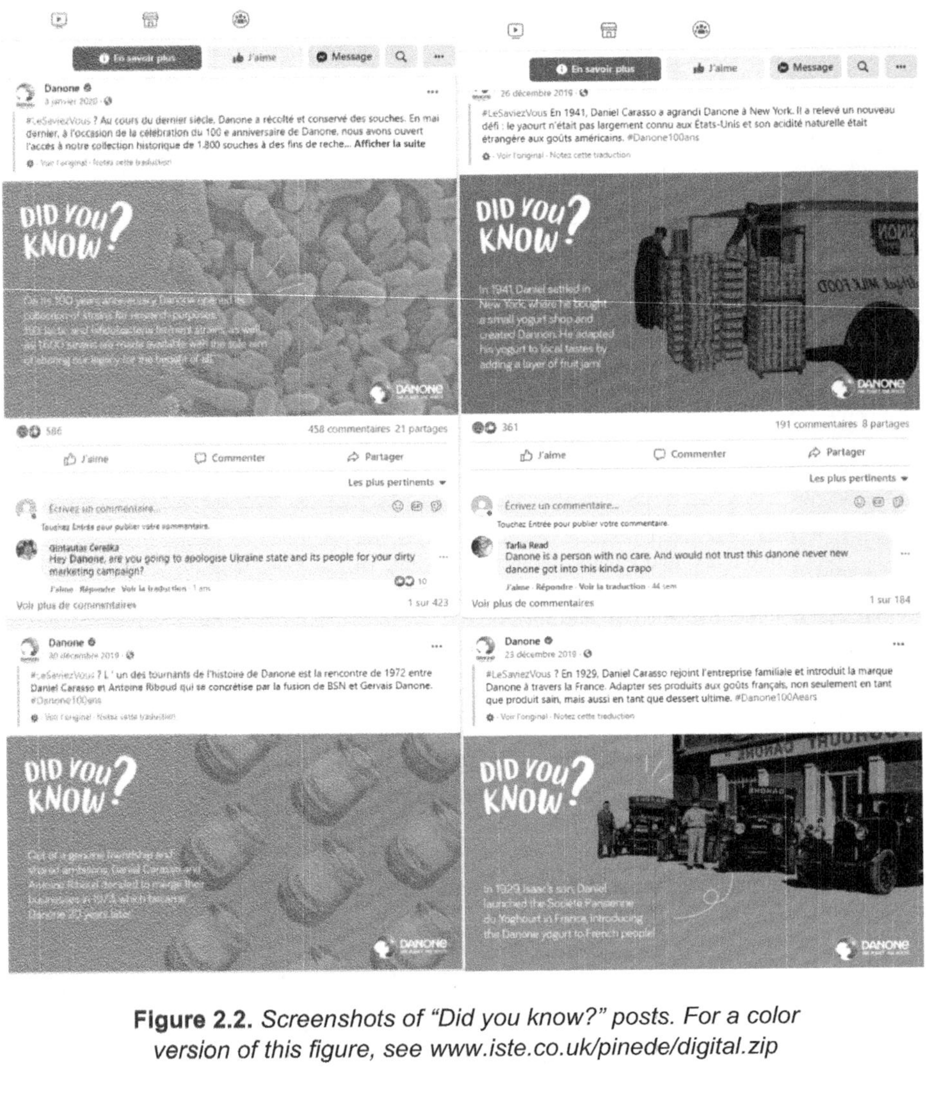

Figure 2.2. *Screenshots of "Did you know?" posts. For a color version of this figure, see www.iste.co.uk/pinede/digital.zip*

In this first period, we are looking at a conversation between families. The narrator is external to the message, certainly, but they share with those around them the extraordinary longevity of the company's products. The product is simple and natural. It is possible to draw a parallel between these messages and the exchange of a few words of good advice between friends. Parental emotions are leveraged to attract attention and interest. The founder of the company shares the concerns of parents through the ages. It is not so much about giving information on Danone's history as introducing the Carasso family, responsive to the concerns of parents of yesterday and today and offering wholesome, less processed foods. The messages are short, not only to conform to the standard usage of social media, but also to arouse curiosity, either by making reference to the website's institutional pages, or by following the thread of the messages posted.

2.4.2. *From April 26 to May 8, 2019*

One event seems to give the Facebook posts a new direction: *The Love behind Food Summit*, organized on May 8. The messages emphasize the gravitas and the use of the results of scientific research for Danone's historic products. It is in this context that the first "Did you know?" insets appear. It is likely that organizing this event, the purpose of which was to mark the Danone's centenary, gave the company's communications team the idea of linking history and science in terms of not only content, but also form with "Did you know?" While a "Did you know?" publication is not necessarily linked to a scientific discovery, it is often associated with verifiable but forgotten facts. The summit, like the "Did you know?" insets, plays a role in marking the importance of Danone's centenary. While it fixes Danone in its time or rather in the time of the food revolution, the "Did you know?" insets fixes (or seeks to fix) Danone in popular history through the recollection of intriguing facts.

2.4.3. *From May 9 to May 25, 2019*

We can observe that during this period, the "Did you know?" insets focus not on intriguing facts from the past, but on information about recent or even ongoing items, always verifiable facts. The text therefore answers the question "Do you know?" rather than the question "Did you know?" However, retaining the past tense of the question presumes that these business activities of Danone are sustainable. If we focus on the thread of messages from this period, we can note the intertextuality between the Facebook page and the institutional website. Video intertextuality seems to be a form of quoting an entire text. To avoid redundancies, this makes the assumption that the readers of the institutional website are not the same as those of the Facebook page. These videos are probably considered by their creators to be an emblem of Danone that must be pushed at audiences. They seem to have acquired the status of cultural products with a value that makes it possible to take them out of the context of their original creation (the institutional website) and disseminate them in the mediatic space[10]. While on the institutional website the videos could be analyzed as a form of performance of the introductory text, on the Facebook page, these are themselves performed by the text that accompanies them. For example, the pioneers video is introduced by the fact that a father, for love for his son, creates a simple, healthy product and suggests an emotional, humanistic reading of the video about the entrepreneur's spirit. Likewise, the video about the encounters is introduced with keys to understanding that put marketing in the background. Finally, the third video is underscored by the current vision of the organization, which steers the temporal dimension of the message. The fourth video reinforces this new, more emotional, more horizontal reading of the three previous narratives with the anniversary celebrations and the committed employees. The four videos follow each other over 4 days, which allows a consecutive reading one day apart so as to link them to a global narrative of Danone whose essence is science, health and humanism.

However, it would certainly have been inappropriate to post them on the same day, because the message would probably have been too long in relation to the usage of social media, with the risk of appearing as monological, thus losing any resemblance to a conversation. A week later, the four "Did you know?" insets serve as factual evidence of the commitments outlined in the videos. The "Did you know?" layout makes Danone's actions part of facts that are high impact but not necessarily known by the general public. It must be stressed that "Did you know?" becomes a fixed form, marking a genre, even when it is used creatively.

2.4.4. *From August 12 to September 2, 2019*

During this period, there is no reference to Danone's centenary, only its local brands scattered all over the world. The "Did you know?" section inscribes these brands within local popular cultures or highlights their positive impact. In other words, the leverage of "Did you know?" is dual, sometimes in its classic usage trialed in the period from April 26 to May 8, 2019, and sometimes in its new usage tried in the period from May 9 to 25, 2019. It seems to be a form of marketing leveraging institutional brand communication.

10 Indeed, it is technically more difficult to modify a video than a text.

2.4.5. *From December 20 to December 30, 2019*

The repetition of "Did you know?" insets with those for the period from April 26 to May 8, 2019, leads us to query the motivation behind this structure. However, this duplication is not complete and it is likely either that this is a deliberate communication strategy or that it results from instability in the Facebook audiences' relationship to time. Nevertheless, if we study the four insets as a series from a single narrative, we realize that it is in fact the succinct version of the first two periods of the company's development as told in the main narrative (from 1919 to 1973) or the "First Steps" of Danone (in the detailed narrative) on the institutional website. In other words, our understanding of the last two new insets would not have the same historical significance without the first two repeated insets. The succession of colors along with images like the first and fourth "Did you know?" visually highlight the link between the four insets, the importance of the brand and the rapid growth of the group.

2.5. A coherent communication strategy

Are Danone's narratives the result of a communication strategy or strategic communication? Ultimately, both. The stories and the corporate culture partly shape the strategy, and the strategy encourages a re-reading or reinterpretation of the former. The series of narratives leveraged during this campaign by Danone shows the company's desire to appear as a precursor and a leader in the field of corporate social responsibility (CSR). The whole construction of these narratives leans toward this idea that Danone has always placed great importance on its societal role. Having been there for many consumers around the world at every stage in their lives, from birth to old age, for more than 100 years, the company wants to set out its values and make them understood, to share them with all its stakeholders, its consumers first and foremost, but also, although less directly, its shareholders, for instance the public authorities in all the countries concerned. Danone's equity is very fragmented; shareholders were relatively dormant until 2015, the strong performance of the group providing them with a security that is always attractive in a share portfolio. The entrance of American pension funds into the equity disturbed this tranquility. These shareholders do not have the same vision of CSR as Europeans. The company and its shareholders, on the basis of their profits, must take on this responsibility toward society and/or nature, indirectly through funding or supporting initiatives taken by other citizens or directly by establishing foundations. Pension fund analysts are well aware that a group that is well placed in terms of CSR is more likely to make a profit, but that is not a sufficient reason to support this strategy as shareholders. The US funds, which are however a small minority in

Danone's capital (a few percent in total), consider the French group to be undervalued on the stock market compared to its competitors. The danger for Danone's management is that these can bring other shareholders onboard with them to force them to a management more focused on stock market movements, traditionally by pushing for job cuts or abandoning the least profitable activities, but more strategically by positioning themselves differently in terms of CSR, especially in its social dimension[11].

The communication from Danone's management, focused, on the one hand, on the perennity of their positions in favor of CSR and their societal commitments and, on the other hand, on the economic success story, has two objectives. It makes it possible to strengthen the image of the company as a creator of value for consumers and to alert European shareholders and politicians, particularly the French, of the risk that could be posed in the medium term by the strategy advocated by the American pension funds. The narratives used, and in particular the "Did you know?" format, are especially pertinent because they reinforce the credibility of the discourse. Each of these facts is intrinsically correct. It is essentially good news. It is verifiable today (hence the abundance of present tense in narratives and archival elements). The interpretation that is made of it should, in all strategic and scientific rationality, be equally verifiable in the past or correspond to previous knowledge shared, if not by all, at least by those who know (hence the past tense of "Did you know?") which can guarantee its veracity. The abundance of media leveraged, the cross-referencing of given information, replace to some extent this process of authentication by readers and Internet users. The fact stated is no longer in isolation and susceptible to critical analysis on the real positioning of the company's value system in its specific, verifiable and operational context. It is integrated into a patchwork, a mass that gives substance to the interpretations put forward by the management.

Analyzing texts about the history of an organization as the performance of a cultural narrative allows us to consider the polysemy of corporate cultures. With Danone's texts, this multitude of interpretations and performances is reinforced both by the splitting of narrative into episodes and by the multimedia (text, visuals, website, social media). Intertextuality makes it possible both to steer the reading, and also to influence it. Another strategy leveraged by Danone is that of the reification of an essence, of the qualities of the leaders, nowadays extended to the products. Through the different uses of "Did you know?" and the narratives of

11 Two shareholders, the activist fund Bluebell Capital and the management company Artisan Partners, pressed Danone to separate the roles of President and CEO at the beginning of March 2021, before the board of directors voted to replace Emmanuel Faber on March 14, 2021.

the recent history of the group, Danone's marketing is evolving toward social marketing and product communication is developing an institutional aspect. In other words, innovations in terms of communication practices seem to us to be due less to ideas that break away from what is already there than to a process of "entextualization", improvization and intertextuality between everyday media. In this context of analysis, contingencies (the "Did you know?" insets that proliferate on social media and the food summit are opportunities for appropriation by Danone's communicators and at least partially re-orientate their narrative modes. If we study the form taken by intermedia quotes, we can observe that the intertextuality of the texts from the institutional website and the Facebook page is indirect, reinterpreted, while that of the videos is direct. The videos are regarded as autonomous cultural products, to be watched in full so as to understand the meaning. This direct quotation and the circulation of these videos give them all the more authority and stabilize their messages through their dissemination. On the other hand, indirect quotations of messages in textual form make it possible to exploit their polysemic dimension and to allow the preservation not only of distanced relationships (informative, monological) with audiences, but also of proximity, involvement, etc.

The "Did you know?" section guides without determining the communicational modes in both its discursive and its material nature. In its discursive form, this question is associated with a specific rhetorical and informational usage: intriguing facts and anecdotes that are part of general culture. Its usage gives this quality to Danone's messages. The information contained in the "Did you know?" is worth knowing. This mark of importance is leveraged both on the Facebook page and on the institutional website, here definitely more sparingly than on social media. In its material form, this section steers messages with a short, factual presentation. Moreover, Danone develops a specific graphic charter and combines the message with a visual. The "Did you know?" posts on the Facebook page thus become products in their own right and can only be quoted directly on other Facebook pages (like the videos found on YouTube).

2.6. Conclusion

This chapter offers an analysis of a number of narratives that relate to the same story, that of Danone. We have tried to take into account the potential consequences of these different narratives on the process of stabilizing a corporate culture. We have adopted a processual perspective by considering this culture as being the result of a multitude of performances that become meaningful not taken in isolation but by considering a series of other texts.

While an isolated text is relatively easy to monitor in its production (but not necessarily in its reception), considering institutional communication not as a text but as a co-production by interrelated texts that were or were not produced by the organization requires us to reject the illusion of a communication department that is in control of contents referring to the company. Thus, official or institutional communication becomes shared or co-oriented by employees, ambassadors, cultural artifacts or conjunctural phenomena. While the department does not have a monopoly on dialogue, it could claim expertise in it.

By considering the texts produced by organizations not as isolated elements, written for their own sakes, but as elements of a network of texts, when developing a communication strategy, it might be useful to think about the temporality of actions in relation to the temporary attention of audiences, but also the insertion of new performances (texts, videos, events) in a pre-existing network of contexts.

Similarly, it is important to take into account not only the semiotic aspects of texts, but also their material form. Once a mode of communication has been "packaged", it implies a linked set of the elements that must be put in place for it to be recognized: graphics, type of message, genre. Once this linked set of elements is stabilized, it produces cultural artifacts that can no longer circulate as a performance in the here and now ("Did you know?" or videos, for example), but as a text independent of its context of origin.

There are a number of limitations to this study. We were not able to access ethnographic information at the production phase of the texts studied or at the precise time when they were written (except on the Facebook page, where the date is explicit). We do not claim to have studied the intentions of the authors of these texts, but rather a number of consequences induced by cross-analyzing them. Another limitation of this study is that we did not analyze the comments of users, their evaluations, the repetitions of Danone texts on other Facebook pages or on other social media. Similarly, other approaches to narrative analysis can be leveraged. This work can be enriched by expanding both the scale of the digital space (other networks, other pages, user comments) and the timescale. Indeed, it may be of interest to follow up the work of legitimization and strategic-cultural stabilization post-intervention of the investment funds on the functioning of the group.

Thus, we can envisage a continuation of this investigation which focuses on cultural dialogue by taking into account interactions with Internet users on the many social media on which a company interacts with its audiences. It is also possible to take into account the socio-material aspects of digital media in the cultural practices of dialogue, inclusion or cultural bifurcation where social and ecological issues take a front seat. Of course, one project could be to look at other cases besides Danone, especially to take part in research on responsible companies.

2.7. References

Abbott, H.P. (2014). *Narrative*. Cambridge University Press, Cambridge.

Abdelwahed, M.A. and Antit, I. (2016). La culture organisationnelle revisitée : esquisse d'une culture située. In *XXVe Conférence de l'AIMS*, Hammamet.

Alvesson, M. (2002). *Understanding Organisational Culture*. SAGE, London.

Alvesson, M. and Sveningsson, S. (2008). *Changing Organisational Culture*. Routledge, London.

Angermuller (2014). *Poststructuralist Discourse Analysis: Subjectivity in Enunciative Pragmatics*. Palgrave Macmillian, London.

Barthes, R. (1991). *Introduction à l'analyse structurale du récit*. Le Seuil, Paris.

Bastard, I., Cardon, D., Charbey, R., Cointet, J.-P., Prieur, C. (2017). Facebook, pour quoi faire ? Configurations d'activités et structures relationnelles. *Sociologie*, 1(8), 57–82.

Beauvisage, T., Beuscart, J., Cardon, D. (2013). Notes et avis des consommateurs sur le Web. Les métriques du web. *Réseaux*, 1(177), 131–161.

Bertrand, Y. (1991). *Culture organisationnelle*. Presses de l'Université du Québec, Quebec.

Bordeau, J. (2012). *Storytelling et contenu de marque : la puissance du langage à l'ère numérique*. Éditions Ellipses, Paris.

Bruna, M.G. (2021). Quelques thèses récentes sur la culture organisationnelle. *Question(s) de management*, 1(31), 211–214.

Cardon, D. (2019). *Culture numérique*. Presses de Sciences Po, Paris.

Chanal, V. and Tannery, F. (2005). La communication de la stratégie ou l'art de persuader. *Revue française de gestion*, 6(159), 165–186.

Chédotel, F. (2004). L'ambivalence de l'identification organisationnelle : revue de littérature et pistes de recherche. *Management & avenir*, 1(1), 59–75.

Cohendet, P. and Diani, M. (2003). L'organisation comme une communauté de communautés. Croyances collectives et culture d'entreprise. *Revue d'économie politique*, 5(113), 697–720.

Daiute, C. (2014). *Narrative Inquiry: A Dynamic Approach*. SAGE, Thousand Oaks.

Eyries, A. (2021). Entreprise et management : formes culturelles et/ou enjeux communicationnels ? *Question(s) de management*, 1(30), 143–150.

Gabriel, Y. (2011). *Storytelling in Organizations: Facts, Fictions and Fantasies*. Oxford University Press, Oxford.

Garfinkel, H. (2007). *Recherches en ethnométhodologie*. PUF, Paris.

Girard, D. (2007). Culture organisationnelle, contexte d'affaires et prise de décision éthique. *Gestion*, 1(32), 101–111.

Godelier, E. (2006). *La Culture d'entreprise*. La Découverte, Paris.

Godelier, E. (2009). La culture d'entreprise. Source de pérennité ou source d'inertie ? *Revue française de gestion*, 2(192), 95–111.

Kahane, B. (2005). Les conditions de cohérence des récits stratégiques de la narration à la naraction. *Revue française de gestion*, 6(159), 125–147.

Kohler Riessman, C. (2008). *Narrative Methods for the Human Sciences*. SAGE, Thousand Oaks.

Lehtonen, M. (2000). *The Cultural Analysis of Texts*. SAGE, Thousand Oaks.

Martin, J. (1992). *Cultures in Organizations: Three Perspectives*. Oxford University Press, Oxford.

Peirce, C. (1998). *The Essential Peirce: Selected Philosophical Writings, V2 (1893-1913)*. The Peirce Edition Project, Bloomington.

Pettigrew, A.M. (1979). On studying organizational cultures. *Administrative Science Quartely*, 24(4), 570–581.

Pohl, S. and Battistelli, A. (2019). Culture organisationnelle. In *Psychologie du travail et des organisations : 110 notions clés*, Vallèry, G., Bobillier-Chaumon, M., Brangier, É., Dubois, M. (eds). Dunod, Paris.

Rouet, G. (2018). L'organisation est communication. *Hermès*, 1(80), 252–254.

Silberzahn, P. (2014). Identité, culture organisationnelle et surprises stratégiques : l'exemple de la CIA. *Le Journal de l'école de Paris du management*, 5(109), 37–44.

Silverstein, M. and Urban, G. (eds) (1996). *Natural Histories of Discourse*. The University of Chicago Press, Chicago.

Sleiman, M.W., Aloui, A., Baruel Bencherqui, D. (2020). Sens et performativité dans les discours de RSE. *Recherches en sciences de gestion*, 2(137), 369–396.

Taylor, J. and Van Every, E. (2000). *The Emergent Organization: Communication as Its Site and Surface*. Lauwrence Erlbaum Associates, Mahwah.

Thevenet, B. (2015). La mise en évidence de la culture. In *La culture d'entreprise*, Thevenet, B. (ed.). PUF, Paris.

3

Website and Media Ethos: A Case Study of Photographic Equipment Manufacturers

Marion ROLLANDIN
Communication et Societiés, Université Clermont Auvergne, Clermont-Ferrand, France

3.1. Introduction

Photography is a technique that first and foremost has evolved as a result of the work of scientists who have each worked on various stages leading up to the production of a photograph. In the early 20th century, some people took up this complex and expensive technique in order to make it their job, becoming professional photographers. Thus, they needed to buy equipment, which gave rise to the creation of photographic equipment companies. We can identify six major companies that are still in business: Nikon, Canon, Fujifilm, Olympus, Pentax and Sony. With the exception of Sony, they all started their business in this sector in the first half of the century. These manufacturers are now recognized as rightfully entitled to design, distribute and market cameras and optics, and they were already in existence before the Internet. With the miniaturization of components and the decrease in production costs, the camera arrived in families, ushering in practices that differ from those of professionals. The transition to digital accentuated this popularization of the practice, making the taking of a snapshot simpler and more automated. It is now possible to take numerous snaps of a scene instead of one, thus limiting the thought process prior to taking the shot. Photography has also changed – as a practice and as an object. Thus, the intention is no longer necessarily

Digital Presences of Organizations,
coordinated by Nathalie PINÈDE, Luc MASSOU and Patrick MPONDO-DICKA. © ISTE Ltd 2024.

for it to printed it on paper; it can be circulated on social media or end up forgotten on a hard drive.

Digital technology – through the design of cameras or the creation of online image-sharing websites – leads to a diversification of practices and audiences. In fact, professionals and amateurs alike will adopt a practice and sometimes use the same equipment. The term "amateur" is used here to refer to a person with a keen interest in the practice without making a living from it, and it is in no way used to define a level of competence. While a critical analysis of the use of this term by commercial organizations would be relevant, it is not the purpose of this study. These multiple changes are leading manufacturers to evolve and communicate with these differing audiences in a sector that has become competitive. The stakes are high for these companies, which have to seduce old and new audiences in order to encourage them to make purchases, at the same time responding to the development of smartphones that can sometimes rival them in terms of practices, for a smaller footprint[1]. Looking at these findings, we began an exploratory survey on photography practices in the digital age. Our intention is to report our early work on this, which focuses on the analysis of photographic equipment manufacturers' websites. The idea is to understand the presentations conveyed by the companies through the prism of their website, now an essential tool for an online presence. Our research falls within the theoretical field of computer-based media (see section 3.2 for more details). We answer the following question: how do the websites of photographic equipment manufacturers deliver their representations of themselves, which constitutes an element that can play a role in the act of making a purchase? In order to answer this question, we conducted a semio-pragmatic analysis consisting of a detailed analysis of the meaning of the computer-based media system through its use by subjects (Odin 2000, pp. 52–53) in 2018 and then in 2021 on the six company websites: Nikon, Canon, Olympus, Pentax, Fujifilm and Sony[2]. We took into account the differences in interpretation related to the potential knowledge levels of individuals when looking at what can be read on the screen and when engaging with the action possibilities made possible by the technological substrate.

This investigation led to detailed studies on various sections of our corpus. We took screenshots that we annotated, in order to consider the various levels of meaning that could be taken on by the visible signs, depending on the relationship to

1 While the weight is undeniably less for a smartphone, this comment should be qualified according to the range into which the product fits and the type of usage.

2 Here are the URLs of the websites of the corpus: Nikon (www.nikon.fr/fr_FR/), Canon (www.canon.fr/), Fujifilm (www.fujifilm.com/fr/fr#), Pentax (www.ricoh-imaging.eu/fr_fr/), Sony (www.sony.fr/) and Olympus (www.shop.olympus.eu/fr_FR/index.html). All the pages, in the French version, were analyzed.

practical experience of photography, but also to knowledge of digital tools. We opted to transcribe only a summary of this work through excerpts from the corpus analysis. Some of the results are presented in the form of comparisons between manufacturers and others simply focus on one specificity. It should be noted that on the six websites studied, some products not dedicated to photography are offered and lead to the creation of specific pages on the website, which we will not take into account. The manufacturers offer various types of camera – hybrid, reflex and compact – with various image formats – APS-C, large format and medium format. While we analyzed all these pages, the results relating to compact cameras and medium format cameras will receive little attention. These are two types of cameras positioned at the extreme ends of the pricing spectrum that were seldom or never encountered during our own interactions with the photographic industry. In fact, this website analysis forms part of a more general research investigation involving participative observation in this sector (visiting exhibitions, attending photography clubs, discussions with professional and amateur photographers, joining online practice groups, etc.). Some of our findings or deductions will thus be derived from this field experience that cannot be dismissed.

This chapter is divided into four sections. In the first section, we will explain the notions leveraged in this work by describing the communication situation induced by the consultation of a website: media ethos, promises and commitment, the interpretative skills of the audience. In the second section, we will look at the basis of the construction of commercial organizations' media ethos, focusing on the first impressions left by a consultation of the home page and the spaces explicitly identified as being part of the company's discourse on itself. In the third section, we will highlight the link between the organization's media ethos and its product promotion strategies through various levels of discourse (discourse from the organization, discourse from controlled or autonomous third parties, etc.). Finally, in the fourth section, we will study the link between the organization's media ethos and the presentation of a segmentation of the website's audiences through personalizing the navigation path, showing usages and photographic practices, and the specific place given to the image of the professional.

3.2. The communication situation induced by a photographic equipment manufacturer's website

An organizational website is a media system that allows an asynchronous relationship between its discourse and its customers or potential customers. It is a third party at the encounter, accessible at any time of the day, for visitors who may follow different paths between pages. While they may start their navigation on the home page, they can equally well land on another page if they have a link to it. The purpose of this section is to define the concepts and notions that help in understanding the issues at play in this encounter, which is centered around commercial products, in this case cameras. Three elements seem to us essential: the promise/commitment generated by the media communication situation, the organization's media ethos and the interpretive abilities of the visitors.

3.2.1. *The website's promise and commitment*

The computerized media to which the object being analyzed (the website) belongs can be defined as follows:

> These "communication machines", to use Pierre Schaeffer's expression, are not like other technological objects, they organize the communication space; as such, they constitute a social technology in themselves However, the organization of the communication space that they present is done through writing ("screen writing") and "text" ("network text") and presupposes sign-bearing objects, input by interpreters and not simply instruments given an operating framework and implemented, in one way or another, by users. (Souchier et al. 2003, p. 34)

A website is therefore not a neutral entity, but a system that sets up a communication situation, in this case, between the manufacturer identified as the enunciator – who is in charge of the message conveyed on the website – and the visitor. It carries an "ostension of a readable communicative intention" (Jeanneret 2008, p. 161); in other words, "the fact that formal configurations are capable, in a given context, of manifesting a communicative intention and a proposal for metacommunication" (Jeanneret 2008, p. 167). The website conveys an intention of communication, a set of representations and it stimulates the imagination around the activities of the organization to which it belongs. In the case being studied, the website enables a presentation of the products that are manufactured. This promise, which denotes here "the way in which the communication actors intervene to make explicit the meaning and the purposes of the communication process itself and to state their own way of engaging in it" (Jeanneret 2014, pp. 66–67), is perceptible prior to accessing the website, be it in the imagination of the visitor who builds up certain expectations when they type the website address into the address bar of their browser or when they read the description given in the search engine, as shown in Figure 3.1.

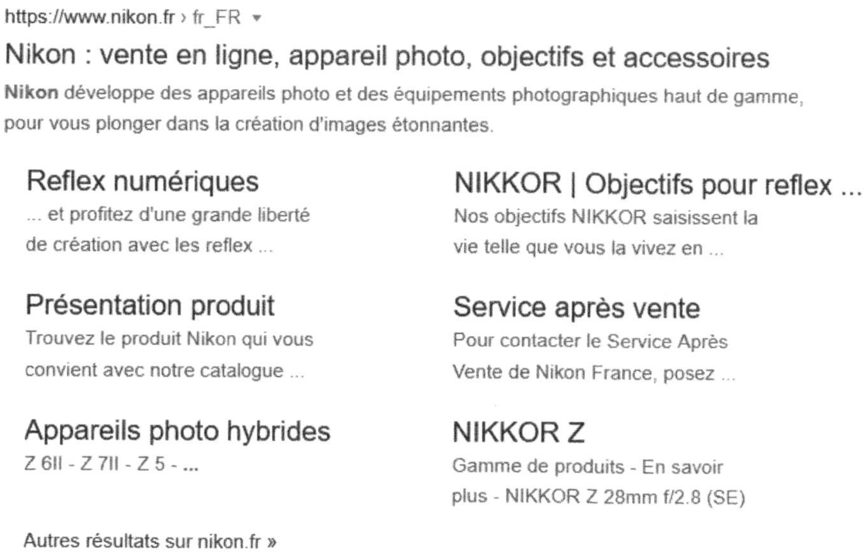

Figure 3.1. *Search results for the brand name "Nikon" in the French Google search engine, which gives a summary of the subject matter of the website. For a color version of this figure, see www.iste.co.uk/pinede/digital.zip*

The stated purpose of the website is very clear: to present the brand's various cameras. This induces in the visitor the promise of discovering the brand's products and is confirmed in what is called the commitment of the system, which places the visitor in an activity and a specific way of communicating. These two notions, promise and commitment, "answer each other. The promise consists of making public a definition of the act of communication and its purpose; the commitment consists of creating a system of objects and discourse that embodies such a claim and that above all convenes the objects of the communication in a posture, a situation, a context of expression" (Jeanneret 2014, p. 64.) In the case of our study, the visitor places themself in an active posture of accessing information that will be presented from the promotional angle. Indeed, as Mouratidou (2018, p. 28) points out, with regard to our "various promotional strategies", "the items for sale and more generally the commercial domain are thus displayed and in consequence represented". The website visitor, potentially accustomed to consuming and being confronted by advertising discourse, expects to see the product and brand put on display to enter into the representation. This representation depicts, through the prism of the system, on the one hand, a visitor who embodies the role of the potential customer and, on the other hand, the brand in the role of shop assistant/sales representative. This role is based on social suggestion or "communication arising from the bringing into play of the implicit meanings attached to all social conduct" (Winkin 1996, p. 42). Thus "each communication situation involves the mobilization of a role according to the social representations we have of it, or what we have learned" (Rollandin 2015, p. 136). This role refers to perceived values or behaviors relating to the commercial communication scenario.

It should also be noted that while product promotion is done through product specification sheets, it is not always possible to make a purchase: this can only be done at Pentax. For Canon, Olympus and Nikon, the purchase is made on an annex to the website, a shop accessible via the product sheets, identifiable by the addition of the word "store" in the URL. At Sony, the only proposal is to purchase the product from online retailers, who are listed on the website. At Fujifilm, there is no mention of making a purchase at the level of the product specification sheets. There is only a "shop" tab included in the menu, which lists the stores that sell their products online and instore. Thus, it is possible to buy products from these companies or to find retailers, but the visitor does not seem pressured to buy. The website thus may not necessarily have the mission of selling the product, but rather of promoting it. It should be borne in mind that visitors, whatever their relationship to photography and their skills with regard to media communication, expect to find themselves in a situation where they will obtain information on a product, presented through the commercial organization's discourse that will be seductive and promotional, going beyond a simple factual presentation.

3.2.2. *Organizations' constructed and perceived media ethos*

The various website visitors thus expect to find an advertising discourse put forward by an organization that seems to have the main role of salesperson or in any case marketing representative. This role, presented through action possibilities, is based on a preliminary consideration of way of being, to which are attached values and suppositions that constitute the media ethos of the organizations that are the enunciators. Before looking in more detail at the characteristics of this ethos in a scenario, let us return to the very construction of the notion, then to the issues that arise.

3.2.2.1. *The notion of media ethos*

We have used the notion of media ethos (Rollandin 2015, pp. 148–152) to describe the self-image that users construct of themselves by leaving traces of their visits in participatory spaces. This image makes it easier or more difficult to make posts, be accepted in groups and develop their sociability. We have defined this notion using the studies of Goffman (1973) and Amossy (2010). Without going back over the entire thought process, let us set out a few fundamental elements. First, we agree with Amossy (2010), who proposes broadening the notion of ethos to a construction that happens through each operation of verbal enunciation:

> A second point from Goffman's microsociology leads to an important redevelopment of the traditional notion of ethos: it is the idea that in any interaction, even the most mundane and informal, the individual makes a presentation of him/herself that is in the interests of the goal being sought in the conversation. Thus, ethos is a notion that arises from every type of conversation and is involved in every situation to function properly. (p. 31)

Our proposal was to extend this to any operation that will leave traces in online spaces. These traces left in the systems are recorded by computer processes and are then given visibility at various times and in various spaces, thus allowing them to be interpreted. Second, we believe that an individual's media ethos, unlike the traditional definition of ethos, is not fundamentally aimed at persuasion. However, its characterization will be essential for the way it will be perceived before and during the communicational exchange. Thus, a person who engages in an online conversation seeks to define the media ethos of their interlocutor, who "appears here as a semiosis acting on two levels: defining the purpose of communicating with a subject and helping them to act during media interaction" (Rollandin 2015, p. 151). Third, the definition of the notion of media ethos moves away from the work of Ruth Amossy and Erving Goffman insofar as they are interested in different facets of identity construction: "Self-presentation according to Erving Goffman is related to behavioral and contextual elements while Ruth Amossy develops a discursive analysis of the phenomenon" (Rollandin 2015, p. 151). We have chosen to consider both these dimensions, and not only these: media ethos is an image of oneself that is built and enriched from preliminary elements, discursive, behavioral, contextual, but also technological (the latter aspect refers to the degree of mastery of mediated systems), which have meaning for the user before and at the time of their engagement in a mediated system. Let us look at how this can apply to a commercial organization.

3.2.2.2. *The media ethos of a commercial organization and issues arising*

We consider that all the elements displayed on the screen, in other words, the website itself, by its construction, formatting, content and functionalities, will constitute traces of presence in the eyes of the visitors who access it and will condition their experience. The organization – the main enunciator and the owner of the website – constructs the whole with care, working on the content according to its editorial policy and defining the possibilities for action and interaction open to the audiences that it hopes to attract. Thus, we distinguish two aspects of this media ethos: that which the enunciator seeks to build through the website, which we call the "constructed media ethos", and that which each website visitor will unconsciously reconstruct to form their own image of the organization expressing itself on the website they consult, which we call "perceived media ethos".

The challenge for the organization is to shape a constructed media ethos that will be perceived, when interpreted, as sufficiently favorable to encourage its visitors to accept the act of communication, to continue to circulate from page to page on the website, and thus to more easily buy in to the promotional discourses put forward. For this, it is necessary to design a website that makes it possible to display varied traces, "object[s] inscribed in materiality" (Galinon-Mélénec 2011, p. 61); in other words, easily decipherable traces that will take on the expected meanings, so that the constructed and the perceived media ethos will be as close as possible. These traces have "a triple status [...] (index, inscription, route) which mediates between uses made and uses anticipated" (Galinon-Mélénec 2011, p. 72) and are diverse in nature: graphic elements, discourses, the functionalities made available, mastery of technological systems, etc. While this may seem quite simple to achieve, three parameters must be given careful consideration: the first is that some traces may be caused by an involuntary action, such as an error related to the website interface which will nonetheless be interpreted by the visitor, which will widen the gap between the two aspects of the ethos. In this example, the media ethos will shift away from professionalism, which is one of the expected values for a commercial organization. The second parameter is that the media ethos is constructed in time and space. The organization must control the various traces left on its website over time, but also in other spaces, where messages are not always within control and cannot always be instrumentalized. The third parameter is that even if the organization is careful to build its website and leave easily interpretable traces in relation to the audiences it expects to have on its website, it must take into account that within each audience category, visitors' interpretative skills and knowledge of photography and digital systems are varied.

3.2.3. *Visitors with varying interpretative skills*

Commitment, embodied in the organization's system and discourses, must be consistent with the promise made and easily detectable through a range of information that will allow visitors to pursue their interpretations in order to proceed serenely in the proposed communication situation. It is, however, complex to ensure that these interpretations will match what the company had hoped for. In fact, the action path on a photographic equipment manufacturer's website is constructed according to fairly broad categorizations (which we will return to in section 3.5.2.2):

beginner, amateur and professional. Thus, the pathways are designed for audiences expected to have relatively similar reactions, whereas in reality, audiences have neither the same expectations nor the same interpretative skills. In addition to the fact that website visitors will have varying knowledge of the practice and the equipment, the same is the case for their relationship to advertising messaging and their susceptibility to discourses of this type. The greatest novices to the practice will be susceptible to the plethora of information displayed, allowing them to glimpse an abundance of possibilities opened up by the potential future purchase, without however being able to grasp their full concreteness. Others, conversely, having already made a purchase or being better informed, will be able to identify more accurately the value added to the product by the information displayed for promotional purposes. We feel that visitors who are "beginners" or who have little practical experience of photography or are not necessarily interested in competitors' products will be more easily seduced by the displays and the promotional discourses than more experienced or professional visitors. It should be noted that discernment skills when looking at promotional and advertising discourses are not identical for all visitors, as is the case for their mastery of digital interfaces. Even if the website is designed to suggest a specific action scenario tailored to the target audience, if the visitor does not have the skills or desire to embark on the suggested path, they will not access the complete range of information.

The website therefore crystallizes various issues that enable smooth rollout of the envisaged media communication situation. If its main purpose is to put the organization in contact with audiences so that it can promote its products, it is necessary for the organization to take care in the construction of its media ethos and the traces that will be shown on the screen, so that they are interpretable and acceptable to the various visitors, irrespective of the audience category to which they belong. The next part looks at how the construction of the media ethos is initiated, and let us not forget that this must then be upheld over time.

3.3. Initiating the photographic equipment manufacturer's media ethos

The perceived media ethos of an organization begins to take form in the mind of the visitor as soon as they decide to access their website. This first step will differ according to their motivation (to buy a product, find out what is new or take part in an event organized by the brand) and the modalities of access (link from search engine or social media, etc.). Before seeing how this image is nuanced via the traces of the website's home page (which is usually the first page consulted) and what values it covers, it must be understood that the media ethos is steered by the ethos of the brand, which predates it.

3.3.1. *An organization with a pre-digital existence*

The corporate image can pre-date the media ethos that is constructed on its website. Through the circulation of discourses in the media or through conversations with others in the company, we note that we already know manufacturers by name even without having purchased any equipment. Given their longstanding presence on the market and the various testimonials that may have circulated, they do not need to convince audiences and future audiences of their right to sell products (without exception, most products are recognized as being of a quality in line with the advertised price segment). Rather, they need to show what differentiates them from the competition. We have noted that photographers will develop brand loyalty after being satisfied with their first purchase. Several photographers interviewed in clubs also mention growing accustomed to using equipment. The comments gathered illustrate Dujarier's (2014) statement: "When re-purchasing, the consumer will prefer to remain loyal to a brand to reduce their learning costs. Thus, paradoxically, the more effort required to learn about a product, the more loyal the consumer will be to the brand" (p. 61). In fact, even though it is possible to do more or less the same things with a camera of an equivalent range, the features are not identified by the same name from one brand to another and are not accessible by the same buttons or action sequence. Companies must retain the fidelity of existing customers by introducing them to new products and innovations while at the same time illustrating the permitted usage in order to attract new buyers. The media ethos will also be approached from a less neutral interpretative angle if an image of the brand has already been created in visitors' minds. The way in which the elements will be interpreted may be less objective, and it will be easier or harder to convince and/or seduce. Let us look at what impressions and values are coveted starting from the first page.

3.3.2. *First impressions of navigation*

The home page features several pieces of information: what can be done via the menu, how products and photography are dealt with under main heading, etc. We note, from this page, that companies' constructed media ethos presents them as being more than simply commercial organizations. They position themselves as potential sources of stimulation of creativity and inspiration (whether through the cameras as described in section 3.4.1 or through testimonial discourses as presented in section 3.4.2). Each manufacturer makes available from the home page various content formats, which will help their audiences to find inspiration. Of the six websites, four make mention of a category or section named "Get Inspired". The companies all seem willing to go beyond simply providing equipment and to offer various solutions to access creativity. The impressions that emerge from these first steps on the website can easily be linked back to the enunciator, which is the company. In addition to the URL on which the visitor clicks to access the site, thus giving them an initial identity marker, the media ethos built by the manufacturers starts and is anchored, for all the websites analyzed, by the same type of sign: the brand logo, displayed top left. This is one of the first elements the visitor discovers. This logo, as well as some of the graphic codes used, is linked to the graphic charter that predated the website; it is also used in other types of communication. In fact, businesses tend to use the identifying elements already known by the company, such as the yellow and black color coding very visible on the Nikon website.

Figure 3.2. *Commentary on the brand logo on the French Nikon website*[3]. *For a color version of this figure, see www.iste.co.uk/pinede/digital.zip*

3 "Company Profile" page: available at: www.nikon.fr/fr_EN/about/company_profile.page [Accessed 23 March 2021].

The retention of this is also mentioned on its "Company Profile" page, in a section devoted to portraying the history and values of the brand, which explains that "the Nikon logo and the yellow color have been retained, because they are globally recognized visual elements that are today synonymous with high quality and trust", as we can see in Figure 3.2. Even though the logo has evolved since its creation, some elements are retained, to ensure continuity in the minds of customers. The pre-existing identity therefore guides the graphic choices used for the design of a website, just like the universes linked to the companies' business activities. For example, the Fujifilm and Olympus websites, parts of which are dedicated to medical products, will have a layout that brings this universe to mind, whether by the cold, bluish colors or by visuals showing medical staff. For these two brands, this positioning is explained in a dedicated part of their website, focusing on the company, its values and its history. They position themselves as figures of innovation and research in the field of medical imaging, exploiting the notions of technologies, advances in research and development. Since these universes generally need high-performance equipment, the visitor can assume that the brand applies the same degree of expertise in these fields as in the field of photography, where there are products for them. The constructed media ethos is based on values of professionalism, linked to the brand's past history, in particular through the design, but also through the discourses present in spaces devoted to the history of the brand.

3.3.3. *Space for explaining values*

Each of the websites has a section devoted to its history and corporate culture, which is usually found at the bottom of the page – the traditional place to find elements about the enunciator and the legal notices, usually called "About". For example, in this section, Canon highlights its corporate philosophy, which is presented as steering the brand's values and activities toward societal causes such as sustainable development. It is also through information on the history of companies experiencing international expansion that they position themselves in relation to their service provision in France, thus playing on the notion of proximity with their audiences.

While each of the companies has an English website, we observe differing strategies: some brands develop specific content for the French website and translate the entire website, at the same time positioning themselves as an attentive brand that is close to each one of their customers. Fujifilm, for example, in its company profile, states that "Fujifilm, while always close to you, has a global network"[4], while others

4 "About Fujifilm" page: available at: www.fujifilm.eu/en/about-fujifilm [Accessed 1 April 2021].

include less content in the French version of their website and redirect you straight to the English version of the website in some sections, as is the case of the "Sony History" section. We can see in most of them this wish to adapt to the visitor's country of origin, with the attempt at translation. Sometimes this is done only on the surface, which could destabilize the visitor and connote negatively to the perceived media ethos. These sections dedicated to the manufacturers' history show that the constructed media ethos is developed by giving prominence to company values and reiterating pre-existing codes. This ethos is perceived as more favorable when the brand plays on the principle of proximity or regularly puts new content online. Showing its international influence also conveys the idea that its competence and know-how are already proven worldwide. By focusing on their evolution through values that adapt to contemporary concerns, manufacturers suggest that products also evolve in their design.

The media ethos, from first steps on the website, is based on an image of the professional who promotes their products by making their action policy readable and their societal concerns visible. Companies also seek to construct a media ethos linked to creativity. Thus, rather than promoting products, they seek to transmit a portrayal of a way of practicing through their products, but also through a diverse range of content on their website.

3.4. Media ethos and discursive strategy

One facet of an organization's media ethos will be developed through the variety of discourses on their website. Through an analysis of the various discursive strategies that run through the subtle constructions of a universe of practice centered around their products and through the instrumentalization of the work of third parties, let us see how the manufacturers seek to position themselves as mediators, intermediaries and community initiators.

3.4.1. *Carefully presented products*

The company can develop its image through the care taken in its product promotion. The trend is no longer toward the presentation of factual information, but toward placing products in a scenario, aiming to seduce specific audiences, and this is confirmed on the six websites analyzed. The visitor is waiting for this approach and will seek to identify what vision of the practice of photography they would be able to access by purchasing the product. This is exactly what the company encourages them to discover, through product specification sheets in which the imagination is aroused and universes of meaning are built.

Figure 3.3. *Product specification of the EOS 90D: highlighting the camera's ergonomics through a staged scenario and an onscreen display*[5]*. For a color version of this figure, see www.iste.co.uk/pinede/digital.zip*

Cameras are primarily portrayed as technological objects. This degree of technology is shown by the use of visuals of different formats: diagrams or cutaways of the camera, depictions of non-visible elements, close-ups or inserts of data in figures, etc. These elements reinforce the idea that the product is very complex to design, which can help justify the price of the product.

Cameras are also presented as intuitive and ergonomic, often through a staged scenario of the product in use, putting the visitor in the shoes of the photographer, as in Figure 3.3. Digital cameras with a live view screen, showing what is in front of the lens, heighten the feeling of being the user in the act of taking the photo. The presence of a hand positioned on the buttons is important, because it provides information about the measurements and makes it possible to imagine the position of the camera when handled. The lexical field of innovation has been frequently described and often associated with the terms "perspectives", "horizon", "possibilities". Manufacturers also showcase the idea that their products are intelligent, like Sony, which describes them as having "intelligent features"[6] to suggest the fact that their functionalities will assist the photographer to achieve technical shots by automating certain actions, such as with autofocus, which can allow continuous focus. The quality of the images is also praised, irrespective of the

5 Available at: www.canon.fr/cameras/eos-90d/.

6 The "Cameras with interchangeable lenses" page from the French Sony website: available at: www.sony.fr/electronics/appareils-photo-a-objectifs-interchangeables/ilca-99m2 [Accessed 17 March 2021].

price range of the camera. If we analyze the specification sheets at entry level, we note that the photographs shown are all taken under favorable conditions: outdoors, in a good light, with people who freeze in front of the lens, striking a pose. However, under these ideal conditions, any camera would allow one to take good photographs. Thus, the proposed scenario will not necessarily convince a photographer who already has some knowledge and experience of photography, but it will have a stronger impact on a novice. Certain criteria are mentioned, especially in the higher ranges, criteria that are essential to help immortalize something outside everyday life. The first is the shutter speed, which is important for scenes where you have to take a shot fast to capture the movement, as is the case for sports photography (sports shown are basketball, fencing, kayaking, rafting, motor racing, etc.) or animal photography (for instance, birds in flight). The second is the light sensitivity of the sensor, a factor that comes into play when light conditions are difficult, as is the case for sunrises or sunsets, or in places without much light (interiors, caves, etc.).

If we focus on the presentation of products according to which range they fall into, we note that entry-level and mid-range cameras are shown as helping to stimulate creativity and put the emphasis on sharing images online, unlike the top-of-the-range cameras. Photographers who have this type of equipment are presented as knowing what they want to do, being in need of a powerful tool rather than assistance. The instrument allows them to achieve their ambitions. The practice of photography is thus presented as the power to "capture the moment your way" and "designed to inspire" as Sony puts it, or to "see the world in a new light" as Nikon puts it. This presentation of the practical experience and objects suggests an apparent concern on the part of the company to help its audiences to project themselves into the activity with the coveted object, which visitors will be able to perceive as being consistent with their expectations and with the perceived media ethos of the professional. We also identified other discursive strategies to present the practice or products and seek to affiliate audiences, while positioning themselves in the niche of initiator of creativity.

3.4.2. *Controlled instrumentalized work and discourses*

The presentation of products and the brand can be done by means of displaying the work of a third party: this person can be a professional or simply a customer.

3.4.2.1. *Leveraging the work and discourses of the professional*

Some professional photographers, recognized by the brand, are instrumentalized by it, through the prism of their work and discourse, in order to enhance its products and give more substance to its media ethos. Two formats can be identified: testimonial marketing and endorsement. Petters (2018) explains these two notions:

> "Testimonial advertising" and the "testimonial" are defined as a type of marketing message that uses a third party to vouch for and give value to the brand or product being advertised, in the same way as endorsement, defined as messaging that uses a celebrity or expert to promote a brand or product. (p. 73)

She also explains that "it could be said that the person giving the testimony functions as an example while the endorser serves as an illustration" (Petters 2018, p. 76). These formats are exploited on the websites studied in a space dedicated to articles where the discourse is taken over by a professional photographer. At Fujifilm, this person is clearly identified in advance, with their name on the thumbnail of the article, and by their biography which appears in the preface to the article. A range of topics are covered (weddings, architecture, sport, etc.) with stories that combine the exhibition of photographs with videos taken from their YouTube channel. Most of the articles are in English and each anecdote is related to a Fujifilm product. The overriding impression is that the work of the photographer is being showcased. One feature of testimonial discourse emerges clearly: "The testimonial is a first-person singular utterance, based on a supposed experience of the advertising spokesperson who testifies to their statements and the sales discourse in which they are involved" (Petters 2018, p. 74). It should be noted that the simple fact that the article is there on the brand's website endows the speech with a strong sales connotation. Indeed, the instrumentalization of the photographer's discourse by the brand makes itself felt by very configuration of the system, which is composed of an element displayed on a website by the page, as Fournout (2012) points out: "The whiteness of the page, while determining the common background of the medium, simultaneously contributes to the functions of stepping to one side, of a place of possible rapprochement and of a logocentric point of view" (p. 104). Thus, by its configuration, the website shown on the screen becomes a space introducing a common background, in other words an element that "confirms the physical medium and gives unity" (Fournout 2012, p. 108). The company is therefore positioned as prescriptive vis-à-vis the visitor, offering them a selection of photographers they recognize and who are allowed to speak. By this process, the photographer is legitimized as a professional worthy of our interest, while the photographer's act of speaking in turn legitimizes the company (and its equipment at the same time). The strategy is quite similar with Olympus, with two differences: the titles of the articles do not always mention the equipment in question and the articles give more prominence to the advantages of the equipment used and its technical features. With

Canon and Nikon, we can also identify discourse that is instrumentalized. However, this is more akin to endorsement than testimonial discourse.

Figure 3.4. *Canon's "Get Inspired" section, with two discourse formats on the French website*[7]. *For a color version of this figure, see www.iste.co.uk/pinede/digital.zip*

7 Available at: www.canon.fr/get-inspired/.

With Canon, as shown by Figure 3.4, the "Get Inspired" section is divided into two parts: the first picks up the principle of the testimonial described above and the second presents a discourse that can be classed as endorsement. Tips are offered for carrying out a photographic project such as "Play with your food; healthy, edible photo projects to print and frame"[8], by an enunciator who is identified as an expert, only cited at the end. This can be classed as endorsement and not testimonial discourse, because the photographer does not present their work and seems to efface themself behind an exhibition of knowledge presented point by point, without any form of the first person, like the forms of address towards the visitor. Nikon takes a similar approach with articles offering advice in a "Discover and Explore" section. There is no mention of inspiration at this point, but of "stimulating your creativity". Some articles give advice, without mentioning any of the brand's equipment. But these references to the equipment, typical of promotional discourse, can nonetheless still be found in the image captions. The discourse is also endorsed by a photographer presented as a professional, whose name is cited at the end and beneath the photographs shown, in the copyright credit.

In general, the articles presented in these sections will establish an asymmetric relationship between the speaker (the professional photographer) and the visitor:

> In this sense, despite the fact that the person giving the testimony may not necessarily be known to the audience before featuring in the sales message, they can be recognized by virtue of a specific knowledge or skill that is attributed to them through the marketing presentation. Here we are close to the figure of the expert, who hovers between scientist and old-timer, the former deriving their legitimacy from their scientific knowledge, the latter from their experience and their long association with the environment in which they consider themself an "expert"; they thus leverage "both theoretical competence and technical know-how. (Petters 2018, p. 78)

Whether the professional photographer is speaking about their experience or offering advice (through endorsement or testimonial form), the visitor thus has the opportunity of expanding their knowledge with regard to their photographic culture or their future practice. These two forms of instrumentalization of the work and discourse of the photographer give the information presented a sociocentric rather than egocentric aim (the latter aim is strongly in evidence in the case with the product specification sheets), which means that the discourse, even though serving the interests of the brand, is presented as bringing knowledge to the visitor,

8 Canon's "Get Inspired" page: available at: www.canon.fr/get-inspired/tips-and-techniques/fun-with-food-photography/ [Accessed 10 March 2021].

transcending the sales dimension of the exchange. This value added to the communication situation, motivated by an act that is commercial in origin, can be perceived favorably and can help to seduce audiences. This can be a basis for usage for the person about to purchase a product of the brand. The amateur or the owner of a camera will have sufficient skill to partially understand what is written and will easily be able to follow the advice, and the neophyte who has not yet purchased any equipment can see a prospect of progress for later. The professionals, for their part, do not seem to us to be the target audience of these sections, unless they in turn wish to present their work (in which case, they would contact the brand directly).

3.4.2.2. *The customer at work*

Two other forms of instrumentalization of the work of photographers were identified, but do not involve professionals, simply customers of the brand. In both cases, this is part of what Dujarier (2014) regards as a form of putting the customer to work, without the company asking them to work: "It 'offers' them an opportunity to act and to get involved" (p. 118).

The primary instrumentalization of customers' work occurs as part of the construction of a brand community such as "Nikon Club", "Ricoh Pentax", "My Sony" or "My Canon".

Figure 3.5. *Incentive to register the product, giving access to the My Sony community*[9]*. For a color version of this figure, see www.iste.co.uk/pinede/digital.zip*

9 Available at: www.sony.fr/electronics/appareils-photo-a-objectifs-interchangeables/slt-a99-a99v.

The customer who accesses this community through the action of registering the product they have purchased, as shown in Figure 3.5, under the pretext of benefiting from traceability that will facilitate after-sales service operations, accesses a photo-sharing gallery, where they can themself become an actor-contributor by posting their work. Several amateur photographers told us that they first shared their photos in this space in order to gain confidence in their work, before subsequently posting them on social networks, where comments can be less benevolent. While this appears beneficial for customers, it also allows the brand to increase the visibility of productions taken with its products, in a relationship that is no longer actually perceived as asymmetrical, unlike the instrumentalization of the work of photographers identified as professionals mentioned in the previous part. Here, the photographer, no matter what their level, can become involved, which will make the relationship appear more genuine, since the customer is not a professional.

The second instrumentalization of customers' work occurs when companies put on events presented as aiming to encourage people to practice photography. This is the case for competitions open to all members of the community. Let us use the example of Canon's Redline Challenge, where the endowment was over €10,000. There are challenges where less is at stake, such as Nikon's #CreateYourLight, where contestants who win the challenge will see their productions posted on the official Nikon website. The customer will throw themself into the game and submit their photos, which will thus circulate on a page or a space dedicated to the contest. There is a certain interest in this:

> The expressive, public and political functions of the activity can be so significant that they are enough to put them to work. The reward is not monetary, but essentially subjective and social. The consumer "treats" themself through the pleasure of achieving something beautiful or useful and by the benefits they derive from it in their relationship with others (forging links, forming collectives, networks, social recognition, etc.). (Dujarier 2014, p. 119)

The fact that customers agree to show their production in galleries or through taking part in a contest makes it possible, on the one hand, to create content at a lower cost and, on the other hand, to participate in the strengthening of a community focused on one's products. The brand, through these various initiatives involving the instrumentalization of works and discourses, thus improves its media ethos by offering content and positioning itself as an online facilitator, prescriber and mediator of photographic practice.

3.4.3. *Potentially beneficial autonomous speeches*

The website is not the only space where the company's media ethos continues its development. Social media are also important spaces for customers who wish to expand their experience by sharing photos. Companies can be the initiators of these exchanges, such as Pentax, which gives suggestions to its visitors on how to become part of its community by suggesting the use of specific hashtags on Instagram. These platforms enable the dissemination of many snapshots and facilitate the creation of interactivity. Audiences' attention is thus captured even outside the institution's website, for those audiences who use social media. While identification may be required by the company, in practice, we have noted that identification of the modalities of production of photography disseminated on social media leads photographers to quote the brand in hashtags or give information about the modalities of taking the shots on sharing platforms such as the 500px website.

This gives additional visibility, putting into the minds of visitors that, if they like the image, it will be possible to produce a similar shot by buying the same camera. Thus, the manufacturer's perceived media ethos is enriched by traces which it cannot monitor. This unmonitored speech, outside of the website or a space managed by the company, is perceived as more genuine and can encourage the act of purchase. Customers become ambassadors in spite of themselves. We have also noted the existence of many groups on the social medium of Facebook, with a connection to the brand's products, managed by people presenting themselves as customers, apparently not mandated by the brand (this is what is claimed, but is difficult to verify). In these spaces, the testimonial discourses do not seem to be monitored and we found several traces indicating that the conversations actually did guide future photographers in their choice of equipment and could even contribute to reinforcing the ethos mediated in a favorable way. This is evidenced by the following situation: although companies communicate on their after-sales service, which is a parameter of their constructed mediatized ethos, some customers may not necessarily dare to use it, for various reasons, thus creating for themselves an image of the service that is far from what the brand hoped. It is through asking questions and requesting feedback on experiences in these unmonitored spaces that they end up contacting the service, then giving feedback in their turn. This thus reflects a reduction in the gap between the constructed media ethos and the perceived media ethos.

Figure 3.6. *Information provided about the equipment used to take the photograph on a 500px sharing website – here the Nikon D810, with data about the lens and the settings used. For a color version of this figure, see www.iste.co.uk/pinede/digital.zip*

The work and discourses, whether selected by the brand or evolving outside the institutional space making reference to the latter, contribute to the development of its media ethos and to its maintenance over the long term (if possible in a favorable light). The fact that the brand does not monitor all the discourse can be favorable, on condition that its products are up to the standard advertised. The constructed media ethos, as well as promises relating to the products' performance, should be fulfilled when the customer uses the camera. Not everything is played out in online spaces: in order for the perceived media ethos to endure in the long term, the brand must in its concrete interactions with its customers honor its promises so as not to lose its credibility and legitimacy. Thus, through these various processes where the brand is not always a protagonist, it sees itself positioned as a mediating entity to creativity and a unifying entity. Let us now address the link between the media ethos of companies and the segmentation of audiences.

3.5. Media ethos and audience segmentation

The constructed media ethos is also created from the basis of the care given to the action pathways and the personalization of information according to audience. In fact, we note that differing levels of actions, discourses and universes make it possible to seduce and guide differing audiences. Through this desire for personalization, the perceived media ethos could be considered favorably and will facilitate the creation of a feeling of affiliation with the discourse and the brand. Let us look, in this final part, at how the company seeks to position itself as being attentive to its audiences.

3.5.1. *Willingness to provide support as part of the package*

We noted the existence of a selection help tool on the Canon and Nikon websites. What interests us here is the way each company portrays its potential audiences. This mediation tool is introduced as being able to help the visitor find the ideal product among the vast and varied range in the catalog. Analyzing the results and the positioning of this tool, the strategies of the two manufacturers seem comparatively different.

This tool is visible from the scroll-down menu at Canon, under the heading "Help me make a choice", as shown in Figure 3.7. It makes it possible, through a system of questions about requirements and skills, to filter products. It is very visible and leads to some variety of responses, depending on the choices made, leaving us with the impression that the visitor could find this really helpful. At Nikon, the role of this tool is more debatable. It is less visible and its use seems to be part of a rather obvious commercial strategy: the prioritization of the promotion of hybrid cameras, as compared to digital reflex and compact cameras. While each category has a dedicated page, we note that the tool exists only on the pages of the latter two categories. We see in that the idea that the visitor is already on the page where they will find the ideal camera. Thus, if the claimed intention is to help "Find the ideal camera" through a tool that asks the visitor to describe their type of practical experience, the results are unconvincing. While certain compacts or reflex cameras can sometimes be the recommended product, a large area is left to similar products that could also be suitable, in which hybrid cameras keep on reappearing. If we repeat the test several times, choosing different answers, we can easily see that the primary motivation of this tool is not to guide, but to lure us towards products from their latest range. Thus, this analysis of the selection help tool reinforces one of Dujarier's (2014) conclusions: "In fact, the companies' interest is that the customer purchases their products, but it does not make it a priority that the consumer knows how to use them correctly and fully" (p. 61).

Figure 3.7. *Canon's help tool to enable the user to find a camera, directly integrated into the menu (third choice on the right[10], in blue). A French website. For a color version of this figure, see www.iste.co.uk/pinede/digital.zip*

While offering a selection tool seems a positive approach toward the visitor, as at Canon which, by guiding them, gives prominence to its ability to meet the needs of its users, the way in which the results are returned for Nikon will not be positive.

10 Available at: www.canon.fr.

Whereas the company used this tool to give itself the image of an advisor, the tool will be perceived only as a pretext to disseminate a promotional message. This can have negative connotations for the media ethos perceived by the visitor, who will feel slightly abused by a too-obvious business strategy, when they might have expected genuine recommendations based on a match between the possibilities of the cameras and their own needs. Let us now look at how companies portray their audiences and practices.

3.5.2. *Representations of practices and audiences*

As a professional, the company seeks to facilitate the affiliation of its audiences and to encourage the act of purchase. To do this, it will leverage imaginations and portray universes of practice for each camera or type of camera, to allow visitors to understand whether the product shown can match their expectations and their practices. Without querying the segments chosen to categorize their products, we would like to highlight how the typical indicators of a practice when connected to products included in a range (entry level to high end) will make it possible to use anecdotes that allow potential customers to project themselves into an act of purchase, thus guiding them. We see different strategies across the six websites. Pentax, Sony and Fujifilm use little or no segmentation based on level of experience, unlike Olympus, Nikon and Canon. Let us look in turn at the advantages and disadvantages of these two strategies.

3.5.2.1. *Low segmentation based on product characteristics*

Some brands do not segment audiences, or not to any great extent, according to their level of practical experience. At Pentax, equipment is classified based on features such as geolocation or environmental resistance and on the type of practice permitted. The product is at the heart of the classification. This, however, requires that you have thought about the use you want to make of your future camera and understand the importance of the presence or absence of certain features and functionalities. At Sony, it is possible to filter the products in the catalog according to the technical characteristics that we wish to have. This filtering clearly requires prior knowledge of the potential specificities of the equipment. Features such as "electronic OLED viewfinder" will in fact be meaningless to someone who is just starting out or who practices occasionally. At Fujifilm, digital cameras are classified in the "general consumer products" section. However, we note the presence of the "medium format" range, which they describe as professional cameras, and a range of hybrid cameras that are "an alternative recognized by both professionals and amateurs". The former are at a much higher price than the hybrids, which suggests to us that they are not sought after by the general public. If we look at the presentation page of the second range, we notice that it is labeled "hybrid compact for the expert and professional". Some cameras even include the term "pro" in their name. Ultimately Fujifilm's products seem to be aimed at people who already have some expertise, an idea that we also found in the discourses of the amateur photographers we met. It should be noted, however, that a parallel can be drawn between the product presentations of these three manufacturers and the classifications established on the other three websites, which differentiate the products according to a classification that combines level of experience and usage. In fact, it is easy to make a comparison between products in the same price range and to see that the presentations of product specification sheets are similar.

3.5.2.2. *Explicit segmentation of audiences based on their skills and experience*

The other three manufacturers in our corpus opt for audience segmentation according to their usage and their level of practical experience. While Olympus opts for this apparent segmentation, some vagueness emerges from the classification adopted, with cameras for professionals, which "meet all the needs of demanding photographers"[11], amateurs and inspired amateurs. The products for amateurs, which are equivalent to entry-level products if we look at the prices, convey via images an idea of guided practice, centering on the immortalization of their daily lives.

Within the category of cameras for professionals, we note an attempt to describe each product that introduces vagueness. Each is referred to differently, in a way that is not very clear: "passionate professionals", "professional photographers" and "professionals". In these names, there seems to be a mix between level in photography and the fact of being a photographer by profession. Through not being very clear, Olympus positions its product as potentially being up to the standard required by a professional photographer, but also for an amateur photographer who has skills that allow them to make use of the features that are present. This segmentation does not really seem to work. At Nikon and Canon, which are the brands we have noticed most frequently among amateur photographers, we observe that audience segmentation is done in several places on the site: the search filter, the product specification sheets and the selection tool mentioned above. Three very similar categories appear. For both brands, we have the "amateur" and "professional" categories. The third category is called "casual photographer" at Nikon and "beginner" at Canon.

11 Olympus OMD Cameras page: available at: www.olympus.fr/site/fr/c/cameras/om_d_system_cameras/index.html [Accessed 23 April 2021].

Figure 3.8. *Segmentation of audiences according to their experience of photography, through images and denomination – Nikon camera selection tool. For a color version of this figure, see www.iste.co.uk/pinede/digital.zip*

Here is a summary made from the texts and images of the characteristics of these audience categories, from the three spaces identified above:

– Beginner or casual photographer: the term "casual" may be perceived as less devaluing. A person who is discovering the tool and seeking to learn to use it to immortalize everyday life is presented as an "aspiring" photographer. This can be either a child under adult supervision, or a person in the company of friends, who approaches the practice of photography as a secondary concern. In several images, the person seems to be laughing at what has been said by those next to them, as shown in Figure 3.8. The photos are ready for publication and can be shared with one click. The mention of the "pleasure of real photography" in one of Nikon's product description sheets begs the question of what unreal photography would be. Is it a photograph taken with a smartphone or with a camera that is not this brand? Or is it about suggesting that if one does not put oneself in a scenario of composing one's photographs properly, the tool is so effective that it will compensate for a certain lack of concentration or competence and allow seamless processing?

– The amateur seems to seek more creativity and tries to explore practices that require a certain commitment (photography of "accessible" animals that are liable to move, such as ducks, taking wildlife photography as their example). They are shown as trying to use specific features of the camera, opting for shots that are starting to rise above the ordinary. The photographer is alone, concentrating, in environments whose conditions can make the shots complex: a place used for sport, a landscape with low light, etc. They no longer use the automatic mode, as is shown by close-ups of the camera being used, which implies a certain level of understanding of the various features. Sharing functionality is also present, while the emphasis is put not on simplicity, but on the technology that enables it.

– The professional, on the other hand, is looking at nature in the far distance. Equipped with gear that allows them to adapt to their environment and climatic conditions, they usually have a bag that allows them to carry a number of lenses. The camera they use is also equipped with a heavy, impressive lens, as can be seen in Figure 3.8, giving rise to a degree of complexity in the shooting. The practical experiences showcased are varied: sport, nature, wedding, the Milky Way, etc. The photographer is like an explorer, setting out in search of a shot where there is only vastness. However, we have noted paradoxes in some description sheets, for example Nikon's. While one of the cameras "adapts to all the requirements of professionals looking for the perfect combination of speed and precision", it mentions that "no matter what your level of experience or preparation, your results are based on the responsiveness and versatility of your camera"[12]. This paradox leads us to believe that one underlying strategy is to not eliminate amateurs from the potential audience of this product.

Thus, beneath an apparent segmentation that is done either by camera features, or by level and type of usage, some paradoxes and inaccuracies are concealed. In the first strategy, it seems to us that the discourse can be more easily appropriated by an

12 Presentation page for the Nikon D6 camera: available at: www.olympus.fr/site/fr/c/cameras/om_d_system_cameras/index.html [Accessed 23 April 2021].

amateur already well informed on the vocabulary and the issues relating to practical experience.

This is also the case with the second strategy, where the amateur photographer seems to have more choice in the products offered to them. The beginner will in any case have difficulty in projecting themself, whether through lack of understanding or by mismatch with a universe that seems quite limiting within the margin of progress envisaged. The professional is presented as an explorer, which does not seem to correspond to the reality on the ground: many do studio or neighborhood photography. Let us look closely at this image of the professional through the services offered to them and question the rapprochement between the profession and the expected level of skills.

3.5.3. *The professional, a figure with sought-after skills*

The perceptions that are mobilized present differences depending on the audience for which the camera is intended, while paradoxically putting forward the idea that any product makes it possible to take good quality photographs, as Canon writes about all its cameras, which make it possible to capture details to obtain "professional results". These phrases show the rapprochement that is made in the collective imagination between quality, level and profession. The rapprochement between professionalism and quality of shooting and the photograph is one of the perceptions we have frequently encountered amongst club photographers and on Facebook sharing groups. Indeed, many non-professional photographers develop this vision, which will be accentuated by (or which will justify) certain slants adopted by manufacturers in their communication strategy, such as: the high price of equipment leads to a higher quality shot, equipment for professionals guarantees professional quality photographs (by implication more aesthetic than those that an amateur would take), the purchase of a camera that does not correspond to one's level means one will be able go further without having to invest again even if using it will be very difficult at first.

Thus, the image of the professional, through what this image represents in terms of photographic production, is coveted by amateurs, which manifests itself in a desire to acquire the same type of equipment. Companies thus seem to cherish the perception that the public have of their photographic skills and their usages by giving them access to professional equipment, even going so far as to offer them advantages reserved in theory to professionals, such as Nikon which has a "pro card", the first level of which is accessible without professional credentials, only on a basis of points gained by purchases. Of course, professionals have other benefits, via two other levels of the card, accessible subject to providing evidence of their professional activity, such as access to specific after-sales services. On the Canon website, there are two routes to accessing professional equipment, via the product presentations or via an area dedicated to professionals, which presents the same products as for the general public, but without the company's discourse on the topics of sharing, memory and mutual support. The company probably feels that these topics will be of no interest to a professional audience. This strategy leads us to believe that the main discourses on websites are above all aimed at seducing amateurs, even when the products are dedicated to professionals. It is possible that professionals have a level of skills and knowledge of the equipment that allows them to be very discerning when confronted by discourses. They might potentially prioritize product efficiency and after-sales service responsiveness so as to be able to practice their profession even in the event of an occasional equipment failure.

The perceptions conveyed are stereotypical and can, in our opinion, pose a problem for visitors, especially for amateur photographers. When the question of budget is not a consideration, audiences do not like being regarded as beginners or casual photographers. For many of the people questioned, there is still a fear of having to replace equipment too quickly and of being disappointed by the quality of cameras intended for casual photographers. The cameras marked out as being for professionals attract an audience that is not necessarily professional, that is seeking performance and quality, to be "at the professional level", without claiming that level. In fact, these cameras are often designed specifically for special and intensive uses, which a non-professional photographer will not have. But the idea that a camera dedicated to professionals and with a high price-tag takes better photographs – which will put you on a par with the achievements of professionals – remains very rooted in perceptions, especially when it is equipped with a large lens. As an anecdote, we went and positioned ourselves on the edge of an area where a competition was being held, where a lot of people were on the fringes with their cameras with fairly standard lenses. When we took out our camera fitted with a very large lens, the company officially responsible for photographing the event came to ask us to stop our practice, fearing that we would seek to sell our work through the media, thus generating unfair competition. Thus, the strategy of presenting products in this costly category, which the various manufacturers opt for, seems to us to make sense rather as a way of inducing the affiliation of a section of photographers whose budget will not be a brake to their choice of the camera.

3.6. Conclusion

To conclude, the website allows each manufacturer to construct for itself a media ethos that is as favorable as possible, while seeking to differentiate itself from its competitors. This media ethos is inseparable from the identity of the company developed offline and from its role, in the communication situation, of salesman. It can evolve positively by playing on the values and perceptions that are most seductive to the audiences, which are embodied through features and action possibilities, positioning them as having complementary roles that go beyond that of the simple manufacturer. Companies then become content producers, mediators, prescribers of information, go-betweens and creators of communities. They then play on notions of proximity, interactivity, transmission, creativity and going beyond the simple image of what we expect of a company that manufactures cameras.

Two points complicate the task, besides the fact of competing with other actors engaged in the same process of constructing a media ethos. On the one hand, depending on their knowledge of the sector, online communication, commercial discourse and their picture of photography, audiences may have different perceptions of the traces left by companies. This introduces the risk of a gap opening up between the image they are trying to construct and the image perceived. On the other hand, it is complex to control the media ethos, because it is not fixed in time and its perception is not limited solely to the space of the company's website. It will evolve as the company posts messages, discourses and instrumentalized work on its website, but also in other spaces, such as social media. The media ethos can even evolve to the disadvantage of the company, in spaces where it is indirectly present, such as photograph sharing websites. It is therefore necessary to control the meanings of the traces left, to know its audiences, but also to take into account in its strategies the impact of these audiences, by considering giving them a role, because their productions and messages can constitute free added value that will favorably reinforce the media ethos.

The website also makes it possible to draw up a panel of practices enabled by its products, and to draw up profiles of the audiences that the brand seeks to reach. We have however found that while three categories of audience may emerge (implicitly or explicitly), the amateur photographer seemed to be the one toward whom the brand seemed to be directing much of its communication effort. Since this audience category is quite large, we can assume that companies hope that beginners will acquire amateur equipment, so as to quickly join this sector (except for those whose budget does not allow it). The professional photographer, coming to the website to make a purchase, would probably not need the brand to offer a presentation of potential practices, because they have the discernment and knowledge to make their own choices. Camera manufacturers, however, make full use of this image of the professional, whether in the instrumentalization of their discourses or in terms of being an aspirational model in terms of practice and competence. This strategy, correlated with the idea that purchasing a camera can be a long-term investment, will thus encourage casual and amateur audiences to lean toward the purchase of cameras that fall into the category above their needs.

3.7. References

Amossy, R. (2010). *La présentation de soi – Éthos et identité verbale*. Presse Universitaires de France, Paris.

Dujarier, M.-A. (2014). *Le travail du consommateur*. La Découverte, Paris.

Fournout, O. (2012). *Théorie de la communication et éthique relationnelle*. Hermes Lavoisier, Cachan.

Galinon-Mélénec, B. (ed.) (2011). *L'homme trace – Perspectives anthropologiques des traces contemporaines*. CNRS Éditions, Paris.

Galinon-Mélénec, B. and Zlitni, S. (eds) (2013). *Traces numériques. De la production à l'interprétation*. CNRS Éditions, Paris.

Goffman, E. (1973). *La mise en scène de la vie quotidienne, volume 1 : La présentation de soi*. Les Editions de Minuit, Paris.

Jeanneret, Y. (2008). *Penser la trivialité, volume 1 : La vie triviale des êtres culturels*. Hermès-Lavoisier, Paris.

Jeanneret, Y. (2014). *Critique de la trivialité – Les médiations de la communication, enjeu de pouvoir*. Editions Non Standard, Paris.

Mouratidou, E. (2018). Le spectacle de la marchandise : imitations, illusions et croyances. *Communication & Langages*, 198, 27–34.

Odin, R. (2000). La question du public. Approche sémio-pragmatique. *Réseaux*, 18(99), 49–72.

Petters, L. (2018). Les figures d'autorité dans la publicité testimoniale. *Communication & Langages*, 198, 71–84.

Rollandin, M. (2015). La réflexivité communicationnelle induite par les échanges en ligne : pratique, médiation et médiatisation, vers une posture d'ethnologue-amateur. PhD Thesis, Université Paris Sorbonne, Paris.

Souchier, E., Jeanneret, Y., Le Marec, J. (eds) (2003). *Lire, écrire, récrire*. Bibliothèque publique d'information, Paris.

Winkin, Y. (1996). *Anthropologie de la communication : de la théorie au terrain*. De Boeck-Westnael, Brussels.

4

Analyses of Digital Communication Strategies for Family Caregivers

Sébastien ROUQUETTE and Christelle CHAUZAL-LARGUIER
Communication et Sociétés, Université Clermont Auvergne, Clermont-Ferrand, France

4.1. Introduction

This research focuses on the communication issues of websites dedicated to family caregivers and is justified by the mismatch decried by Atifi and Gaglio (2012) between "the abundance of online spaces for caregivers and the lack of research on this topic". According to Article L. 113-1-3 of France's Code of Social Action and Families, "Shall be considered as a family caregiver of an elderly person their spouse, the partner with whom they have entered into a civil solidarity pact or their partner, a relative or a friend, defined as family caregivers [...], who assists them, regularly and frequently, on a non-professional basis, to perform all or some of the actions or activities of daily life".

In France, "nearly three out of ten French people, aged 18 and over, making 11 million people" take on this role (Ipsos/Macif survey, *Aidants : le temps des solutions?*, 2020) justifying the growing interest they are receiving from actors in the private sector who, through their digital communication strategies, deliver what Romeyer (2008) calls "health information" aimed at the general public, easily

Digital Presences of Organizations,
coordinated by Nathalie PINÈDE, Luc MASSOU and Patrick MPONDO-DICKA. © ISTE Ltd 2024.

accessible on the Internet and subject to little or no monitoring. But who are these private actors?

The associative environment has led to the emergence of actors who lead the way in giving support to caregivers. These generalist or specialized associations, bringing together patients and families, "wish to play a role in improving the health system and call for better recognition of the role of friends and family and their needs. They play a significant part in the development of innovative approaches that are being developed based on the needs of users such as mutual support groups (MSGs) with Una-fam"[1] (Bloch 2012, p. 14). Profit-making organizations have joined the associations on the Web. These are essentially mutual societies, insurance companies and banks who take an interest in the needs of this target group likely to become a commercial target in terms of insurance, savings, provident schemes and services in the broad sense. Finally, regional health agencies have a role insofar as they coordinate medico-social activities (assistance and support for elderly and disabled persons) and allocate the operating budget of facilities for elderly, disabled and dependent persons[2].

What are the digital communication tools are used by the private actors in this ecosystem to address the target audience of caregivers, that Hassan Atifi and Gérald Gaglio draw together under the term "caregivers' Internet"? This term encompasses the Internet spaces offered to caregivers by associations and more recently profit-making organizations. It also includes the approach taken by caregivers who "use the Internet, appropriate it, in order to resource their position as caregiver, and do so beyond the spaces designed for them" (Atifi and Gaglio 2012, p. 311).

Traditionally, associations and, more recently, profit-making organizations have reached caregivers through websites and on social media. These days there is still a high level of stakeholder investment in websites, even though "on the whole, social media channels seem to have created opportunities for interpersonal engagement, interactivity and dialogue that are qualitatively different from those offered by traditional websites" (Lovejoy and Saxton 2012, p. 337).

What role do websites play in the digital strategy of these organizations: in the age of social media, is it still central or is it becoming secondary? In fact, a social media channel is – at first glance – a communication system that is perfectly suited to the communication objectives of these institutions, particularly family caregiver associations which have less financial resources and professional skills for their

1 Union nationale de familles et amis de personnes malades et/ou handicapées psychiques.

2 Available at: www.ars.sante.fr/quest-ce-quune-agence-regionale-de-sante [Accessed 1 January 2021].

communication (some operating solely with volunteers) than profit-making organizations. At the same time, are there distinctions to be made between the websites adopted by these two types of organizations?

4.2. Methodology

In order to carry out this comparative analysis successfully, this research combines two methodologies. The first carries out a comparative study of the websites and social media of these organizations. In order to determine the place given to the websites in their digital communication strategies, this analysis focuses on the content published on the pages: headings, types of information (Rouquette 2009). The website content is examined using the tool outiref.fr ("textual content" tab). This maps the main fields of the website's domains by studying all the words and phrases used in the Web page submitted for analysis. This SEO tool will study the text of the Web page – unique keywords, combinations of two keywords – with the aim of identifying the main lexical fields used on the page. In addition, the study considers how often the information is refreshed: instantaneous or deferred communication, number of posts published (Campbell et al. 2014).

The activity that this content generates among subscribers is the subject of two specific analyses. The first is based on the study of sitelinks (Rouquette 2010). This is part of a website usage analysis. It allows us to compare productions and usages; contents published by these websites and the interest that these contents arouse among users. According to Google, websites' sitelinks are the most visited internal sections of the website. Shown below in addition to the homepage URL, they can be analyzed manually. Google calculates these sitelinks from user behavior, and in particular – according to the analysis by Erik Wilde and Anuradha Roy – from the number of times a page has been viewed, the time spent on the page, and the content of the page itself (Wilde and Roy 2019). These data "have the advantage both of being available for all information websites with sufficient traffic [...] and of being based on the same (quantitative) data ranking criteria. In other words, of giving a similar bias to all the results obtained (overestimation of the number of 'unique visitors', unstable boundaries of the 'website perimeters', etc.). These biases, moreover, are limited by the fact that the results are not delivered in absolute values (audience figures) but in relative values, by ranking the audience of one heading in relation to another on each website" (Rouquette 2010, p. 161).

The second analysis is based on a study of the natural referencing of the website, in other words the position in which each website appears in the rankings in targeted searches. It is necessary to determine beforehand the information searched for most often by French Internet users on the subject of caregivers. Over the past 14 years, the two queries asked most often according to the Google index tool Trends are "caregivers" and "family caregivers"[3]. These data provided by the search engine can be exploited all the more reliably in France since the Google search engine is still the one used by 91% of French Internet users in the last month, far ahead of Yahoo (14%) and Bing (12%)[4]. The position in the search results is significant because it determines the audience of each of these websites, the number of pages viewed and thus their online visibility.

All these criteria are included in Table 4.1. The number of criteria used here is less than that usually used for a strict website analysis, but it is appropriate for establishing the desired comparison.

Analysis tools	Questions asked
Website content analysis	Which headings and information are preferred? What proportion does the website assign more specifically to information relating to caregivers: administrative procedures, scientific health news, setting out administrative procedures, scientific news items on health subjects, publication of reports, advertising symposia, the opening of nursing homes, etc.?
Website visibility analysis	Where is the website positioned in the search rankings?
Analysis of the main contents consulted on these websites	Which pages of the website are most visited?

Table 4.1. *Criteria for analyzing caregiver websites*

The second part examines, through six in-depth interviews, the viewpoint of persons holding leadership roles in structures working with caregivers, or communication or liaison roles with caregivers in private organizations, as shown in Table 4.2.

During these interviews conducted between 2017 and 2021, three main topics relating to online communication on the subject of caregivers were addressed:

3 Specifically, these two requests are twice as high as "aide aux aidants" (help for caregivers), "Alzheimer" (Alzheimer's), "les aidants familiaux" (family caregivers), "maison des aidants" (caregiver's home), etc.: available at: www.trends.google.com/trends/?geo=FR [Accessed 1 January 2021].

4 Available at: www.statista.com/infographic/20508/motors-de-recherche-les-plus-utilises-en-france/.

– the objectives of this online communication: this topic is addressed through the objectives of the media (Internet and digital social media) and the people in charge of communication;

– the content of online communication: for this, we look at the intended target groups (on the Internet, on digital social media), the discourse conveyed in both cases and also areas for improving and developing the discourse;

– the technical aspects of online communication. Various points are examined: SEO and its strategy, complementarity between the Internet and digital social media, notification count, profile of those who viewed the page, number of actions taken on the page and their scope.

Structure	Name of structure	Role within structure	Interview number
Union Départementale des Associations Familiales	Union Départementale des Associations Familiales du Maine-et-Loire	Liaison and information officer	Interview 1
Association	La Maison des Aidants	Founding president	Interview 2
Association	Association des Aidants et Malades à Corps de Lewy	President	Interview 3
Association	"Je t'aide" co-operative	Project manager of National Day	Interview 4
Association	France Alzheimer Allier	President of departmental branch	Interview 5
Private company	Novartis	Communications officer	Interview 6

Table 4.2. *Corpus of interviewees*

This research combines the study of the online content and actors' strategy, in order to understand whether, in their view, digital media are seen as complementary to websites or, going forward, sufficient in themselves and if so, why.

4.3. Analytical corpus

This study is based on a specific field with a corpus composed of a total of eight family caregiver associations and four profit-making organizations (mutual societies, insurance companies) presented briefly in Table 4.3 and more at length in section 4.7. It will consider what differentiated strategies (content, services, interaction) are deployed on the Internet by these two types of organizations.

A first category of websites sets out to be generalist, oriented toward and on caregivers ("because on the Internet, there is only general information" (interview 1, 2017)), such as La Maison des Aidants, La Compagnie des Aidants, Udaf 49, Aidant Attitude, for example. This type of website is "intended to provide information, present news items and provide discussion spaces for caregivers if they want to comment. There are mood posts, reactions, feedback; they can also give their feelings on all the headings of the website" (interview 2, 2017). This category of websites offers information of a very practical nature such as the calendar of caregiver training sessions, with its heading on the first page for example but also referring, in some cases, to other websites, always aimed at caregivers.

	Structure	Website URLs
Associations	Association Française des Aidants	www.aidants.fr/
	La Maison des Aidants/Aidants en Mouvement	www.lamaisondesaidants.com/
	Udaf 49 (Union Départementale des Associations Familiales du Maine-et-Loire)	www.udaf49.fr/
	La Compagnie des Aidants	www.lacompagniedesaidants.org
	Aidant Attitude	www.aidantattitude.fr/
	France Alzheimer Allier	www.francealzheimer.org/allier/
	Association des Aidants et Malades à Corps de Lewy	www.a2mcl.org
	"Je t'aide" co-operative	www.associationjetaide.org/
For-profit organizations (banks, insurance companies)	Capgeris	www.capgeris.com/aidants-and-aids-1689/
	Novartis: NovaSenior Group	www.novasenior.com/aidants.htm
	Malakoff Médéric	www.malakoffhumanis.com/solutions/social-assistance-services/line-info-assistants/
	AG2R	www.ag2rlamondiale.fr/sante-prevoyance/dependence/conseil-aidants-familiaux-quelles-sont-les-aides

Table 4.3. *Corpus of Web pages of associations and profit-making organizations dedicated to family caregivers*

These websites have headings dedicated to caregivers (e.g. on the Compagnie des Aidants website, we can read: "Always tell the person what you are doing or are going to do. Before helping them with anything, ask if they want your help. Be patient. Do not rush the person, even if they are slow to respond to your requests"), but that is not all. More broadly, advice for the elderly is given: how to wash your hands, protect yourself from the cold, etc.

If the websites of private profit-making organizations are also generalist and aimed at caregivers, the content is very close to the above case. Indeed, these websites have an abundance of information of an administrative nature (mobility aids, applying for assistance, home help, tax allowances, etc.) or financial advice. They provide free and open access to a wide range of qualified information (geolocation service, fact sheets, self-assessment tools, etc.) and participatory spaces, a calendar of events ("When we were able to offer services (action support, home adaptation service, etc.), we communicated). We follow the example of how things are done across the Atlantic, where there is communication about what exists, what works or what does not" (interview 6, 2017). However, what differentiates the websites of associations from those of private profit-making organizations is that the latter use this communication tool to promote accommodation facilities (residences for the elderly, retirement homes) for dependent persons, with paid access to the website for professionals who wish to be inventoried (Novasenior group) and/or spaces for caregivers who are already clients. Thus, for example, Malakoff Médéric's caregiver website gives caregivers who are clients access to a list of the group's social actions.

A second category of more specialized websites is not considered from the point of view of target (making them feel concerned, putting themselves in their place) because "on the website, the target group is not composed only of caregivers. It's a bit of a mix, we have physiotherapists, nurses, speech therapists who contact us to ask for information. As it is a poorly understood disease, there are also doctors" (interview 3, 2021). So, the website of the association is the one that is preferred. This category of websites concentrates more on a specific disease (medical research, the patient's life, etc.) in order to give more technical information and refocuses on its problems (appeals for donations, volunteer recruitment). France Alzheimer, for example, addresses through its website three potential target groups: professionals in the medical and social sector, potential France Alzheimer volunteers and caregivers to whom the association offers training.

On the websites of both profit-making and not-for-profit actors, the volume of information is large, but particular attention is paid to access to information for this audience of caregivers, 76% of whom are under 65 years old and 43% under 50 years old (BVA barometer April 2018). Thus, the tree structure of the websites is designed so as to organize the information under headings that can be very numerous, sometimes 15 or more. Many visuals are presented. Videos are also frequently made available on these websites. Websites, with their accessible and abundant information, are thus an essential digital communication tool ("If we want to offer technical information, we cannot manage without a website because it makes the information permanently accessible" (interview 3, 2021)) because it can evolve in real time.

In the first part, this study compares the websites and social media pages deployed by these organizations, concluding in highlighting the advantages of websites, digital communication tools that are far from being outstripped by the advent of social media. The second part of this work proposes explanations for this result.

4.4. The central position of websites in digital communication strategies

4.4.1. *Digital communication pre-adapted to its target audiences*

> It must be remembered that the caregiver is a third party in the care and support relationship. It is not the caregiver who is sick, elderly, disabled or socially vulnerable. Consequently, the caregiver is not naturally a protagonist in the relationship that unites the patient or user and the professionals. (Rousset 2015, p. 96)

Suffering from a lack of recognition, caregivers have long remained in the shadows (Bloch 2012) and isolated (Atifi and Gaglio 2012). The government, mindful of the considerable costs likely to be incurred by caring for an increasing number of people in need of assistance (Minozio 2004), prefers to keep care recipients at home and is pressing ahead with legislation through the 2015 Act pertaining to the adaptation of society to aging and the 2016 Act pertaining to labor, the modernization of social dialogue and the safeguarding of professional pathways.

> Leveraging the experience of associations and actors on the ground, public policies have focused on two areas of action: on the one

> hand initiatives relating to information, training and support for caregivers, and on the other hand the creation of mechanisms such as day care or temporary housing for people with Alzheimer's disease. (Kenigsberg et al. 2013, p. 59)

In this context, associations have seen the size of their field of action increase sharply. While the caregiver gives support to a loved one, they fear, forget and put off seeking help for themself. Yet what is commonly referred to as "caregiver support" is essential and associations have contributed greatly to its implementation (Ghent et al. 2014), because "supporting this informal work, long invisible, prevents these neighborhood caregivers – true close-at-hand protection – from becoming exhausted" (Campéon and Le Bihan 2016, p. 88). The family caregiver, even when exhausted, can be resistant to an alternative (a respite facility, for example) (Mollard 2009) at the risk of jeopardizing their health (Pinquart and Sörensen 2003; Schulz and Sherwood 2008). How can we support, inform and more generally provide assistance to a family caregiver who, because of their position, can more often than not no longer go anywhere, due to lack of time and respite? The caregiver like "the patient gives consideration to the cost of entry into this or that information-gathering process. It is measured in time, in money, and in intangible costs (pain, apprehension)" (Nabarette 2002, p. 262). In all these respects, digital communication offers many advantages.

Taking on the role of caregiver is a big decision, which has a significant impact as much on professional life (loss of employment, absenteeism, adjustment of working time, loss of access to the labor market) as on personal life for the person who has to assume the role. While the caregiver knows that a decision such as this is going to disrupt everyday life, they do not necessarily know in what ways. This leap into the unknown is accompanied by a lack of information and difficulty in knowing who to contact. Thus, 85% of caregivers experience a feeling of discouragement[5]. In this context, does the digital communication of associations and profit-making organizations make greater use of websites or of social media?

4.4.2. *Social media comparatively disadvantageous to associations*

In our earlier research, we showed (Chauzal-Larguier and Rouquette 2017) that social media does not give these associations visibility commensurate with their

5 Study carried out among 509 caregivers by Opinion Way for the Espace national de réflexion ethique sur la maladie d'Alzheimer and Espace ethique Île-de-France.

investments and their role on the ground. They fail to form a real social bond with the caregivers they seek to reach. Measured in number of "friends" (subscribers) or comments, caregiver associations are much less visible than the Facebook accounts of profit-making organizations. Only the latter succeed in promoting their messages, including the services they provide (nursing home room, credit, medical equipment, home care) by initiating and developing digital conversations on topics of concern to caregivers and their loved ones. On the other hand, this promotion is – on a social medium like Facebook – more uncertain in the case of family caregiver associations. "Such that the risk for family caregiver associations is less of losing their souls in communicating on social media than of being much less visible than profit-making organizations. The main reason is to do with lack of time, strategy and the skills needed to put in place a structured approach to communication including social media" (Chauzal-Larguier and Rouquette 2017, p. 100). Do websites enable a better response to the primary need of caregivers, namely a need for structured information?

This research published in 2017 is complementary to the aforementioned study. Some clarification is needed. On the one hand, the corpus of associations and companies studied is almost the same, but enriched (Association des Aidants, Malades à Corps de Lewy and Équité pour les Aidants) and excludes Natixis, which does not have a dedicated website for caregivers. On the other hand, the methodologies used to study the Facebook pages and Twitter accounts of these associations and companies and the results of this study are set out in this earlier research.

4.4.3. *Association websites with greater visibility than those of profit-making organizations*

Let us look at the results of the comparative analysis of websites of caregiver associations and profit-making organizations that we carried out in November and December 2020, analyzed and laid out in Table 4.4.

Thus, contrary to what has been observed on social media, the visibility of association websites is better than that of profit-making organizations. On the first two queries submitted by French Internet users on these topics via Google ("caregivers" and "family caregivers"), the Association Française des Aidants has the best placed website (first and sixth), the association La Maison des Aidants is ranked third for the most frequently formulated request ("caregivers"), the association Compagnie des Aidants 12th, the association Aidant Attitude 10th. Conversely, several profit-making organizations' websites are ranked extremely poorly (placed at 100+ on both requests): Capgeris and Malakoff Médéric. None (except AG2R at 14th on the "family caregivers" request) achieves a respectable natural indexing that is good enough to hope for the slightest visibility in a general search.

	Structure	Natural indexing for the request "caregivers"	Natural indexing for the request "family caregivers"
Caregiver associations	Association Française des Aidants	1	6
	La Maison des Aidants	3	100+
	Udaf 49	100+	74
	Compagnie des Aidants	12	100+
	Aidant Attitude	19	55
	France Alzheimer Allier	86	100+
	Association des aidants et malades à corps de Lewy	100+	100+
	"Je t'aide" co-operative	44	100+
Profit-making organizations	Capgeris	100+	100+
	Novartis: Novasenior Group	100+	50
	Malakoff Médéric	100+	100+
	AG2R	100+	14

Table 4.4. *Comparative analysis of the visibility of websites of caregivers' associations and profit-making organizations, dated January 3, 2021*

This observation is all the more important because, while in France the dissemination of information on and for caregivers is still a recent phenomenon ("Only [13] years ago, when you typed "family caregiver" into Google, you would find nothing except on North American websites thanks to the medico-social networks that took an interest in the topic" (interview 2, 2017)), it is becoming more and more widespread. As shown in Figure 4.1, in 5 years (2014–2019) the French have submitted twice as many queries on these topics. Because, as Colette Eynard (2010, p. 119) points out, "Beyond information, some family caregivers are seeking to understand what is happening" in order to move ahead in their personal journey and project themselves into the unknown.

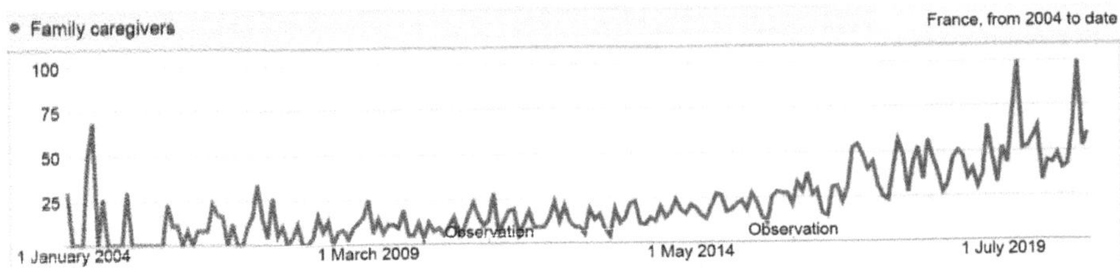

Figure 4.1. *Requests for information about caregivers are rising steeply online. Source: Google Trends, last consulted January 7, 2021*

4.5. Websites: advantages for associative actors

4.5.1. *Content focused on caregivers' expectations, the main strength of associations' websites*

A major explanation emerges from the comparison between the columns "main content disseminated by websites" and "main headings consulted by Internet users" (Table 4.5).

Analysis grid of websites	**Website content (via the study of the site's lexical fields with the Outiref website content analysis tool)**	**Number of headings preferentially consulted by Internet users relating to caregivers**
	Proportion of lexical fields primarily devoted to caregivers among the ten most frequently occurring lexical fields on the site	**Proportion of sitelinks primarily devoted to caregivers among the website headings most consulted by Internet users**
Association Française des Aidants	10/10 (help in understanding, caregivers, help for caregivers, help to understand, family caregivers, caregiver support, helper, helping caregivers, accompanying caregivers, family caregivers)	9/10 (caregiver café, for your loved one, useful links, training for caregivers, factsheets, caregiver health, our policies, respite for young caregivers)
La Maison des Aidants	7/10 (caregivers, caregiver accompaniment, help for caregivers, helping caregivers, caregiver support, supporting caregivers, gerontology, respite, family caregivers)	8/10 (welcome to the website ..., tools for caregivers, the toolkit, useful links, presentation, what is, "domaidants", take time out, Lyon will start)
Udaf 49	0/10 Main field: Udaf. Secondary fields: family associations, departmental union, Unaf, national union of associations, APF France handicap, family association, national union, community center, family action	0/10 (social and other services, our services remain open, Udaf is recruiting, manage services, organization chart, measures, general presentation, read and get others to read, family mediation, Angers, funding)

Analysis grid of websites	Website content (via the study of the site's lexical fields with the Outiref website content analysis tool)	Number of headings preferentially consulted by Internet users relating to caregivers
	Proportion of lexical fields primarily devoted to caregivers among the ten most frequently occurring lexical fields on the site	Proportion of sitelinks primarily devoted to caregivers among the website headings most consulted by Internet users
Compagnie des Aidants	6/10 Main fields: caregivers, family caregivers, neighborhood caregivers, caregiver, respite. Secondary fields: ADMR, caregiver, France Alzheimer, family caregiver, personal independence	4/10 (who are we, train with the company, the "Tous Aidants" caravan, caregiver registration, guide, HR solutions, contact us, my training pathway, services, volunteer registration)
Aidant Attitude	9/10 (caregivers, caregiver, neighborhood caregiver, help for caregivers, neighborhood caregivers, helping caregivers, family caregivers, caregiver support, personal independence, role of the caregiver)	4/5 (the Aidant Attitude team, rights and assistance, caregivers in our society, reading material)
France Alzheimer Allier	1/10 Main fields: association France Alzheimer, France Alzheimer, Alzheimer France, related. Secondary fields: related diseases, Alzheimer, our missions, neurodegenerative, help for caregivers	1/10 (contact your association, holiday breaks, become a donor, contact us, Alzheimer's disease, all France Alzheimer's news, social and financial aid, caregiver training, what are our missions, France Alzheimer)

Analysis grid of websites	Website content (via the study of the site's lexical fields with the Outiref website content analysis tool)	Number of headings preferentially consulted by Internet users relating to caregivers
	Proportion of lexical fields primarily devoted to caregivers among the ten most frequently occurring lexical fields on the site	Proportion of sitelinks primarily devoted to caregivers among the website headings most consulted by Internet users
Association des aidants et malades à corps de Lewy	0/10 Main fields: related, related diseases, Alzheimer's. Secondary fields: disease sufferers, Alzheimer's disease, body dementia, Alzheimer's type dementia, related disease, neurodegenerative, Alzheimer's type	1/10 (the symptoms, medical research, news, treatments, about us, support us, useful links, Lewy body dementia, documentation, how to manage)
"Je t'aide" co-operative	4/10 (Main fields: help for caregivers; caregivers; family caregivers; caregiver. Secondary fields: Respite; gerontology; social action; France Alzheimer; medico-social; CCAS)	2/4 (caregiver kit, about us, contact, National Caregiver Day)
Capgeris	7/10 (caregivers, dependents, caregiver, helping caregivers, family caregivers, help for caregivers, personal independence, loss of independence, personal care, personal assistance)	0/10 (recruitment, residential care, host family, Capgeris.com, …. portal, accommodation for the elderly, retirement home/nursing home ..., senior village, news, meal delivery)

Analysis grid of websites	Website content (via the study of the site's lexical fields with the Outiref website content analysis tool)	Number of headings preferentially consulted by Internet users relating to caregivers
	Proportion of lexical fields primarily devoted to caregivers among the ten most frequently occurring lexical fields on the site	Proportion of sitelinks primarily devoted to caregivers among the website headings most consulted by Internet users
Novartis: NovaSenior Group	1/10 Main fields: temporary accommodation, gerontology, seniors, personal independence, finding a retirement home, help for caregivers, nursing homes, local center, dependent person, supporting the elderly	1/10 (home help, financial help at home, about us, cost of home help, retirement home, ... residences, ... caregiver directories, find a retirement home, Yvelines 78, home help agencies, state or private nursing home)
Malakoff Médéric	0/10 Main fields: health and provident planning, Malakoff Médéric provident schemes, insurance fund, mutual health insurance. Secondary fields: health insurance, our solutions, healthcare costs, complementary mutual insurance, compulsory scheme	1/10 (individual, mutual health insurance, how to access my..., Covid-19: help ..., Malakoff Médéric, learn more about us, contact us, retirement pension, supplementary pension, make a claim)
AG2R	5/10 Main fields: family caregiver, neighborhood caregiver, family caregivers, caregiver, caregivers, provident schemes, old-age insurance. Secondary fields: personal independence payment, right to respite, PIP)	0/5 (all our services, online service: ... designation, mutual health insurance, provident scheme)

Table 4.5. *Comparative analysis of the content of the websites of caregivers' associations and profit-making organizations, January 3, 2021*

The study of sitelinks, the headings of a website most consulted by Internet users, makes it clear: the content of associative websites is, on the whole, much more focused on the issue of caregivers than that of more generalist profit-making organizations. Only four of the 12 organizations have at least six sitelinks out of 10 that directly concern caregivers. These are four associations: the Association Française des Aidants, the Compagnie des Aidants, Aidant Attitude, and La Maison des Aidants. Conversely, only one of the five profit-making organizations manages to have good visibility on two of the most frequent requests (AG2R, 14th, therefore on the second page of results, for the request "family caregivers"). For others, visibility is extremely low on the most common and the most generalist queries (ranked 100+). Under these conditions, the possibility of reaching neophyte Internet users – those who have general questions – or who are unaware of the existence of these profit-making organizations – and who therefore do not put it in their keywords – is therefore very small.

From this point of view, what is a good website? Ahead of being aesthetically pleasing, interactive, open, fun to use or even secure, it is above all a website whose content meets the expectations of Internet users. Unlike a billboard ad placed in the path of a passerby, the Internet user does not need to click on the website URL. "On the Internet, the user goes in search of information" (interview 3, 2021): if the content of the website does not interest him, he will pass it by or will not stay long. Hence this axiom that should be taught in every digital communication training course: a good website is first and foremost a website that answers the main questions that its main target groups ask themselves. This axiom is easy to give but not easy to put into practice. It involves first correctly identifying its main target groups (here, what audience will connect to my website: elderly ladies? caregivers' children?). It also involves having a proper knowledge of their expectations (what information are they looking for primarily?) and not falling back on a vague and undefined "I know my audience". Finally, it involves building a home page that showcases this information by putting it on the first page of the website and under the first headings of the menu bar, and not at the third level of the website.

To translate this in concrete terms in the Internet of health: what is a good website from the point of view of caregivers looking for information? Compiling a list of which "sublinks" (sitelinks) reoccur among the best indexed websites provides an initial answer to this question. Which headings do caregivers consult primarily? Those that talk about training (caregiver training), health (caregiver health, taking time out), psychological help (caregiver café) or that provide practical resources (useful links, factsheets, toolkit) and legal advice (rights and support). In other words, practical information – to help individuals manage their daily lives

(Rouquette 2010) – and specific information to help caregivers. The content of these associative websites thus echoes the research that had identified the nature of the information that caregivers need. This is what was written in the specialized literature on these issues in 2013: "[Caregivers] seek medical information about their sick relative, the most suitable care networks, addresses of doctors or medical institutions, or they share their feelings about the difficulty of their situation as a caregiver, trying to find comfort, an understanding listener through the fact of sharing a situation common to both" (Dubreuil and Hazif-Thomas 2013, p. 252).

In fact, through the content of their websites, caregivers' associations aim to achieve this informational objective, "namely to break the feeling of isolation by helping the caregiver/care-recipient couple to rebuild a new relational fabric and a new affiliation to a social group, to take the necessary step back to avoid getting into that situation and to work on the limits of their role as caregiver, to provide a space for the expression of emotions" (Coudin and Mollard 2011, p. 369).

Their websites prove to be a very suitable tool to meet this informational need, because of their round-the-clock access to information and the unparalleled amount of information offered (Nabarette 2002). They also make it possible "to compensate for several gaps: availability of staff, family caregivers, lack of premises and the problem of reimbursement for a psycho-social intervention" (Wu et al. 2009, p. 189). However, profit-making actors do not adopt the same content and do not achieve the same visibility. How can these differences be explained?

4.5.2. *Well-pitched websites to interest the target group*

To reach the target audience, looking for practical information, websites must, in addition to finding topics of interest to caregivers, pitch themselves appropriately. Indeed, "the exceptional success of these websites is based on a new form of navigation that, recognizing the imperfections of search engines, is rooted in an experience much closer to the expectations and ordinary practices of users" (Cardon 2011, p. 142).

The analysis of marketing pitches plays a full role on websites. According to Lescourret's (2017) typology of marketing pitches (p. 102), a company promotes itself "through its promises (manipulation), its expertise (skill), its achievements (performance) or through customer reactions (response)", as summarized in Table 4.6.

Among the not-for-profit actors, some are engaged in representation, others much less so. Thus, some opt for a marketing pitch based on their actions and are more engaged and animated by a form of activism. For example, since its creation in 2003, the Association Française des Aidants has campaigned for the recognition of the role and the place of caregivers in society and puts its structure at the service of this cause. Others opt more for an informative marketing pitch related to their skills (Udaf 49, Aidant Attitude). Thus, for example, over the period 2010–2017, the website of Aidant Attitude essentially lists the principle sources of assistance available to caregivers, disabled care-recipients and dependent care-recipients. Over time, the structure develops and becomes more impactful. Others, finally, like La Maison des Aidants, view themselves as both professional (helping caregivers) and committed through mood posts for instance. Profit-making organizations' websites are professional websites that use a certain amount of manipulation. In fact, the marketing pitch is focused on caregivers and it is not clear that a profit-making actor is hiding behind it. The marketing pitch is made with the enunciator concealed, as in the case of La Macif. "A commitment to support each other. […] This website was created so that caregivers can, day after day, carry out their role while at the same time preserving their quality of life"[6]. Sometimes, attempts by profit-making organizations to try for greater individualization emerge. Thus, on the Novasenior site, the user can fill out a questionnaire about me, my loved one, my situation, my needs (job, employee, etc.), the objective being to offer personalized information. Is this the future of big websites? The question is worth asking, because, on the associative websites, the enunciators are shown, for example, as from 2010, on Aidant Attitude's website. It is less impersonal. "Annick Toczé (care assistant) and Pierre Denis (family caregiver) have put at your disposal practical advice and information that will enable you to get answers to some of the questions and situations for which you will have to find solutions".

Action	Manipulation	Skill	Performance	Response
Promoting the indexed institution	Promise of caregiver support	Presentation and detailed description of the range of services offered	Presentation of the press review and illustrative function of the photographic modules	Positive Presentation of video reports within the press review

Table 4.6. *Classification of publication areas in terms of their narrative function in the promotional discourse of the indexed institution (Balnéa and Lescourret 2017, p. 107)*

6 Available at: www.aveclesaidants.fr/services/service-daide-memoire/.

To reach caregivers, new websites are emerging, alongside those of existing associations, on more targeted themes. "Since these caregivers are not, by nature, professionals, training is essential for them so that they can support their loved one in the best way possible without putting themselves in difficulty or even in danger" (Rousset 2015, p. 97). Also, associations' websites are changing the training headings, because as we have mentioned, initiatives are multiplying on the ground. This is the experience reported by the journalist L. Boccara on "La Maison des Aidants in metropolitan Lille-Roubaix-Tourcoing [which] offers the services of 'stand-in home caregivers'. For a modest fee, from €4 to €6 per hour, a member of the association with knowledge of these diseases acts as stand-in for the caregiver at the home of the loved one for half a day or an evening to allow them to spend time away without worrying. After the passing of their loved one, many former caregivers do not forget this feeling of desperation. Many sign up as volunteers to help others who are sometimes facing difficult situations". Also, existing associations are creating new websites for training purposes, to which reference is made on the association's website. This is the case for the Association Française des Aidants, which in September 2017 launched an online training course consisting of six modules. "Free of charge and open to all, online training for caregivers aims to question and analyze the situations experienced in the relationship with the loved one in a situation of disability or dependence, in order to find the appropriate responses"[7]. "Conceived by the association for the National Day of Caregivers, this new website takes the form of a pathway with the modules: 'At work', 'At home', 'Find support', 'Need for respite', etc. Each module corresponds to a moment in the life of a person who is caring for an elderly or disabled person in their circle of acquaintances"[8].

The actors attach great importance to the layout and the colors but also the animation on websites, giving prominence to videos, testimonies (videos featuring caregivers which take the form of interviews, including interviews with the caregiver at home) and reports. "Eighty percent of caregivers take charge of personal and toilet needs, and bandaging. You can hurt yourself and your loved one. Therefore, we provide videos showing the correct handling techniques", explains Claudie Kulak, President of the Association for the National Caregiver Day[9]. Videos are also available on Facebook accounts, because social media is good for disseminating videos. Thus, the selected headings appear twice, under two different

7 Available at: www.aidants.fr/vous-etes-aidant/participer-action-pres-de-chez-soi/formation-aidants.

8 Available at: www.faire-face.fr/2017/03/08/aidants-familiaux-kit-internet.

9 Available at: www.francetvinfo.fr/sante/handicap/aidants-un-site-internet-pour aider_2107990.html.

headings: reception centers and the home helps are placed in "information and advice" (which seems more neutral) and in "useful contacts".

Consequently, medical experts cannot ignore the new expectations of caregivers and their knowledge that is not only empirical but also intersubjective, arising from discussions between "e-caregiver" based around feedback from them on their experiences (Dubreuil and Hazif-Thomas 2013, p. 252). "The increase in the number of websites dedicated to healthcare shows that patients, their loved ones and caregivers want to be involved in their care journey and in the management of their health. The patient's circle of acquaintances will easily, in a few clicks, obtain the information being sought on pathologies, treatments, care providers. The "e-caregiver" appropriates medical knowledge, becomes better informed about the pathology of the patient they care for and more engaged in their medical care and treatment. "The appropriation of power, as the Quebecers translate "empowerment", is the keyword to a change of outlook on psychic suffering and on the people who carry this suffering", summarize Dutoi-Sola and Deutsch (2012), for whom the emergence of the user in the healthcare democracy goes hand-in-hand with the evolution from psychiatry to mental health. We will add, for our part, that it is a catalyst for the evolution from mental health to relational e-health because, with the Internet, it is indeed a trigger that leads to information gaining momentum allowing a person to orient themself toward the best possible help, hence this "internal movement that allows the person to move from their potential abilities to their actual abilities" (Dubreuil and Hazif-Thomas 2013, p. 253).

4.5.3. *Level of updates: a non-prohibitive weakness of associative websites*

One final point remains: in order to be visible, must these websites constantly enrich their content, for instance through a regularly refreshed news section? Porter and Edirippulige (2007) take the view that caregivers are looking for positive stories to cheer themselves up and forget the issue of the support process, an idea taken up and reinforced by Atifi and Gaglio (2012, p. 319): "Caregiver who use the Internet often confine themselves to reading posts to reassure themselves". Since the caregiver's experience is forged on a daily basis, information related to that experience predominates (helpful tips, aids). Thus, only a tiny proportion of the information available is consulted at one time.

In fact, updating does happen but at very variable intervals, more frequently for profit-making organizations (see Table 4.7).

Three out of four websites of profit-making actors have a news section or a newsfeed. Of the seven not-for-profit actors in the corpus, only one association disseminates ten or more news items per month (Aidant Attitude).

Indeed, for small associations, the lack of skills ("To start with, I had created a website on OVH. Then we decided to move to the business platform. We subcontract the technical side and in addition, the platform handles membership management, subscriptions, cash management, online payments" (interview 3, 2021)) and sometimes dictates the selection of the information to be updated. "Not all the headings need the same updating work. For example, the calendar heading lists conferences, wellness workshops, special events. This heading is updated once or twice a week. I remove, I update. The information itself, the content, for certain headings to be updated, I only do that annually, such as the totals for example" (interview 1, 2017).

Type of structure	Structure	Website updating: presence of a newsfeed and number articles published between November and December 2020
Associations	Association Française des Aidants	Yes, four items
	La Maison des Aidants	Yes, three items
	Udaf 49	Yes, no items
	Compagnie des Aidants	Yes, 10 articles
	Aidant Attitude	Yes, 19 (page linked to Facebook page)
	France Alzheimer Allier	Yes, 11
	Association des aidants et malades à corps de Lewy	None
	"Je t'aide" co-operative	Yes, three
Profit-making organizations	Capgeris	Yes (one heading "caregivers and care recipients"), 27
	Novartis: Novasenior Group	No
	Malakoff Médéric	Yes, two
	AG2R	Yes, 71

Table 4.7. *Comparative analysis of website updating of the websites of caregiver associations and of profit-making organizations, January 3, 2021*

However, these associative websites are the most frequently consulted, which shows that it is to the advantage of Internet sites to focus the architecture of their website on the main expectations of caregivers rather than investing in a time-consuming activity of continuous updating in order to be visible and effective.

4.5.4. *The interactional limits of associative sites*

However, the limits of a website have been reached when we focus not on the quality of the information disseminated but on the interactions with family caregivers of the same type as those put forward by social networks. "The Internet opens up 'spaces' with no physical location, in which anonymous discussions between disembodied individuals can take place" (Jauréguiberry 2000, p. 136) but the websites remain shop windows that cannot not used for discussion.

> The website has an additional advantage over the telephone in the way it delivers a program of intervention thanks to its interactive possibilities. This change in Internet practices, which has been identified as a turning point of 'Web 2.0', is characterized by significant user participation in the production of content and by them establishing contact with each other. (Cardon 2011, p. 141)

Nowadays, associations find it quite hard to progress beyond the limits of the tools made available on the Internet (forums, discussion groups) that are better suited to the target group of caregivers than social media but often at the expense of the interactivity that can break the isolation.

4.6 Conclusion

Does this analysis of the online communication of family caregiver associations and profit-making organizations support the idea of a planned obsolescence of websites? On the contrary, websites that bring help to family caregivers have good times ahead. Nowadays, especially for associations, the website is a tool that gives wide visibility.

The reasons are diverse. The primary reasons relate to the communication strengths of websites in several registers. A website is an appropriate tool for every organization that wishes to disseminate a large amount of information in a structured way. This is the case of associations and profit-making organizations addressing an audience of caregivers who are very often isolated, do not have much time to spare, yet who need advice on financial matters, health, care programs, etc. Websites make it possible to make a great many headings visible from the home page, while at the same time helping to prioritize information. This is done by having multiple access paths to the most important headings – such as information on "home helps", placed under two different headings on the Aidant Attitude website – or by positioning them in the most visible places on a home page (at the top rather than at the bottom of a long page).

The secondary reasons relate to the functions devolved to the Twitter and Facebook accounts of these organizations, in particular by profit-making organizations. These accounts are regarded more – here – as outposts of the website, procurers of Internet users for the main website rather than innovative tools to create new relationships with Internet users. This policy shows the primacy that these associations and profit-making organizations give to their websites. This is the case for Facebook accounts that are seen by profit-making organizations as appropriate communication tools to reach the main audience that is targeted in their case, particularly women aged between 25 and 60. Conversely, this is not the case for Twitter accounts, which, for these same profit-making organizations, are perceived as unprofitable in terms of time required to manage these accounts and users reached. This social media channel is, compared to Facebook, used more by target groups already aware of caregivers' problems (professionals, other associations, journalists, etc.) than by the general public that these organizations seek to reach.

Thus, social media is, here, more in a position of being made use of by existing websites than of replacing these systems. This observation is all the more significant since the communication departments of profit-making organizations in particular are obliged to decide on their priorities among the available systems (Instagram, Twitter, blog, website, etc.), since this multiplication proves so time consuming. This choice clearly shows that in the eyes of the communication managers of profit-making organizations, the promotion of websites remains a priority.

This choice should come as no surprise insofar as, generally speaking, social media, like websites, are seen as possible communication tools among others. "To communicate the results of research we use the Internet but not only that [...]. Our communication is multichannel: digital internationally but also brochures, leaflets and CDs. There is interesting information on the Internet but it is not always appropriate. A person may want it in written form because it is easier for administrative procedures. Administrative procedures are not simple. This equates to a need to be able to read in comfort because sometimes the content can be dense and voluminous. Not everything is confined to the Internet. Some information given on leaflets is not available on the Internet. [...] If we are involved in communication, we are transmitting information and therefore we may need to leverage different channels" (interview 6, 2017). In other words, if we have to relativize the place we accord to social media, it is – at the end of the day – because usually every new system is inserted among existing uses, which causes them to evolve or complements them but does not remove them.

4.7. Appendix

	Presentation of the associations
Association Française des Aidants	Founded in 2003, this association, which consists of 120 members in the regions in 2016, campaigns for measures that make life easier for family caregivers.
La Maison des Aidants/Aidants en Mouvement	La Maison des Aidants, based in Bergerac, supports between 200 and 250 caregivers per year "through their communication, workshops that we organize to train and inform, the telephone helpline that generally accompanies people over a period of several months". Interview conducted with P.J., founding president.
Udaf 49	The Departmental Union of Family Associations of Maine-et-Loire is a departmental offshoot of Unaf, a national public interest association responsible for promoting, defending and representing the interests of all families.
Compagnie des Aidants	The Compagnie des Aidants, an association founded in 2015, has the primary objective of creating a database of care professionals through member caregivers. From year one, this self-help network had 4,000 members. Interview with Claudie Kulak, founder of the Compagnie des Aidants[10].
Aidant Attitude	According to the founder of this association, Pierre Denis, "Aidant Attitude gives itself a mission of information and prevention and has no vocation to go in the field or provide personal services. E-caregivers share their experiences on the website so that they can be used by others, irrespective of the illness of the loved one"[11].
France Alzheimer Allier	"The France Alzheimer Union oversees the 96 departmental associations and assists them. The departments must retain the name France Alzheimer, followed by the department number [...]. When I was appointed president, we had 90 members, now we have 130". Interview with S. L., president of a departmental section of France Alzheimer, on February 28, 2017.

10 Available at: www.gpma-asso.fr/un-reseau-pour-les-aidants [April 22, 2016].

11 Available at: www.canalfnapaef.webnode.fr/news/aidons-les-aidants-une-conference-debat-organisee-par-vedibe-le-12-october-2013/.

Presentation of the associations	
Association des Aidants et Malades à Corps de Lewy	Created in 2019: "We are a small association. Every day people call us, even though we are four volunteers plus one employee on a skills sponsorship program. [...] We have kept our Google group, which currently has 400 members who post". Interview conducted with P. de L., president of the association, on January 19, 2021.
"Je t'aide" co-operative	Originally known as National Caregivers Day, starting in 2010, the Je t'aide Co-operative was launched in 2017. It is a national association responsible, among other things, for coordinating and promoting all events organized for National Caregivers Day, held in France on October 6 each year since 2010.
Profit-making organizations (banks, insurance companies)	
Macif	Mutual insurance company of French traders and industrialists and also executives and employees in industry and commerce. Developed a website dedicated to caregivers (www.aveclesaidants.fr) and launched in 2020 the Caregiver Observatory, a monitoring structure dedicated to caregivers.
Capgeris	Capgeris.com is published by Australis, a consulting company specialized in the field of marketing intelligence and Web marketing, offering companies an innovative approach in the implementation of an effective digital strategy.
Novartis: NovaSenior Group	The NovaSenior platform is free for families, and for partners (retirement homes, senior residences, home helps) it is paid for.
Malakoff Médéric	Malakoff Médéric, the second largest French social protection group, is the insurer used by 200,000 companies for health insurance and provident schemes.
AG2R	Insurance company whose acronym means General Association of Distributed Retirement, which covers 15 million individuals and 500,000 corporate clients. Developed a website dedicated to caregivers (www.aidonslesnotres.fr).

Table 4.8. *Presentation of the associations and profit-making organizations of the corpus studied*

4.8. References

Atifi, H. and Gaglio, G. (2012). L'Internet des aidants. In *Internet et santé : acteurs, usages et appropriations*, Lévy, J.J., Thoër, C. (eds). Presses de l'Université du Québec, Québec.

Bloch, M.-A. (2012). Les aidants et l'émergence d'un nouveau champ de recherche interdisciplinaire. *Vie sociale*, 4(4), 11–29.

Campbell, D.A., Lambright, K.T., Wells, C.J. (2014). Looking for friends, fans, and followers? Social media use in public and nonprofit human services. *Public Administration Review*, 74, 555–663.

Campéon, A. and Le Bihan-Youinou, B. (2016). Le développement des dispositifs d'aide aux aidants : une démarche d'investissement social ? *Informations sociales*, 1(192), 88–97.

Cardon, D. (2011). Réseaux sociaux de l'Internet. *Communications*, 1(88), 141–148.

Chauzal-Larguier, C. and Rouquette, S. (2017). Médias sociaux et associations d'aidants familiaux. Risques opportunités ? *Les cahiers du numérique*, 13(2), 75–104.

Coudin, G. and Mollard, J. (2011). Être aidant de malade Alzheimer : difficultés, stratégies de faire face et gratifications. *Geriatrie et Psychologie Neuropsychiatrie du Vieillissement*, 9(3), 363–378.

Dubreuil, A. and Hazif-Thomas, C. (2013). Les aidants et la santé sur Internet ou les "aidantnautes" s'entraident. *Neurologie/Psychiatrie/Gériatrie*, 13, 250–255.

Eynard, C. (2010). Les familles et la notion d'aidant familial : représentations et vécu. In *Les Aidants familiaux*, Blanc, A. (ed.). Presses Universitaires de Grenoble, Clamecy.

Gand, S., Hénaut, L., Sardas, J.-C. (2014). *Aider les proches aidants : comprendre les besoins et organiser les services sur les territoires*. Presses des Mines, Paris.

Jauréguiberry, F. (2000). Le moi, le soi et Internet. *Sociologie et sociétés*, 32(2), 136–152.

Kenigsberg, P.-A., Ngatcha-Ribert, L., Villez, M., Gzil, F., Bérard, A., Frémontier, M. (2013). Le répit : des réponses pour les personnes atteintes de la maladie d'alzheimer ou de maladies apparentées, et leurs aidants – Évolutions de 2000 à 2011. *Recherches familiales*, 1(10), 57–69.

Lescourret, M. (2017). L'analyse des stratégies de communication opérées sur les réseaux sociaux. In *Site internet : audit et stratégie*, Rouquette, S. (ed.). De Boeck, Louvain.

Lovejoy, K. and Saxton, G. (2012). Information, community, and action: How nonprofit organizations use social media. *Journal of Computer-Mediated Communication*, 17(3), 337–353.

Mollard, J. (2009). Aider les proches. *Gérontologie et société*, 32(128–129), 257–272.

Minozio, J. (2004). Les solidarités familiales dans l'espace public. *Recherches et prévisions*, 77, 7–19.

Nabarette, H. (2002). L'internet médical et la consommation d'information par les patients. *Réseaux*, 4(114), 249–286.

Pinquart, M. and Sörensen, S. (2003). Differences between caregivers and noncaregivers in psychological health and physical health: A meta-analysis. *Psychology and Aging*, 18(2), 250–267.

Porter, A. and Edirippulige, S. (2007). Parents of deaf children seeking hearing loss-related information on the Internet: The Australian experience. *Journal of Deaf Studies and Deaf Education*, 12(4), 518–529.

Romeyer, H. (2008). TIC et santé : entre information médicale et information de santé. *TIC & Société* [Online]. Available at: https://journals.openedition.org/ticetsociete/365 [Accessed 5 January 2021].

Rousset, G. (2015). Focus – Le rôle des proches aidants, une réponse à la vulnérabilité reconnue et encouragée par le droit. *Informations sociales*, 2(188), 96–98.

Rouquette, S. (2009). *L'analyse des sites Internet. Une radiographie du cyberesp@ce*. Ina, Paris, and De Boeck, Louvain.

Rouquette, S. (2010). *L'hypermédia internet*. Ina, Paris.

Schulz, R. and Sherwood, P.R. (2008). Physical and mental health effects of family caregiving. *American Journal of Nursing*, 108(9), 23–27.

Wilde, E. and Roy, A. (2019). Web side metadata [Online]. Available at: https://www.ischool.berkeley.edu/sites [Accessed 5 January 2021].

Wu, Y.-H., Faucounau, V., De Rotrou, J., Riguet, M., Rigaud, A.-S. (2009). Intervention psychosociale auprès de proches aidants de patients atteints de la maladie d'Alzheimer et technologies de l'information et de la communication : une revue de la littérature. *Gériatrie et Psychologie Neuropsychiatrie du Vieillissement*, 7(3), 185–192.

5

Associations' Online Communication and Discursive Strategies: A Case Study

Marcy Delsione OVOUNDAGA
GRESEC, Université Grenoble Alpes, Échirolles, France

5.1. Introduction

In an article in the periodical *Jusqu'à la mort accompagner la vie*, entitled "L'art de communiquer, un enjeu associatif et interassociatif", Le Pelley Fonteny (2015) states:

> Communication merits deep consideration from our associations and our national movement to ensure that our messages to institutions, elected officials, health professionals, the medico-social sector and our fellow citizens are readable, coherent and effective. It is a matter of taking a critical and constructive look at how we communicate and measuring the results through simple indicators over time in order to change anything that does not work properly or adequately.

While this statement, although focusing on the French online space, is about the effectiveness of communication in the associative world, it should be noted that it also highlights actors involved in this process. Above all, it shows how central communication is to this sector. At present, the associative sector is growing rapidly.

Digital Presences of Organizations,
coordinated by Nathalie PINÈDE, Luc MASSOU and Patrick MPONDO-DICKA.

There are more and more social actors taking an interest in political, economic, social, ecological, medico-social, etc., issues. This trend has led to the creation of associations and also not-for-profit organizations. An association can be defined as a group of people having a common object or project. There are several forms of associations.

In this study, far from claiming to deal with all associative structures – and beyond their legal status as not-for-profit associations – we will focus on structures with functions of public interest that are able, on the one hand, to work together with the State or territorial administrations and, on the other hand, are able to benefit from public subsidies. Whatever its nature, an association has an obligation to communicate. Since it is essentially public-facing, it must continually work to promote its activities, establish its reputation and maintain its image. It is for this reason above all that communication occupies a prominent position, for its functioning and its societal positioning, but also to support it in its development strategies.

Since the digital revolution and the advent of social media, organizational communication has entered a new era. Indeed, digitalization has significantly impacted the business world. As some observers demonstrate, the appropriation of digital tools by companies took a two-pronged approach: websites were created but at the same time community spaces such as Facebook and blogs were set up (Omrane 2010).

Associative organizations have not been left out of this race to conquer tools and socio-digital spaces. Companies in the tertiary sector are leveraging digital tools to inform, share information and animate communities (Dolbeau-Bandin 2017). In some associations, communication strategies are now being effected through leveraging the various opportunities offered by online digital systems. Thus, in this context of widespread digitization, is it not appropriate to assess how associations are appropriating these online digital systems? Is it not logical to make the link between the communication of associations and socio-digital tools?

It was to address these concerns that we decided to investigate the following topic: the online communication of associations and their discursive strategies, studying the case of La Chaîne de l'Espoir and Action Contre la Faim. Our aim is to determine the modes of appropriation of socio-digital media by associative organizations and to see how they have adopted them as a communication tool. Ultimately, it is a question of understanding the various strategies implemented by these associations. In this complex sociological environment, how do associative organizations make use of discursive strategies to communicate effectively? Do these strategies include semio-discursive narratives? If so, in what forms? More specifically, how is this online communication carried out for La Chaîne de l'Espoir and Action Contre la Faim? And how do the discursive strategies employed online support a form of social marketing?

5.2. Theoretical framework

The study of communication of associations in the era of socio-digital media, means being prepared in advance to embrace the field of social communication in general. This field of research is often viewed more favorably in the vast field of the socio-cognitive psychology of communication. For many years, this approach has sought to bring together social psychology, information and communication sciences and social marketing in order to understand the impact mechanisms of public health campaigns, on the one hand, and social prevention campaigns, on the other hand (Courbet et al. 2014). It is based on persuasive communication, meaning the ability to modify social representations, beliefs and attitudes, and engaging communication that aims to modify or reinforce personal and social actions (Courbet et al. 2014). The value of engaging communication, as some researchers demonstrate, is to promote behavioral intention and attitude (Girandola and Joule 2012). In terms of the place occupied by communication in the functioning of associative organizations, the current leveraging of social marketing seems to feed to a significant extent on the strategies of persuasive and engaging communication. The aim of social communication is to change attitudes and to urge action. And in studies to do with persuasion, the change in attitude happens as a result of receiving a persuasive message (Girandola and Joule 2012). In particular, it is this intentionality that underpins the communications of social organizations in traditional media and on digital social media. Our present investigation is part of this perspective of assessing the mechanisms of inserting persuasive and engaging communication in the promotional and preventive campaigns of certain associative organizations through the use of discursive strategies. To do this, it is also relevant to determine in theory how communication and social marketing strategies (discursive and semio-discursive methods) are combined therein.

Associative structures have often expressed the need to communicate. They have always found a way to adapt or seek adaptation to the techniques and tools of the moment. One of the major developments was to give very early consideration to developing social marketing. This technique has been defined by social entrepreneurs as being the application of techniques used in commercial marketing to analyze, plan, execute and evaluate programs aimed at modifying the behavior of a target group of individuals in order to improve their personal well-being and that of society (Gallopel-Morvan 2014). Although it is very difficult to change behaviors or garner support with pure sales techniques, this initiative is still commendable in its ambition to boost the communication of associations.

The current challenge in the communication of associative organizations has to do with the adoption of digital tools, on the one hand, and digital social media, on the other hand. Several approaches are proposed to describe the modes of appropriation and use of these digital systems. In a more global perspective, the use of socio-digital media by organizations is often apprehended under two communication strategies: inter-user and controlling (Omrane 2010). These two techniques, as Dorsaf Omrane explains, are based on an online communication monitoring strategy. The inter-user communication rationale seeks to monitor the opinions of Internet users and the e-reputation. And the controlling rationale sets out to identify online interactions between an organization's customers or potential audiences and the organization. Focusing on the associative environment, Cécile Dolbeau-Bandin suggests that social media are leveraged in this sector according to two communication models: functional communication based on the principles of marketing and relational communication based on participation and awareness-raising (2017).

But the communication that happens on digital platforms is complex. Because it produces a form of semio-discursive mediation that involves two types of discourse: escort discourse and accompanying discourse (Omrane 2010). Accompanying discourse, in its accepted sense, is perceived as the entire collection of statements characterized by the fact that they are made in the public space and are formed from external comments on a technique, its use, the context and the consequences of its use (Omrane 2010). Thus, the study of modes of appropriation of socio-digital media by associations is not a simple undertaking. It puts at the heart of the analysis a semio-discursive aspect that is fundamental in order to grasp communicative intentions in the form of verbal and visual mediations. The study of discursive strategies will thus involve all verbal, textual, pictorial, iconic and symbolic elements leveraged by associations to produce meaning.

5.3. Methodological approach

To deal with this topic, we based our work essentially on the study of the Facebook platforms of two associations: La Chaîne de l'Espoir and Action Contre la Faim.

5.3.1. *Justification for the choice of corpus*

The choice of these two associations was made on the basis of three main criteria. In the first place, we chose entrepreneurial management. In other words, choosing NGOs or associations that use purely entrepreneurial management in their operating fabric. And the Action Contre la Faim association is characteristic of this change in operating system, which began in the 1980s with a massive use of the media.

The second criterion is that of humanitarian associations that are striving for a real professionalization of communication. This professionalization is marked by the leveraging of direct marketing techniques for fundraising. But this use of direct marketing techniques is expensive and often not within the reach of all associations. Hence, the interest in associations is indicative of an industrialization of the associative sector based on economic autonomy in which fundraising is the main activity of the marketing and communication departments (Ferenczy 2005). Thus, the leverage of traditional media and digital social media by La Chaîne de l'Espoir was a point in favor of including it in this study.

Finally, the third criterion arises from an investigation of social and digital platforms, and Facebook in particular. In fact, as Anna Ferenczy clarifies, communication and image are the two common elements through which humanitarian work comes together (2005). The utilization of new media is thus a necessity in order to be visible in these digital and virtual spaces. The choice therefore focused on associations that were early adopters of the social medium of Facebook: La Chaîne de l'Espoir's Facebook page was created on November 16, 2007, and Action Contre la Faim's on August 5, 2009. Thus, settling the choice on the social medium of Facebook is not without significance. In addition to being the most popular social medium in the world (2.6 billion users), it appears as one of the first tools leveraged by the actors of the associative world.

5.3.2. *Presentation of the corpus and analysis protocol*

As for corpus composition and analysis protocol, we used here an exploratory approach to the Facebook pages of these two associations. This approach was carried out on the content disseminated on these two platforms from January 1 to December 31, 2020. This made it possible to pick out certain occurrences from the thematic and semio-discursive point of view. In other words, this exploratory work allowed us to categorize the communication content, taking into consideration their discursive and semiotic structure, on the one hand, and differentiating between images, texts, and videos, on the other hand (Jeanne-Perrier 2015).

It is principally on this basis that we compiled a corpus of 56 publications and 942 comments in the period from December 1 to December 31, 2020. The choice of this period is justified by the abundance of elements to be analyzed in terms of the exploratory work carried out from December 1 to December 31, 2020. As some specialists have demonstrated, online data are not constituted only from verbal processes; they are composites of a technical nature (written, audio and visual) (Develotte and Paveau 2017). One of the tasks here was to initiate a data analysis methodology that allows us to grasp this complexity.

Then, based on the two registers of use of the social media used by the associations, namely functional and relational communication (Dolbeau-Bandin and Lochon 2017), we identified four content models that seem to fit with the discursive and marketing strategies used by these two associations. This identification was made on the basis of communication monitoring carried out on the Facebook platforms of these two associations from January to December 2020. This approach allowed us to identify certain occurrences that we used to propose the thematic categorization presented in Table 5.1.

Categorization of models of content disseminated online	Types of content considered
Dissemination of daily news	Objectives and missions of the association, daily activities
Active search for donors for specific cases	Campaign appealing for donors for children in need
Self-congratulation following the success of an initiative	Thanking members or donors Presentations of children after the success of an initiative Thanks from partners
Seeking interactivity in the virtual community	Questions posed to the virtual community Topics for discussion, opinion questions

Table 5.1. *Categorization of models for content disseminated online*

These are the dissemination of daily news, the active search for donors for specific cases, self-congratulation following the success of an initiative and seeking interactivity in the virtual community. These models constituted the categories with which we carried out an initial content analysis to better evaluate the dominant registers. In order to better apprehend the aspect of online techno-discourses, our second analysis focused on the semio-discursive aspect and its various communicational aims. To do this, two analytical tables were designed based on certain discursive models of posting comments on Facebook (Le Caroff 2015) and on the empathic aspect that characterizes expression in associative environments. It should be clarified here that the terms discursive models and semio-discursive signs refer to the techno-discourses found on socio-digital media (Jeanne-Perrier 2015). Thus, when we talk about discursive models, the focus will be on verbal processes and when it comes to semio-discursive signs, it will be on audiovisual elements (texts, photos and videos).

Table 5.2 presents the different analytical variables taken into consideration. These variables were selected based on Facebook posting patterns developed by Coralie Le Caroff (2015) and the discursive models and semio-discursive signs of social media techno-discourses as presented by Valérie Jeanne-Perrier (2015). By basing ourselves on these two models and on the investigation of our corpus, we were able to define variables and quantify the data. The quantification was made on the basis of 56 publications identified from December 1 to December 31, 2020. Specifically, this includes a group of 45 publications from La Chaîne de l'Espoir's Facebook page and 11 publications from Action Contre la Faim's Facebook page. The data collected are set out here globally but in the development of the argument the comparative significance of the observed trends is given prominence and is substantiated. It should be noted that in view of their polysemic nature, some data may have two values. Thus, we were able to obtain the global quantification of Table 5.2.

Discursive models	Quantification
Empathy	14
Affect	2
Argument	45
Attention	18

Table 5.2. *Discursive model analysis*

To better understand the functions of the visual content and their use as a visual mediation device, we have classified, on the basis of 56 publications, the various registers of usage according to three objectives: illustrative, empathetic and attention-seeking. For the whole of the content of these two associations, we obtained the following data (Table 5.3).

Image targets	Quantification
Illustration	43
Empathy	16
Attention	13

Table 5.3. *Analysis of the communicative objectives of the images*

These three analytical categories were chosen after an exploratory survey and based on the mediatic dimension of socio-numeric networks. Here, as Joffe (2007) demonstrates for mass media:

> Images serve to illustrate the news items and articles on page one, but they also appear in advertising and in health, safety or charitable campaigns, where they seek to persuade and/or influence behaviors and attitudes. (p. 102)

This method enabled us to apprehend the escort and accompaniment discourses used by these two organizations and to better evaluate the online discursive strategies. The initial results obtained show that these associations have identified the challenges of the discursive digital world.

These results show that socio-digital media are taking on more and more importance in online communication strategies. In the associative environment, the two corpuses studied (56 publications) showed that socio-digital media are essentially used for traditional purposes, specifically the presentation of the activities and the mission of each association, specifically 63% of the content disseminated by Action Contre la Faim and 53% of that disseminated by La Chaîne de l'Espoir. In terms of online discursive strategies, the argumentative model appears most dominant in the various types of rhetoric deployed by these two associations. Finally, as far as semio-discursive aims are concerned, the various visual elements that are used play more of an illustrative function alongside an empathic dimension that remains very vivid.

5.4. Digital social media at the heart of organizations' new communication strategy

We will introduce our argument with these words from Le Pelley Fonteny (2012):

> Communicating means having an active position so that the image perceived by volunteers, supporters, donors or institutions is the image sought by our organization. Are we doing enough to proclaim our charter, our values that constitute the foundation of our association/federation?

These remarks show, and rightly so, how central communication is in the operational fabric of associative organizations, and by questioning its effectiveness, this author highlights the merits of good communication and the need to equip oneself with the best tools. Associative organizations have always found ways to use new means of communication to their advantage. From printed media to audiovisual media, strategies have always been put in place to better exploit the potential of the media. Today, particular attention is paid to socio-digital platforms, because these are now at the heart of societal functioning. Hence, it is of value here to understand the way in which associative structures are appropriating it.

5.4.1. *Changes in communication strategies in the associative environment: the appropriation of digital social media*

Communication enables the internal and external functioning of an association. Its purpose is therefore functional and strategic. It helps to raise audience awareness, recruit volunteers, retain them, become well known and achieve the objectives defined by each organization. In a broader perspective, by focusing on certain social topics, communication makes it possible to bring certain issues onto the agenda of public authorities' priorities. Faced with such varied functions and missions, the communication strategies and resources used by these structures are equally diverse. This central position of communication leads to a continual questioning of the methods and media used. The arrival of the Internet and socio-digital media has really fueled the questioning and brought changes in the various communication protocols. The questions formulated by Le Pelley Fonteny (2012) for the actors of the associative world are very edifying on this point:

> Are we aware of the changes in our society? We are in the participatory age, the age of networking, of horizontal communication. We should not think only about top-down communication.

These allegations show the need to make use of the new communication tools. And in particular digital systems, which are causing a paradigm shift between the traditionally vertical communication inspired by marketing methods to lean toward much more participatory methods, which put the relationship at the center of conversations.

For Le Pelley Fonteny, it is imperative for associative actors to transition from the role of sender to that of communications co-ordinator (2012). This reality is now visible, because the majority of associative organizations have adopted socio-digital media and put them at the service of their communication. Indeed, for associations, these social media have become means of communication that are complementary to their corporate websites (Bazin and Mollet 2014). They are used in the two fundamental facets of the associative sector, that is, in a functional and a relational way. Their usefulness is thus appreciable in promoting projects, in fundraising, in animating a community or modernizing the association's management and putting out an attractive image (Dolbeau-Bandin and Lochon 2017). But far beyond this rollout of the use of socio-digital media, we should assess the modes of appropriation according to social media typology and to the specificity of the associative organization (Bazin and Mollet 2014; Dolbeau-Bandin and Lochon 2017). For our part, we will focus here on the use of Facebook.

5.4.2. *The associations' Facebook pages*

In associative structures, socio-digital networks provide complementarity between functional communication based on marketing principles and relational communication based on participation and awareness (Cairon 2010). The capabilities of these media are used internally within the organization and especially in external deployment. This is the case with the use of Facebook pages. These, beyond their multiple functionalities (texts, images and videos), are regarded as moral entities. Having a presence on Facebook and a number of other social media channels has encouraged the emergence of a new type of volunteer: the cybervolunteer (Viallon 2017), as can be seen through the usage made of it by volunteers at the individual or collective level, by acting as levers for online associative campaigns.

With regard to usage, an organization's Facebook page fulfills the functions of a media agenda in terms of information management and a sharing function for event management. It is officially established as an informational tool that revolves around the dissemination of past and present elements, and future events. It also serves to relay partners' posts and as self-promotion (Figure 5.1).

Figure 5.1. *Presentation of Facebook cover pages. For a color version of this figure, see www.iste.co.uk/pinede/digital.zip*

We are focusing here on elements of the layout in section headings not as elements of enunciation and mediation but rather in a socio-technological perspective in an attempt to evaluate the various functionalities of the digital system. The two pages display the same functional layout offering, in a different order, the home page, a presentation of the social media (about), photos, videos, events, fundraising, a presentation of the community, feedback and publications. By analyzing all of these features, one of the first observations is the concentration in the virtual public space of tasks that recommend much more organization in the physical public space. Second, there is the feedback element where the participatory nature seems to give an active role to the community of members and supporters. This aspect, although achievable without socio-digital media, used to be costly in terms of equipment and financial resources. Viallon (2017) neatly sums up this simplicity drawn off by social media in general, and Facebook in particular, when he says:

> Digital social media can support the work of the small local association whilst at the same time being, for international NGOs, a global tool whose professional usage is in no way inferior to the use made of it by the large multinationals. (p. 15)

The concentration of the functional and relational dimension is clear evidence of this. Even better, the creation of a community of members that overcomes the obstacle of territoriality also attests to this.

The different Facebook pages present a precise accompanying message whose objective is to lead the user into each associative universe. They openly present themselves as promotional spaces for their websites, given the inclusion of links from the official websites on the home page, but also and above all for their activities. They play the role of a mainstage platform and thus they make it possible for associations to maintain a high profile. In addition, the presentation also plays on the online and offline continuum. It gives all possible information on the geographical location of the head office in the French capital, Paris, together with the address details and a pictorial itinerary available to Internet users.

5.5. Online discursive strategies at the heart of associations' social marketing

The advent of socio-digital media has changed the ways in which social marketing is appropriated by organizations in general and by associative structures in particular. This technique no longer seems to be leveraged solely in the vertical plane that links a company to its audience. A horizontal plane has gradually taken over by establishing a complementarity between functional communication and relational communication (Viallon 2011; Dolbeau-Bandin and Lochon 2017). As a result, social marketing on socio-digital media differentiates itself from traditional social marketing, which is essentially based on the adoption of marketing techniques with the aim of changing behavior. This marketing register has been successful in health prevention campaigns, despite certain limitations. Now and in the future, it is digital marketing that is at work in socio-digital spaces. It gives more emphasis to the discursive and semio-discursive content of websites, through texts, images and videos. This marketing essentially draws its essence from the semio-discursive dimension of socio-digital media.

For some associative structures, the leverage of online social marketing strategies seems to be based on seeking visibility, demonstrating activity and keeping a high profile. It is on this basis in particular that we established the following analytical categories: dissemination of daily news, the active search for donors for specific cases, self-congratulation after the success of an initiative, seeking the interaction of the virtual community. Although these different models try to grasp different realities, they rely on fundamental aspects of marketing, specifically to generate action or support. On Facebook, the key principle is seeking interaction using the viral marketing method (Barabel et al. 2010). What emerges from our analysis on the Facebook pages of Action Contre la Faim and La Chaîne de l'Espoir is therefore akin to viral social media marketing.

5.5.1. *Viral social media marketing on Facebook*

From our analysis, it emerges that Action Contre la Faim and La Chaîne de l'Espoir make strategic use of Facebook. First, in a framework of traditional communication: this includes raising public awareness about their missions and activities. Then, in a purely functional dimension that consists of engaging in specific communication campaigns in line with the associations' projects.

Finally, this social medium is used above all in order to be visible in a digital space that has henceforth gained prominence as the new public space. In doing this, it appears that the seeking of conversation, interaction or public outcry presents itself as the primary intention on this online platform. This aspect gives the various strategies deployed a virality in which centrality is given to audience discussion or reaction. But despite this combination of functional and relational communication, it must be noted that traditional communication based on the presentation of news items and association activities is still heavily used. The analysis carried out from December 1 to December 31, 2020, which enabled us to list 56 publications, better illustrates our point. The results set out below have been calculated on the basis of 45 publications published on La Chaîne de l'Espoir's Facebook page and 11 publications for Action Contre la Faim, and they were distributed according to the four analytical categories identified from the exploratory approach.

For Action Contre la Faim, seven publications focused on daily activities, three on self-congratulation following the success of an activity and one publication was aimed at seeking the interaction of the virtual community. This distribution is shown in Figure 5.2.

In the diagram in Figure 5.3, it can be seen that the results obtained basically show the same trend in terms of published content and especially in terms of the predominant category in this daily stream of disseminated news items. The distributed data among the 43 publications we identified are as follows: dissemination of daily news (25), active search for donors for specific cases (2), self-congratulation following the success of an activity (9), and seven publications focusing on seeking the interaction of the virtual community.

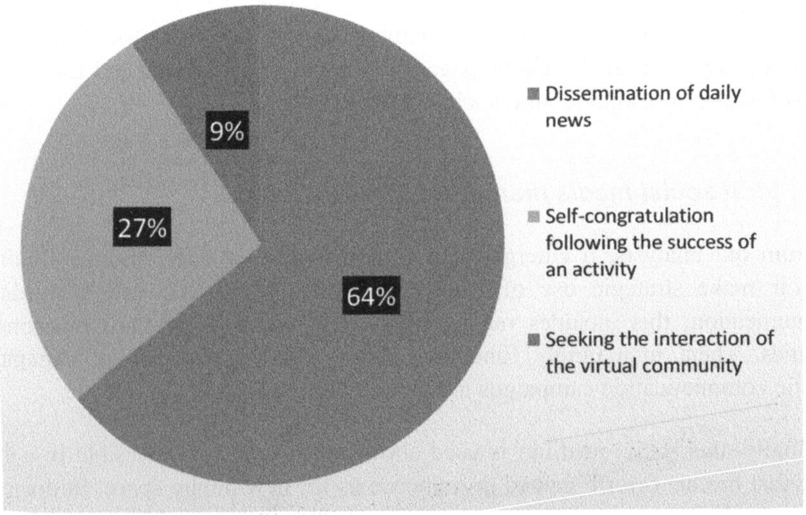

Figure 5.2. *Action Contre la Faim social marketing strategy. For a color version of this figure, see www.iste.co.uk/pinede/digital.zip*

Based on the chosen categorization, it appears that the dissemination of daily news is the most dominant type of post. In fact, for Action Contre la Faim, nearly 64% of the content posted on Facebook focuses on showcasing daily activities and relaying posts on initiatives carried out in certain regions of the world. The same facts can be observed for La Chaîne de l'Espoir. Here, more than 58% of Facebook posts showcase the various care initiatives carried out to help children. This type of content is consistent with the basic principle of communication. It is primarily intended to be a catalyst for the search for potential members, donors and volunteers. And the publication of each association's activities is targeted primarily at this objective. In other words, to reach a community of sympathizers who are likely to join and act as benefactors.

Also, in order to retain and thank the online member community, one of the practices leveraged by these two associations is self-congratulation following the success of an activity; this accounts for 27% of posts for Action Contre la Faim and 21% of La Chaîne de l'Espoir's content. These posts often mention the various donors or partners who have contributed to the success of an initiative.

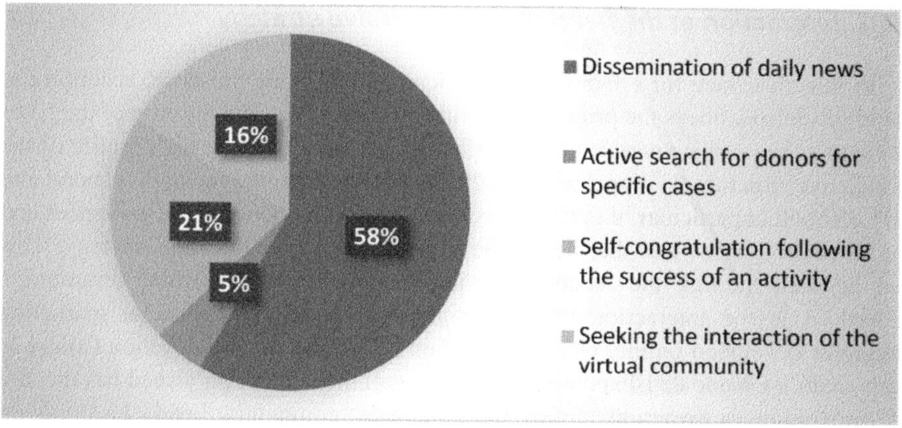

Figure 5.3. *La Chaîne de l'Espoir social marketing strategy. For a color version of this figure, see www.iste.co.uk/pinede/digital.zip*

In addition, some publications clearly aim to elicit reactions from Web users. This is the search for interaction. They are discernible in the questions posed to the virtual community, topics for debate and controversial news items. In our corpus, this content represents 9% of the content disseminated by Action Contre la Faim and 16% of the content published by La Chaîne de l'Espoir.

Finally, although these two associations play on several registers to ensure good visibility for their informative and communicative content on Facebook, we observe that there is a dominance of the traditional register, which puts the emphasis on the publication of associative activities. This tendency seems to draw its essence from the functionalities offered by social media in general and by Facebook in particular. There is thus the need to always incite affiliation (search for cyber-volunteers) and motivate action (search for donors). But all social marketing strategies on Facebook are based on the quest for interaction. The issue is no longer merely to distil messages for audiences but to animate a virtual community. In reality, the presentation of daily news online is based on a persuasive and engaging communication strategy that imperatively spurs Internet users to action. It is probably this tendency that gives a sense of virality to the social marketing strategy deployed online.

5.5.2. *Interaction at the heart of the discursive strategy*

In this clear race for effective communication, an online presence, according to some specialists, obeys the principle of strategic marketing. The purpose of the latter being to achieve objectives, it thus contributes to maintaining the high profile of the associative structure (Gallopel-Morvan 2013). On socio-digital media in general and on Facebook in particular, it is the horizontal relationship between the audiences and the associative structures that lies at the heart of the communication strategy. This can be seen through the feedback or interactivity with the virtual community. Indeed, it is the interaction that gives another aspect to the social marketing strategies developed online. Our investigation on the associations Action Contre la Faim and La Chaîne de l'Espoir has shown that all the content published has the aim of provoking a reaction from the member community and encouraging conversations. This in particular is what corresponds to the strategies of engaging communication embraced by humanitarian associations. Thus, likes and comments act as barometers by which one can judge the favorable echo received by an item of content and the commitment it can generate. But far beyond this observation, there is also the possibility offered to the community to become involved, proactively in some cases. This, at the physical level, used to be difficult to achieve. This is the case, for example, of the following message from a follower of Action Contre la Faim's Facebook page, giving their approval to the story of a young immigrant who left Venezuela because of the economic crisis and malnutrition. The poster says this:

> This will not happen overnight, nor without organization, nor without ending the conflict, but if humanity is willing to go and live in reclaimed desert such as in the Emirates, to destroy the cities where the land is fertile to turn it into fields so that humanity has enough to eat.

Through this comment, this Internet user is seeking to draw the attention of leaders and political figureheads to the need to show humanism and prioritize agriculture in their projects.

These conversations can also involve testimonies in which the member community recognizes the benefits of an initiative or welcomes the completion of a project whose birth it witnessed. These types of conversation can be found very frequently in the comments on La Chaîne de l'Espoir's Facebook page. While they may not take stock of the evacuation process of a child or a successful health initiative, they are interested in setting up parallel associative cells that support the action of the mother association. The testimony of one user, below, illustrates this perfectly:

> In 2019, Yvick Pourmesamis founded the association Yezibreizh which enabled a family of seven including three small children to be welcomed to a village in Brittany. Very happy to learn of the reconstruction of the hospital that will help this population make a fresh start at home.

In this comment, the user is not only highlighting the merits of these associative structures, which allow La Chaîne de l'Espoir to achieve its objectives, but it is also spotlighting the reconstruction of a health facility that allows this association to carry out its missions. This comment thus clearly shows both facets of La Chaîne de l'Espoir's activity, namely the social aspect, which consists of providing living accommodation for a child, and the medical aspect, which remains the epicenter of its activity.

Figure 5.4. *The role of the online facilitator. For a color version of this figure, see www.iste.co.uk/pinede/digital.zip*

This centrality of interaction as a mode of online communication is encouraging associations to change paradigms in their communication strategy. As we mentioned above, there is a rejection of vertical communication, which placed only the actors of associative communication in the role of sender. Going forward, the advice is to be a facilitator, a communication coordinator and the link will be stronger for it (Le Pelley Fonteny 2015). This new communication model introduces a new communication professional, the community manager. They are responsible for keeping a watch over communication on Facebook to animate the community and respond to any concerns. On the Facebook pages of Action Contre la Faim and La Chaîne de l'Espoir, we can clearly see the active presence of online facilitators, who constantly keep up conversations by responding to congratulations, replying to specific requests about membership or by giving the procedure to be followed to obtain support from the association. The various screenshots in Figure 5.4 explain in more detail how this operates in practice.

In these screenshots, the community managers are playing a full role in giving communicative content its maximum social and relational impact. They give a meaning to conversations by coordinating Facebook communication. The facilitator posts content and ensures that the member community is upheld by providing answers to the concerns raised. In most of the comments, the main requests are about membership terms and conditions and especially the protocol to be followed to become fully involved in these associative structures.

In short, on the Facebook pages of the two structures studied, there is a dynamic and retroactive communication between the senders and recipients of the content published online. This mode of communication is essentially based on conversations and a direct relationship with the community of members and sympathizers. From passive audience to active audience, socio-digital media thus give audiences a voice by offering them the opportunity to be proactive on crucial topics and to have direct, person-to-person contact with the associative structures. Functionally, they form a bridge between top-down and bottom-up communication by placing interaction at the center of the new communication strategy.

But these media channels do not confine themselves to establishing a horizontality of relationships and conversations, they also touch on a semio-discursive aspect that puts the spotlight on a number of issues both at the level of discursive strategies and at the level of semio-discursive objectives. It is these aspects that we will investigate in the following paragraphs.

5.5.3. *Discursive models at work*

In terms of online discourse, researchers stress the permeability of borders between the professional discourse of specialists and the ordinary discourse of audiences (Oprea 2019). Thus, the various discursive models leveraged by some associations adhere to this reality, in particular between a professional narrative and a purely ordinary narrative based essentially on their own moral, social, affective, rational, etc., filters (Oprea 2019). Exploring these associations allowed us to identify five discursive patterns that seem to fit with the various online social marketing strategies. These tend to highlight the empathetic, affective, argumentative, attentive and polemical dimensions of discourse. Thus, using the 56 publications gathered on these two digital platforms, we have distributed them according to the discursive models set out above. For Action Contre la Faim, the data obtained were calculated from the 11 publications identified from December 1 to December 31, 2020. Again, the polysemic nature of the data means that they can be included under several headings at the same time. And for La Chaîne de l'Espoir, the distribution was based on 45 publications.

In both the situations studied, the argumentative, attentive and empathic dimensions are very dominant. The two charts presented in Figure 5.5 better explain this reality.

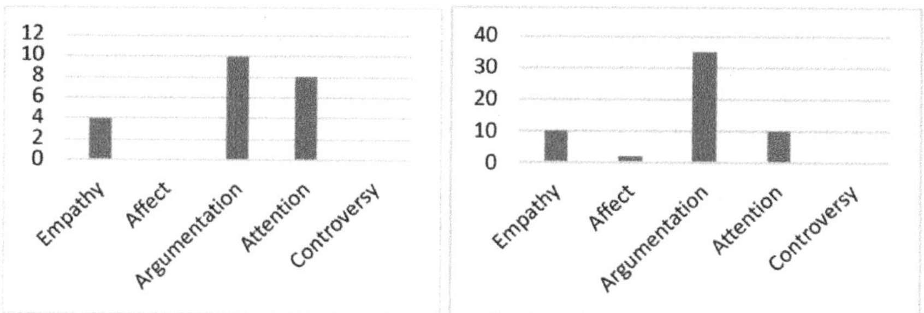

a) b)

Figure 5.5. *Discursive models for Action Contre la Faim (a) and La Chaîne de l'Espoir (b)*

There is, in fact, a tangible dominance of the argumentative register in the types of discourse used by these two associations. This strategy could be explained by the functional dimension, which relies mainly on explanation and raising the awareness of online audiences. Each post on Facebook is an argumentative construct that is always linked to the purpose of associative communication: attracting members, volunteers and donors. This mode of communication draws on the persuasive register of discourse. It is a narrative construct that, in most cases, is dense and is centered around an explanatory dimension. The following examples illustrate this quite well:

> Hunger is not a cause, we know we can eliminate it. Fardosa, our mission manager in Somalia, explains how to cure a child of

> malnutrition in six weeks! Support us. (Action Contre la Faim Facebook post from December 17, 2020)

> For the International Year of Midwives and Nurses, we introduce Dr. Agnès Simon, midwife and essential link in La Chaîne de l'Espoir. During her missions, in Afghanistan or Bangladesh in particular, she transmits her knowledge and continues to learn from others. (La Chaîne de l'Espoir Facebook post from December 29, 2020)

Argumentative rhetoric focuses on presenting events or promoting associative activities. The same goal is pursued through the quest for empathy and attention from online audiences. The empathetic dimension of the discourse can be seen in several items of content published on Facebook. Although leveraged less frequently than the argumentative register, the empathic dimension underpins some publications by looking for an outcry from the virtual community and seeking above all to touch its sensibilities. It is present in the lexicon used and in the topics discussed. This is the case of this post from December 15, 2020, published on La Chaîne de l'Espoir's Facebook page:

> Like Precious, Doudedji or Laurencia recently arrived in France, Steven, aged 5, reached the French mainland on December 9 to undergo surgery for a serious heart condition.

In this post, the news is not only sad but the lexicon used hovers between worry and empathy. Between gravity and a glimmer of hope, most of this type of content calls upon a strong empathetic register.

The same observation can be made of many items of content that seek to attract attention. A discursive register is also very frequently used at Action Contre la Faim. Here, in order to generate buy-in and action, the discourse deployed attracts the full attention of Internet users by revealing facts or producing data in the form of figures: "52 million children are suffering from severe hunger. Support them and make a donation before December 31 2020", "By making a donation, you enable us to take concrete action. Learn about the care given by our teams to undernourished children in Somalia" (Publication by Action Contre la Faim from December 23, 2020).

This communication thus attracts attention by focusing on the theme of hunger with precise statistics before setting out the merits of aid or solidarity intervention. Alternatively, the persuasive aspect can be mixed with an argument that attracts attention by setting out concrete facts linked to associative action. Such is the case with this publication, which draws a clear parallel between donor action and the deployment of teams in Somalia. This dominance of the argumentative register as a discursive strategy hides a form of persuasive communication in the background that draws upon the argumentative register, not only to touch the affect of Internet users and trigger their reactions. In this situation, in particular, we can see the viral nature of social marketing developed to appeal to members and donors.

Some content uses several discursive models to appeal for donations. This strategy is very much in evidence on the Facebook pages of associations. In our case, as we have seen in Figure 5.5, discourses remain marked by strong argumentation that, at many junctures, espouses an empathetic and affective dimension, when they are not simply seeking to attract attention. These discursive models are more pertinent when assessed in their semio-discursive dimensions.

5.5.4. *Semio-discursive signs*

The various online communication strategies have their foundations in the potential of the image. The various visual signs are not used by chance. They follow a strategy or semio-discursive aims. As explained by Cécile Dolbeau-Bandin and Annie Lochon (2017), associative communication on social media brings to the fore the role of the image in accordance with the principle of three sentences and one image. Some also stress the advent of an image society to show how important photos and videos are (Jeanne-Perrier 2015). This importance begins with the affirmation of a visual identity; in other words, the logo that represents the association's identity. It is part of the visual mediation system. It allows a recognition of the structure, the affirmation of its values and its personality through the medium of its shapes, its colors and its symbols (Gallopel-Morvan 2013). These logotypes are the first visual elements that constitute escort messages to the communicative and informative content. All associative structures have them. As the first mediator elements, they thus assure the identification of the online platforms of associations. Apart from these fixed visual elements, there is the image as a purely informational element that can be understood as a semio-discursive sign.

These days the image is the strongest force in the attention economy. It embellishes presentation of facts by illustrating them or by being the perfect reflection of social realities. In fact, the various visual elements take on a media function that gives credibility to online communication campaigns. Thus, the image is effective in another way. It can testify to the veracity of the news items and it brings greater impact to discursive content. This is part of the role of photography, which is a tangible capture of a societal moment, to the realities in pictorial form that accompany the testimony of a lived experience. It can also be a video, a news report describing any social situation. On socio-digital media in general and on

Facebook in particular, it is these visual elements that are leveraged to give greater authentication to the content disseminated.

On the Facebook pages of Action Contre la Faim and La Chaîne de l'Espoir, the semio-discursive dimension of the content disseminated is fully mastered. Communication is based on the photos-texts-videos triptych. No content is published without this combination of text and image or text and visual elements. Photos, illustrations and videos emerge as key factors for communication.

This mobilization obeys a text-image relationship that supports each act of communication through focusing essentially on illustrative and empathetic aims. The data quantification strategy was based on a total of 56 publications for all associations and specifically those collected on Action Pour la Faim (11 posts) and those from La Chaîne de l'Espoir (45 posts). The thematic classification yielded the following results: for Action Contre la Faim, nine publications had visual content with illustrative impact, four had an empathetic dimension and only three sought rather to attract the attention of Internet users.

For La Chaîne de l'Espoir, the classification is as follows: 34 posts in which the visual elements have an illustrative impact, 12 have espoused an empathetic dimension and three have included visual elements in order to attract attention. The trend observed in the online communication of Action Contre la Faim seems to be clearly taking shape in La Chaîne de l'Espoir. The same visual aims are dominant. This is the reality that can be seen in Figure 5.6.

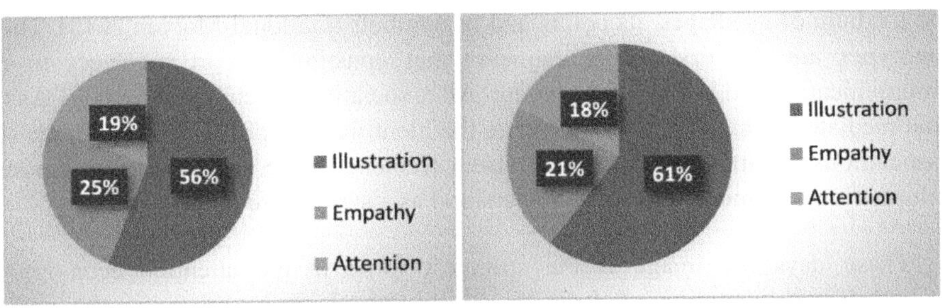

a) b)

Figure 5.6. *Semio-discursive aims Action Contre la Faim (a) and La Chaîne de l'Espoir (b). For a color version of this figure, see www.iste.co.uk/pinede/digital.zip*

Thus, of the illustrative, empathic and attentional purposes, it emerges that image is much more used in its illustrative dimension, whether for Action Contre la Faim or La Chaîne de l'Espoir. More than 56% of the visual elements in Action Contre la Faim have an illustrative scope. For La Chaîne de l'Espoir, there are illustrative purposes in more than 61% of visual content.

Exploring the empathetic dimension of the visual material by taking into account the empathetic expression that predominates in the associative environment has, to some extent, confirmed a trend. Because for Action Contre la Faim, in the corpus used, more than 25% of the visual elements disseminated had an empathic value. And the investigation done on the Facebook platform of La Chaîne de l'Espoir counted more than 21% of visuals with an empathetic aim.

In terms of seeking attention, the various items of visual content posted on Facebook by Action Contre la Faim and La Chaîne de l'Espoir leveraged this dimension, at the level of 19% for the former and 18% for the latter. In fact, in this semio-discursive collection, a good proportion of the visual elements are designed to capture the attention of the online virtual community.

This visual material is essentially composed of photographs, pictorial illustrations and videos. These visual elements provide text and image complementarity and they give videos a demonstrative scope that makes it possible to bring a quotient of authenticity to the facts presented. The associative community works on social issues that affect every layer of society. Photographic illustrations and video reports make it possible to make greater impact on the social body and above all to testify to the truth of the facts.

For these two associations, the semio-discursive elements are mobilized first in an illustrative dimension to better establish the argumentative register by supporting each piece of text with an image. Next, in an empathic dimension, to encourage affiliation in line with the dominance of empathic expression in an associative environment (Viallon 2017). In its end purpose, the complementarity of text and image seeks to arouse interest, attract the attention of the target audiences and motivate donors to action.

In exploring the visual corpus, several observations were made on the use of these elements by Action Contre la Faim or by La Chaîne de l'Espoir. In fact, the grouping of presentations of varying visual content is different. The gallery of subjects photographed according to whether we are on the one structure or the other is not the same. In the two cases studied, the visual strategy is essentially based on the objectives and missions of each structure. Thus, the visual narration focuses on the main beneficiaries of associative action, on the one hand (La Chaîne de l'Espoir), and the work in the social space, on the other hand (Action Contre la Faim).

By doing this, the semio-discursive aims are essentially based on putting the focus on the figure of the subject. This is the case of the Chaîne de l'Espoir and the highlighting of work in the field for Action Contre la Faim. The two images presented in Figure 5.7, chosen from among the visuals mobilized by this association from December 1 to 31, 2020, illustrate our point well.

Depending on the objectives of each association, the image is used here to illustrate and support the textual argumentation. There is a tangible focus on the figure of the subject at La Chaîne de l'Espoir, while Action Contre la Faim alternates between presenting fieldwork and presenting boxed data in figures. The majority of photographs showing children focus on the presentation of the subject by revealing their facial expressions. This emphasis did not happen by chance. It can actually be evaluated in the approach of seeking interest and emotion as developed by Tcherkassof and Frijda (2014). These two authors have demonstrated that, for a news item or event to stimulate interest at the psychological level, it must excite feelings by arousing emotions. And this interest lies in several variables that can be sociocultural, stem from personal experiences or even be the result of cognitive and affective skills. For affective interest, the authors cite as an example the sight of a vulnerable child or images of the transience of feelings. In focusing on the face of the photographed subject, it seems that it is this emotional interest that is sought. This is taking into account the affect that arises from the sight of a child in a situation of distress. These appeals to the emotions are aimed directly at attracting attention, on the one hand, and motivating action, on the other hand. In doing this, the image of children is presented in all possible situations in La Chaîne de l'Espoir's chain of intervention, focusing on postures and facial expressions.

Figure 5.7. *Visual illustrations from Action Contre la Faim. For a color version of this figure, see www.iste.co.uk/pinede/digital.zip*

The accentuated presentation of fieldwork in the visual elements for Action Contre la Faim also helps to generate interest on the basis of a topic with a benchmark value, in this case hunger. Putting it into the context of finding solutions to the problems posed, the visual content, as a whole, puts the emphasis on direct interventions in the social space. In the majority of situations, the images show the work of the structure in regions of political and armed conflict. Just as with La Chaîne de l'Espoir, the focus on fieldwork seems to demonstrate the urgent need to take action.

To sum up, the semio-discursive signs leveraged by these two structures have aims that are fully aligned with their online communication strategy. They essentially have an illustrative function. As a visual mediation device, these various signs aim to arouse interest and motivate the member community to action. The various photographs, illustrations and videos embellish the texts by presenting the realities of the activities and missions of each of these associations.

5.6. Conclusion

Concluding our analysis, we can say that communication is at the center of associative activity. It is even consubstantial with its functioning. This centrality of the communicative function has always been understood by professionals in the associative environment to the point of always adapting communication methods and tools to better achieve their objectives. This was the case with the development of social marketing, the aim of which was to appropriate commercial marketing techniques to change the behaviors of individuals in a social context. This technique has been developed extensively during public health campaigns by the public authorities and by some non-governmental organizations. The advent of socio-digital networks has also led to a paradigm shift in the communication strategies of the tertiary sector. From our investigation, it emerges that associative organizations have appropriated digital social platforms. Today, these social media channels seem to be establishing themselves as the new preferred tools of associative communication. In view of their different functionalities, they have succeeded in changing the traditional communication circuit between the sender and targets by moving from a vertical communication model to a horizontal communication model.

Our study has shown that social media channels constitute the new space of expression and the place in which associative organizations develop new social marketing strategies. For some structures, it is imperative to be on these new platforms not only to uphold their reputation but also to ensure good visibility. Several organizations have appropriated these networks, at the head of which Facebook appears to be the most used. The two associative structures used for our investigation (Action Contre la Faim and La Chaîne de l'Espoir) use the social medium of Facebook as a communication tool that makes it possible, on the one hand, to establish functional communication and, on the other hand, to permit a new form of relationship with the member communities. In this new perspective, there is therefore a form of online social marketing that, in many ways, has a viral aspect that prioritizes the search for interaction, conversation or seeking to elicit reactions.

The content models published on the Facebook platforms of these two associations can be divided into four categories. First, the dissemination of daily news, which is responsible for publishing content directly related to the activity and missions of the organization, and then the active search for donors for specific cases. It acts as a special communication campaign when one of the organizations is facing an emergency. Then, self-congratulation after the success of an activity that is most often used to thank partners, donors and the online member community. Finally, there is the direct quest for the interaction of the virtual community, which is discernable through questions, discussion topics and other content that calls for opinions. All this content revolves around the search for conversation, which now places the association and its members in a horizontality of relationships, in which the work of coordination and animation occupies a very important place. In doing this, the social marketing strategy on Facebook is thus a pure fusion between functional communication that obeys the traditional principles of social marketing and relational communication that highlights the task of animating the online community: this is the role of the community manager.

It is the latter who is responsible for taking into account the opinions of the community, responding to their requests and thus giving a more appreciable place to an online audience, which shows a renewed interest in the activities of an organization. This rollout on the socio-digital networks also allows us to evaluate the various discursive strategies that are at work there. In this perspective, by pinpointing these new platforms as verbal and visual mediation devices, we have thus highlighted the discursive strategies, which are a mixture between a discourse of professionals and a social discourse, on the one hand, and we have identified the semio-discursive aims, on the other hand.

Reading the online discursive strategies has shown that these two organizations rely more on the argumentative and empathetic dimensions of discourse. In terms of the aims of the visual material, our examination shows that text-image complementarity has more of a purely illustrative function before seeking to arouse empathy or attract attention.

5.7. References

Barabel, M., Mayol, S., Meier, O. (2012). Les médias sociaux au service du marketing territorial : une approche exploratoire. *Management & avenir*, 32, 233–253.

Bazin, C. and Mollet, J. (eds) (2014). Développement du numérique dans les associations et nouvelles formes de mobilisations citoyennes. Final report, Ministère de la Ville, de la Jeunesse et des Sports.

Carion, F. (2010). La communication associative. *Communication*, 28(1), 193–206.

Courbet, D., Fourquet-Courbet, M.-F., Joule, R.V., Bernard, F. (2014). Communication persuasive et communication engageante pour la santé : favoriser des comportements sains avec les médias, internet et les serious games. In *Publicité et santé : des liaisons dangereuses ? Le point de vue de la psychologie*, 21–46 [Online]. Available at: https://archivesic.ccsd.cnrs.fr/sic_01076750 [Accessed 17 March 2021].

Dessinges, C. (2008). Émotion, collectif et lien social : vers une approche sociologique du don humanitaire. *Revue du MAUSS*, 32, 303–321.

Develotte, C. and Paveau, M.-A. (2017). Pratiques discursives et interactionnelles en contexte numérique. Questionnements linguistiques. *Langage et société*, 160–161, 199–215.

Dolbeau-Bandin, C., Lochon, A., Krebs, V. (2017). Médias sociaux et associations : conjugaison réussie d'une communication fonctionnelle et relationnelle ? *Les Cahiers du numérique*, 13, 51–74.

Dumont, C. (2016). Le défi de la transition sociétale : les associations s'affirment dans l'innovation. *VST – Vie sociale et traitements*, 131, 61–64.

Ferenczy, A. (2005). Les ONG humanitaires, leur financement et les médias. Master's dissertation, Institut Européen des Hautes Etudes Internationales, Nice.

Gallopel-Morvan, K. (2014). Marketing social et marketing social critique : quelle utilité pour la santé publique ? *Les Tribunes de la santé*, 45, 37–43.

Gallopel-Morvan, K., Birambeau, P., Larceneux, F., Rieunier, S. (2013). Introduction. Pourquoi intégrer une démarche marketing dans les associations ? In *Marketing et communication des associations*, Gallopel-Morvan, K., Birambeau, P., Larceneux, F. Rieunier, S. (eds). Dunod, Paris.

Girandola, F. and Joule, R.-V. (2012). La communication engageante : aspects théoriques et pratiques. *L'Année psychologique*, 112, 117–144.

Jeanne-Perrier, V. (2015). Des discours et des signes : pour une évaluation critique de Twitter et de Facebook. *Communication & Langages*, 183, 111–131.

Joffe, H. (2007). Le pouvoir de l'image : persuasion, émotion et identification. *Diogène*, 217(1), 102–115.

Le Caroff, C. (2015). Le genre et la prise de parole politique sur Facebook. *Participations*, 12, 109–137.

Le Pelley Fonteny, P. (2015). L'art de communiquer, un enjeu associatif et interassociatif. *Jusqu'à la mort accompagner la vie*, 122, 99–108.

Michelik, F. (2011). La communication engageante : effets sur les dimensions cognitives et comportementales. PhD Thesis, Université de Franche-Comté, Besançon.

Ollivier-Yanniv, C. and Rinn, M. (eds) (2009). *Communication de l'état et gouvernement du social : pour une société parfaite ?* PUG, Grenoble.

Omrane, D. (2010). Communication des entreprises. Logiques d'interactions à l'ère du web social. *Les Cahiers du numérique*, 6, 39–48.

Oprea, D. (2019). Le renouveau du narratif dans les réseaux sociaux : l'action civique roumaine #noifacemunspital [#onbatitunhopital] en récit. Approche socio-discursive. *Les Cahiers du numérique*, 15, 161–184.

Tcherkassof, A. and Frijda, N.H. (2014). Les émotions : une conception relationnelle. *L'Année psychologique*, 114, 501–535.

Viallon, P. (2010). Le monde à portée de clic : la communication touristique. In *La communication touristique : vers des nouvelles interfaces ?* Aquilina, M., Pugnière-Saavedra, F. (eds). PUL, Paris.

Viallon, P. (2017). Introduction. Bénévolat, lien social et numérique. *Cahiers du numérique*, 13(2), 9–23.

PART 2

Websites and Cultural Dynamics

6

Website Localization and the Cultural Dimension: Professional Skills

Alexander FRAME and Will NOONAN
TIL, Université de Bourgogne, Dijon, France

6.1. Introduction

The aim of this contribution is to examine the way in which researchers and companies approach the cultural dimension of website localization, by raising what we believe to be a fundamental problem for the sector but also for training future translators/localizers capable of working in an increasingly globalized and all-digital environment. Localization can be defined as "a complex communicative, cognitive, textual and technological process by which interactive digital texts are modified to be used in different linguistic and socio-cultural contexts" (Jiménez-Crespo 2013, p. 20) and includes the adaptation into another language and culture of computer products, Web pages, websites and user guides (Alshtaiwi 2017). Closely linked to a rationale of digital "distribution" that typically includes a process of translation or "transfer" (Pym 2004, p. 14), localization implies a skill set complementary to but distinct from that of specialized translation, as well as a specific consideration of the importance of culture. While it may appear more "intractable" (Cronin 2003, p. 18) than the purely technical and linguistic aspects of the localization process, the problem of adapting websites to cultural differences has occupied researchers and practitioners for several decades, as can be seen in the scientific literature (Barber and Badre 1998; Baack and Singh 2007; Tigre Moura et al. 2016) and in the sales pitches displayed on service provider websites. This chapter is a result of an ongoing

Digital Presences of Organizations,
coordinated by Nathalie PINÈDE, Luc MASSOU and Patrick MPONDO-DICKA.

reflection by its authors, as academics specialized in intercultural communication and translation studies, on the ways in which the relationship between these disciplines may contribute to translation and localization training[1].

Intercultural studies have long taken an interest in the cultural dimension of websites. However, a review of the literature suggests that taking stock of this dimension remains a complex matter. This literature is mainly composed of (i) deductive approaches based on a national, essentialist definition of culture, via comparative theoretical models, regarded by the intercultural specialists as outdated and unsuitable for this kind of application (McSweeney 2002; Dervin 2014), and (ii) inductive empirical approaches, which are not able to identify consistent "cultural" differences, aside from details that are often superficial and/or technical in nature (colors of national flags, direction of writing, etc.). Relatively few studies seem to take into account the influence of multiple factors (Shneor 2012), including marketing or communication strategies, and only a few mention the importance to target audiences of representations of the organization or its national identity (Tigre Moura et al. 2015).

In a globalized context in which identity markers are becoming increasingly important (Wolton 2003) and where societies are becoming increasingly connected, diasporic and multicultural, it is important to consider how much importance should be given to the national-level cultural dimension of websites and what model(s) of culture should be applied when designing and localizing websites. Once the concept of plural identities is factored in (Lahire 2001), stereotyped generalizations may prove too simplistic to concretely engage audiences that are in fact far less culturally homogeneous than communication or marketing professionals would sometimes like to believe (Frame 2013). Macro-social approaches to national cultures must therefore make way for meso- or micro-social approaches, open to contexts of enunciation and reception. Identities appear just as important in this context as (multiple and emerging) cultures.

In the light of this, and given the context of our multicultural societies, we can also question how best to prepare future translator/localizers to take into account the cultural dimension of localization, which can, strictly speaking, be thought of as a communicational issue that is connected to advertisers' communication strategies

1 While the latter can and must integrate lessons from the field of intercultural studies (and vice versa (Liddicoat 2014; García Ochoa 2016; Walravens 2017)), the way in which this supposed interdisciplinarity is reflected in both scientific and commercial discourse on website localization raises some doubts and questions. These doubts are often confirmed by freelance translation colleagues who carry out translation-localization assignments for agencies.

and other questions of brand identity. Through an analysis of the scientific and professional literature on the cultural dimension of localization, looking at corporate discourse in the sector and perspectives from practitioners and trainers, this chapter reviews the main approaches recommended and practices adopted by researchers, trainers and practitioners. It then opens perspectives to better reconcile these approaches and practices with a more holistic vision of localization as a communicational activity situated in a social and geographical context, but that is often also marked by commercial and identity-based considerations. The aim is to identify directions that could potentially be useful in a training context, but that are for the most part yet to be implemented in practice.

6.2. Field-testing cultural localization: from words to action

6.2.1. *The "cultural" skills of the localizer*

When focusing on the localization industry, dominated by agencies and companies subcontracting usually large multilingual projects to a number of freelance translator/localizers, we can question the extent to which scientific approaches to culture are really used to structure working practices. Are they primarily part of a sales pitch, a discourse aimed at prospective clients? Do agencies position themselves in contrast to the traditional "native" skill of the specialized translator, trained and expected to translate only into their mother tongue (or culture or locale) (Samuelsson-Brown 2005; Gouadec 2009a; McKay 2011; SFT n.d.)? In comparison with the translation of written texts, the multimodal and interactive dimension that is characteristic of websites and other digital productions calls for the application not only of technical and linguistic skills but also of cultural skills. This skill set would seem to make the localizer "the most accomplished translator" (Gouadec 2003; Duclos 2017), even though the exact nature of these "cultural skills" is rather more difficult to identify or analyze.

Mazur (2007) points out that the metalanguage used in the field of localization owes its origins more to practitioners than to academia, though we can also note a growing trend toward theorization within the industry. The publications and events of organizations such as LISA (Localization Industry Standards Association, dissolved in 2011) and its successor GALA (Globalization and Localization Association, www.gala-global.org/), which began to offer free subscription to academic programs in the field in 2020, show evidence of a reflexive approach to practice, though this is largely focused on linguistic and technological rather than on cultural issues. The GILT model (Globalization, Internationalization, Localization, Translation: see LISA (2003) and Figure 6.1) represents the adaptation of a website (or other product) in the form of a cycle, where an "internationalization" phase aimed at facilitating adaptation (in particular on the technical level) to the largest possible number of markets is followed by the "localization" phase as such, which consists of adapting the product to a specific target market. This second phase clearly involves a cultural dimension, though the mechanics of how this is taken into account are rarely explained in detail. While researchers such as Miguel Jiménez-Crespo have tried to explain the nature and typology of this cultural dimension (Jiménez-Crespo 2013, 2019), the theoretical perspectives heard in seminars and other "professional" discussions more often resemble the inductive and deductive approaches mentioned above.

Figure 6.1. *Global product development cycle (LISA 2003, p. 15)*[2]

6.2.2. *Culture, culture and training of translators*

The notion of Culture (with a capital C)[3] remains very much in evidence in the websites and publications of professional bodies such as the International Federation of Translators (2014) and within some areas of translation studies, particularly prominent in France, that have remained close to traditional literary studies (Lederer

2 For a more detailed discussion of the model in French, see Freitas et al. (2008), pp. 5–7.

3 The heuristic distinction between "Culture" and "culture" here refers respectively to artistic and literary conceptions ("Culture") and anthropological conceptions ("culture"), even though this kind of distinction in everyday language may also have its limits on the analytical level (Frame 2017).

and Stratford 2020). With regard to pragmatic texts (and websites), on the other hand, the notion of a problematized approach to culture (with a small c) is often obscured by the notion of a "native" competence that established practices and codes of ethics within the industry do not encourage practitioners to question.

Perhaps as a consequence, frameworks and manuals designed to train translators and localizers show a very variable degree of interest in the concept of culture. The *Guide des Métiers de la Traduction-Localisation* (Gouadec 2009, pp. 137–139) differentiates mainly between the linguistic and technical aspects of the website localizer's profession, without explicitly addressing the question of an approach to culture. The skills framework in force at the time of writing for the European Master's in Translation network (EMT 2017) presents "Language and Culture" as a "competence [which] encompasses all the general or language-specific linguistic, sociolinguistic, cultural and transcultural knowledge and skills that constitute the basis for advanced translation competence", without dwelling further on the possible definitions or issues of "culture". Interestingly, the previous version of the EMT framework (EMT 2009) identifies an intercultural competence in its own right, incorporating a sociolinguistic dimension ("Knowing how to identify the rules for interaction relating to a specific community, including non-verbal elements (useful knowledge for negotiation)") and a textual dimension ("Knowing how to understand and analyse the macrostructure of a document and its overall coherence (including where it consists of visual and sound elements)"). As seems to be the case among localization practitioners (and despite a few attempts discussed below), the cultural dimension of website localization – or even of the translation of traditional written texts – does not seem to be addressed sufficiently in competence frameworks or other studies dealing with translator training, even though the need for and usefulness of intercultural skills seem to be recognized by trainers, students and practitioners in the field (Chodkiewicz 2012, p. 48). The same implicit recognition can be found in translator training textbooks, though it is rare to see a dedicated chapter on or substantial treatment of the question. For example, Baker's (2011) authoritative work *In Other Words: A Coursebook on Translation*[4] offers a sub-sub-subsection on "translation though cultural substitution" within the chapter on word-level equivalence (section 2.3.2.2.[c], pp. 29–32). The more recent edited collection *Teaching Translation: Programs, Courses, Pedagogies* offers a somewhat cursory discussion of localization, restricted mostly to technical aspects (Massardier-Kenney 2017, pp. 35–36). The same book offers an overview of strategies for teaching translation (Colina and Venuti 2017) and recent translator training textbooks (Maitland 2017) with no explicit reference to a cultural dimension.

4 First edition published 1992.

6.2.3. *The range of cultural localization services*

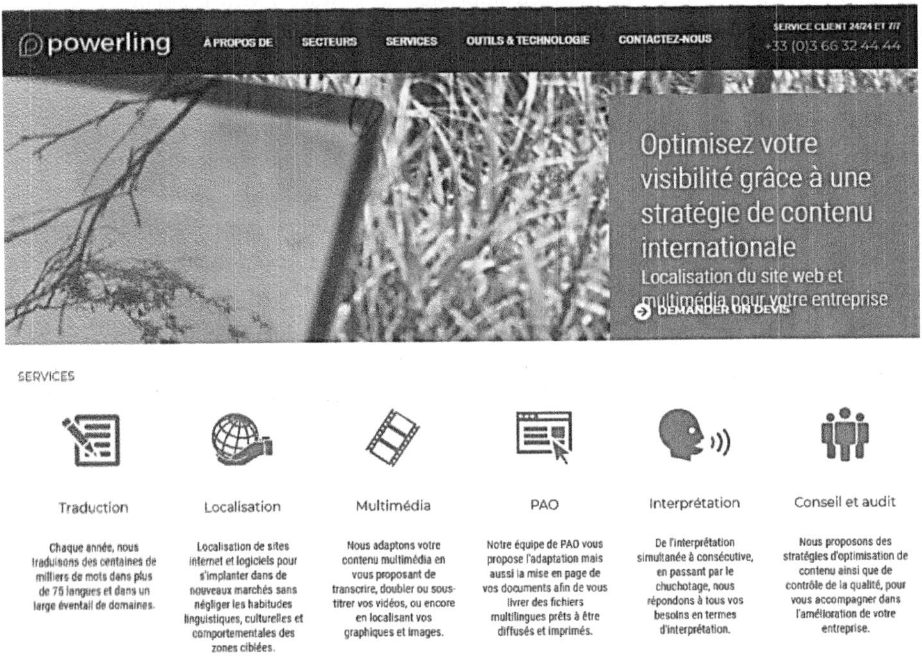

Figure 6.2. *Homepage of www.powerling.com/fr/ (accessed 15 October 2021); "Location" tab on the homepage. For a color version of this figure, see www.iste.co.uk/pinede/digital.zip*

Among companies offering website localization services, it is not surprising to see more interest in the question of culture, even if the arguments offered to clients rarely go beyond the frameworks already mentioned. Although this chapter does not claim to offer an exhaustive study of the discourse on website localization found on such corporate websites, an overview of a few websites that are highly ranked by search engines allows us to identify two principal arguments. The first, more widespread in medium-sized companies, is based on the already mentioned notion of native competence, inherited from the paradigm of written translation and applied with a greater or lesser degree of adaptation to digital texts: the native speaker is supposed to know how to adapt the contents to the specificities and needs of their language, market or locale of origin. The second argument, more widespread among large companies, puts forward an allegedly scientific model supposed to serve as a guarantee of "(inter)cultural expertise", inspired, often loosely, by LISA's internationalization-localization cycle, by Geert Hofstede and/or by other concepts mentioned above. These two arguments are by no means mutually exclusive: some companies' websites use both, either simultaneously or at different points in time, as websites are periodically updated to provide relevant content but also, presumably, to improve their search engine ranking.

The choice of websites studied here is not based on any specific methodology other than the observation, over the course of recent years, of the work of second-year MA Translation students, who are asked to cite elements supporting and benchmarking their choice of cultural adaptation strategy for Web localization projects that are carried out in almost all cases toward their native language or locale.

A quick check when marking these students' work showed us that these websites appeared systematically in the top results of a query using keywords such as "culture, localization, Web". The websites studied here include, in particular, those of Powerling (www.powerling.com/fr/, Figure 6.2) and Global Voices (www.globalvoices.fr/, Figure 6.3), medium-sized agencies that are active in a number of markets, and RWS (www.rws.com/) and Transperfect (www.transperfect.com/), larger language service providers with a global presence[5]. The discourse of these companies would certainly merit a more in-depth study to enable comparisons between the status and size of the company, its presence and its discourse in various markets, etc., but this would entail studying each company's geographical situation and global offer and would constitute an article in its own right.

A recent blog post, entitled "What is a localized translation?", published on the Powerling agency's website, notes that localization consists of a "more advanced translation" that takes into account factors including graphic design, involving a greater level of finesse along with a cultural dimension[6]. While such an observation can be aligned intuitively with the "translation plus…" competency advanced by some trainers and practitioners (Gouadec 2003; Duclos 2017), the detail and especially the methodology for assessing the mysterious "cultural factor" are not explained further[7]. The same post puts forward "five essential reasons why the work

5 Other companies offering more specialized localization services are also highly ranked by search engines under the same keywords but are less relevant to this discussion. Examples include www.transifex.com/, a specialist in semi-automatic translation services for websites by proxy server.

6 www.powerling.com/fr/blog/entry/qu-est-ce-qu-une-traduction-localisee/ [Accessed 10 June 2021]. Translations are our own.

7 The post goes on to explain its findings with an example that may sound more like an advertising slogan than a considered approach to culture: "To make it simple, if you choose to have an English translation, you have to choose between British English and American English."

of a native speaker will make a difference", each of them touching intuitively upon culture without problematizing or making explicit the link: regional linguistic subtleties, degree of adaptation of the content, compliance of the graphical elements, user experience and improving the brand image.

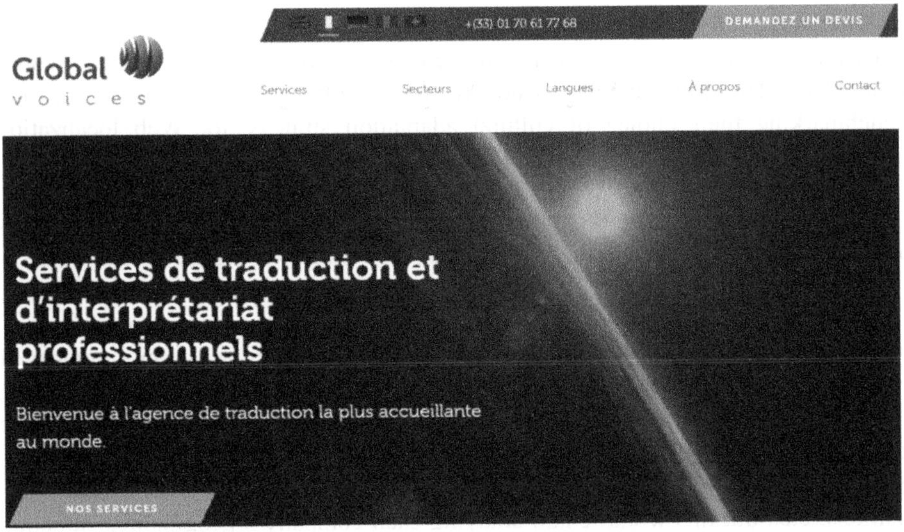

Figure 6.3. *Homepage of the website www.globalvoices.com/fr/ (accessed 15 October 2021); "Localization" section under the "Services" menu. For a color version of this figure, see www.iste.co.uk/pinede/digital.zip*

We can find the same type of argument on many other websites, such as that of the company Global Voices, where we read that "localization goes way beyond translating text and also takes cultural and aesthetic factors into consideration", without however finding an explanation of the notion of "culture", beyond details such as regional expressions or currencies and units of measurement[8]. An earlier iteration of the same company's website refers more specifically to the competence of a "professional translator born and raised in the country into which [the corporate clients] wish to export"[9]. Here again, the reader is led to read the pedigree of such a translator as a guarantee of "native" cultural competency, even if a glance at Internet

8 Available at: https://www.globalvoices.co.uk/localisation/website-localisation/ [Accessed 8 May 2020].

9 Page archived under the link https://web.archive.org/web/20161122112241/https:/www.globalvoices.fr/localisation-siteweb.php [Accessed 10 June 2021]. Translations are our own.

Archive's Wayback Machine suggests that this message is not, in fact, present in all language versions at all times.

Other companies offering localization services, mostly large agencies offering a full range of language services on an international scale, tend more toward selling the idea of cultural expertise, using models that recall the influence of Geert Hofstede, the Global Product Development Cycle (LISA 2003), or sometimes both. Figure 6.4 presents the graphic used until recently to present RWS's Go Global Model, which puts the "Localize" element at the center of a five-step process: "Plan – Create – Localize – Engage – Optimize". This process strongly recalls the internationalization/localization cycle proposed by LISA, rendered in a slider-like form that, perhaps, better reflects fashions in corporate website design.

Figure 6.4. *The RWS Go Global Model*[10]*. For a color version of this figure, see www.iste.co.uk/pinede/digital.zip*

The text accompanying the "Localize" label stresses the need to take linguistic nuances and cultural differences into account; the corresponding link takes us to a page where we find a brief text highlighting the need to use human skills as well as digital tools to meet the needs of the international market. This is followed by a list of services offered, with no further mention of culture. The text associated with the "Optimize" phase places a strong emphasis on the communication strategy but also on the importance of "gathering and acting on the right insights", an expression that reminds us of the importance of data collection and analysis, but at the same time, perhaps not coincidentally, of the importance of "insights", a word that is difficult to translate or even define but that remains closely associated with the influence of www.hofstede-insights.com/. The RWS website was completely refurbished following its acquisition in 2020 of SDL, another global language service provider and it is interesting to compare the model just cited with the current version of the website, whose French version appears to have abandoned the framework of the Go Global Model to focus once again on a network of "native linguistic experts [...]

10 Page archived under the link: https://web.archive.org/web/20190729194052/https:/www.rws.com/what-we-do/rws-moravia/go-global-model/ [Accessed June 10 2021] and on the company's website [Accessed November 5 2018].

based in our network of offices across the top 30 global translation markets [whose] expertise in unique language nuances ensures translated content will resonate with in-market audiences"[11]. The "Consulting and Insights" tab on the English version of the site, again reminiscent of Geert Hofstede's insights, still underlines the importance of choosing a model and strategy adapted to the project and the target market, but ultimately seems to focus less on one particular model and more on the work of local consultants (perhaps the same as the "native language experts" highlighted in the "Translation" tab?) capable of "producing culturally appropriate content across all markets".

The sometimes unclear relationship between skills in translation, localization and cultural consultancy applied to website localization is visible on the website of the multinational company Transperfect, where the website localization process is presented in the form of a cycle that, once more, is reminiscent of LISA's website, though placing a stronger emphasis on the provision of services beyond traditional translation (SEO, social media, customer support, etc.: see Figure 6.5).

It is interesting to note a marked separation between the essentially technical and technological services shown here and those presented on the same website's "Multicultural marketing" page, where mention is made of the work of "linguists who are experts in copywriting and marketing" but also that of "cultural advisors" who "possess or gather current, reliable, and insightful information about your concepts, your target market, and how to best adapt existing copy or create original copy and creative that will produce the desired result"[12]. While the boundaries between localization, cultural consultancy and Web marketing are not always distinct, it nonetheless seems quite difficult to pinpoint the difference between the competencies assigned to each type of expert and to understand what companies selling localization services mean when they address the notion of culture.

The various models and practices highlighted in this section suggest that cultural competency is necessary for the activity of a professional translator and more particularly a website localizer. However, the nature and the means of acquiring this competency are less clearly identified, whether in the professional literature aimed at translator-localizer training or in the commercial discourse of the industry itself. On the other hand, the scientific literature opens up some avenues for reflection on the nature of this competency.

11 Available at: www.rws.com/translation/localization/ [Accessed June 18, 2021]. Translations are our own.

12 Available at: https://www.transperfect.com/solutions/global-brand-management/multicultural-marketing [Accessed 23 March 2023].

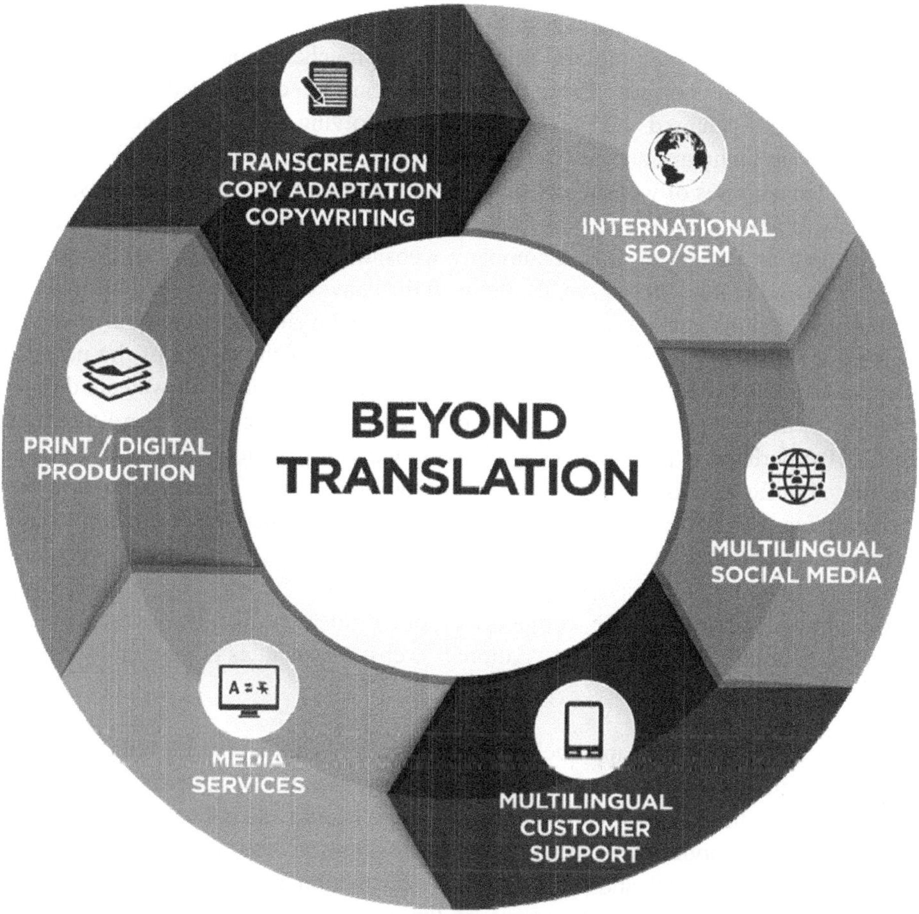

Figure 6.5. *Cycle of a localization project ("beyond translation") on the Transperfect website*[13]*. For a color version of this figure, see www.iste.co.uk/pinede/digital.zip*

6.3. From (intercultural) communication to localization services

6.3.1. *Three scientific approaches to cultural localization*

A large part of the literature focusing on the cultural dimension of website localization is covered in a comprehensive literature review based on 90 scientific

13 Available at: www.transperfect.com/services/website-localization.html [Accessed 10 June 2021].

articles published between 2000 and 2015 (Tigre Moura et al. 2016). These articles were classified by the authors into three approaches, approximately equally represented in the corpus. These approaches can be categorized as inductive, deductive and centered on usage. Studies involving the inductive approach, including one landmark article (Barber and Badre 1998), seek to identify "cultural markers" in a corpus of websites associated with different countries or locales, either generally, as in the study cited, or focused on specific countries only and a specific sector, such as a study of airline company websites between the United States and China (Lo and Gong 2005). Overall, these studies have identified a small number of similarities and differences according to countries and business sectors, but at such a general level (language used, direction of writing, use of the colors of the national flag on some websites, etc.) that they have no major implications for website design. Moreover, this type of approach seems to have attracted much less interest beyond the 2010s, perhaps in the light of its relatively weak explanatory powers in the face of the significance of other factors. As communicators – and the marketing departments of major language service agencies (if the above examples are reliable) – know, the creative brief behind the design of a professional website is usually based on a sector-specific or market-specific strategy, target audiences, positioning compared to the competition, brand identity, etc. It is certainly not possible to reduce everything to a "national" website format, as is implied by certain studies of this type.

Adopting the opposite approach, deductive studies aim to identify manifestations of cultural differences predicted by certain comparative theories of national cultures. Among the studies inventoried by Francisco Tigre Moura and colleagues (2016), the Geert Hofstede model is used in about 88% of these, followed by the Shalom Schwartz (1994) model and Edward Hall's distinction between high-context and low-context cultures, or combinations of these models, such as that proposed by Nitish Singh (Baack and Singh 2007). However, most of the researchers cited in the review are specialists in Web design or marketing, and not in intercultural questions as such. A critical reading reveals a marked stance of methodological nationalism (Beck 2007; Dervin 2014)[14] in most of these studies, which tend toward essentialism, as well as a lack of understanding, on occasions, of the actual models used and how to use them appropriately.

As an example not to be followed, an article published in the *International Journal of Scientific and Engineering Research* claims to apply Geert Hofstede's

14 Methodological nationalism consists in positing that differences necessarily exist due to the fact of national affiliation, and then implementing a methodology to seek to identify and characterize such differences, without questioning similarity between national groups or diversity at other levels of social organization.

model to website analysis in order to highlight distinct cultural rationales, presented in the form of advice for Web designers. The article recommends, for instance, the use of colors described as "masculine", such as black, gray, brown, blue or green, on websites aimed at audiences in "masculine" societies, whereas there should be a preference for "soft" colors such as pink, peach or shades of red, it explains, for websites aimed at "feminine" societies (Alao Olujimi et al. 2013). The same article advises opting to include mainly photographs of individuals when targeting an individualistic society and photographs of groups for collectivist societies. Quite clearly, recommendations such as this both defy common sense and reveal their authors' fundamental misunderstanding of Geert Hofstede's model in itself. They also overlook the criticisms that have been made of this model (Livian 2011; McSweeney 2002), as well as Geert Hofstede's warnings about the differences in scale between macro and micro and therefore the fact that such a model cannot be applied on the level of a communication tool that must be designed in relation to multiple levels of context: commercial, communicational, technological, social, etc. However, such supposedly scientific articles, advocating essentialist approaches to national cultures, continue to appear, particularly in journals with little scientific rigor. They are apparently aimed at filling a gap in the literature and a commercial/professional need in relation to a research question that has not yet been answered satisfactorily elsewhere[15].

The third type of research inventoried by Tigre Moura and colleagues concerns the practices of users representing different national groups, and in particular their reactions to interfaces developed in or for different national contexts. Despite a few exceptions, the majority of these studies converge around the idea that, even if no cultural specificities can be very easily detected through the inductive approach (see above), the degree of satisfaction reported and the degree of effectiveness in navigation and searching for information seem higher for localized websites (Tigre Moura et al. 2016, p. 317). The attitude of users is then more positive, more trusting, their intentions to make a purchase or come back to the website are more marked, the authors write. According to these results, it seems that adapting the form and contents of a website to its audiences is a factor in the engagement of these audiences via the ergonomic user experience, but it is also clear that this goes beyond mere macro-social considerations of national culture in Web design.

6.3.2. *A necessary consideration of complexity in Web communication*

In order to fill the apparent gap in scientific literature able to shed light on the cultural dimension of localization, it may be appropriate to reformulate the research

15 See section 6.3.2 for a discussion of some recent approaches to this question.

question initially stated. Instead of studying the influence of national cultures on Web design and localization, it would seem more appropriate and useful to look instead at the influence on this process of a whole range of other factors: cultural, but also social, economic, commercial or strategic. As we see it, it is only by addressing the complexity of this question, particularly from a strategic point of view on the micro-social level, that we will be able to understand the dynamics of sensemaking (Weick et al. 2005). By taking into consideration the communication strategy and the positioning of an organization in a more global landscape, in relation to brand identity but also to the identity of the target audiences, we will better understand certain creative choices that go far beyond questions of individualism or collectivism.

By opening up to issues of standardization or "glocalization" of communication materials, for example, we can assess the strategic value of a global policy of heavy website standardization at Microsoft[16]. The company's reputation rests on the equipment it sells being able to be used internationally, with interchangeable language interfaces but full interoperability. Its website understandably respects the same principle. Similarly, the United Nations has a unique position in the world, operating independently of individual nation states. This position makes it inconceivable for it to change its discourse between its different language versions. It needs to carry the same message all around the world[17]. On the other hand, the same degree of standardization would be totally inappropriate in the various national websites of McDonald's restaurants[18], where adapting the product offer and associated communication to local tastes and eating habits constitutes a major factor in competitiveness. Depending on whether or not a brand image has national connotations, non-adaptation can also be embraced as a strategy. This is the case, for example, of the Bureau Interprofessionnel des Vins de Bourgogne[19] which, in the English and German versions of its website, retains language elements in French and relies on the notions of terroir and traditional know-how associated with French and Burgundy wines, just as much as in the original version, with typical images of hills lined with vineyards in the Burgundy countryside and recognizably French typography. The French identity is here a selling point and a guarantee of quality for the foreign consumer, which it is appropriate to keep, and even underline, in the

16 Available at: www.microsoft.com. Various geographical versions consulted on March 10, 2021.

17 Available at: www.un.org. Various language versions consulted on March 10, 2021.

18 See, for example: www.mcdonalds.fr, www.mcdonalds.de, www.mcdonalds.com, www.mcdonaldsindia.com [Accessed 10 March 2021].

19 Available at: www.vins-bourgogne.fr/ [Accessed 10 March 2021].

foreign versions of the website (Bô et al. 2013, p. 105). As Tigre Moura and colleagues note in an article that analyzes user reactions to versions of travel websites that are or are not "culturally adapted", sometimes the perceived exoticism becomes a guarantee of authenticity that increases the attractiveness of the product or service being sold (Tigre Moura et al. 2015).

The cultural dimension must clearly be taken into account in a study of this kind in order to analyze how communication materials and the messages they seek to convey can be interpreted from the point of view of "cultural framing" (Van Gorp 2007). Cultural framing studies how various elements in a given enunciative setting can work together to take form and make sense in a particular way, to a given audience, in a given sociohistorical context. By taking into account the dominant social representations in a given locale makes it possible to adapt communication materials by anticipating various possible interpretations the target audience might make, and trying to choose discursive elements that will "make sense" for them. Reducing this dimension to questions of Hofstede-style values, as much of the scientific literature in the field does, seems highly reductive and largely inappropriate. On the other hand, a more complex approach to relationships between cultures – in the plural – and communication, which gives full importance to the context of enunciation and the rhetorical and identity positioning of all the parties involved, can open up other horizons for localization.

6.4. Attempts and experiments for a complex, non-essentialist approach to cultural localization

As already stated, the need to take cultural differences into consideration, preferably in their complexity and linked to the specificities of the product and the target audience, seems to be commonly taken for granted, intuitively at least, by professional translators and language service providers. For a company such as Transperfect and for practitioners such as Martin (2005), the notion of translation already encompasses that of cultural adaptation, with the notion of localization sometimes taking on a narrower technical meaning limited to one language, one geographical region and one character set, originally applied to desktop computer software and to some extent to websites (Esselink 2000, p. 1). But whatever meaning is given to the words, the recognition of a cultural dimension and even the need for expertise in intercultural communication is not always supported by a nuanced approach to culture.

6.4.1. *Intercultural studies and translator training*

This issue has nevertheless given rise to several attempted solutions, such as the European PICT (Promoting Intercultural Competence for Translators) project, launched in 2012 and aimed at developing methods and resources to train translators on the issues of intercultural communication by stressing the link between the role of the translator and the intercultural mediator (Tomozeiu et al. 2016). The project's website (offline since 2020 but fully archived by Wayback Machine)[20] gives details of a standard teaching program constructed around three key aspects (theoretical, textual, interpersonal) that "put limited emphasis on linguistic competence [since] the main focus is the complex network of cultural perspectives involved when each of these languages is approached from a plurilingual perspective – that is, loaded with cultural meanings that inevitably reach beyond the boundaries of one single culture" (PICT 2012, p. 6). The aim of sensitizing translation students to the issue of intercultural communication is certainly commendable, but the teaching activities offered on the website are for the most part confined to raising awareness and, to some extent, to fostering a reflexive approach. For example, one of the proposed activities asks participants to translate a recipe and to compare the cultural assumptions of source and target audiences while trying to identify the conventions and choices that might cause problems (PICT 2012, pp. 15–17). While such an approach clearly has some application in the classroom in terms of raising awareness about intercultural issues, it does not represent a radical step beyond the models and frameworks for translator training identified above.

The PICT project does not claim specifically to address the issue of localization. Its reflexive approach could certainly extend to the graphical and interactive content of websites but would presumably need to offer an analytical framework beyond the simplistic essentialism of some of the works already cited. Its recommended reading list (PICT 2012, pp. 20–24) and the recommended exercise "Comparing cultural values using Hofstede's theories" are probable evidence of the approaches, which we have already criticized being taken at face value. While more recent studies in the wake of the PICT project highlight the need for concrete implementation (Tomozeiu and Kumpulainen 2016) and the establishment of a critical framework for assessing intercultural competency in translator training (Angelone 2016), the application of these approaches to the field of localization in particular still appears to be some distance away.

20 Available at: https://web.archive.org/web/20160410175619/http:/pictllp.eu/en [Accessed 10 June 2021].

6.4.2. *From translation to intercultural expertise*

Jiménez-Crespo's *Translation and Web Localization* (2013) remains a key reference for Web localization training despite the many developments in digital and multimodal communication since the book was first published. While underlining the tension between the processes of internationalization (favoring standardization, at least at the technical level, particularly visible on Microsoft's websites) and localization (favoring adaptation to cultural and sectoral specificities, such as the website of the Bureau Interprofessionnel des Vins de Bourgogne), Jiménez-Crespo (2013) suggests a cyclic model inspired by that of LISA but whose acronym, GILT (Globalization – Internationalization – Localization – Translation), formalizes translation as a separate step that can take place once a localization strategy has been perfected, possibly in parallel with other approaches to adapting to the local market (p. 27).

The LISA model, based on a rationale derived from a product development cycle, moves from its localization phase straight into a new phase of internationalization through a "product requirements analysis (global/local)". However, Jiménez-Crespo's variant involves two intermediate stages that demonstrate not only the particularities of a website compared to other types of products marketed on a global scale, but also the somewhat unusual status of the translator/localizer within the globalization cycle and in relation to intercultural communication.

Internationalization > Localization > Translation > *Feedback from experts on intercultural communication* >…

Box 6.1. *Linear representation of the GILT cycle adapted from Jiménez-Crespo (2013, p. 27)*

Box 6.1 shows a linear representation of the cycle that, according to Jiménez-Crespo, constitutes the globalization process, where localization leads to a translation phase and where the transition from this translation phase to a new phase of internationalization happens via an intermediate stage entitled "feedback from experts on intercultural communication". The exact nature and especially the identity of those providing this feedback is not made explicit but, in a sector where the translator-localizer may carry out a greater or lesser number of the technical tasks required for website localization, depending on the organization and the scope of the project, and given the scientific and commercial discourses cited above, it is easy to form the impression that this expert is often – perhaps for lack of any other expert – the actual translator.

Jiménez-Crespo (2013, pp. 31–33) outlines a pragmatic framework for analyzing cultural adaptation, setting out the arguments and underlining the influence of Singh and Pereira (2005) and of Geert Hofstede among localization practitioners, although without explicitly subscribing to them. His discussion of "levels" of localization (Jiménez-Crespo 2013, pp. 33–36) seems to confirm this ambiguous positioning. The complete "cultural customization" of a website would represent, following Singh and Pereira's typology, a level of localization above the simple "cloning" obtained by a complete and faithful translation of the site's contents, but the criteria used for this adaptation are not developed in further detail. More recent studies continue the analysis of localized websites in sectors such as international NGOs (Charalampidou 2019) and French tourism websites (Cowan 2019), drawing on the perspectives of researchers including Singh, Pereira and Hofstede while continuing to recognize the difficulty of substantiating general conclusions from specific examples.

6.4.3. *From localization to transcreation*

In the first chapter of the *Routledge Handbook of Translation and Culture*, David Katan (2004, 2018) acknowledges the influence of Hofstede's thinking while at the same time bemoaning, for the same reasons cited above, a tendency to overinterpret it by confusing the macro- and micro-scales (pp. 22–28). In other works, Katan identifies a shift in the field, caused by the increasingly widespread use of machine translation and post-editing, with the potential for profound effect on the relationship between translation and culture in a world where the means of dissemination and even production of texts are increasingly dominated by digital technologies. Presented as something of a thought experiment, this "transcreational turn" (Katan 2016) envisages a split between purely pragmatic texts (and translation tasks), whose primary aim is comprehension and which could be assigned to machines, and texts (and translation tasks) that present a particular creative or cultural value, whose adaptation would need to be assigned to human translators liberated from boring, repetitive tasks and whose creative intelligence would thus be better harnessed and valued.

Digital culture has brought with it new tools for automatic natural language processing but also an abundance of interactive multi-modal products, including websites, for which cultural representations are potentially more complex than for most written texts. This vision of transcreation as the recreation of content adapted to a target audience comes close to Kaindl's (2019) recasting of the role of the multimedia translator as one of a "text designer", also echoing the complex nature of the localization process highlighted by Jiménez-Crespo in the definition cited in the introduction to this chapter. The precise relationship between transcreation (a concept focused primarily on the translator-creator and on the process) and website localization (a concept focused primarily on the product, the target user and the customer) is outside the scope of this chapter, but it is worth mentioning one promising attempt to apply Katan's perspective to a training module on transcreation, adopting a project-based learning approach (Huertas Barros and Vine 2019). The idea of a "transcreational turn" applied to the field of localization seems to imply both a return to human skills, as opposed to machine translation and, by extension, a return to the notion of "native competence". However, there are also cultural models that can be operationalized to study websites.

6.4.4. *Toward a liquid approach to localization*

The field of intercultural communication, and in particular its critical studies, offers a theoretical framework providing a complex vision of the relationship between cultures and communication, applied to localization. Faced with models deemed too essentialist or "solid", many scholars advocate adopting a "liquid" approach to cultures and identities. This rejects a more traditional conception of cultures as stable, static – often national – "essences", with a supposedly strong influence over behaviors and representations within (national or other) social groups.

This distinction between "solid" and "liquid" approaches to culture is proposed, for example, by Fred Dervin, based on the concept of "liquidity" popularized by Bauman and which he himself applies to culture (Bauman 1999, 2011). "Liquid" approaches, according to Dervin (2011), lean toward complexity, dynamism, processes or completely reject the category of culture as heuristic for a conception of social relations (pp. 33–35). A liquid vision of cultures highlights their elusive nature, their continuous evolution through microsocial interactions and the way in which social actors make use of them while at the same time negotiating them, on account of the vagueness that surrounds them. From this point of view, cultures can be summarized as idealized, expected traits, grouping together representations, behavioral styles, values and affects, which are projected onto others to make them predictable on the intersubjective level, because of their presumed affiliation to this or that social group. We can then speak of cultural "repertoires" or even "toolkits" (Swidler 1986), which individuals mobilize to "make sense", according to the situation. Finally, the liquid approach puts the emphasis on the creativity of social actors who play with presumed cultural traits, conforming or not conforming to the expectations of others to create effect, acting out roles in a particular way to emphasize idiosyncrasy, thus “performing” cultures through their interactions (Frame 2013).

Between these two visions, solid and liquid, Dervin denounces what he calls the “Janusian” or “simplex” approaches, open to both perspectives but which he presents as “schizophrenic” or unresolved. These approaches seem to wish to defend, implicitly or explicitly, apparently irreconcilable positions, refusing to settle on either a (“solid”) vision of a culture shared by the members of a group and acting on them, or a (“liquid”) vision based on the intersubjective negotiation of cultural traits idealized through interactions.

The recent non-essentialist models of localization cited in the earlier discussion seem to correspond in this respect to the Janusian approaches described by Fred Dervin. They seek to avoid the application of national categories which are too rigid, taking other factors into account. The “transcreational turn” opens localization to creativity and the richness of communication with complex messages and plural audiences. However, to escape the shortcomings that Dervin denounces, these approaches should also undertake the paradigm shift that involves deconstructing the national, taken as a socially constructed category projected onto oneself and others, rather than as a marker of a fundamental ontological difference.

By refocusing the analysis on identities and the way in which national cultures are foregrounded in terms of identity alongside other cultures, the liquid approach allows us to take into account the complexity of audiences within the cosmopolitan societies of late modernity (Bauman 2011). This vision is potentially valuable for performing localization that seeks to come as close as possible to the diverse audiences targeted, while at the same time remaining alert to identity-related risks, such as “cultural appropriation” (Rogers 2006).

Such an approach can also seem more reliable and consistent in terms of adapting contents than a purely intuitive approach by an “artist”. Approaching nationality not as a key cognitive operator, but as a source of possible representations (cultural framing) and a sense of belonging, makes it possible to link it to other vectors of socialization and possible sources of social belonging, such as age groups, leisure pursuits or brand affinity, among others. These elements can prove equally relevant to the ways in which people interpret a localized website, which must be positioned in relation to various possible codes and readings, and in accordance with a communication strategy specific to the targeted locale.

6.4.5. *Teaching vocational skills for cultural localization*

Having established the limitations of the dominant approaches in this area, and having taken into consideration current avenues for rethinking cultures and localization, we can now start to draw up some concrete proposals for vocational localizer training. Table 6.1 summarizes these proposals, centered around three "pedagogical axes", involving empirical analysis activities, topics for discussion in the light of the analysis carried out, and elements to be highlighted during ongoing discussions.

This pedagogical approach is fundamentally pragmatic, with a focus on three complementary dimensions of the localization process that is designed to encourage students of translation-localization to ask themselves the right questions. First, studying websites associated with the same organization in different countries, such as those mentioned above (section 6.2.2), allows us to highlight localization strategies specific to each organization. For instance, as already highlighted, McDonald's develops very different websites according to the locale, which reflect food-related habits and representations that vary considerably from one country to another, whereas Microsoft practices standardization in the structure and content of its websites, managed centrally, which reflects the commercial promise of perfect interoperability between different language versions of the software sold around the world. The respective national identities of the various actors (of the organization and of the target audience) can also come into play, since localization must take into account these identities and the way in which it may or may not be appropriate, strategically, to play on this or that provenance, from one locale to another.

Armed with these pragmatic findings on the way localization functions in concrete terms, in light of the advertiser's strategy, students can then easily perceive the limitations of comparative approaches to national cultures, when applied blindly and out of all context, to website localization. It can then be entertaining to look for counterexamples to set against the disembodied theories advocated in a deductive approach, or at any rate to note that these theories cannot be applied straight out of the box to the websites studied. By taking a few examples of sectoral websites that mobilize some of the same codes from one country to another (industrial websites, e-commerce websites, video games websites, etc.), we can look for the specific codes they use, in order to re-examine the notion of specialized "audiences", transnationally from one place to another. This, in turn, can lead students to reflect on the organization of the professional translation sector, which dictates a national or at least a linguistic prism, but which also takes into account the notion of specialization: cultural repertoires can help to interpret content at different levels.

Pedagogical axis	Empirical analysis activity	Discussion of results	Central elements to be highlighted
1. Case studies of international localization	Work on a corpus of websites to measure the relative importance of national and other cultural representations, according to organization, sector of activity, product or service	Discussion of institutional and organizational communication strategies that shed light on the localization options chosen, making reference to social representations that may underlie the image that the speaker wishes to give	Approach the communication strategy as a whole: brand positioning, identities rendered salient (those of the organization and those projected onto the Internet users)
2. Development of a non-essentialist vision of cultures linked to the multiplicity of audiences	Review the applied scientific literature of comparative inspiration, in the light of website analyses carried out, in order to note the paucity of explanatory factors put forward	Approach culture as a "repertoire" or "toolkit" that constitutes a presumed communality. In a given situation or when looking at particular communication materials, the way meaning is constructed by the audience is linked to the identities of the actors, to the context and not to some kind of cultural "formatting"	Question the national viewpoint taken by the industry toward translation-localization (notion of "native speaker") and its institutional basis, in order to open up this viewpoint to the diversity inherent in target audiences
3. Discussions of the (cultural) limitations of the algorithmic automation of localization	Analyze from a cultural localization perspective the way that corpus-trained translation tools based on deep learning actually function: what are the limitations?	Reflect on marketing or communication techniques based on audience segmentation: toward a consideration of the intersectionality and diversity of populations	Question and identify the added value of human intervention in a transcreational perspective

Table 6.1. *Pedagogical axes proposed for vocational training in localization*

Our proposals remain, at least for the moment, focused on the analysis and reflection phase necessary to define an internationalization and localization strategy. Our experience in the training context suggests that (a) there is pedagogical work to be done to promote a clear understanding of the need to integrate this reflexive dimension into projects, since it can be perceived as excessively abstract by students enrolled in so-called "vocational" training, and (b) there are bridges to be built between this analysis phase, which represents the first stage of the development cycle identified by LISA (2003), and the concrete, constructive and often creative work of defining, implementing and testing localized content. While we regret that some future localizers express mistrust of theoretical models, especially where this leads them to adopt, without sufficient critical distance, the essentialist postures proposed by certain "professional" sources, we are working toward setting up pedagogical practices through which these principles can be clearly presented and implemented in concrete terms. As Jiménez-Crespo's (2013) definition points out, localization is a complex process and is often constrained by the requirements specified by the client and by economic considerations. It is thus not always possible for localizers to produce what they would see as the ideal localization solution, but a better understanding of cultural issues among localizers should help them to better explain these issues to their clients.

Finally, taking into account the complex nature of these analyses, we can consider where and how to situate the limits of machine translation and computer-assisted translation tools, especially in cases where audiences are diverse and where client identities and communication strategies need to be considered carefully, and where meanings are often multiple and unstable. To draw a parallel with the rise of neural machine translation, how might deep learning eventually meet, or not meet, such challenges? How far and when can these tools facilitate the task of localization? A discussion that compares marketing to translation can explore how these activities segment and stereotype their audiences, the better to address them collectively. How should the diversity and intersectionality of audiences be taken into account in translation? These questions can lead back to the notion of transcreation and to a discussion of its possible added value. For example, what place can transcreation have in the business model of a translation agency that seeks to optimize costs by redefining the way humans and machines interact in the translation-localization process?

6.5. Conclusion

This contribution set out to show that there is no simple answer to the question initially posed about the professional competencies needed to deal with the cultural dimension of website localization. The cultural dimension is implicit in the construction of meaning, when looking at a website or in any other communication situation. However, different cultures (not only national, but also professional, organizational, regional, family, generational, religious, etc.) can constitute markers of meaning that are leveraged by diverse audiences to "make sense" of a website or other communication tool. These cultures are connected to identities (of the individuals themselves, of the brand or of the organization) that have greater or lesser salience in a given context, a context that can also be commercial, competitive, inter-ethnic, geopolitical, etc. For this reason, and in spite of a body of scientific literature applied to the field that still seems to support such simplistic perspectives, we have rejected as the dominant paradigm the comparative approaches of national cultures, in favor of a more complex, liquid vision of cultures and identities. Since Internet communication is, in a sense, re-territorialized by the virtual space of the Web, professionals must remain attentive to the need to adapt a localized website or digital product for a given locale and to avoid limiting adaptations to details such as currency, date format or character encoding. The risk of methodological nationalism is associated with the way that the translation and localization industry is structured. The concept of (linguistic) locales, which often correspond to the spaces of national states, tends to strengthen the status and the consideration of national cultures in the minds of both customers and professionals in the sector. These representations of national cultural differences are part of our world awareness and must be taken into account as such, but not as "solid" differences or as the only cultural vectors at play in localization.

The transcreational paradigm offers a partial answer to these concerns, relying on human intelligence to deal with a complexity that is difficult to model using simple categories or even, to date, by means of deep learning. The division of tasks between man and machine and the "creative" posture of the "copywriter", enacted by a native speaker, allows multiple factors to be taken into account, including an awareness of mixed audiences, and the strategic considerations of advertisers. However, in the field of vocational training, such use of "intuitive" faculties, learned during primary socialization, poses obvious issues to do with transferability of skills. In an attempt to resolve these issues, we have formulated recommendations for localizer training programs around three pedagogical axes that can be implemented in the classroom:

1) analysis of case studies of international localization;

2) the development of a liquid, non-essentialist vision of cultures and localization, acknowledging the multiplicity of potential audiences;

3) analysis of the (cultural) limits of machine-performed or machine-assisted localization, viewed in the light of a transcreational approach.

Despite the lack of scientific literature dealing with the issue of cultural localization in these terms, what encourages the authors of this chapter to continue their reflection is the observation that the students we train have no difficulty in recognizing the paucity of an essentialist approach once we encourage them to take a step back. Seeking to avoid falling into the trap of advocating a reductive model of a complex phenomenon, we hope that the principles outlined here, based on a theoretical reflection that links recent approaches from intercultural studies and translation/localization studies, can help future professionals to better understand this dimension of their work, so rich in meaning. There is certainly still much more to be done between the development of these principles and their implementation in a training context – and, further, empirical testing of their effectiveness and perhaps the development of a competence framework for localizer training – but we remain optimistic insofar as the search for ways to assess the cultural dimension of websites represents a fertile ground for testing different solutions.

6.6. References

Alao Olujimi, D., Adekunle, Y., Ibikunle, F., Shodiya, A. (2013). Culture-based adaptive web design. *International Journal of Scientific and Engineering Research*, 4(2) [Online]. Available at: http://www.ijser.org/researchpaper/CULTURE-BASED-ADAPTIVE-WEB-DESIGN.pdf.

Alshtaiwi, M. (2017). Parlons du localisateur : rôle et profil. *Traduire*, 237, 38–47 [Online]. Available at: http://journals.openedition.org/translate/945.

Angelone, E. (2016). A process-oriented approach for documenting and gauging inter-cultural competence in translation. *The Interpreter and Translator Trainer*, 10(3), 304–317.

Baack, D.W. and Singh, N. (2007). Culture and web communications. *Journal of Business Research*, 60(3), 181–188.

Baker, M. (2011). *In Other Words: A Coursebook in Translation*. Routledge, New York.

Barber, W. and Badre, A. (1998). Culturability: The merging of culture and usability. In *Conference on Human Factors and the Web (AtetT Conference Proceedings)*. Basking Ridge, New Jersey [Online]. Available at: https://zing.ncsl.nist.gov/hfweb/att4/proceedings/barber/.

Bauman, Z. (1999). *Culture as Praxis*. SAGE, London.

Bauman, Z. (2011). *Culture in a Liquid Modern World*. Polity Press, Cambridge.

Beck, U. (2007). La condition cosmopolite et le piège du nationalisme méthodologique. In *Les sciences sociales en mutation*, Wieviorka, M. (ed.). Editions Sciences Humaines, Paris.

Bô, D., Lellouche, R., Guével, M. (2013). *Brand Culture : développer le potentiel culturel des marques*. Dunod, Paris.

Charalampidou, P. (2019). Culture and persuasive discourse in localized NGO websites. *Journal of Internationalization and Localization*, 6(1), 25–44.

Chodkiewicz, M. (2012). The EMT framework of reference for competences applied to translation: Perceptions by professional and student translators. *JoSTrans – Journal of Specialized Translation*, 17, 37–54 [Online]. Available at: https://www.jostrans.org/issue17/art_chodkiewicz.php.

Colina, S. and Venuti, L. (2017). A survey of translation pedagogies. In *Teaching Translation: Programs, Courses, Pedagogies*, Venuti, L. (ed.). Routledge, New York.

Cowan, S.E. (2019). Cultural localisation as a strategy to preserve the persuasive function in the translation of tourism websites from French into English. *Journal of Internationalization and Localization*, 6(2), 131–152.

Cronin, M. (2003). *Translation and Globalization*. Routledge, New York.

Dervin, F. (2011). *Impostures interculturelles*. L'Harmattan, Paris.

Dervin, F. (2014). Au-delà du nationalisme méthodologique : l'interculturel sans essentialisme. *Raisons Politiques*, 54(2), 121–132 [Online].

Duclos, A. (2017). Guide pratique pour traduire un site web. *Traduire*, 237, 15–22 [Online]. Available at: https://journals.openedition.org/translate/937.

EMT (2009). EMT competence framework. European Commission [Online]. Available at: https://ec.europa.eu/info/sites/default/files/emt_competences_translators_en.pdf.

EMT (2017). European Master's in Translation – EMT competence framework. European Commission [Online]. Available at: https://commission.europa.eu/system/files/2018-02/emt_competence_fwk_2017_en_web.pdf.

Esselink, B. (2000). *A Practical Guide to Localization*. John Benjamins, Amsterdam.

Frame, A. (2013). *Communication et interculturalité. Cultures et interactions interpersonnelles*. Hermès Lavoisier, Paris.

Frame, A. (2017). What future for the concept of culture in the social sciences? *Epistémè*, 17, 151–172.

Freitas, P.H., Freitas, H., Janissek-Muiniz, R., Kuhn Andriotti, F., Krafta, L. (2008). Comment adapter une application Web pour un nouveau marché ? *Annais do 5° IFBAE – Congresso do IFBAE*, 1–16 [Online]. Available at: https://docplayer.fr/1891268-Comment-adapter-une-application-web-pour-un-nouveau-marche.html.

García Ochoa, G. (2016). Reading across cultures: "Self localization" in the higher education curriculum. *Journal of Internationalization and Localization*, 3(2), 165–181.

Gouadec, D. (2003). Le bagage spécifique du localiseur/localisateur : le vrai "nouveau profil" requis. *Meta*, 48(4), 526–545.

Gouadec, D. (2009a). *Guide des métiers de la traduction-localisation et de la communication multilingue et multimédia*. Maison du dictionnaire, Paris.

Gouadec, D. (2009b). *Profession : Traducteur*, 2nd edition. Maison du dictionnaire, Paris.

Huertas Barros, E. and Vine, J. (2019). Training the trainers in embedding assessment literacy into module design: A case study of a collaborative transcreation project. *The Interpreter and Translator Trainer*, 13(3), 271–291.

International Federation of Translators (2014). Translator's Charter [Online]. Available at: https://www.dpts.si/en/home/the-translator-s-code-of-ethics.

Jiménez-Crespo, M. (2013). *Translation and Web Localization*. Routledge, New York.

Jiménez-Crespo, M. (2019). Localisation research in translation studies: Expanding the limits or blurring the lines? In *Moving Boundaries in Translation Studies*, Dam, H.V., Brøgger, M.N., Korning Zethsen, K. (eds). Routledge, New York.

Kaindl, K. (2019). A theoretical framework for a multimodal design of translation. In *Translation and Multimodality: Beyond Words*, Boria, M., Carreres, Á., Noriega-Sánchez, M., Tomalin, M. (eds). Routledge, New York.

Katan, D. (2004). *Translating Cultures: An Introduction for Translators, Interpreters and Mediators*. Routledge, New York.

Katan, D. (2016). Translation at the crossroads: Time for the transcreational turn? *Perspectives*, 24(3), 365–381.

Katan, D. (2018). Defining culture, defining translation. In *The Routledge Handbook of Translation and Culture*, Harding, S.-A., Carbonell Cortés, O. (eds). Routledge, New York.

Lahire, B. (2001). *L'homme pluriel : les ressorts de l'action*. Armand Colin – Nathan, Paris.

Lederer, M. and Stratford, M. (ed.) (2020). *Culture et traduction. Au-delà des mots*. Classiques Garnier, Paris.

Liddicoat, A.J. (2016). Intercultural mediation, intercultural communication and translation. *Perspectives*, 24(3), 354–364.

LISA (2003). The localization industry primer [Online]. Available at: https://docplayer.net/5650852-Lisa-the-localization-industry-primer-2nd-edition-http-www-lisa-org.html.

Livian, Y. (2011). Pour en finir avec Hofstede : renouveler les références en management interculturel. In *Conférence francophone sur le management international* [Online]. Available at: https://hal.archives-ouvertes.fr/halshs-00643593.

Lo, B.W. and Gong, P. (2005). Cultural impact on the design of e-commerce sites: Part I – Site format and layout. *Issues in Information Systems*, 6(2), 182–189 [Online]. Available at: http://www.uwec.edu/CFSA/Documents/IACIS2005%20%20Cultural%20impact.pdf.

Maitland, S. (2017). A review of textbooks in translation studies. In *Teaching Translation: Programs, Courses, Pedagogies*, Venuti, L. (ed.). Routledge, New York.

Martin, C. (2005). De la trad' à la loca'. In *Traduire pour le web*, Gouadec, D. (ed.). La Maison du Dictionnaire, Paris.

Massardier-Kenney, F. (2017). An MA in translation. In *Teaching Translation: Programs, Courses, Pedagogies*, Venuti, L. (ed.). Routledge, New York.

Mazur, I. (2007). The metalanguage of localization: Theory and practice. *Target*, 19(2), 337–357.

McKay, C. (2011). *How to Succeed as a Freelance Translator*, 2nd edition. Lulu Press, Morrisville.

McSweeney, B. (2002). Hofstede's model of national cultural differences and their consequences: A triumph of faith – a failure of analysis. *Human Relations*, 55(1), 89–118.

PICT (2012). Intercultural competence curriculum framework [Online]. Available at: https://web.archive.org/web/20170427135447/http://pictllp.eu/curriculum-framework.

Pym, A. (2004). *The Moving Text: Localization, Translation and Distribution*. John Benjamins, Amsterdam.

Rogers, R.A. (2006). From cultural exchange to transculturation: A review and reconceptualization of cultural appropriation. *Communication Theory*, 16(4), 474–503.

Samuelsson-Brown, G. (2005). *A Practical Guide for Translators*, 4th edition. Multilingual Matters, London.

Schwartz, S. (1994). Beyond individualism/collectivism: New cultural dimensions of values. In *Individualism and Collectivism: Theory Application and Methods*, Kim, U., Triandis, H., Kagitçibasi, C., Choi, S., Yoon, G. (eds). SAGE, London.

SFT (n.d.). Code de déontologie général des adhérents de la SFT [Online]. Available at: https://www.sft.fr/code-de-deontologie-des-traducteurs-et-interpretes.html.

Shneor, R. (2012). Influences of culture, geography and infrastructure on website localization decisions. *Cross Cultural Management: An International Journal*, 19(3), 352–374.

Singh, N. and Pereira, A. (2005). *The Culturally Customised Web Site*. Elsevier Butterworth-Heinemann, New York.

Swidler, A. (1986). Culture in action: Symbols and strategies. *American Sociological Review*, 51(2), 273–286.

Tigre Moura, F., Gnoth, J., Deans, K.R. (2015). Localizing cultural values on tourism destination websites: The effects on users' willingness to travel and destination image. *Journal of Travel Research*, 54(4), 528–542.

Tigre Moura, F., Singh, N., Chun, W. (2016). The influence of culture in website design and users' perceptions: Three systematic reviews. *Journal of Electronic Commerce Research*, 17(4), 312–339.

Tomozeiu, D. and Kumpulainen, M. (2016). Operationalising intercultural competence for translation pedagogy. *The Translator and Interpreter Trainer*, 10(3), 268–284.

Tomozeiu, D., Koskinen, K., D'Arcangelo, A. (2016). Teaching intercultural competence in translator training. *The Interpreter and Translator Trainer*, 10(3), 251–267.

Van Gorp, B. (2007). The constructionist approach to framing: Bringing culture back in. *Journal of Communication*, 57(1), 60–78 [Online]. Available at: http://journals.ohiolink.edu.proxy.lib.ohio-state.edu/ejc/article.cgi?issn=00219916etissue=v57i0001etarticle=60_tcatfbcbi.

Walravens, J. (2017). Towards a culture-based paradigm for translator training. In *Towards Transcultural Awareness in Translation Pedagogy*, Deconnick, J., Humblé, P., Sepp, A., Stengers, H. (eds). Lit Verlag, Zürich.

Weick, K.E., Sutcliffe, K.M., Obstfeld, D. (2005). Organizing and the process of sense-making. *Organization Science*, 16(4), 409–421 [Online]. Available at: http://pubsonline.informs.org/doi/abs/10.1287/orsc.1050.0133.

Wolton, D. (2003). *L'autre mondialisation*. Flammarion, Paris.

7

Representativity of Indigenous Minorities and Cultural Identity on the Web

Cécile-Marie MARTIN
Université des Antilles, Pointe-à-Pitre, France

7.1. Introduction

In order to interrogate the place of indigenous minorities on the Web, we will focus on the importance assumed by the place of states in managing this online space. Indeed, despite the attempts of those who support a Web intended as a global space, governed by laws aimed at ensuring universal access (Berners-Lee et al. 1991), the question of the construction and expression of collective identities such as cultural identity remains eminently political (Vinsonneau 2012). From there, we will consider to what extent the Web can be a space of expression for indigenous minorities when the management of this system is operated by, among others, states where these communities struggle to be recognized.

We will seek to define and justify the terms identifying the populations targeted by our analysis, specifically the indigenous aspect and the minority aspect, and we will explain their distinctions (Abu Ramadan 2016; de Lespinay 2016; Bellier 2018).

We will present a state of the art of the evolution of the term associated with the definition and nomination of these communities, each federated around a common heritage and having begun a process to be recognized as such.

Digital Presences of Organizations,
coordinated by Nathalie PINÈDE, Luc MASSOU and Patrick MPONDO-DICKA.

The main levels (Brondizio 2013), hardware and software, that constitute the Web system, such as the network infrastructure, terminals, protocols, programming languages, interfaces and search engines, will serve as our framework for discussion of the place occupied by state apparatus in the definition of its architecture, access management and conditions of use. If, for some people, the Web enshrines the notion of a global village (MacLuhan 2004), or a system to globalize culture (Warnier 2017), in the sense of a space of expression free of national borders, in reality we will see that the disruptive character of this territory can be relativized. Many elements are intrinsically linked to the state apparatus, from domain names to email addresses, via the modalities of network access.

Examples of initiatives enabling indigenous minorities to establish their representativity on the Web will serve to illustrate our argument and identify the possibilities of a digital presence (Merzeau 2010) for these communities, without them having to take the path of acculturation but rather in the implementation of an alternative form of modernity (Habermas 1998).

7.2. "Indigenous minorities", a terminology to designate without discriminating

In the first place, it seems important to us to justify the use of specific terms to identify the communities to which reference will be made in our research. Indeed, whenever the issue of designation of a human group is approached in the cultural context, its lexicon must be chosen carefully. Observing the stumbling blocks that arise when creating a discourse in the field of intercultural communication, we ask ourselves how we can identify without stigmatizing.

7.2.1. *Minority and indigenousness: from self-determination to the recognition of rights*

Since our objective is to analyze the modalities of expression on the Web of communities encountering difficulties in being recognized as such in the physical space, these difficulties will thus be used to define them, while seeking to avoid them being discriminatory (Ringelheim 2018).

The first term frequently encountered in the literature that we consulted on these communities is that of minority (Marquardt 1991; Rigoni 2010; de Lespinay 2016; Bellier 2018). In fact, the minority aspect includes the notions of domination and dependence that are of interest to us here. But we should note that the notion of number is also attached to this term, sometimes implicitly. In reality, it can be seen that in the texts governing international relations, these two aspects are most often dealt with separately. There are indeed communities that are outnumbered in a given territory, but their culture is not threatened. These minorities, like the Francophone community in Burkina Faso (Guissou 2002), the White community in South Africa or the Alawite community in Syria, are regarded as being dominant economically, politically and culturally (Abu Ramadan 2016). They are not covered by legislation concerned with the protection of minorities. Conversely, a minority can evaluate itself in terms of the domination to which it is subjected, without the criterion of numerical inferiority being necessarily conclusive, as in the case of Hawaii's Kānaka Maoli community (20% of the state's population)[1] or the Inuit community of Nunavut in Canada (85% of the territory's population)[2]. As Bizeul (2016) reminds us, "The fact of being a minority is not based primarily on an exact count of the number of members of a group; it is above all the result of an imaginary social construct. A community becomes a minority [...] only when a reflective process of self-definition and identity self-perception has taken place".

Moreover, it seems to us of interest to recall that under international law, the law of minorities derives from human rights. The Declaration on the Rights of Persons Belonging to National or Ethnic, Religious and Linguistic Minorities, adopted by the United Nations in 1992, enshrines this separation between individual and collective rights. This choice is not without significance because the granting of collective rights to a community raises major issues. It opens the possibility for certain communities to claim entitlement to rights and provisions relating to territorial management, access to employment as in the United States and Canada or the method of obtaining seats in Parliament in Poland (Bellier 2018). The attribution of the designation of minority brings consequences in terms of national law, which leads some States such as France to reject or strictly regulate its use, the argument put forward being the risk of undermining the security and oneness of the State (de Lespinay 2016).

Finally, at the European level, two texts have been adopted that state two conditions for assessing the existence of minority status: nationality and language. The States that have ratified the Framework Convention for the Protection of National Minorities presented to the Council of Europe in 1991, 39 out of 47, thus undertake to recognize and protect national minorities, except for foreign incomers. However, since the term minority is not defined in the Convention, it is open to each State to interpret it, which leads to situations of inequality as in the

1 Available at: www.data.census.gov/cedsci/ [Accessed 20 September 2021].

2 Available at: www.www12.statcan.gc.ca/ [Accessed 20 September 2021].

case of the Sami, who live in Sweden, Norway, Finland and Russia and do not enjoy the same rights according to their nationality (Bellier 2020). The European Charter for Regional or Minority Languages, adopted by the Council of Europe in 1992, has been ratified by 25 out of 47 states and permits the protection and promotion of minority languages regarded as part of Europe's cultural heritage. The State's role in acknowledging the existence of one or more minority communities in its territory is therefore essential. Confronted by the reluctance of some States to ratify the texts that would instigate constitutional reforms, an alternative has been found in the use of the term indigenous.

The date generally taken as the start, at the international level, of the recognition of a cultural community that is different from the majority in power within a state, is the date of the study carried out by the International Labor Organization (ILO) in 1921. At that time, the term indigenous population was used by Albert Thomas, in his proposal to draft a "charter of indigenous working conditions" (Ricciardi 2019). In 1957, a new convention was adopted with aboriginal and tribal populations replacing the term indigenous population (Organisation internationale du travail 1957). The term *indigène* was then gradually abandoned in the French language, in favor of the term *autochtone*. Francophone indigenous representatives who had taken part in the working group on the Déclaration des Nations Unies sur les Droits des Peuples Autochtones [Declaration on the Rights of Indigenous Peoples] at the United Nations, adopted in 2007, made their voices heard on the issue of this pejorative connotation and expressly asked for the term *autochtone* to be used in the official texts of international bodies (Gergaud 2016). This term is still used, but that is in the case of word for word translations of the English word indigenous, as in the ILO Convention No. 169 of 1989. As for the terms tribal or semi-tribal people, these notions have no meaning in the French law. However, they are sometimes found in literal translations of the English word tribe to designate nomadic populations ruled by an organization of their own, depending on one or more chiefs of the said tribe. To translate this state of affairs, the term *population nomade*, nomadic population, is more appropriate in French. We also come across the term ethnicity, whose use is regularly contested in English and Spanish as well as in French, where it remains problematic (as for the term race, it is associated with the risk of hierarchization).

The term *autochtone* is therefore the one on which there is consensus. It also responds to the various concerns listed in the preamble, namely that the negative connotations on the historical level have been neutralized by the participation of the communities concerned in the choice of this term for use in international communication; it is not polysemous on the multilingual level; it comes from the ancient Greek, where its meaning is part of the history of Indo-European languages; it means "one who is attached to the land" – unlike indigenous, which emphasizes the fact of belonging to a lineage. Also worthy of note is the importance of the use of the plural, as in the United Nations Declaration on the Rights of Indigenous Peoples. This declaration is the result of the work of representatives of very diverse groups, for whom it is important not to be amalgamated. It is important to recall that while it is essential that an indigenous collective voice can be formed, this grouping is merely a step that helps make it possible to take up a position in relation to all states. As they regularly reiterate, their wish is to be called by their names.

Figure 7.1. *Poster for International Day of the World's Indigenous Peoples, 2020. The poster discusses the use of the term* autochtone *but how it is not part of Ludovic's identity. For a color version of this figure, see www.iste.co.uk/pinede/digital.zip*

7.2.2. Communities within a society

Finally, among the terms to designate all the individuals who share a heritage, we will focus on certain factors that make the difference between them. "People" has important legal implications, since it is a reference in international law to the "rights of peoples to self-determination", regularly reiterated in international texts, but these rights still struggle to be applied. In reality, some states avoid using the term, so as not to have to recognize the rights of certain communities. France has thus opted to substitute the term *population* in Article 72-3 of the Constitution[3].

Similarly, the designation of nation can also be misleading. Used in the title of international organizations such as the League of Nations (LoN) and then the United Nations (UN), it supposes the existence of a state. It is also used in a specific context to designate the Canadian Aboriginal communities. The wish expressed by the latter, moreover, is that the term First Nations replaces that of Indians or Amerindians[4].

It seems to us that this interest taken in ethnonymy finds an interesting echo in the conceptual pairing of community and society (Tönnies 2015) and in the main analyses that have been drawn from this pairing (Durkheim 2013; Weber 2015). Thus, for these late 19th-century thinkers and most of their contemporary readers, the indigenous minorities were organized as communities, as opposed to the Western or Westernized dominant populations which were organized as a society.

It is true that this concept is now outdated, but re-reading it can help us to apprehend the structural changes undergone by the institutional framework (Habermas 2002), from the local scale to the international scale. These terms can indeed be considered symbols at work in the world of communication (Habermas 2002) in the form of vectors of intercultural media interactions. By supporting or rejecting the use of these terms, indigenous minorities are reclaiming them and leading the majorities to interrogate their conception of intercultural dialogue.

Depending on the media usage of these terms in a particular context (especially colonization or genocide), some of them are weighted in a way that makes their usage problematic since it may impact the interpretation of the reader or speaker. Another problem arises from the circulation of terms between different languages. Special attention must therefore be paid to consideration of the enunciating body, the issue being whether identification with a community is a quality imposed from the outside or whether it is claimed and whether it is self-identification[5].

---

3 This is a provision added on 28 March 2003 concerning the recognition of overseas populations within the French people.

4 "Indian or Native American designations can be problematic, as some have a negative connotation and others (Indian in particular) have a particular legal meaning in Canada". Source: www.thecanadianencyclopedia.ca/fr/article/premieres-nations [Accessed 5 May 2021].

5 We translate self-identification here as *auto-identification*, although it is sometimes translated as a sense of belonging, as in ILO Convention No. 169 of 27 June 1989.

The role of self-determination in the choice of terms used to name, distinguish and ultimately identify oneself is crucial. It may be recalled that there are many examples of the names given to peoples by Westerners, which are actually pejorative terms in the language of those they designate. Throughout the 20th century, peoples were named by Western ethnologists and then renamed after consultation with those concerned. For example, the term Eskimo has been replaced by Inuit (Mailhot 1978); likewise, the Kaliña, peoples settled in South America, were until recently called Galibis (Collomb 2000), or the Lapps self-designated as Sami (Fagherazzi-Pagel 2010).

Thus, the main pitfalls in initiating a process of intercultural communication, that is, a framework of establishing intercultural contacts where each party positions itself in relation to the others (Vinsonneau 2012), are as follows: the use of a term with connotations arising from a particular usage at a given period; the use of an exogenous term, derived from an external language, without considering the endogenous meaning of this term for the people who coined this term; or the use of a term that is homographic or is the result of a literal translation. Hence, it seems that the main biases for the establishment of an adequate terminology can be neutralized, at least in part, by subscribing to an approach consisting of learning the history of the term (diachronic perspective) and the meaning it has acquired by the time of the analysis (synchronic perspective).

In a space of expression such as that of the Web, the issue of mastery of language, as one of the elements in this intercultural communication system, appears as a fundamental factor in defining cultural identity. The Web becomes an emerging whole on the principle of recursivity (Morin 1999) at work in the communicational process.

In the light of this review of the lexicon associated with the designation of indigenous minorities, we will now attempt to produce a summary review. The first element that underpins this collective identity is the relationship of domination experienced by these communities, often subjected against their will to states confronting the paradoxes of assimilationist ideology. The second element concerns the reasons behind this confrontation, namely their claims to be able to express a singular cultural identity, in particular through languages that themselves are a part of the heritage they aim to transmit. This "meta-ethnonymic" analysis allowed us to emphasize the importance of the role of states in these situations of intercultural communication, of states that are at liberty to recognize and validate the cultural identity of their citizens, the right to self-determination itself being prescribed in agreements between states and communities.

Faced with the alternative that the Web can represent a space of expression, we can ask ourselves to what extent the transition of the context of expression from physical space to online space can influence the balance of power between cultural majorities and minorities. Do the criteria used to define these communities retain their relevance on the Web? We will now see how conflicts related to the links between the definition of identity and territories, the latter being both a field of cultural expression and an element of this culture, can be transposed or potentially resolved on the Web.

7.3. Web access routes for indigenous minorities

In order to be able to identify the possibilities of representativity on the Web for indigenous minorities, we should look at the modalities of access to this space of expression. The Web being understood as one of the applications of the Internet, we will begin with an examination of the definition of this technical object as a prerequisite for accessing the Web.

7.3.1. *The Internet, a network of networks*

Endorsing here a definition of the Internet that is as accurate and as concise as possible, we note that it is a network infrastructure that links computers together on the basis of communication protocols (Serres 2000). We will focus on the technical and cultural origins of these three elements, the pillars of the Internet. Currently, the Internet relies on various technical connectivity solutions such as fixed and mobile telephone networks, fiber optics or satellite links. Access to the Internet, and ultimately to the Web, therefore requires a connection to a network infrastructure. At this level, disparities between major territorial masses can be observed, particularly in Africa or Central and Southern Asia (Wearesocial and Hootsuite 2020). A more detailed level of analysis also makes it possible to identify variances between regions of the same country. From degree of urbanization to average standard of living of the inhabitants, many factors contribute to the digital divide (Peugeot 2001; Ben Youssef 2004; Houzet and Grasland 2004; Methamen 2004; Rallet and Rochelandet 2004; Franco 2006).

When some regions are not covered by a wired network, the development of the mobile network can then compensate for this deficiency and can serve as a lever to support the development of Internet access (Kiyindou et al. 2015; Berrou and Mellet 2020). However, in both cases, establishing provision is dependent on measures that are subject to decision-making at the government level (Benhamou and Sorbier 2006; de La Coste 2006). In the case of the French overseas territories, it should be noted, for example, that while in 2020 4G coverage was improving for Guadeloupe, Martinique or Réunion, it was still very little developed in Guyana, where only 8% of the territory was covered by an operator, compared to 94% for metropolitan France (ARCEP 2021).

This situation is explained by the smaller sizes of the markets and meteorological and geographical conditions that differ from those of the mainland. Access to the Internet, whether via the wired network or the mobile telephone network, thus depends primarily on decisions taken by the public authorities. In fact, it is actually, on the one hand, the State that gives approval for operators to set up and, on the other hand, when a territory is of little interest to private investors, it is the public authorities that can complete the chain. In France, for example, the 2004 law for confidence in the digital economy (LCEN) introduced the possibility of setting up Public Initiative Networks (PINs). Local authorities can thus decide to take charge of the construction of the network and then make it available to telecommunications operators.

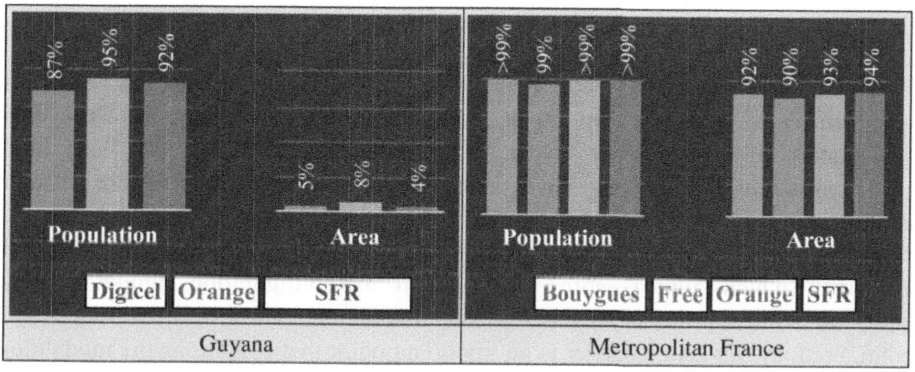

Figure 7.2. *4G coverage (source: ARCEP data, September 2021). For a color version of this figure, see www.iste.co.uk/pinede/digital.zip*

This situation has various implications for indigenous minorities. In the case of populations that have managed to obtain rights in the territories they occupy, this can give them a degree of autonomy in the development of the network infrastructure. However, factors of population density and territorial accessibility will have an impact on negotiations with private operators[6]. Moreover, cultural

6 In this regard, the shutdown of Google's Project Loon, tested in Puerto Rico, Peru and Kenya, is quite significant. These helium balloons were to fly over territories that were remote or had become difficult to access following a natural disaster to offer populations Internet access replacing fixed and mobile connections. After being tested from 2011 to 2019, the project was stopped for lack of profitability. Information on Project Loon: www.x.company/projects/loon/ [Accessed 15 September 2021].

specificities give rise to the need to adapt practices and set up a dialogue between community representatives and operators, a commitment that the latter are not always ready to make. For example, the Federal Communications Commission (FCC), the US telecommunications certification and regulatory body, set up an agreement in 2012, the Tribal Government Engagement Obligation, aimed at facilitating the setting up of a network across the reserves of indigenous communities in the United States. In 2019, the picture was still mixed, with most of the reserves having 10% coverage (Native Nations Communications Task Force 2019).

7.3.2. *Individual and collective equipment*

It is understood that the primary gateway to the Web is the gateway to Internet access. Once this step has been taken, the second main element to be considered is the question of equipment: access to a computer or mobile terminal.

For Internet access via a mobile phone device, the access process can be set out in a number of steps. Acquisition of the device, together with the purchase of a subscription or a prepaid card, depends on both access to a point of sale and sufficient purchasing power to cover these two items of expenditure, the fixed cost and the operating cost. But once this step has been taken, learning to use the device raises the principle of autonomy. While most smartphones are sold with a virtual keyboard (which allows more flexibility in its configuration, unlike models equipped with a physical keyboard) and a search engine already installed and configured, the language barrier is an important point that conditions the modalities of Web access, as we will see below, especially for speakers of minority languages.

For access via a computer, while investment in the device and the subscription can prove obstacles, it should be remembered that unlike a mobile phone, usage and costs can be shared between a number of users, within the family unit, for example (Lelong et al. 2004). Furthermore, Internet access via a computer does not require the user to own the equipment used. Thus, the use of collective equipment at a dedicated public access point (Houzet and Grasland 2004) inside public institutions (universities, libraries and employment agencies) or private institutions (cybercafes) is one of the levers identified to facilitate Internet access.

In addition to the economic aspect, these places generally offer support and guidance in using the equipment with a view to achieving autonomy (Raoul et al.

2004). Public institutions thus have a role in making access to the Web more widespread, technical skills being considered de facto as a "discriminating factor in participation" (Le Crosnier and Schafer 2011). The discovery and initiation phases can be supervised and supported by a support program. The value of these collective access points, despite having proved a success in Europe, must be qualified when rolled out in other geographical areas. We will cite as an example the Bluezones or Blue Points installed by the Bolloré Group in West Africa. In fact, these access points, far from reducing inequalities across a territory, have contrived to strengthen them, their installation being done at the expense of the development of individual access[7].

Where there is a connection point and a terminal, we can however note that the user can be exempted from acquiring certain intermediate skills. Upstream of access to Web interfaces such as browsers, search engines and websites, whether the equipment is for individual or collective, personal or public use, it should in any case be borne in mind that the TCP/IP protocol, which was imposed in preference to Open Systems Interconnection (Schafer 2014), enables a connection that does not require prior technical knowledge on the part of the user, in the same way as Ethernet, 3G, 4G and Wi-Fi technologies, which were designed to be interoperable.

Ultimately, if the geographical, financial or socio-cultural situation of the user has an influence on access to the Web, it is more of a brake than a block. But while the wide range of existing options in terms of access to devices make it possible to circumvent some obstacles, this does not solve the issue of network access, which remains a barrier to entry. The development of the Internet is in fact conditioned by power struggles and competing interests and raises geopolitical questions (de La Coste 2006), with control of the Web at stake.

7.3.3. *Web technologies, a Western heritage*

If the Internet represents the first level of the Web access system, the second level consists of the main Web technologies, Hypertext Markup Language (HTML), Uniform Resource Locator (URL) and Hypertext Transfer Protocol (HTTP) (Migayrou 2018). The markup language representing Web pages (HTML), the paths

7 The Bolloré Group's investments are subject to agreements with governments concerning, among other things, the Internet access market, which seem to aim to encourage a monopoly situation. See in particular the conclusions of the hearing of 26 February 2021 on corruption in Togo [Online]. Available at: www.lesechos.fr/industrie-services/services-conseils/corruption-au-togo-le-groupe-bollore-va-sacquitter-dune-amende-de-12-millions-deuros-1293925 [Accessed 15 September 2021].

to those pages (URLs) and the protocol enabling client-server communication (HTTP) is generally regarded as the "backbone" technologies of the Web. These three technologies are complementary, in the sense that the HTTP protocol allows circulation between various resources, identified by URLs, themselves structured in an HTML language. The articulation between these technologies makes it possible to navigate the Web, in other words to access resources. This articulation has been described in a number of documents (Berners-Lee 1989; Berners-Lee and Cailliau 1990; Berners-Lee and Connolly 1993) written and presented in the early 1990s.

A URL is an online resource locator tool. It takes the form of a string of characters for which a specific syntax applies, regulated by a technical standard. The first link corresponds to the HTTP communication protocol, which gives access to a Web server. After the protocol, we have the subdomain (www), the second-level domain name (the domain name) and the first-level domain name (extension). HTML is a language that makes it possible to structure the writing and reading of Web pages. While these technologies have been developed with the aim of democratizing access to knowledge, a number of observations on the influence of their cultural origins are necessary. First, the main contributors were Tim Berners-Lee, a British computer scientist; Robert Caillau, a Belgian computer engineer; and Daniel Connolly, an American computer scientist. The early research was developed at the European Center for Nuclear Research (CERN), located in France and Switzerland. The aim was to put forward technical solutions to improve information sharing between the various research teams communicating mainly in English.

The first community for which this tool was intended was therefore initially composed mainly of Western, European and American individuals, sharing an interest in computer science and using English to communicate. This was the kernel from which the Web gradually opened up to a wider audience. As for the syntax of HTML and URL technologies, and computer code in general, this is part of the history of programming, which uses English for the terms and abbreviations used. For example, CTRL stands for control in English, *contrôle* in French. This word is derived from the contraction of two Latin words, *contra* and *rotulus*. It also seems important to mention the page layout rationale, which assumes mastery of the Latin alphabet, practicing writing and reading horizontally from left to right, experience of the page concept (Grafton 2015) and so on, various points to which we will return later.

Finally, while the management of second-level domain names has been delegated to state institutions, the United States has retained the exclusive management of top-level domain names (we will expand on this point later). Looking at these elements, the issues of the cultural origins of the Web are taking shape. Although Web technologies are intended to be used by everybody, regardless of the community to which they belong, they nonetheless seem to be the product of Western or even Anglo-Saxon culture, insofar as digital culture is essentially textual.

7.3.4. *Governance and democracy*

In 1993, in order to encourage Web development and democratization, in the sense of popular participation, CERN surrendered all intellectual property rights, authorizing the use, duplication, modification and dissemination of the three components of Web software (Smith and Flückiger 2021). The following year, Tim Berners-Lee founded the World Wide Web Consortium (W3C), whose motto is "One Web Everywhere for Everyone". Initially housed at the Massachusetts Institute of Technology (MIT) and supported by DARPA, an agency of the United States Department of Defense, branches have gradually opened in different countries. Over the years, the organization has become quite complex, with the main governing bodies being, to summarize, MIT in the United States, ERCIM in Europe, Keio University in Japan and Beihang University in China. Its members are private IT companies and public research centers. Its mission is to check the compatibility of Web technologies to test and validate standards affecting the evolution of languages and document formats.

The role of the W3C is therefore of capital importance in the governance of the Web. The fact that most of its offices are located in Europe, the United States and Australia[8] does not plead in favor of the intercultural openness originally proclaimed. In 2009, a new structure dedicated to this theme, that is, promoting Web access for all, was created: the World Wide Web Foundation. But in 2021, it has to be said that it is not (yet?) in a position to offer sustainable solutions that are in line with its ambitions. Among the various projects, we can observe that the defense of minority rights is not approached from the angle of indigenous issues but through the prism of gender (the Women's Rights Online project for the defense of Web access for women, started in 2020) or individual rights (the Web We Want project initiated in 2013, for the freedom of expression)[9].

Alongside W3C, a number of institutions are involved in the governance of the Internet and thus have a major influence on the Web. These are the Internet Engineering Task Force (IETF), the Internet Architecture Board (IAB), the Internet

8 In 2021, of the 92 antennas, there are three in Asia (India, China, Korea), one in the Middle East (Kuwait), two in Africa (Morocco and Senegal) and one in South America (Brazil). Available at: www.w3.org/Consortium/Offices/Staff/ [Accessed 15 September 2021].

9 Available at: www.webfoundation.org/our-work/ [Accessed 15 September 2021].

Society (ISOC), the Internet Engineering Steering Group (IESG) and the Internet Corporation for Assigned Names and Numbers (ICANN). The first four form a group (ISOC controls IESG and IAB, IAB controls IETF). ISOC has nearly 70,000 members, representing 170 countries. But behind this apparent interculturality, we should not lose sight of the fact that it is an association under American law, founded by American engineers, led by Americans. We might add that Andrew Sullivan, who has been director since 2018, previously worked at ICANN, an institution long described as an "unidentified legal object" (Massit-Folléa 2012), being a private structure, under contract to the United States Department of Commerce up to 2016. Its role is to manage the root servers, that is, the five blocks corresponding to the geopolitical sectors of North America, South America, Europe, Africa and Asia-Pacific. It is thus at the head of a pyramid organization since it is from these entities that the management of domain names (DNS) is then delegated to national registries and private operators, who market them to end users, physical persons or legal entities.

While the nature of this current model of governance makes it apt to interrogate users, governments and the UN[10], does it have an impact on indigenous minorities? Using a few examples, we propose to illustrate some of the impacts stemming from the position occupied by the United States. First, we can cite the suspension by ICANN of the ".iq" domain belonging to Iraq, which was "returned" to it in 2005 (de La Coste 2006). First-level domain names, instrumentalized, thus emerged as a leading political issue. For indigenous minorities, this has no negative impact, and on the contrary this situation has encouraged the development of generic domain names, such as .org, which has been open to the whole world without restriction since 2019. Then, the Snowden affair caused ICANN to request independence and break the contract that tied the association to the U.S. government[11]. ICANN retains its prerogatives for the time being, but this example suggests that if it were to lose its

10 The UN, since 1947, has been responsible for the International Telecommunication Union (ITU) agency, the institution that is ICANN's main competitor (Massit-Folléa 2012).

11 In 2013, after Edward Snowden's revelations, the major players in Internet management, such as ICANN or W3C, signed the Montevideo Declaration on the Future of Internet Cooperation. Their representatives demanded emancipation from the American government in this declaration co-signed with nine other organizations. To recap, Edward Snowden was an American whistleblower, a computer scientist, formerly employed by the Central Intelligence Agency (CIA) and the National Security Agency (NSA). Through the media, he made public information about the existence of several American and British mass surveillance programs. Charged by the US government, he has been in exile in Russia since 2013. These events inspired the film *Snowden*, directed by Oliver Stone and released in 2016.

supremacy to another institution, clearly there would be a strong temptation for other States to seek to appropriate its missions.

In this example, it can also be pointed out that the international rivalries at play led to media coverage of this abuse of power and protection of the whistleblower. Could a deconcentration of powers and a reorganization of ICANN's missions at the national level help to ensure greater respect for freedom of expression in the long term? In most cases, it is to be feared that this will only aggravate the situation, as in China where Internet boundaries were designed by the government, with the support of foreign private companies such as Cisco, Google or Microsoft (Douzet 2007).

The fears of a Chinese independence, "creating an Internet of its own, obeying different rules and principles, and more easily lockable", "an autonomous system [that] would communicate with the rest of the Internet only through gateways necessary for the functioning of the Chinese economy" (de La Coste 2006) is already a reality. The fate in store for representatives of indigenous minorities engaged in Web-based activities that could be considered harmful to the regime is the same as that for the defenders of freedom of expression and human rights, such as Liu Xiaobo or Huang Qi, who were imprisoned, or Lhadon Tethong, who was expelled for his support of the Tibetan community (Wangkhang 2015).

It is to be feared that Web censorship more specifically affects indigenous minorities in regions where a situation of conflict already exists within the national territory. Among the various ways in which it is possible for States to block access to content, in addition to blocking certain websites such as social media platforms, we can point to slowing down the loading of pages by limiting the speed or simply temporary shutdowns. These usually affect the country or entire regions. But they can also be targeted, as in Sudan or Ethiopia[12] (Giles and Mwai 2020).

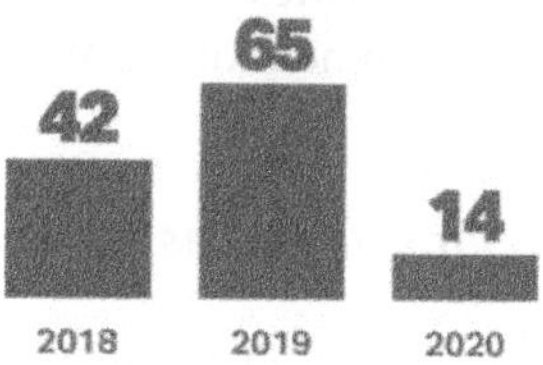

Figure 7.3. *Annual number of Internet shutdowns implemented by governments in the wake of social movements (source: KeepItOn annual report 2020)*

12 See in particular the shutdown in June 2020 in Ethiopia in response to the riots following the murder of Hachalu Hundessa, an activist from the Oromo indigenous minority. Available at: www.bbc.com/afrique/region-54793807 [Accessed 20 September 2021].

In these cases, the existence of a supranational body, even if it does not have the power to sanction or prevent blockages, would at least serve to ensure that indigenous minorities can be represented at the international level. Another remedy, alongside this, could be to benefit from the support of a non-governmental organization in investigating and rolling out circumvention solutions, such as the use of virtual private networks (VPNs), proxy configuration or the implementation of a keyword management strategy.

At present, even though Web technologies are considered "common property" (Le Crosnier and Schafer 2011; Musitelli 2014), access to the Web remains a national and international issue and an attribute of power for dominant communities. In terms of freedom of access in a dematerialized space, they reproduce the Western-style model of private property, a topic that has been high on the agenda for debate since the Internet Governance Forum in 2006. States' insistence on retaining "control over intellectual property within networks" and over "filtering and cybersecurity" (Le Crosnier and Schafer 2011) has long clouded the issue of indigenous minorities' freedom of expression on the Web in international debate. Moreover, while the importance of the issues to do with domain name ownership is still topical, the rise in power of another kind of major players in Web governance, such as search engines and social media, merits discussion.

7.4. Access strategies, from consultation to contribution

In spite of the central position occupied by cultural majorities in the governance and steering of the Web project, its accessibility for indigenous minorities is supported by the progressive implementation of services either dedicated to them or that they are able to appropriate. A number of examples of completed projects created for or by indigenous minorities will allow us to take stock of the opportunities for a democratic development of the Web.

7.4.1. *Google, openness to languages as an economic lever*

Among the major innovations that stud the history of the Web, search engines hold a place of honor. The transition from the manual referencing proposed by Yahoo! to the first full-text database search based on keywords in HTML pages created by AltaVista (Ifrah 2010) then opened the way for other refinements for finding relevant resources online, such as the results ranking system based on popularity rating: PageRank. Since 1998, this algorithm has gradually assured the

Google search engine of a quasi-monopoly in the world market, with the exception of China and Russia[13].

Google's global strategy, including financial and legal management and communication, is of course not unconnected to its success. Here, we will focus on the user interface and Google's interest in languages. It is no coincidence that the holding company created in 2015 to manage Google's various business activities was called Alphabet. Languages lie at the center of numerous projects. Examples include Google Books, a project to scan and OCR-ize books[14]. Like the search engine, the interface is configured to allow a search in 150 languages. Google Books also serves as the basis for the Ngram Viewer project, which generates graphical representations to illustrate the evolution of the frequency of use of a word or group of words. Google also offers a translation tool, Google Translate. Although teams are constantly working to improve translation equivalencies at the level of complex expressions, the approach of using English as the pivot language (the text is translated into English and then from English into the requested target language) (Poibeau 2016) affects the quality of translations. In fact, even though competitors such as DeepL offer more pertinent translations[15], Google Translate has two advantages: the application supports 109 languages (compared to 26 for DeepL) and its breakdown into modular form can be implemented on a website to generate an automatic translation of the pages. Finally, the design has been conceived to be as simple and streamlined as possible, as is the case for the search engine.

The benefits that indigenous minorities can derive from this application are obvious: we will simply add two nuances, namely the centrality of English in the method used and the fact that the quality of translations depends directly on the level of user participation. The user actually has a role to play in selecting, from the proposed terms, the one that seems to them to be the most correct in the context of the sentence. They can also add suggestions.

The Woolaroo app, currently being developed by Google Arts & Culture[16], is an app for preserving endangered languages. This is not a new idea; it had for example

13 Available at: www.gs.statcounter.com/search-engine-market-share/ [Accessed 20 September 2021].

14 *OCR-ize*: neologism formed from the acronym OCR, for "optical character recognition"

15 Available at: www.lemonde.fr/pixels/article/2017/08/29/quel-est-le-meilleur-service-de-traduction-en-ligne_5177956_4408996.html [Accessed 20 September 2021].

16 Link to the Woolaroo Project: www.woolaroo-project.appspot.com/woolaroo/intro/about [Accessed 20 September 2021]. Note: Google Arts & Culture is not dedicated specifically to supporting indigenous minorities, and Google has developed other projects that target them

already been developed in France with the website sorosoro.org, launched by the Chirac Foundation in 2009. But Google's experience in developing quality user interfaces and democratizing Web practices on mobile devices suggests that the project could take off rapidly. Although only 10 languages are currently supported (Louisiana Creole, Calabrian Greek, Maori, Nawat, Berber, Sicilian, Yang Zhuang, Rapa Nui, Yiddish and Yugambeh), the architecture, inspired by that of Wikipedia (see below), facilitates the addition of new languages.

7.4.2. *The role of social media in the formation of language communities on the Web*

Indigenous Tweets[17] is a website project by the researcher Kevin Scannell, which aims to connect speakers of minority languages. The interface is relatively simple: it consists of a table that lists a selection of languages. Launched in 2011, the website listed 35 minority languages. This list is growing steadily, with 185 in 2021. To begin with, for each language, a certain amount of data are shown: number of Twitter users who speak the language, number of tweets, most active user, number of posts by this "super-user" and finally the first user to have posted a tweet in this language. The table is dynamic, and it is possible to sort the results in ascending or descending order for the number of tweets, and in alphabetical order for languages and usernames. An additional level of detail can be obtained for each of the languages. By clicking on the corresponding row in the table, we obtain the list of Twitter users associated with this given language, the number of posts in this language and the percentage that these posts represent of their total activity on Twitter, the number of people who follow them and who they follow and the date of their most recent tweet. Finally, for each of these users listed as using a minority language on Twitter, there is a link to their account. Indigenous Tweets users thus have the opportunity to interact with speakers of the identified languages by following the link to their Twitter accounts.

This tool has two advantages. It makes it possible to obtain quantitative data on the use of minority languages on Twitter (number of speakers, number of tweets). But it also allows posters to be identified by giving useful information on their notoriety (number of "followers" and "following"), the proportion of their posts in a minority language compared to their total activity and the date of their most recent activity. Beyond an aggregation of data, suitable for "consultation" purposes, by making it possible to cross-reference these data, Indigenous Tweets acts as a

more directly. Google.org, a philanthropic foundation, is dedicated to sustainable development and supporting public services and SMEs in countries that seek their help.

17 Available at: www.indigenoustweets.com/ [Accessed 20 September 2021].

go-between to enable a user to identify a linguistic community and join it if appropriate. In this specific case, the contribution of Indigenous Tweets is not only informative. In addition to providing information on the existence of the use of certain languages, the user has the opportunity to use one of these languages. Indigenous Tweets plays a role in, if not strengthening, at least preserving the intangible cultural heritage (ICH) in one of its manifestations, that is, language (Diémoz 2013). As a factor of identification with a community, the use of a common language reinforces the feeling of belonging and slows down the acculturation process (de Lespinay 2016).

7.4.3. *Hypertext as an interlingual and intercultural gateway*

Indigenous Tweets and Woolaroo have points in common with the Wikipedia project[18], which offers two levels of use, a "consultation" level and a "contribution" level. When using Wikipedia, the user can thus identify with a community of users through the intermediary of sharing of a common language by consulting resources in that language. Second, the user can then contribute to the preservation of the cultural heritage by creating pages, adding comments or making changes to an existing page. In addition, the website implements a judicious use of hypertext links, which offer several levels of navigation. Classic navigation on the one hand, intra-linguistic, leads to a deepening of knowledge on the principle of the network of associations between articles, as Vannevar Bush imagined it for Memex (Bush 1945). This model brings with it the possibility of inter-linguistic navigation, since the permanence of the page structure makes it possible to maintain the overall coherence and user recognition of the blocks of information.

Thus, in these three projects, the identification of user communities who are speakers of minority languages is supported by a quite simple, streamlined system. There are different access pathways to the pages, making it easier for users to connect with the content, or even with other users. In the case of Indigenous Tweets and Wikipedia, it should be added that the pages are indexed and they are accessible from a search engine, so it is much easier to access the contents. But it is also possible to enter through the portal of these websites, whose simplified design makes it possible to quickly understand it and learn to use it. Although their designers are from the Anglo-Saxon culture, the amount of English language in the interface is reduced almost to the domain name and the title of the project.

These three projects are evidence of the status of English as a pivot language, unavoidable due to the position it occupies at the interface level. Its role as a bridge

18 Available at: www.fr.wikipedia.org/ [Accessed 20 September 2021].

between cultures is rooted in a tradition inherited, as seen previously, from Web governance, but is also explained by a deeper legacy, that of computer programming and especially the conception of the input system.

7.4.4. *Computer code, a key to Web access*

As mentioned above, programming languages are directly inherited from the culture of the earliest computer engineers, and it is within this community that the use of English has been democratized. English, as the working language, has carved out for itself the leading position in the product of their work, itself conditioned by their input tool, the keyboard.

The configuration of computer keyboards was not originally based, let us remember, on intrinsic qualities but on an accumulation of learning and networking effects (Flichy 1998), like so many cultural factors. The design of keyboards for computing was based on the mode of use of the "typewriter" object. However, the hardware constraints that led to the QWERTY or AZERTY arrangement of keys were no longer relevant when applied to the computer domain, since the main concern of keyboard manufacturers in the 19th century was to reduce the frequency of collisions between type bars (David 1998). Thus, the average number of keys, their arrangement in rows and their placement gradually became standard with the development of the practice of shorthand typing. However, alternatives have been proposed, such as Douglas Engelbart's chorded keyboard in the 1960s (Bardini 1998), but have not managed to usurp this design that is the legacy of typing habits. These habits, supported by the provision of the central unit-screen-mouse-keyboard kit first in the work context and then in the home context, have enshrined the adoption of keyboards designed in a way that defies common sense but in a kind of blind loyalty to an object that has ended up as part of the heritage.

In this long series of chain reactions, the creation of the American Standard Code for Information Interchange (ASCII) is a major step. ASCII is a character encoding that dates back to the 1960s. It consists of 128 characters encoded in 7 bits, 95 of which are printable, distributed as follows: the 26 letters of the Latin alphabet in lowercase and uppercase, the figures 0–9 and some mathematical symbols and punctuation marks. Although ASCII only enables comprehensive writing in English, this computerized alphabet has nevertheless become the subject of a standard and then an international standard, ISO 646 (Baste 2002).

Partially resolved by the adoption of Unicode in the 1990s, ASCII's monopoly position greatly impacted the circulation of apps and documents written in other alphabets. It is also at the origin of the generalization of practices that have direct consequences on the practice of writing since it is this standard that has long defined, and still partially defines, file names, URLs and email addresses[19]. Indeed, as Ben Henda (2014) reminds us, it was not until the 1980s that researchers and industrialists began to pay attention to “linguistic balance in the digital world”.

In an attempt to remedy the widespread use of English as an input language, a number of solutions exist. Inspired by the work of August Dvorak, many working groups have proposed their versions of key arrangements optimized to their alphabet, such as de-ergo for German, DAS for Finnish and BEPO for French. However, the input device must be capable of adapting to these layouts. For several years, customizable keyboards have been marketed, such as the Nemeio, offered by the company LDLC from 2020. E Ink screens allow each key of this keyboard to be reversibly customized.

This leaves the question of the number of keys, which can be limiting for some alphabets. To address this problem, the widespread use of touch screens with the adoption of smartphones and tablets could have led manufacturers to simply offer software customization of keyboards. But most of the time, it is the app providers who offer their own built-in keyboard interface. If we add to this the restricted size of the smartphone screen, we understand why Arabic-speaking or Chinese-speaking communities have developed cultural poaching techniques (de Certeau 1990). We can cite the creation of Franco-Arabic or Arabizi, born from the Romanization of Arabic, mainly used for discussion on social media, or the generalization of voice messages and intuitive typing in Asiatic countries.

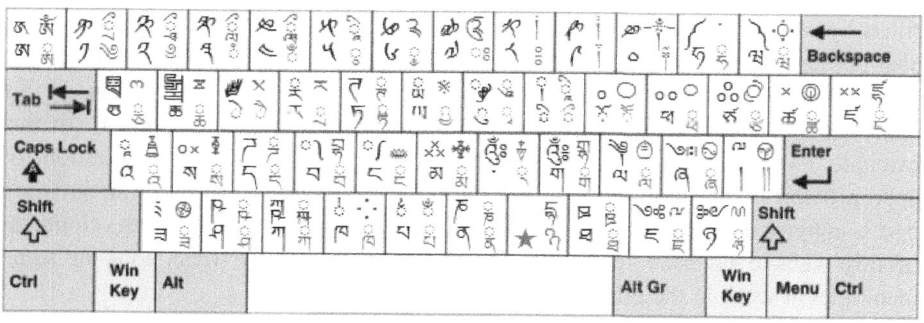

Figure 7.4. Tibetan keyboard layout. For a color version of this figure, see www.iste.co.uk/pinede/digital.zip

19 The first URL in non-Latin characters was to be created in 2010 (Ben Henda 2014). For technical details, see RFC 6530: www.datatracker.ietf.org/doc/html/rfc6530 [Accessed 20 September 2021].

7.4.5. *"Never again without us", systems designed by indigenous minorities*

The Mukurtu Content Management System (CMS) resulted from a collaboration between the Warumungu Aboriginal community and researcher Kimberley Christen (Christen 2005). The team's objective was to develop a solution for administering the community's digitized heritage, a solution that had to be aligned with the Warumungu culture. Indeed, in the classic approach to website design, navigation is planned in such a way as to simplify access to content. The view taken is that the speed with which the user can find a resource is a guarantee of quality. But in the Warumungu culture, to access content, the user must be identified by gender, age and relationship to the community (are they a member of the community or not? what place do they occupy within it?). Access is conditional upon a number of parameters, some relating to the visitor's identity and others being external factors such as the time of year or geographical location.

The Mukurtu CMS was therefore designed to meet specific needs, and the team achieved the feat of coordinating the response to these needs through integration into the Web system, while also enabling a variant of the tool and facilitating its reappropriation by other communities[20]. The website design work has been analyzed from both a technical and a cultural point of view. The CMS architecture has been designed for an optimal articulation of these three levels: database, administrator–controller interface and visitor interface.

One function thus allows the administrator to manage access rights by applying filters by content or for a selection of content, for a given period, and reversibly. It is also possible to use the same basis to develop various websites, private or public pages. Attention has been paid to ensuring content integrity, in the event of this content being exploited by third parties (simplified addition of metadata). In this example, we see that particular care has been taken over the question of appropriation of the tool, but also the question of autonomy. In fact, the software part is copyright-free, but training is offered to learn how to use it. The development of this website creation tool was an opportunity to take a fresh look at some ideologies at work in the principles of website design.

These are in fact developed to serve two objectives: the sharing but also the protection of resources that, as soon as they are published on the Web, become common property. However, this ideology of open access, championed by the Web pioneers in order to oppose it being turned into a commodity or privatized, may in

20 Mainly in the United States and Canada. See the list at www.mukurtu.org/showcase.

some cases amount to a form of domination over the cultural heritage of indigenous minorities. The World Heritage of Humanity and the public domain are amalgamated and hailed as progress, a goal to be achieved for all humanity, while part of humanity has not been consulted on whether it intends to endorse it (Martin 2018).

7.5. Conclusion

Over the past three decades, declarations in support of a Web open to all have proliferated. However, the implementation of this project and the fight against discrimination for access to this space of expression make it necessary to give consideration to the complexity of this system, which is made up of a great many levels (Brondizio 2013). Encouraging the publication of information on its functioning, at least on the technical level and as far as possible on its governance, may prove judicious because by having an informed vision of the functioning of this system and the role played in it by private and public actors, some barriers to entry for indigenous minorities could be lifted.

In order to be able to express their identity and envisage appropriating these tools and this space of communication, some knowledge of the identity and culture of those who created them and who exercise their power over them seems to be a prerequisite that current infrastructures could help to bring about. By combining generalist tools for the publication of contributory and multilingual content, such as Wikipedia, and for connecting people on the basis of the sharing of information around common interests, such as Twitter, customized design tools such as Mukurtu and input devices that are technically and culturally interoperable, a number of conditions could be met to achieve a mesh supporting the construction of a common space of expression. If the universal dimension of the Web is to be relativized (Lenoble-Bart and Damome 2014), the challenge is to try to maintain a coherence and a balance between autonomous areas connected by gateways, access being conditioned by the acquisition of "vehicular" technical and linguistic skills, guaranteeing a form of intercultural linkage.

7.6. References

Abu Ramadan, M. (2016). La définition des minorités en droit international. In *Minorité et communauté en religion*, Obadia, L., Zwilling, A. (eds). Strasbourg University Press, Strasbourg.

ARCEP (2021). Mesures de qualité de service. Qualité de service mobile (S2 2020). Autorité de régulation des communications électroniques et des Postes, Paris [Online]. Available at: https://www.arcep.fr/fileadmin/user_upload/grands_dossiers/qualite-services-mobiles/Fiche-QoS-outre-mer_mars_2021.pdf [Accessed 15 April 2021].

Baste, S. (2002). Enjeux de la normalisation internationale de la numérisation des écritures et langue française, appropriation d'Unicode. *Digital document*, 3(3–4), 255–284.

Bellier, I. (2018). Les droits des peuples autochtones : entre reconnaissance internationale, visibilité nouvelle et violations ordinaires. *L'Homme & la Société*, 206(1), 137–174.

Bellier, I. (2020). L'Europe et les droits des peuples autochtones. *Ethnologie française*, 50, 513–528.

Ben Henda, M. (2014). Langues en danger et multilinguisme numérique. In *Les oubliés de l'Internet. Cultures et langues sur l'Internet oubli ou déni ?* Laulan, A.M., Lenoble-Bart, A. (eds). Les Etudes hospitalières, Bordeaux.

Ben Youssef, A. (2004). Les quatre dimensions de la fracture numérique. *Réseaux*, 5(5–6), 181–209.

Benhamou, B. and Sorbier, L. (2006). Souveraineté et réseaux numériques. *Politique étrangère*, 3(3), 519–530.

Berners-Lee, T. (1989). Information management: A proposal. Report, CERN [Online]. Available at: https://cds.cern.ch/record/2665088 [Accessed 15 April 2021].

Berners-Lee, T. and Cailliau, R. (1990). WorldWideWeb. Proposal for a HyperText Project. Report, CERN [Online]. Available at: http://cds.cern.ch/record/2639699/files/Proposal_Nov-1990.pdf [Accessed 15 April 2021].

Berners-Lee, T., Cailliau, R., Groff, J.-F., Pollermann, B. (1992). World Wide Web: The information universe. *Internet Research*, 2(1), 52–58.

Berners-Lee, T. and Connolly, D. (1993). Hypertext Markup Language (HTML). A representation of textual information and metainformation for retrieval and interchange. Report, CERN, Atrium, IEEE Group [Online]. Available at: https://www.w3.org/MarkUp/draft-ietf-iiir-html-01.txt [Accessed 15 April 2021].

Berrou, J. and Mellet, K. (2020). Une révolution mobile en Afrique subsaharienne ? *Réseaux*, 1(1), 11–38.

Bizeul, Y. (2016). Réflexions sur le phénomène minoritaire. In *Minorité et communauté en religion*, Obadia, L., Zwilling, A. (eds). Strasbourg University Press, Strasbourg.

Brondizio, E., Ostrom, E., Young, O. (2013). Connectivité et gouvernance des systèmes socio-écologiques multiniveaux : le rôle du capital social. *Management & avenir*, 7(7), 108–140.

Bush, V. (1945). As we may think. *Atlantic Monthly*, 176(1), 101–108.

de Certeau, M. (1990). *L'Invention du quotidien. 1 : Arts de faire.* Gallimard, Paris.

Christen, K. (2005). Gone digital. Aboriginal remix and the cultural commons. *International Journal of Cultural Property*, 12(3), 315–345.

Collomb, G. and Tiouka, F. (2000). *Na'na Kali'na. Une histoire des Kali'na en Guyane.* Ibis Rouge, Matoury.

David, P. (1998). Comprendre les aspects économiques de QWERTY : la contrainte de l'histoire. *Networks*, 16(87), 5–6.

Diémoz, F. (2013). Langue et "patrimoine" immatériel. *Études de lettres*, 2(1), 143–166.

Douzet, F. (2007). Les frontières chinoises de l'Internet. *Hérodote*, 125, 127–142.

Durkheim, E. (2013). Communauté et société selon Tönnies, *Sociologie*, 2(4) [Online]. Available at: http://journals.openedition.org/sociologie/1820 [Accessed 15 April 2021].

Fagherazzi-Pagel, H. (2010). Sauvegarder la culture des Samis, plus grand peuple autochtone d'Europe. *Recherches Arctiques, Actualités de la recherche scientifique*. Inist-CNRS [Online]. Available at: http://recherchespolaires.inist.fr/?Sauvegarder-la-culture-des-Samis,541 [Accessed 15 April 2021].

Flichy, P. (1998). Présentation. *Réseaux*, 16(87), 5–6.

Franco, R. (2006). La fracture numérique : diagnostic et parades. *Politique étrangère*, 3(3), 531–544.

Gergaud, S. (2016). De l'usage des termes "indigène" et "autochtone". Groupe international de travail pour les peuples autochtones [Online]. Available at: http://delaplumealecran.org/IMG/pdf/indigeneautochtone.pdf [Accessed 15 April 2021].

Giles, G. and Mwai, P. (2020). Où et comment les gouvernements bloquent ils Internet ? [Online]. Available at: https://www.bbc.com/afrique/region-54793807 [Accessed 30 April 2021].

Grafton, A. (2015). *La page, de l'antiquité à l'ère du numérique.* Editions Hazan, Paris.

Guissou, B. (2002). Histoire et pauvreté au Burkina Faso. In *La pauvreté, une fatalité. Promouvoir l'autonomie et la sécurité humaine des groupes défavorisés*, UNESCO (ed.). Karthala, Paris.

Habermas, J. (1998). *L'intégration républicaine. Essais de théorie politique.* Fayard, Paris.

Habermas, J. (2002). *La technique et la science comme "idéologie".* Gallimard, Paris.

Houzet, S. and Grasland, L. (2004). Les dimensions spatiales de la fracture numérique en France. *Réseaux*, 5(5–6), 115–140.

Ifrah, L. (2010). Histoire des moteurs de recherche. In *L'information et le renseignement par Internet*, Ifrah, L. (ed.). Presses universitaires de France, Paris.

Kiyindou, A., Anaté, K., Capo-Chich, A. (eds) (2015). *Quand l'Afrique réinvente la téléphonie mobile.* L'Harmattan, Paris.

de La Coste, P. (2006). La gouvernance internationale de l'Internet. *Politique étrangère*, 3(3), 507–518.

Le Crosnier, H. and Schafer, V. (2011). Gouvernance et neutralité de l'internet. In *La neutralité de l'internet : un enjeux de communication*, Le Crosnier, H., Schafer, V. (eds). CNRS Éditions, Paris.

Lelong, B., Thomas, F., Ziemlicki, C. (2004). Des technologies inégalitaires : l'intégration de l'internet dans l'univers domestique et les pratiques relationnelles. *Réseaux*, 5(5–6), 141–180.

Lenoble-Bart, A. and Damome, E. (2014). Cultures minoritaires au risque de l'oubli en ligne. In *Les oubliés de l'Internet. Cultures et langues sur l'Internet oubli ou déni ?* Laulan, A.M., Lenoble-Bart, A. (eds), Les Etudes hospitalières, Bordeaux.

de Lespinay, C. (2016). Les concepts d'autochtone (indigenous) et de minorité (minority). *Droit et cultures*, 72, 19–42.

MacLuhan, M. (2004). *Pour comprendre les médias*. Le Seuil, Paris.

Mailhot, J. (1978). L'étymologie de "Esquimau" revue et corrigée. *Études Inuit Studies*, 2(2), 59–69.

Marquardt, S. (1991). La protection des minorités en droit international. In *La Question kurde*, Picard, E. (ed.). Éditions Complexe, Paris.

Martin, C.M. (2018). Le système Mukurtu : une ouverture sur l'interculturel. *Hermès*, 3(3), 238–243.

Massit-Folléa, F. (2012). La gouvernance de l'Internet. Une internationalisation inachevée. *Le Temps des médias*, 1(1), 29–40.

Merzeau, L., Le Crosnier, H., Denis, V., Picard, J., Juanals, B., Mercier, S. (2010). Une nouvelle dimension de l'information. *Documentaliste – sciences de l'information*, 1(1), 32–41.

Methamem, R. (2004). Note critique sur les indicateurs de la fracture numérique. *Réseaux*, 5(5–6), 211–229.

Migayrou, F. (ed.) (2018). *Coder le monde*. Editions du Centre Pompidou/Editions HYX, Paris.

Morin, E. (1999). Science et conscience de la complexité. In *L'Intelligence de la complexité*, Morin E., Le Moigne, J.-L. (eds). L'Harmattan, Paris.

Musitelli, J. (2014). La Convention de 2005 sur la diversité culturelle au défi du numérique. In *Les oubliés de l'Internet. Cultures et langues sur l'Internet oubli ou déni ?* Laulan, A.M., Lenoble-Bart, A. (eds). Les Etudes hospitalières, Bordeaux.

Native Nations Communications Task Force (2019). Improving and increasing broadband deployment on tribal lands. Report to the Federal Communications Commission [Online]. Available at: https://www.fcc.gov/sites/default/files/nnctf_tribal_broadband_report.pdf [Accessed 15 April 2021].

Organisation internationale du travail (1957). Convention relative aux populations aborigènes et tribales [Online]. Available at: https://www.ilo.org/dyn/normlex/en/f?p=1000:12100:0::NO::P12100_INSTRUMENT_ID,P12100_LANG_CODE:312252,fr:NO [Accessed 15 April 2021].

Peugeot, V. (2001). L'internet citoyen : de la fracture numérique au projet de société. *Les Cahiers du numérique*, 3(3), 163–184.

Poibeau, T. (2016). Traduire sans comprendre ? La place de la sémantique en traduction automatique. *Langages*, 1(1), 77–90.

Rallet, A. and Rochelandet, F. (2004). La fracture numérique : une faille sans fondement ? *Réseaux*, 5(5–6), 19–54.

Raoul, B., Benrahhal, Z., Guignard, T. (2004). Le cybercentre comme lieu : un "espace public" à l'épreuve des pratiques d'usagers. *Réseaux*, 5(5–6), 297–325.

Ricciardi, F. (2019). Travail indigène / travail colonial. L'invention du "travail indigène". In *Les zones grises des relations de travail et d'emploi. Un dictionnaire sociologique*, Bureau, M.C., Corsani, A., Giraud, O., Rey, F. (eds). Editorial Teseo, Buenos Aires [Online]. Available at: https://www.teseopress.com/dictionnaire/ [Accessed 15 September 2021].

Rigoni, I. (2010). Éditorial. Les médias des minorités ethniques. Représenter l'identité collective sur la scène publique. *Revue européenne des migrations internationales*, 26(1), 7–16.

Ringelheim, J. (2018). Nommer les groupes discriminés pour mieux combattre la discrimination : la fin d'un tabou ? *Recherche & formation*, 3(3), 83–94.

Schafer, V. (2014) Histoire et oubli : la place de la diversité linguistique et culturelle dans l'histoire d'Internet. In *Les oubliés de l'Internet. Cultures et langues sur l'Internet oubli ou déni ?* Laulan, A.M., Lenoble-Bart, A. (eds). Les Etudes hospitalières, Bordeaux.

Serres, A. (2000). Aux sources d'Internet : l'émergence d'ARPANET. Exploration du processus d'émergence d'une infrastructure informationnelle. Description des trajectoires des acteurs et actants, des filières et des réseaux constitutifs de la naissance d'ARPANET. Problèmes critiques et épistémologiques posés par l'histoire des innovations. PhD Thesis, Université Rennes 2, Rennes.

Smith, T. and Flückiger, F. (2021). Les versions publiques du logiciel du web [Online]. Available at: https://home.cern/fr/science/computing/birth-web/icensing-web [Accessed 15 April 2021].

Tönnies, F. (2010). *Communauté et société*. PUF, Paris.

Vinsonneau, G. (2012). *Mondialisation et identité culturelle*. De Boeck Supérieur, Louvain-la-Neuve.

Wangkhang, R. (2015). Renforcer le numérique au Tibet : un entretien avec l'activiste Lhadon Tethong [Online]. Available at: https://ifex.org/fr/renforcer-le-numerique-au-tibet-un-entretien-avec-lactiviste-lhadon-tethong/ [Accessed 30 April 2021].

Warnier, J.-P. (2017). *La mondialisation de la culture*. La Découverte, Paris.

Wearesocial, H. (2021). Digital 2020. Global digital overview [Online]. Available at: https://wearesocial.com/digital-2020 [Accessed 30 April 2021].

Weber, M. (1995). *Economie et société.* Pocket, Paris.

8

Cultural and Political Anchors of Environmental Communication on the Web

Sandra MELLOT[1], Anh Ngoc HOANG[2], Magali PRODHOMME[2] and Anaïs THEVIOT[2]

[1] *ESMA, CinéCréatis Nantes, France*

[2] *CHUS, Université Catholique de l'Ouest, Angers, France*

8.1. Introduction

The proliferation of environmental non-governmental organizations (NGOs) can be linked to the transition from a materialist society to a post-industrial society: while "past" militancy focused more on the redistribution of wealth and materialist demands (increase in wages, for example), the "new" militants have more expressive or qualitative, post-materialist demands, focusing more on the quality of life, identities and so on. Charnovitz (2002) has shown that NGOs have occupied a determining political position from the 1920s onward and have aligned themselves with the "May '68" movements on issues relating to the defense of human rights (abolition of modern slavery, evolution of the rights of women, minorities, etc.). The "newness" of the themes is also accompanied by a "newness" in the organizational structures of the militant collectives. We can say that we have gone from a pyramidal and hierarchical structure – a characteristic of political parties or trades unions – to a networking operation, more horizontal, associated with the concept of deliberation. However, today there is much criticism of the professionalization of NGOs which, under the pretext of environmental or humanitarian emergencies,

Digital Presences of Organizations,
coordinated by Nathalie PINÈDE, Luc MASSOU and Patrick MPONDO-DICKA.

impose an efficiency criterion that may contradict the primary ambition to develop less pyramidal organizations (Freyss 2004).

NGOs have always sought to communicate to raise awareness of their actions and the causes they support. The humanitarian message is generally presented as belonging to three different registers:

> A political discourse that recalls the values and principles of humanitarian action; an expert discourse that situates the action in its geopolitical or medical environment; a compassionate discourse that showcases the action through the victims. (Maillard 2010, p. 68)

However, it is complex to account for these three registers in an online article, referring at the same time to the writing style that is effective on digital tools, which sets out to be more synthetic and simplified, with the emphasis on images. Moreover, Fouchard (2010) has stressed that accounting for these three registers in more in-depth and complex articles is not necessarily effective in appealing for donations. Brauman (2010, p. 155) thus speaks of the "consensual spirit that essentially characterizes humanitarian communication mindful of the need to present clear situations, even if that comes at the cost of sometimes misleading simplifications". We can differentiate between a number of communication techniques that are used:

> Advocacy, which seeks to speak out in the public space and to act in the political arena; fundraising, which seeks to ensure the funding of the organization; and publicity, which seeks to raise the organization's profile. The same action can of course act in all three directions at the same time. (Bruno et al. 2020, p. 53)

The objective is to give visibility to the cause to be supported in order to raise public awareness and make the audience want to make a financial commitment to support the actions of the NGO. The politician Charles Tilly speaks of "repertoires of collective actions" (Tilly 1984) to stress that the means of action are not all utilized in the same way depending on the group being mobilized, its history, the institution under scrutiny, the political context, the funding possibilities, the skills of those being mobilized and so on. He also highlights the historical evolution of modes of protest by distinguishing two major repertoires of action: from 1600 to 1848, "localized and patronized" (having recourse to a mediator via a man of the Church or the State) and from 1848 to 1986, "national and autonomous" (developed through unions formed from among the protestors themselves). Nowadays, we could add to this typology another level of mobilization, with the struggles becoming both localized and internationalized. These would then be international repertoires (with, for example, inter-globalist forums) promoting expertise. As Massiah (2002) points out, since the early 1990s, NGOs have become widely internationalized and have carried out targeted mobilization campaigns: cancellation of the debt of poor countries, reforms of financial institutions and so on.

With the advent of the Internet, NGO activists have a new tool to share their actions without going through the media. Activists are thus encouraged to tweet, post comments on online forums, repost messages on their Facebook account, make videos and disseminate them to as wide an audience as possible on YouTube and so on. The issue is thus not to set online activism against offline activism. Ollitrault (2015) points to the weight of the political context in which engagement takes place and the risks incurred under certain regimes "as much for having been cyber activists as for having demonstrated in the streets" (p. 83). Thus, the political and social context is a determining marker of the forms taken by engagement. The socially established "expectations" of what engagement represents – "French Touch" engagement for example – steer the forms of mobilization:

> French NGOs have a brand image that they want to preserve, based on intense and disinterested engagement, in short the volunteer profile of the 1901 Law on Associations. However, these new ways of engaging in virtual communities, of getting organized in a network structure in order to respond to a blatant injustice, can disrupt NGOs that have their own networks of actors, their textbooks of action that, what is more, tell them to literally "work up a sweat". (Ollitrault 2015, p. 84)

It seems clear that humanitarian organizations cannot bypass, as Ollitrault (2015) points out, "this morphological change in individual engagement. Even if one is a citizen before being an activist, if one does not fit the pattern of the typical ideals of collective action (especially in terms of duration), one takes up positions, including emotionally, that NGOs can channel and then pursue to their advantage" (p. 87).

Digital activism is not a substitute for work on the ground. On the contrary, the use of the Web makes it possible to showcase and publicize militant activity on the ground. It can also give more power and legitimacy to a movement, using Web metrics (number of fans, followers) to highlight the number of supporters. The strength of numbers is thus used to emphasize the collective and its rise in power (or even its representativity compared to other opposing groups). We can see this clearly with online petitions, which make it possible to give a strong visibility to causes that could not have benefited from the same media coverage offline without this strength of the number of signatories, maximized in some cases by their popularity. Digital technology can also be a starting point for the struggle itself, especially in authoritarian regimes: this is what Badouard (2013) calls "keyboard mobilizations", in other words the opportunity for a collective to give substance to a mobilization via hypertext links and potentially to then structure it. These online mobilizations often go beyond cyberspace to take substance in the public space, or vice versa[1].

To understand the specific political and cultural anchors of these online mobilizations, we will analyze the setting of a digital co-enunciative space, in the sense of a meeting place, of dialogue between actors and individuals, configured by the "traditional" NGOs in the environmental battle (Greenpeace and WWF) and recent collectives (L'Affaire du Siècle, On est Prêt). We chose Greenpeace and WWF because their actions are widely disseminated and familiar to citizens, giving them an emblematic status in the environmental battle. We put these familiar speeches into perspective with other discourses, other ways of engaging that have gained a higher profile through collectives such as L'Affaire du Siècle, and personalities such as Camille Étienne, member of On est Prêt and Pensée Sauvage. What ethos, what cultural and social anchors, can be discerned in the analysis of visibility strategies and the rhetoric developed in these environmental messages, enabling citizens to become engaged in a meaningful universe corresponding to their values?

8.2. Methodological approach: analysis of the ecological ethos in a digital regime

Our multimodal semiotic analysis of the websites and video clips disseminated on the Web by these collectives is based on the concept of ethos in order to highlight the construction of ecological values in a digital regime. It is important to point out at the outset that despite its common usage, the word ethos conveys both lexical ambiguity and conceptual ambiguity. As Cornilliat and Lockwood (2000) remind us,

1 Nor is it a question of believing that the Internet gives rise to causes *ex nihilo*: the "Arab Spring" has often been wrongly referred to as a "Facebook revolution", making the rise of social media the main cause of the triggering of such protest movements. Subsequently, it was shown that the online mobilizations relied upstream on well-structured offline underground networks. Digital technology then made it possible to publicize the mobilization, go beyond these militant groups and organize online the action on the ground.

transcribed in French in various orthographic forms (èthos, éthos, êthos, ethos, ithos), the word of Greek origin tends to be confused between ethos (with a short e), which means a custom or a habit, and ethos (with a long e), which means the disposition or character that results from it or creates it. This etymological confusion naturally leads to the difficulty of distinguishing "between the 'real' ethical character of man and the way in which he habitually presents himself, particularly through his discourse" (pp. 9–10). Thus, it seems important to us to clarify the meaning of the term ethos that we adopt in our study. No doubt it is good to remind ourselves first of all of the way in which Aristotle himself defines the rhetorical ethos in his *Rhetoric*:

> We persuade by character (= *ethos*) when the discourse is held in such a way as to make the speaker worthy of trust; in fact we trust good people more quickly, and more, on all subjects in general, and completely, on questions which do not involve certainty, but leave room for doubt (Aristotle, *Rhetoric*, 1356, quoted by Maingueneau 2002, p. 2).

It is therefore a question of "proof by ethos" which "consists in making a good impression, by the way one constructs one's discourse, in giving an image of oneself capable of convincing the audience by gaining its trust" (Maingueneau 2002, p. 1). It is part of the triangle of ancient rhetoric – "we teach by arguments; we move by passions; we insinuate ourselves by mores", to use a formula of Gibert (18th century): the arguments correspond to the *logos*, the passions to the *pathos*, the mores to the *ethos* (Maingueneau 2002).

For our part, following Maingueneau's (2002) work, we choose to situate the ethos in a discourse analysis framework, which allows us, "beyond persuasion by arguments", to "reflect on the more general process of the affiliation of subjects to a certain positioning" (p. 7). In fact, Maingueneau (2014) concludes by pointing out that ethos refers to "a simple, intuitive reality, that of a phenomenon that is coextensive with any use of language: the recipient necessarily constructs a representation of the speaker through what the latter says and their way of saying it" (p. 46). Indeed, the recipient constructs "the figure of a guarantor endowed with physical properties (corporeality) and psychological properties (character) on the basis of a diffuse set of social representations evaluated positively or negatively, of stereotypes that the enunciation helps to reinforce or transform" (Maingueneau 2002, p. 32).

The identification of the ethos becomes more complex on the Web because it is "exploded" and "distributed" in the digital system that has multiple contributors, spaces and modalities. Maingueneau (2016b) states that on a website, "even the possibility of relating this or that page to the ethos of a source becomes uncertain, as the number of contributors on a website is potentially so high". For the author, "it is the consequence of the fact that the specifically verbal ethos loses its importance, in favor of a global ethos, much hazier, which surpasses the characterizations in terms of speaker and individual text" (paragraphs 17 and 18).

In our analysis, we take into account these two dimensions of the ethos on the Web: the global ethos considered by the editorial positioning of actors in the Web strategy and the ethos embodied in the rhetoric developed in the specific media of online videos. Our analysis is enriched from these two approaches.

On the one hand, we perform an analysis of co-enunciation strategies on the Web: what is the design and the editorial positioning of actors in environmental mobilization? Beyond website analysis, it is an explosion in distributed spaces on platforms that is at play on the Web. This ecological ethos invites participation in a world whose modalities of meeting and participating are configured in part by the system itself. Jeanneret (2007) has pointed out, in several analyses, the anticipation of practices at the moment when a system is designed: "The creation of the software and these successive refinements always proceed from a writing of practices" (p. 328). Such a concept of the signs of editorial enunciation refers to the notion of "configuration of practical scenes through design" for Pignier (2014) or "depiction of anticipation of practices" within the system for Saemmer (2016).

The digital strategies of the actors in environmental engagement draw social and cultural constructs (Jeanneret 2011, p. 72) on the Web revealing various conceptions of engagement and ways of connecting with the environment. The structuring configuration of the system builds a multicultural communication of engagement. For Merzeau (2014), "besides the fact that it reintroduces sedimented time into the collaborative gesture, an 'applicative distribution' highlights the transmedia structure of the environment in which the forms of participation are henceforth called upon to be exercised" (p. 231). For Jeanneret (2011, p. 72), the trace on the Web is "an act of inscription": "It is not a natural imprint phenomenon, but a cultural construct derived from a documentary creation". We propose to define the communicational ecosystem of the environmental actors' engagement by highlighting the structuring of their online presence, which we call the strategic distribution "traced" by these organizations.

On the other hand, we complete our study of websites with a corpus composed of the same discursive genre, namely the five video clips disseminated online by these collectives. In terms of content, these clips have one characteristic in common: they all highlight the climate emergency. In terms of form, composed of texts, images and sounds, these clips unfold on the computerized system whose socio-technical and symbolic dimensions are especially meaningful in relation to the rhetorical aim. The specific concept of an "embodied ethos", which involves the ideas of "body", "incorporation", and "community" proves particularly illuminating for the analysis of the ethos operating in these clips. Moreover, in relation to the specific topic of our chapter, it is crucial to examine this "embodied ethos" in the digital discursive regime. Thus, we propose to classify these five clips in a categorization that Maingueneau calls "hyper-genres", which are "modes of textual organization with poor constraints, which are found at very diverse times and places and within which there can develop very varied depictions of speech"[2]. Thus, the clip (or video clip) is indeed a "hyper-genre" of which we can try to describe some major characteristics in the following terms:

– As is shown by the historical origins of the "phonoscenes" created in 1902 in France by Alice Guy, the modern video clip is an audiovisual format where "sound is synchronized with image, for promotional purposes"[3].

– Similar to the original minimalist format of phonoscenes, clips are often very short, 1–2 minutes in duration. Here, we find the etymological meaning of the term "clip", in English, which refers to the idea of "cutting", "trimming" and "shortening"[4].

– Manufactured on the basis of a technological advance of the time (cinematographic technology in the past and digital technology at present), the clips therefore convey a certain collective image on an attractive, "modern", "fashionable" type of "media".

2 Glossary, entry "hypergenre": available at: www.dominique.maingueneau.pagesperso-orange.fr/glossaire.html #Hypergen [Accessed 30 March 2021].

3 Glossary, entry "hypergenre": available at: www.dominique.maingueneau.pagesperso-orange.fr/glossaire.html #Hypergen [Accessed 30 March 2021].

4 The Oxford Learner Dictionaries gives one of the following definitions of the verb *clip*: "To cut something with scissors or shears, in order to make it shorter or neater. Source: www.oxfordlearnersdictionaries.com/definition/english/clip_2 [Accessed 30 March 2021].

– Perceived as shows, like the phonoscenes that served as a “promotional tool for the popular music of the day”[5], today’s clips also help to raise the profile of the actors concerned and give visibility to their “performances” in the space of computerized systems: in the digital age, clips are posted on clip-sharing platforms such as YouTube, and may be intended for online circulation (websites, socio-digital media, etc.).

In a word, if the hyper-genre dialogue, “in the West, has structured a multitude of texts over some 2,500 years”[6], the hyper-genre clip, with a history of more than a hundred years, is now gaining more and more ground by structuring a large number of contemporary discourses, including ecological engagement discourses. In addition, it is significant that the contemporary ecological engagement discourses of our corpus take shape and flesh in the hyper-genre clip. With a very short duration, which varies between 1 minute and more than 2 minutes (with the exception of the clip “Réveillons-nous”), these clips give visibility, in a high density of images, sound and texts, to a message calling for urgent action for the ecological cause. As if this minimalist format best evoked the pressing and urgent nature of the ecological cause, expressed through concise titles with rousing emphasis – “Réveillons-nous”, “#pasledernier”, “[Action] climat…” – or in a solemn voice – “Affaire du siècle” (Table 8.1).

Moreover, the hyper-genre clip is also, by a kind of expansion of the brief, part of a lifestyle of late modernity, characterized by a generalized speeding up of time (Rosa 2013). Finally, the use of the clip-sharing platform YouTube has a strategic goal, that of giving visibility, in the digital space, to a struggle for the recognition of the ecological cause, whose success is largely measured by the viewing figures for each clip. Against this backdrop of the hyper-genre clip, we see several environmental discourses showcased in this corpus. With a view to examining the central question of the “incarnated ethos”, we focus our attention on the pervasiveness of the physical bodies that give voice and vision to the ecological emergency in these clips.

Thus, the analysis of design, clips and discourse aims to show how spaces configured on the Web potentialize ways of connecting with an environmental engagement. By analyzing the various configurations, we render intelligible the planned strategy and the inherent ecological ethos.

5 Glossary, entry “hypergenre”: available at: www.dominique.maingueneau.pagesperso-orange.fr/glossaire.html #Hypergen [Accessed 30 March 2021].

6 Glossary, entry “hypergenre”: available at: www.dominique.maingueneau.pagesperso-orange.fr/glossaire.html #Hypergen [Accessed 30 March 2021].

Clip	Collective	Date	Duration	Number of views as of March 30 2021
"Affaire du siècle 1" https://www.youtube.com/watch?v=l8j-9mPwehw	Affaire du siècle	18 December 2018	2′48″	339,439 views
"Réveillons-nous" https://www.youtube.com/watchv=1Mw5ADaHyFo&vl=fr-FR	Pensée Sauvage	28 May 2020	10′27″	440,787 views
"[Action] climat : Macron, Notre Drame" https://www.greenpeace.fr/action-en-cours-climat-e-macron-notre-drame/	Greenpeace	20 July 2020	1′11″	1,139 views
"#Pasledernier" https://youtu.be/X2bk12ZTUss	WWF	18 September 2020	1′00″	73,981 views
"Affaire du siècle 2" https://youtu.be/WTLIYbsnEP8	Affaire du siècle	3 February 2021	2′43″	82,965 views

Table 8.1. *Description of environmental emergency clips*

8.3. Ethos of action (Greenpeace)

8.3.1. *Passage to action*

The structuring of Greenpeace's online presence addresses the NGO's historical challenges: giving visibility and instant intelligibility to their actions for environmental protection (Mellot 2017). The presentation on the Web is based on an institutional concept of communication: the website, a reflection of the Greenpeace brand, makes it possible to clearly identify the NGO's actions, the petition platform constitutes the passage to action, social media relay the message, and the communication campaigns constitute video evidence, testifying to their existence and importance. The media environment gives resonance to ongoing actions.

The ethos of environmental engagement is here based on action, and the Web strategy sets out on a path that allows the citizen to identify these actions and the passage to action. In our view, this approach should be linked to theories of engagement (Joule et al. 1987), which recognize the interactions as sequences either preparing for the act of engagement or revealing the degree of identification, by the individual, of the expected level of engagement:

> The theory of action identification (Vallacher and Wegner 1987), a central element of the engagement theory, postulates that an action is identified at various levels ranging from a low level ([for example] quitting smoking to save money) to a high level ([for example] quitting smoking to preserve one's health and that of one's associates). (Courbet et al. 2013, p. 9)

Engaging communication builds on these theories to demonstrate that this identification can be accentuated when the individual is asked to perform preparatory acts before the actual act of engagement. The process of this engaging communication consists of an adjustment of user behaviors in line what they themselves have identified as the correct behavior to follow during the preparatory act. Thus, the Greenpeace website configures a performative level of interaction, considering the user is able to produce a response to an issue (Mellot 2015). The user engages in the digital arena through an action that recognizes different levels of investment, actions with a higher or a lower cost. We regard signing a petition, which is the preferred action in Greenpeace's various campaigns, as an engaging statement that prefigures a performative level depending on the action possibilities in the statement (the action program here is generally to click on the statement, fill in and sign the form and send the petition) and on condition of a collective realization of this action. Performativity is understood here as the concretization of the digital gesture in the actual public arena (e.g. the submission of the petition to an authority) and in the everyday space of the individual by the identification of an issue that can lead them to change their lifestyle.

Figure 8.1. *Home page of the Greenpeace.fr website (March 2021). For a color version of this figure, see www.iste.co.uk/pinede/digital.zip*

The depiction of this performative level is generally affected in a simple iconic, plastic space, which we call hyper-intelligible. Indeed, an engaging space helps the user to quickly understand what is expected of them. The operational dimension of the digital space is a characteristic exacerbated by the performative model, focused on putting the user's cooperative qualities to the fore. We have highlighted this structurization in several Greenpeace campaigns (Mellot 2017, 2020): the visuals represent the landscape as Greenpeace's field of experience, the texts localize and target the actions. The NGO is in fusion with this terrain, a fusion directly stated in the image by the banner on the crane in the image on the website's home page (Figure 8.1). The website is built from clear textual statements inviting the user to take up a position in the field of action (engaging statements such as "join the appeal", "support us"). The hyper-intelligible blocks are in the colors of their ecological commitment, a simplicity that does not seek aestheticization of the space thus constructed but a strong operationality.

The call to action is coupled in Greenpeace's Web strategy with an attempt to structure digital commons of the environmental struggle with "Green-voice", the petition platform, and WeGreen, the dedicated social media channel. Online involvement is described there as a program of actions associated with the effort expected of an activist in the public space: "As soon as possible, I set up a small campaign team to help me. I can use WeGreen – the social media channel totally dedicated to ecology – to recruit and coordinate my team"[7].

8.3.2. *Climbing body: a courageous corporeality for an ethos of action*

The NGO Greenpeace denounces, in its clip entitled "[Action] climat : Macron, Notre Drame", the climate inaction of the State, a denunciation limited to the words of two of its activists who climbed the crane beside Notre-Dame Cathedral. The choice of this symbolic, iconic location places the NGO's message into a spectacular contrivance that captures the attention immediately. Two registers typical of epideictic are invested: indignation, first, targeted at the person of Emmanuel Macron ("I have a message to pass on to Emmanuel Macron"), guilty of not acting and of lying. Then the denunciation of a policy that plays with climate issues ("It's no longer a game").

Indeed, following on from Danblon (2001)[8], we maintain that there is "the rationality of epideictic discourse". We know from Aristotle that rhetorical activity is divided into three oratorical genres: deliberative, judicial and epideictic. But while for the first two genres the persuasive aim is obvious, because the deliberative deals with the useful and the detrimental and the judicial with the just and the unjust, the epideictic, whose purpose is aesthetic, namely the beautiful or ugly nature of the actions attributable to the agent, which has to do with non-controversial matters, "seems to have no utility for the city, no political function of its own" (Danblon 2001, p. 27). In epideictic discourse, the decision one is seeking to take will be brought about by a perlocutionary effect, in other words, by the creation of a general disposition to imitate certain fine actions (Danblon 2001, p. 40).

The epideictic orator seeks to put their audience in an emotional state leading to a mindset that is itself likely to induce a passage to action that will require no deliberation, it will be felt to be so obvious (Danblon 2001, p. 40).

In this Greenpeace clip, the impulsiveness of the words, like their power, lies in the expression of a keen, unquenchable anger that, in the NGO's two activists, takes the form of a simmering indignation and echoes, by a mirror effect cleverly constructed by the action and its location, at the foot of Notre-Dame, the action that followed the collapse of its roof. This powerful symbol escorts Greenpeace's discourse of indignation and denunciation, making the connection between its

7 Available at: www.wegreen.fr.

8 In *La mise en scène des valeurs. La rhétorique de l'éloge et du blâme* by Marc Dominicy and Madeleine Frédéric, 2001.

rebuilding and the urgent need to construct another climate policy ("It's time to act").

We are spectators at Greenpeace's performance of a dramatic action to celebrate the "action" dimension in ecological engagement. Putting bodies into a stage-show, which displays, before our eyes, and therefore in a way that involves our senses, "the Greenpeace climbers" who "are climbing to the top of the largest crane in Europe" glorify a courageous corporeality. The message is clear: to truly "act" in support of the ecological cause requires "courage".

It is clear that this illocutionary aim has succeeded when we read, in many comments from visitors to the Greenpeace website, words praising the courageous action of the Greenpeace activists: "Dear friends of Greenpeace, You are brave and lucid people"; "Your activists are fantastic!!! One must indeed have exceptional spiritual and physical qualities in order to be able to say what the common mortal wants to express but cannot!"; "Your determination and courage command admiration and give us new heart"; "Bravo for this courageous action!"[9]

Thus, through showcasing in this clip a courageous corporeality, Greenpeace activists participate in an ethical world and, through the same movement, allow visitors to the website to have access to it: the world of environmental activists acting courageously. The ethos aimed at is a human quality that comes from the heart, as evidenced by the Latin etymology (*cor*) of the term courage, but that must take flesh in an action, a courageous action.

8.4. Ethos of the will (WWF)

8.4.1. *Celebrating nature*

WWF's online presence is also strongly marked by a conception of engagement, values anchored in the organization and shared with its activists. Greenpeace's landscape of experience, the field of all actions, is replaced at WWF by a landscape of contemplation (Mellot 2017), whose aesthetic intention is deployed across the whole website. WWF's Web campaigns liberate the landscape from the enunciative markers that are much in evidence with Greenpeace. The user and the organization do not feature as such on the landscape, and they are thus placed at a distance, as observers. In front of them lie landscapes stretching out endlessly. We are not in "the landscape of experience" but facing "the landscape of expanse", whose meaning is immensity. In it there is the will to reorient ourselves in relation to the

9 Available at: www.greenpeace.fr/action-en-cours-climat-e-macron-notre-drame.

environment: in relation to immensity on the scale of the natural element, to a limited space on the scale of human occupation.

Figure 8.2. *"Fields of action" section on the WWF website[10]. For a color version of this figure, see www.iste.co.uk/pinede/digital.zip*

WWF's ethos is based on this celebration of nature, conveyed by an aesthetic of images and a symbolic strategy (Figure 8.2).

The Earth Hour campaign, on the first page of WWF's website, is characteristic of this. "Earth Hour is generally an opportunity to meet up and by a symbolic gesture, switch off city monuments or the lights at home, to celebrate nature"[11]. Invited in the real world to switch off their lights and in the virtual world to switch off the lights of monuments, users "play" with their power of action. With one click, a light on the Eiffel Tower is symbolically extinguished on the platform (Mellot 2015). Pignier (2012) develops this reflection on the pleasure of interacting with the object linked to a gestural mode of interaction operating by analogy. This is also noted by Saemmer (2013), who proposes iconic couplings between the gesture and the multisensory effects involved, thus accentuating immersion in the environment. While user involvement is, as for Greenpeace, expected in the signing of petitions and making donations to the NGO, the values given greatest prominence are those that allow "reconnection to nature" by daily symbolic gestures. The WAG app created by the NGO (We Act for Good) encourages gestures to "eat better", produce "zero waste", "optimize energy" and is presented as "a personalized transformational program"[12].

10 Available at: www.wwf.fr [Accessed March 2021].

11 Campaign appeal text: on www.wwf.fr.

12 Available at: www.wwf.fr/agir-au-quotidien/we-act-for-good.

The image conveyed by WWF is constructed on the Web by classic strategic distribution, following the same pattern as Greenpeace, in which the website occupies a central place to deploy the aesthetics sought by the organization. The campaigns accentuate the dimension of contemplation and exploration of this nature to which we must reconnect by following the program offered by the WWF platforms (WAG or Earth Hour). If the media permit the dissemination of the image thus constructed of an NGO celebrating nature, they are also a place of controversy that is not controlled by WWF, calling into question this smoothed, estheticized vision of engagement, for example, when France Info has on its website the headline, on 18 February 2021, "WWF: when a nature protection NGO is accused of violating human rights in Central Africa".

8.4.2. *Exhibited and exhibiting body in WWF's "#Pasledernier": voluntary corporeality for an ethos of the will*

The surprising choice in the making of WWF's clip #Pasledernier, which consists of using a voiceover while showing the motionless bodies of figures of athletes and eco-engaged artists, paradoxically forms part of a clearly assumed discursive and rhetorical strategy: these physical bodies, shown in this setting through exemplification, are strictly speaking "mouthpieces" for a message. Indeed, the frozen character of these exhibiting bodies invites an attitude of contemplation, which resonates with the WWF's ethos of the aesthetic celebration of nature: the bodies of the athletes and artists do indeed lead us to contemplate the beauty of a work of corporeal performance, fruit of the human will in a work on oneself.

The capacity of human will is expressed through a linguistic form of negativity "not", and in the same movement, by the manifestation of a strong, determined act of opposition, of resistance: *pasledernier*, not the last. This exaltation of the human will is also embodied in the gesture "X" with the crossing of the index fingers to mean "no"[13], made by an athlete at the end of the clip (Figure 8.3). Here, WWF is inviting Internet users to incorporate, under the effect of viewing the clip, an ethos of the will, which can also be seen, to a large extent, in what this NGO describes as their "DNA" in the formulation of a CODE: "C – Competent; O – Optimistic (positive, ambitious, successful, inspiring others); D – Determined (passionate, with a sense of urgency, results-focused); E – Engaging, open, accessible, listening"[14].

---

13 Originally, this gesture made by the two index fingers forming an "X" means the "end" of a meal, which is called "Shime (〆(し め))" in Japanese.

14 Available at: www.wwf.fr/qui-sommes-nous/adn.

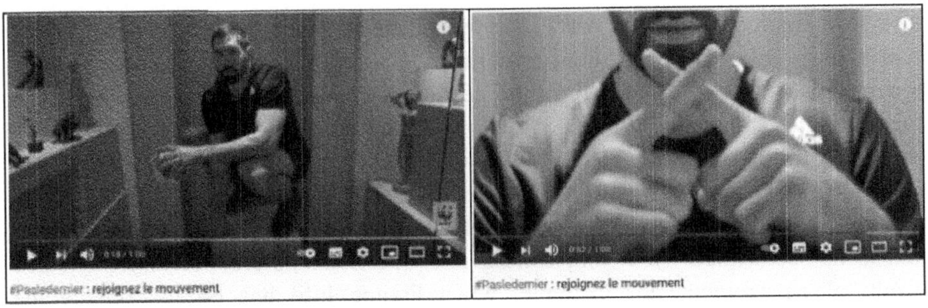

Figure 8.3. *Exhibited and exhibiting body of an athlete and gesture of saying "no" in the clip #Pasledernier. For a color version of this figure, see www.iste.co.uk/pinede/digital.zip*

This campaign by WWF France focuses on the will as a driver of environmental action. This choice to make the will an impulsion was guided by WWF's 2020 Living Planet report, which points to human activities as being primarily responsible for the destruction of nature. It will therefore merge with the image of personalities drawn mainly from the sports world, who already embody, in their respective practices, this ethos of will.

The discourse provided by the voiceovers, which take pride of place in a slick video, uses the device of amplifying repetition: "We do not want to be the last", shortened through the formula #Pasledernier preceded by the technosign # to facilitate its circulation on socio-digital media. This device makes it possible to put the emphasis on the articulation of an action subjected to a wanting that the speakers implicitly steer to raise questions. The speech ends with a direct interpolation from the audience: "You too!" The ecological message becomes a choice that compels everyone to think about their relationship to the environment but also to take responsibility. Choosing to want or not want to join it implies a wider involvement in an ethic of responsibility.

8.5. Ethos of justice (L'Affaire du Siècle)

8.5.1. *Make some noise*

The media resonance sought by NGOs is the lifeblood of the collective L'Affaire du Siècle. Constituted from the organizations Greenpeace, Oxfam, Notre Affaire à Tous and the Nicolas-Hulot Foundation, these "four organizations of general interest are suing the French State before the administrative court of Paris for inaction in the face of climate change. Their objective is to have the judge recognize the State's obligation to act to limit global warming to 1.5°C, in order to protect the people of France from the risks caused by climate change".[15] L'Affaire du Siècle was created on 17 December 2018, and the entire Web strategy is twofold: to mobilize citizens through an extensive petition to express their support and to track the lawsuit act by act.

From that point on, it is a matter of following the event, being part of the group and making a lot of noise in the media. Thus, the strategic distribution on the Web is twofold: on the one side the websites of the founding organizations that relay the case's progress step by step and urge signature of the petition, on the other side a dedicated platform, L'Affaire du Siècle, which handles the stage presentation of the collective, in particular through two videos of the launch and the outcome, which bookend the case. Thus, each mobilizes their media channels to create one single channel for the duration of the case. This hyper-media strategy based on the event is embodied by celebrities who become the spokespersons and "virtual" leaders. The identification of the NGOs is erased in favor of media figures who appear as totally disinterested but fully involved. They in turn mobilize their audience and ensure a resonance beyond the collectives' traditional activists. All citizens have a chance of being reached, whether by the NGO that is aligned with their values or the media figure challenging them. All gather together on social media with the same "kit" that will create visual unity: "mobilization kit for the affair of the century" (Figure 8.4).

A strategy such as this relies on the news channels reporting on the stages and successes engaged by the collective. During the judgment delivered on this case, lemonde.fr was to run the headline on 2 March 2021: "A historic victory for the climate". "It would be an understatement to say that the judgment delivered on Wednesday, February 3 by the administrative court of Paris satisfied the collectives defending the environment and to their lawyers"[16]. The media play their role of contextualizing and nuancing in contrast to the NGOs' hype and the superlatives that are characteristic of the entire campaign, starting with its name. France24.fr asks: "L'Affaire du Siècle: a 'historic' first or a symbolic judgment?"[17] and The Conversation nuances: "This decision was described as 'historic' by the four plaintiff NGOs. It does, however, deserve explanation and nuance"[18].

15 Available at: www.laffairedusiecle.net/qui-sommes-nous/.

16 Available at: www.lemonde.fr/planete/article/2021/02/03/climat-l-etat-condamne-pour-carences-fautives-dans-l-affaire-du-siecle_6068613_3244.html.

17 Available at: www.france24.com/fr/france/20210203-l-affaire-du-si %C3%A8cle-premi% C3%A8re-historique-ou-judgment-symbolique.

18 Available at: www.theconversation.com/decryptage-juridique-de-l-affaire-du-siecle-155053.

Figure 8.4. *Visuals of the L'Affaire du Siècle campaign. For a color version of this figure, see www.iste.co.uk/pinede/digital.zip*

8.5.2. *Demonstrative body in L'Affaire du Siècle: an epideictic corporeality for an ethos of justice*

In the launch clip of L'Affaire du Siècle, we see multiple bodies engaging in an act of blame against the French State for its inaction in ecological matters. Here, the rhetorical epideictic act is a demonstrative act, as in the etymological meaning of the term *epidexis* (demonstration). But these epideictic bodies are those of a specific socio-professional category, namely celebrities (actors, artists, YouTubers, etc.), whose very identity has a high profile in the public space. The exceptional character of these mouthpiece figures is counterbalanced in a way by the stage setting of a wide range of ordinary places of everyday life, from where this enunciation is made: in the private space of the house, in the street, in a workplace, in a park, in front of the building, in the middle of the crowd, in the middle of a wood and so on. A paradox therefore between the singularity of the "celebrity voices" seeking to draw the audience's attention to the environmental struggle and the ordinariness of the "living environments" of the "people" who are crying out for justice.

These epideictic bodies seek embodiment in order to construct, by "making some noise" in the media, an "imaginary community" based on an ethos of justice. Incorporating this ethos and belonging to this imaginary community translates into buying into the ecological message, through the corporeal gesture of signing the petition. The performative effect targeted by this discursive strategy is therefore the construction of a new city. This new city is shown in counterpoint in the photograph of people demonstrating for the ecological cause, forming the "Who are we?" section of L'Affaire du Siècle's website.

Figure 8.5. *Presentation of the collective L'Affaire du Siècle. For a color version of this figure, see www.iste.co.uk/pinede/digital.zip*

L'Affaire du Siècle, through its choral enunciation, proposes affiliation to what the association describes as "a campaign for climate justice" by mobilizing a number of personalities from public life and a single actor to "make a legal attack" on the State, on the grounds of its "inaction in the face of climate change". Here, the epideictic register takes on its full meaning inasmuch as it is generally accepted that the function of this genre is to foster a propensity for action.

The equation is reduced, in this vigilante account, to sophistry. We will summarize:

– "we are in danger";

– "the State has a duty to protect us, but it is not doing";

– so "quite simply we will launch a legal attack on the French State".

The issue here is to facilitate the power of attorney. The discourse of L'Affaire du Siècle presents a conflict, certainly, but offers to be the guarantor of its resolution by "quite simply" launching a legal attack on the French State. The adverbial phrase "quite simply", as a prelude to the narrative in the video clip, may appear as the translation of an illocutionory aim (the passage to action is easy), but it is however destabilizing because to "launch an attack on a State" in practice (and not just saying it) is a complex act completely circumvented in the discourse of L'Affaire du Siècle, which deals with this. The two video clips, the first broadcast on 18 December 2018 and the second on 3 February 2021, obey a discursive strategy that aims, first, to galvanize the audience by the passage to action – "quite simply launch an attack on the State" – and secondly to praise the victory "historic/unprecedented" which must augur others. The collective is therefore introducing the plot of what is to come. The audience holds its breath, kept in suspense until the next episode (not only the legal aspect), serializing its communication ("but it's not over"). The discourse is not challenging the intellect (neither explanation of the procedure nor serious assessment of the ecological damages mentioned) but the evidence, by asking questions (episode 1: "Can it work?"; episode 2: "But in concrete terms, what can it change?") and answering them. The collective is doing our thinking for us ("we have done a lot of thinking") and is seeking the power of attorney to act ("Four associations will do this on our behalf"). This power of attorney anticipated by the collective in order to take the State to court, a sovereign function *par excellence*, requires mobilization that will seek its legitimacy in a radical dichotomy ultimately aimed at changing the balance of power: "We (the collective, scientists, the public, the media – objects of incorporation in the clip) versus the French State". The State is therefore "legitimately" to blame for not acting, not protecting us and talking instead of acting.

8.6. Ethos of belief

8.6.1. *Renew (On est Prêt, Réveillons-nous, Pensée Sauvage)*

The collective On est Prêt appears in the L'Affaire du Siècle as a stakeholder in this action, in particular by making the video, and Camille Étienne, a young French environmental activist and spokesperson for this collective, is one of the media figures involved in the mobilization videos of the case. To understand how the new generation is embracing the Web with or on the fringes of these traditional NGOs, we are interested in this rewriting posted by "On est Prêt", which explicitly states their "message" in these words: "We are ready to act for the planet. We are ready to change our habits. [...] We want to take the whole of society to a new imaginary world. Because it is necessary to imagine a desirable future in order to be able to create it together."[19]

What is this collective's strategic device and what role does it play in the ways of encountering and participating in this ecological ethos? Social networking sites form the heart of the system, YouTube first of all since it is the place of creation for the collective, the space in which the signs of engagement are established by the various productions of its members. This is the opposite process from the strategies embraced by the two traditional NGOs, which base their Web communication on their website and deploy institutional campaigns on social-digital networks. The On est Prêt website acts here as a relay of what has been created elsewhere on the YouTube channel. Personal expression is central, we no longer have the landscape displayed but personalities who create new landscapes. The website opens on a portrait gallery of this young generation (Figure 8.6).

Figure 8.6. *Website home page banner On est Prêt. For a color version of this figure, see www.iste.co.uk/pinede/digital.zip*

"To mobilize using storytelling" is the objective posted on their website to "embody genuine lucid utopias showing with current cultural content approaching dystopia and apocalypse, images that can paralyze citizen action instead of motivating it". The cultural anchorage here is strong, in the sense of creation, art, projects in which individuals express themselves singularly. Thus, everyone is called upon to suggest and submit their project because "we are in dire need of a new narrative of society that is fairer, more ecological and more sustainable".

Camille Étienne contributes to this creative dynamic with the video "Réveillons-nous". Described by some as a "new Greta Thunberg", the activist – a student at Sciences Po Paris – came to the attention of the general public through this video

19 Available at: www.onestpret.com/campagnes/agir-pour-climat.

clip in particularly, co-produced with Solal Moisan as part of their artistic collective Pensée Sauvage. Released on YouTube the day after the end of lockdown (May 28), this clip, which "thus offers a clever mix of art(s) and ecological awareness", has been a great success across social media. Her media popularity grew further following her "resistance" speech as a guest at the Medef Summer School on 27 August 2020.

The strength of engagement of a generation Y ready to change humanity's relationship to nature is expressed above all in the video by aestheticism (dance, images), symbolism (the stability of the mountain echoed in the stability of the young activist in front of her various audiences) and the call to action.

The collective borrows from the two great registers of the environmental struggle (symbolic and performative), which are considered here with the same importance. Engagement no longer takes shelter on an institutional website that gives the keys to collective success but is distilled across various media channels in cadence with the creations and actions of its members. Facebook is thus used to rally without belonging to the various ecological movements by joining pre-existing spaces of action, sketching a form of legacy action.

What they are rewriting is the very history of the environmental struggle, no longer behind an organization but on the front of the stage, by creating "inspiring" spaces from dance, discourse, images and music: composing a narrative of the environmental struggle from personal, emotional stories. During a conference on agriculture, Camille Étienne had no hesitation in presenting her personal experiences with agriculture[20].

This platformization brings visibility outside the target community, generation Y, and thus advances by infiltration into other worlds. Indeed, the speech at the Medef summer school, where she appears as a resistance fighter, shows the place that the individuals involved in this struggle wish to occupy by rewriting the stories of environmental commitment.

The dissemination of the clip and the speeches of Camille Étienne in the public space also arouse the attraction of another generation with the activist being invited onto various media channels (France Inter, in the pages of *Marie Claire*, on the set of *C à vous*, etc.), spaces "visited" by another generation. Founded on the creation of meaning and action, the commitment of this collective is shifting away from the framework of collective action and the "digital commons" of the struggle.

---

20 Repenser l'agriculture à l'intérieur de ses limites – Camille Étienne | Camille Etienne | TEDxPULV [Online]. Available at: www.youtube.com/watch?v=4RxqMSlUI80.

8.6.2. *Double body speaking and dancing in "Réveillons-nous": a professing corporeality for an ethos of belief*

For the artistic collective Pensée Sauvage, in its video clip "Réveillons-nous", the values of courage, boldness, awareness, pride, indignation and disquiet are celebrated, and conversely those of inaction, ignorance and laziness, illustrated by behaviors typical of the target generation Y, are rejected. These illustrations are worth highlighting as they function as signs of hypermodernity, revealing through mirror play the ways of being and doing that belong to the consumer society: our Deliveroo sushis, we "like", we "share", we "stalk", we "swipe", "binge-watching", eating cereal on the couch, YouTube tutorials, pixellated drinks, augmented reality glasses, apps and 5G.

In this frenzied enumeration, driven by amplification rising to a crescendo, the video's other enunciative device, dance, counterbalances the specular logorrhea. Camille Étienne, the scriptwriter, stamps values on a whole environment of actors to be followed or rejected. She continues her discourse making use of opposition and sets up antitheses: "designers/start-uppers versus farmers, nurses or teachers", "policies in cardboard and future in porcelain", "we become blind to what we have before our eyes", "the world before versus the world to come", "doing nothing is already acting", "unplugging the screens, reconnecting to the living".

In this world that she is rearranging, assuming the function of educator, as archaic as it is perilous, of speaker in the epideictic genre, the figures who are disqualified, those affected by negative values, are those "of decision-makers, big companies, the privileged [with whom she associates herself], the State, States, boomers, institutions and their summits, multinationals and millennials". The latter figure is the one that, accused of falling asleep (laziness), blindness (seeing nothing), dumbing-down (ignorance) and inaction, is complicit in "not being part of nature". But as Saint Gérand (2002) reminds us, quoting Emmanuelle Danblon, "calling a person into question through language always leads to undermining the personality and producing related affects – pride, shame, admiration, anger, etc." (p. 179).

Camille Étienne takes the risk of awakening guilty consciences but, in a context of the lifting of lockdown, on 28 May 2020, the date of publication of the video, the mindset on reception of the message is no longer a gamble but an awakening, therefore a form of environmental action that consists of conscientionizing our complicity ("we become accomplices"), what she describes as "a surreptitious validation of this model". In the passage that she organizes from description to explanation of acts in support of a hyper-realistic causality, and an ethos of lucidity (versus when one becomes blind), she instantiates values that configure a communality of destinies ("We are nature", "to be part of this whole"). Concord here is not a rhetorical effect; it becomes a constraint to integrate the ecological struggle.

The video "Réveillons-nous" (Figure 8.7) offers a sensitive perception of a double body, the speaking body of the activist Camille Étienne and the dancing body of the choreographer Léa Durand.

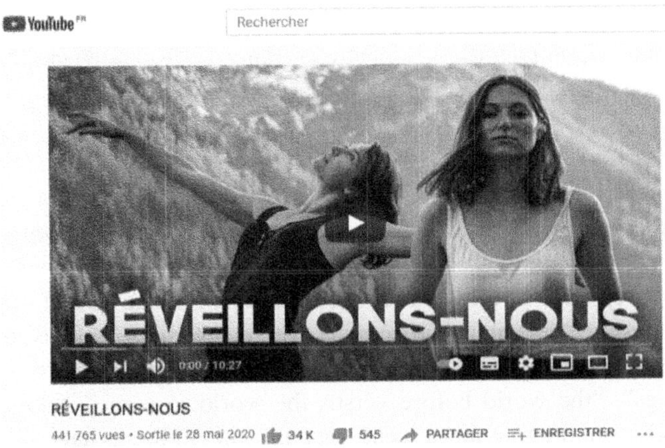

Figure 8.7. *Stage set of the double body speaking and dancing in "Réveillons-nous". For a color version of this figure, see www.iste.co.uk/pinede/digital.zip*

This double body forms one corporeal whole that professes a "great narrative" aimed at emancipation: it is fundamentally about "saving the planet, protecting the environment" by becoming "an intransigent, conscious and indignant generation" and refusing to "put our lives into the hands of a handful of baby-boomers".

Camille Étienne thus lends her voice to declaim this narrative of a "world that is dying" and a "new world to be (re)invented". By declaring that "we are nature, if it disappears, we will disappear with it", the young activist professes her faith in a kind of nature cult that has now become sacred in our time, because as Debray (2020) maintains, "There is always something sacred in a human community, at no matter what era" (p.33).

In this perspective, it seems to us possible to include this scene of enunciation in a scenography of religious preaching where, like a biblical prophet figure, the activist devotes herself to a double mission: on the one hand, to "denounce" the "sins" of her "people" and especially of their leaders in the ecological field (unbridled consumption, political inaction, laziness, complicity with the capitalist system, blind trust in technology, etc.), and on the other hand, to "announce" the good news of "a world to come".

In addition, calling into question our habitual belief in the model of a world that is dying – "Do you really believe in it?" – the activist concludes her profession of faith with an exhortation to believe – "We no longer have time to not believe" – and the final interpellation – "Wake up" – sounds like the call to conversion in the etymological sense of *metanoia,* referring to the idea of a change in thinking, direction, through a transformation, a rebirth.

It must be noted that this profession of belief is not only declaimed verbally, but celebrated corporeally by a dancing body in a space dedicated to ritual: the evocative power of the mountain as a highly symbolic place on the spiritual level (place of worship), corporeal gestures (ceremonial, liturgical gestures) and music. All these elements help Internet users to incorporate an ethos of belief, belief being defined here, as de Certeau (1990) suggests, "not the object of belief (a dogma, a program, etc.), but the investment of the subjects in a proposal, the act of enouncing it by holding it as true – in other words, a 'modality' of affirmation and not its content" (p. 260). The crucial thing is to believe in the ecological narrative, and everything else will follow from this conversion. This ecological belief will also give rise to an "imaginary community" of people believing in the construction of a "world to come".

8.7. Structuring an ecological *homonoia* on the Web: emergency, praise and blame

The notion of an emergency, in our view, puts its mark on the discourse of environmental activists and reconfigures all the driving values, now ringed by temporal markers: "The last generation to be able to do something about it" (Pensée Sauvage, "Réveillons-nous"), "and perhaps the last generation to be able to reverse the trend" (WWF France, "#Pasledernier"), "time to act" (Greenpeace, "Action Climat"), "it's now or never" (L'Affaire du Siècle).

The emergency response in the discourses makes it possible to engage the recipients with a passage to action and contributes to a strategy of amplification specific to the epideictic register. It compresses the relationship to the time of action in the face of the climate emergency and thus guarantees conversion to a new ecological homonoia, in other words a "concord", a "community of feelings" based on "sacred values" of the city of today: the environment.

	Greenpeace	WWF	L'Affaire du Siècle	On est Prêt/Pensée Sauvage
Web strategy	Performative and centralized	Symbolic and centralized	Hypermedia and doubled	Engaged and platformizing
Discursive register	Epideictic	Amplifying	Epideictic	Emancipation narrative
Design	Hyper-intelligible	Aesthetic	Informative	Artistic
Corporeality	Courageous	Exhibited	Demonstrative	Professing
Ethos	Ethos of action	Ethos of will	Ethos of justice	Ethos of belief

Table 8.2. *Synthesis of analyses of the ecological ethos on the Web*

Thus, we observe a double rhetorical mechanism at work:

– On the one hand, the prevalence of epideictic discourses of praise or blame through a staged presentation of values: praise (in the subtle form of self-glorification) of figures of engagement in the ecological cause and blame of the French State and President Macron (L'Affaire du Siècle, "Macron Notre Drame").

– On the other hand, the construction of an ethos embodied by role models ("celebrities" from the media, sports, artistic sectors, etc.) (L'Affaire du Siècle, "#Pasledernier", "Réveillons-nous"), who function as guarantors. They are therefore part of an ethical world and give access to it. More than a means of persuasion, this enveloping ethos allows the reader or listener not only to "decipher the content" but also to "participate in the world configured by the enunciation", to "access an embodied identity" (Maingueneau 2002, p. 16).

The climate issue, nature, life, the environment and the supreme values of ecological *homonoia* therefore pass through the filter of enunciations whose staged presentations and plural incarnations recall the diversity of forms of mobilization and the power of the role of the ethos, including the collective ethos, in a strategy (Table 8.2).

Indeed, the ethos has a prominent place within well-controlled transmedia strategies that tend to smooth the presentations so that people can see and understand the most "obvious" meaning of their action.

Catherine Kerbrat-Orrecchioni reiterates, stressing the difference in conception of ethos between rhetoric and pragmatism, that "the Aristotelian notion applies to individuals, whereas in contrastive pragmatism, it applies to collectives of individuals (speech communities)". According to the linguistics specialist:

> The individual ethos is anchored in the collective ethos (the speaker must draw upon a stock of shared values for it to work) and conversely, the collective ethos can only be apprehended through the individual behaviors in which it becomes incarnate (it is the individuals who through their behavior confirm and consolidate the values of the group, attesting at the same time to their adherence to these collective values). (Kerbrat-Orecchioni 2002, p. 43)

In our case, an ethical engagement of the enunciators is displayed, which appears through the validation of their positions in the fight for the climate and in the name of a rationality informed by values. The individual-collective or collective-individual articulation of the enunciation devices brings the recipient to engage responsibly in the ecological *homonoia*, in an almost Ricoeurian logic of the self as another, of "we are nature".

At the end of our analysis, it emerges that the communication employed within the framework of environmental collectives (NGOs, activist associations, etc.) is characterized by an operational, performative aim. Thus, we see an affirmation of the Austinian maxim "how to do things with words" (Austin 1976), which updates and extends the teaching of the Greek rhetoricians of antiquity on the power of words in the political life of the city. This performativity can be broken down into a similar register of actions from one website to another – sign a petition, repost information, join a community, give testimony and so on – but it is based on values specific to the collectives according to various conceptions of the environmental struggle.

Thus, we note that the ecological ethos in the digital regime stems from two strategic movements.

– The first part from the collective, well-structured and presented on the website to reach individuals, in the new modalities of action on the Web. This pattern prioritizes the website as the main vector of a collective's values from where social-digital media channels amplify visibility and ensure contact with citizens. In this approach, the Web is a way of connecting everyone to the collective with an attempt to structure digital commons dedicated to the environmental struggle.

– The second movement, however, operates from singular initiatives particularly connected to creativity, the expressiveness of each individual to join together in collective spaces for the duration of an event, an action and a media relay. The platformization of the Web is leveraged, leading to an infiltration into various media spaces rather than an organization of dedicated spaces.

This double movement, building consensus and awareness, is part of what Ollitraut (2001) emphasizes, in relation to the "remodeling of militancy", as "a certain adaptation to these contextual effects" in the trajectories that lead to militant enterprise (p. 107). These "master frames" or "dominant frameworks of interpretation" are newly accentuated and marked by an "ecopolitical shift in contemporary thought" that draws its inspiration from ecological disaster and seeks to renew the experience of nature. The ecological crisis, in these "master frames", thus becomes a crisis of sensibility. Through "this ideological disruption..., this change of perspective... and this metaphysical reversal" (*Le Monde* 2020)[21], the opportunity presents itself to change the discursive repertoires and to re-politicize the ecological issue, by creating a community of values, in order to put it at the heart

21 Available at: www.lemonde.fr/idees/article/2020/08/02/le-tournant-ecopolitique-de-la-pensee-francaise_6047969_3232.html.

of the city. In short, it is a question of "governing the climate" through the people by leaving "an economy of perpetual promise" embodied by the political management of the environmental crisis (Akyut 2020)[22]. Cooling the world involves restoring horizontality to counter a verticality of power accused of inaction.

8.8. Conclusion

In this new ecopolitical wave that is in the process of shifting ideological lines and establishing itself in the political, media and socio-digital arena, the notion of affect and the concept of enemy ensure a rewriting of the anchoring of the rhetoric of environmental communication on the Web based on praise and blame and aimed at building a new *homonoia*. This new *homonoia* serves as a reference to produce praise of the ecological activists and blame the French state and its political leaders.

Websites and the various video clips make up the cultural constructs, stabilizing the position of the collective in a co-enunciation space that is symbolic and contemplative for WWF, hyper-intelligible and engaging for Greenpeace, hyper-media for L'Affaire du Siècle, creative for On est Prêt. The images and discourses that populate it are the guarantors of a certain way of envisaging environmental engagement and are based on the need to reinvent a community of consensus, a new *homonoia* founded as a collective rationality in the face of the climate emergency.

The epideictic orientation of ecological activist discourse, as an illocutionary value (therefore a persuasive force), reminds us here that the ecological crisis is first and foremost a crisis of sensibility. To sharing feelings for the environmental cause is to (re)politicize wonder and make it a vector of concrete struggles. "The affect of the conscious wonderment of the conflictuality of the world" (*Le Monde* 2020)[23] becomes the new discursive horizon of ecological activism. It is also a gamble to be taken on the post-modern era marked by what Nicolas (2015) describes as

> a hiatus dug between praise and democratic emotions: we have lost the faculty or, more precisely, the sensibility that enabled audiences of times gone by to share feelings, in other words, to relate, to connect, a singular, occasional glorification to the here and now of the community, therefore to its present. (p. 35)

---

22 Available at: www.aoc.media/entretien/2020/12/11/stefan-aykut-apres-la-cop21-nous-avons-bascule-in-une-economie-de-la-promesse-perpetuelle/.

23 Available at: www.lemonde.fr/idees/article/2020/08/02/le-tournant-ecopolitique-de-la-pensee-francaise_6047969_3232.html.

Ecological *homonoia* is not new because the community exists. But the register of its values and also its boundaries are being redrawn and expanded as a result of a new ecological order singularly marked by the question of its urgency.

Thus, with environmental communication on the Web, we are led to confirm that "when saying, really is doing" (Cassin 2018). Is that the "world-effect" of ecological discourse that has become a "winning discourse", in other words, "a world-changing discourse", according to the happy formula of Cassin (2019, p. 4)? It speaks of and at the same time forges our "entry into the ecological era" where "the profound integration of the ecological into social and political" (Morin 2020, p. 13) is becoming well established.

8.9. References

Austin, J.L. (1976). *How to do things with words*. Oxford University Press, Oxford.

Badouard, R. (2013). Les mobilisations de clavier : le lien hypertexte comme ressource des actions collectives en ligne. *Réseaux*, 181, 87–117.

Brauman, R. (2010). Communication, témoignage et politique. À propos de la guerre du Biafra et du cyclone de Birmanie. In *La Communication des ONG humanitaire*, Dauvin, P. (ed.). L'Harmattan, Paris.

Bruno, C., Garbe, E., Morales, J. (2020). III. Vendre de manière désintéressée : le paradoxe de la communication des ONG. In *Le management des ONG*, Cazenave, B. (ed.). La Découverte, Paris.

Cassin, B. (2018). *Quand dire, c'est vraiment faire. Homère, Gorgias et le peuple arc-en-ciel.* Fayard, Paris.

Cassin, B. (2019). Un discours peut transformer le monde. *Sciences Humaines*, 3(3), 4–4 [Online]. Available at: https://doi.org/10.3917/sh.312.0004 [Accessed 4 July 2021].

de Certeau, M. (1990). *L'Invention du quotidien 1. Arts de faire*. Gallimard, Paris.

Charnovitz, S. (2002). Les ONG : deux siècles et demi de mobilisation. *L'Économie politique*, 1, 6–21.

Cornilliat, F. and Lockwood, R. (2000). Foreword. In *Èthos et pathos : le statut du sujet rhétorique*, Cornilliat, F., Lockwood, R. (eds). Editions Champion, Paris.

Courbet, D., Fourquet-Courbet, M.P., Bernard, F., Joule, R.V. (2013). Communication persuasive et communication engageante pour la santé : favoriser des comportements sains avec les médias, Internet et les serious games. In *Publicité et santé : des liaisons dangereuses ? Le point de vue de la psychologie*, Blanc, N. (ed.). Editions In Press, Paris.

Debray, R. (2020). *Le siècle vert. Un changement de civilisation*. Gallimard, Paris.

Fouchard, A. (2010). Éthique et communication. Quelques leçons à partir d'une expérience singulière. In *La Communication des ONG humanitaire*, Dauvin, P. (ed.). L'Harmattan, Paris.

Fraenkel, B. (2007). Actes d'écriture : quand écrire c'est faire. *Langage et société*, 121–122, 101–112.

Freyss, J. (2004). La solidarité internationale, une profession ? *Revue tiers monde*, 4, 735–772.

Jeanneret, Y. (2007). Cadre pratique, cadre symbolique et cadre technique dans la dite "société de l'information". In *Technique, communication et société : à la recherche d'un modèle de gouvernance*, Goujon, P., Lavelle, S. (eds). Presses universitaires de Namur, Namur.

Jeanneret, Y. (2011). Complexité de la notion de trace. De la traque au tracé. L'homme trace. *Perspectives anthropologiques des traces contemporaines*, 1, 59–86.

Joule, R.V., Beauvois, J.L., Deschamps, J.C. (1987). *Petit traité de manipulation à l'usage des honnêtes gens*. Presses universitaires de Grenoble, Grenoble.

Kerbrat-Orecchioni, C. (2002). Système linguistique et éthos communicatif [Online]. Available at: http://journals.openedition.org/praxematique/540 [Accessed 15 March 2021].

Maillard, D. (2010). Professionnalisation de la communication humanitaire et logiques démocratiques. In *La Communication des ONG humanitaire*, Dauvin, P. (ed.). L'Harmattan, Paris.

Maingueneau, D. (2002). Problèmes d'éthos [Online]. Available at: http://dominique.maingueneau.pagespersoorange.fr/texte06.html [Accessed 4 July 2021].

Maingueneau, D. (2013). Genres de discours et web : existe-t-il des genres web ? In *Manuel d'analyse du web en Sciences Humaines et Sociales*, Barats, C. (ed.). Armand Colin, Paris [Online]. Available at: https://doi-org.srvext.uco.fr/10.3917/arco.barat.2013.01.0074 [Accessed 4 July 2021].

Maingueneau, D. (2014). Retour critique sur l'éthos [Online]. Available at: https://doi-org.srvext.uco.fr/10.3917/ls.149.0031 [Accessed 4 July 2021].

Maingueneau, D. (2016a). *Analyser les textes de communication*. Armand Colin, Paris.

Maingueneau, D. (2016b). L'éthos discursif et le défi du web. Itinéraires. Littérature, textes, cultures [Online]. Available at: https://journals.openedition.org/itineraires/3000 [Accessed 4 July 2021].

Massiah, G. (2002). Le mouvement citoyen mondial. *L'Économie politique*, 1, 22–37.

Mellot, S. (2015). Le parcours d'interaction sur le Web comme expérience d'immersion : entre promesses des interfaces des ONG et mode de perception de l'usager. *Les enjeux de l'information et de la communication*, 17/3A, 179–194.

Mellot, S. (2017). Modes de vie durables : la stratégie des ONG sur le web. In *Formes de vie et modes d'existence durables*, Zinna, A., Darrault-Harris, Y. (eds). Collection Actes, Toulouse.

Mellot, S. (2020). Un don = un like ? Le nouvel imaginaire de la solidarité en ligne. In *Interconnectés ? Numérique et convivialisme*, Wallenhorst, N., Mellot., S, Theviot, A, (eds). Le Bord de l'eau, Lormont.

Merzeau, L. (2014). Entre événement et document : vers l'environnement-support. *Les Cahiers de la SFSIC*, 9, 230–233.

Morin, E. (2020). *L'entrée dans l'ère écologique*. Editions de l'aube, La Tour d'Aigues.

Nicolas, L. (2015). L'épidictique : assise et pivot de l'édifice rhétorique. *Rivista Italiana di Filosofia del Linguaggio* [Online]. Available at: http://www.rifl.unical.it/index.php/rifl/article/view/251.

Ollitrault, S. (2015). Les mobilisations citoyennes au XXIe siècle : un défi pour les ONG ? *Humanitaire. Enjeux, pratiques, débats*, 41, 80–87.

Pignier, N. (2012). Le plaisir de l'interaction entre l'usager et les objets TIC numériques. *Interfaces numériques*, 1(1), 123.

Pignier, N. and Gobert, T. (2014). Sens, supports et dispositifs. Le design des TIC en termes de dessins et de desseins. In *XIXe congrès de la Société française des sciences de l'information et de la communication*. L'Harmattan, Paris.

Rosa, H. (2013). *Accélération. Une critique sociale du temps*. La Découverte, Paris.

Saemmer, A. (2013). Approche sémio-rhétorique du texte animé dans la publicité en ligne. *Recherches en Communication*, 39(39), 165–181.

Saemmer, A. (2016). *Rhétorique du texte numérique : figures de la lecture, anticipations de pratiques*. Presses de l'Enssib, Villeurbanne.

Saint-Gérand, J.P. (2002). Dominicy, Marc & Madeleine Frédéric. La mise en scène des valeurs. La rhétorique de l'éloge et du blâme. *Histoire Épistémologie Langage*, 24(2), 178–180.

Tilly, C. (1984). Les origines du répertoire d'action collective contemporaine en France et en Grande-Bretagne. *Vingtième Siècle. Revue d'histoire*, 4, 89–108.

Tilly, C. (1986). *La France conteste*. Fayard, Paris.

9

Covid-19 and Digital Fundraising: Actors, Strategies and Perspectives

Géraud AHOUANDJINOU, Ornheilia ZOUNON, Agnès BADOU and Ismène KPÉDJO
Université d'Abomey-Calavi, Cotonou, Benin

9.1. Introduction

The year 2019 was very challenging for the French charitable sector because of successive crises that disrupted the usual activities of appeals for charitable donations: the *gilet jaunes* (Yellow Vests) crisis, the tax reforms that led to the abolition of the wealth tax, the pension reforms with the strikes of December 2019 and so on. It was in this context that the Covid-19 crisis occurred a few months later, with the series of exceptional lockdown decisions that posed major questions and imposed massive uncertainty on fundraising in the short and long term. Indeed, measures related to managing the coronavirus pandemic in 2020 slowed the economy and forced the reinvention of new forms of social and professional interactions based on physical distancing and the use of information technologies. Digital technology occupied a preponderant space in all categories of social exchanges.

Digital Presences of Organizations,
coordinated by Nathalie PINÈDE, Luc MASSOU and Patrick MPONDO-DICKA.

The public fundraising sector has been particularly impacted by this situation. On the one hand, the fundraisers continued to call upon the public to support the causes related to the Covid-19 emergency. On the other hand, they had to face the complete halt of normal traditional fundraising activities: galas, sporting events, leaflet drops, street collections and other fundraising gatherings. From mid-March 2020, the NGO Sidaction had already envisaged cancelling its annual media event scheduled for late March. Following that, Solidays, a music festival that takes place in France every year at the end of June, was also cancelled by the promoters, Solidarité Sida. Similar to other business sectors, fundraising organizers had no choice other than to resort to making charitable appeals via digital channels.

Several organizations, foundations and associations began by initiating online fundraising operations through social media particularly to support hospitals and those weakened by the health crisis. In the wake of the shockwave caused by the initial lockdowns in China, Italy and then France, these actions were a response from the charitable sector to accompany the popular support shown toward caregivers, who at the time were applauded every evening at 8 PM. For fundraisers, the Internet was already envisaged as a new, more reactive and more interactive niche that would offer broader perspectives than the traditional marketing channels, which were becoming exhausted (Dupont 2002). Moreover, the health crisis context rendered these old channels inoperative and encouraged the all-digital approach (Alberola-Ila et al. 2020). Following earlier research on the subject, including "Le sale boulot et les bonnes causes, institutionnalisation et légitimation du marketing direct au sein des ONG" (Lefèvre 2007) and "Charity e-business ou la collecte de fonds sur le digital en France" (Ahouandjinou et al. 2018), our study aims to take stock of the new and emerging e-fundraising practices. Through the exploration of digital marketing campaign mechanisms launched between March and May 2020 in France, it is a question of analyzing the Web pages of initiatives dedicated to appealing for donations for Covid-19 belonging to five charities as well as evaluating the interaction between the communication put out by these charities and the public.

Moreover, since the appeal for donations is, for once, part of a generalized and globalized context, it happens that, exceptionally, the potential donors and also the beneficiaries of their donations are all affected by the same unique cause. The donation and its rational are thus disrupted, especially when some of the donation recipients live on the African continent, where the prevalence of Covid-19 did not meet any of the forecasts. "Africa has foiled the most pessimistic predictions" (UN

Info 2020)[1], and indeed, African populations could look at the issue from an unusual perspective. The second part of this study has sought to explore, explain and analyze the aforementioned perspective.

We seek to answer the following questions. How do associations and foundations adopt digital technology to mobilize resources in these times of health crisis? What is the typology of the actors in the campaigns launched to collect donations for the coronavirus crisis? What narrative and conversational mechanisms are at play with the public on the organizations' Facebook pages? How did the opinion of donation recipients in Africa perceive the call for donations for Africa on this cause in particular?

9.2. Theoretical and methodological framework

9.2.1. *Theoretical bases of the positioning and scriptwriting of fundraising communication*

The theoretical basis that underpins our analysis of the communication of organizations related to seeking donors on the Internet is a blend of three theories.

First, we called upon the theory of donation and counter donation (Mauss 2012). According to the author, donation fulfils several purposes and meets several principles:

– it is a strategic way of obtaining a counter donation. In this, it is not completely disinterested or altruistic;

– it is a way to create and maintain the social bond between individuals.

If the donation cannot produce a counter donation from its recipients, one can regard the feeling of usefulness or even superiority that the act of giving can generate, as its counterpart. Donation can be seen as playing a psychological and social function here by raising self-esteem. Moreover, several works in psychology tend to show that "in the secure adult, the most reliable source of good feelings about the Self is found in a reciprocal relationship in which giving and receiving are an integral part" (Guédeney 2011, p. 140). We should remember here that the donation can be motivated by the hope of a counter donation, whose nature can be either material or immaterial.

1 Available at: www.news.un.org/fr/story/2020/10/1079912.

Donation as a catalyst of the social bond mentioned above has been further explored through the theory of positive social action (Gergen and Gergen 1986), which falls within the field of social psychology. Positive social action is defined by the authors as a type of behavior in which one person performs an action for the benefit of another.

We also talk about "pro-social" behavior. This theory has been the subject of numerous studies and publications in social psychology. The authors, following the initiators, have tried to better relate it to their contemporary realities. It has thus been established that it is the interplay between personality traits and certain situations (e.g. dependence on one other in uncertainty) that urges the individual to pro-social behavior (Thielmann et al. 2020).

Finally, the three-dimensional model defining personal involvement (Rouquette 1997) completes our clarification of the issue of donation, particularly in the context of the 2020 pandemic. Basically, the author considers that there are three explanatory dimensions of personal involvement:

– identification of the individual with the object;

– attaching value to the object;

– the perceived possibility of perceived action.

Thus, there is an involvement in relation to an object when the individual feels they are involved strictly rather than diffusely, when the matter is a vital rather than insignificant issue and when they can by their action change something (Vintila 2012). From this analysis, we can note that donation during a pandemic fulfils all the conditions for maximum involvement of all and sundry. This pandemic involves, in one way or another, every individual around the globe. It has changed our habits and has had a visible and enduring impact on our daily lives. Everywhere, it was necessary to limit travel and stay at home, stop social activities and reconfigure social bonding via digital tools. Furthermore, it caused millions of deaths and, during the period over which the present study was conducted, the subject caught the attention of all nations and received heavy media coverage. For example, in France, the proportion of televised news devoted to Covid-19 reached a record 80.5% during the eight weeks of the first lockdown (Poels and Lefort 2021). Finally, participating in a fundraising campaign, in order to support an aggressive response to the disease, was made possible by the mobilization of a number of organizations. The advice at that time, "Stay home!", might have plunged everyone into a fatalistic and potentially pathogenic immobility. Making a donation to support research, coming to the aid of the most vulnerable populations, undoubtedly made it possible to keep active and create the feeling that, from this reclusive situation, the return to normality could be encouraged and envisaged.

The mechanisms of the NGOs' approach and discourse in the context of orchestrated campaigns to raise funds for the emergency connected to the coronavirus crisis are firmly established. They stem from the practices adopted by the world of marketing from the 1980s onward.

> You know, the fundraising pattern is an extremely simple thing. You have an emotional approach that shows suffering, a problem, and opposite, you show a solution. [...] Whatever the medium, you have to show an emotion and a solution: you see someone on the street who is suffering, you are told that there is a possibility for them to suffer less, you are going be interested in this possibility and even promote it. [...] The weight of words, the shock of photos... Actually, it should really be the opposite, first the shock of the photos, then the weight of the words since emotion provides the way in. (Lefèvre 2007, p. 79)

The three theories explained above and combined (see Figure 9.1) have allowed us to give a certain direction to this study.

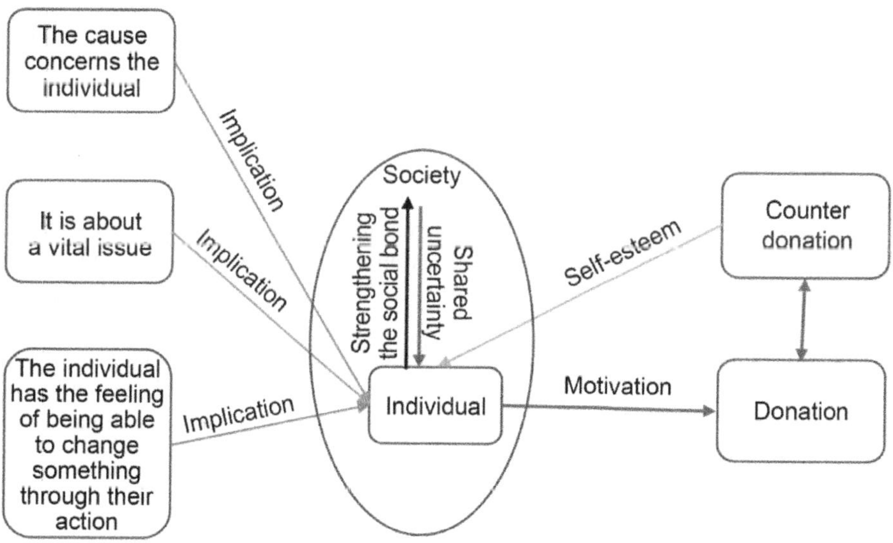

Figure 9.1. *Schematic theoretical framework*

In view of the above, we will take the approach of questioning the strategy of positioning and scriptwriting the messages given out by the charities in their fundraising mechanisms put online on this occasion. However, in terms of the target audience of this method of communication, we do not see it as being inactive and passive. Thus, beyond the emotions aroused, the design, the shapes, the colors and the action buttons (with hypertext links guiding to donation), we also set out to evaluate the influence of the interactional process between the individuals targeted and the digital interfaces relaying the messages of the non-governmental organizations studied in the context of this research. We will thus make use of the contribution of Pignier (2012, p. 151) that analyzes the notion of pleasure of interaction between user and objects of digital ICT: "Interaction perceived as a process, an art of doing, assumes that the bodies of the user and the object find, during the relationship, a dynamic, adjust to each other, in a sort of, no longer operation, but cooperation." Thus, having carried out a content analysis to highlight the communication style that was prevalent at the time and the strategies adopted to encourage donation – in the light of these combined theoretical elements – we looked at donor reactions on digital platforms and the point of view of potential donation beneficiaries in Africa, specifically in an exploratory perspective. The African audience that was among the potential beneficiaries of fundraising is now active on digital social media and, like the (European) donor audience, has access to campaigns. From this point of view, it can adopt a position in relation to the communication sent out, which might sometimes find itself out of step with the real situations experienced on the ground in Africa.

9.2.2. *Methodology*

In order to satisfactorily answer all the research questions formulated above, a mixed qualitative and quantitative study was envisaged; the study is based on two different techniques.

We undertook a content analysis targeting a corpus composed of various campaigns launched (in the aforementioned period) by charities. This analysis is supplemented by a quantitative survey on a mechanism appealing for donations to support healthcare work to manage Covid-19 in Africa.

9.2.2.1. *Content analysis*

9.2.2.1.1. Population

Five of the organizations that set up online fundraising mechanisms for the Covid-19 emergency in the target period were selected to form the corpus for study.

In fact, they are among the organizations that were the first to appeal for charitable donations. We must bear in mind the specific nature of the context, where society as a whole was taken by surprise and seemed shocked by the sudden lockdown and the inherent lack of anticipation. Thus, as in most sectors, the NGOs did not really anticipate the crisis or expect to launch fundraising operations. Among the first organizations to launch online fundraising appeals, here are the five charities selected rationally in order to include in the corpus a diversity of positions, causes and initiatives.

Alliance Urgence

This is a collection of organizations consisting of six non-governmental organizations. Together, they seek to provide quick, easy ways for the French to donate in response to a humanitarian emergency[2]. It is a consortium of organizations composed of Action Contre la Faim, CARE France, Handicap International, Médecins du Monde, Plan International and Solidarités International. It was created just before the coronavirus crisis. It is a melting-pot for pooling resources in order to enable member organizations to create a synergy to mobilize resources together, with the goal of significantly strengthening the coordination, speed and impact of the humanitarian response in emergencies. Covid-19 was the opportunity to launch the very first emergency fundraising initiative. It should be stressed that this consortium is composed of major players operating from France and recognized as such.

Figure 9.2. *Screenshot of the Alliance Urgence campaign website. For a color version of this figure, see www.iste.co.uk/pinede/digital.zip*

2 Available at: www.allianceurgences.org/notre-role/.

The original missions of Alliance Urgence's constitutive NGOs are set out below:

– Action Contre la Faim is an NGO created in 1979 whose mission is to fight against world hunger. It works to eliminate hunger through the prevention, detection and treatment of malnutrition, especially during and after emergencies linked to conflicts and natural disasters[3].

– CARE France was founded in 1983 and is one of the largest humanitarian aid networks in the world. It aims to fight extreme poverty and defend human rights. It builds on the essential levers of communities and women for effective and sustainable action[4].

– Handicap International[5] is involved in helping vulnerable populations, especially people with disabilities all over the world. This association has been working to provide emergency assistance to populations affected by natural disasters to prevent disabilities and disabling diseases; supply equipment and rehabilitation services to persons with disabilities; support school, social and economic integration; support the clearing of mines and remnants of war and promote the rights of people with disabilities since 1982.

– Médecins du Monde was founded in 1980. It is an independent international movement of active campaigners operating through support for the victims of crises and conflicts, the promotion of sexual and reproductive health, risk reduction, care for migrant and displaced populations, and reducing the impact of the environment on health[6].

– Plan International was founded in 1937. It is a non-governmental international solidarity organization, independent of any faith or political party, which has been working for more than 80 years to advance children's rights and equality between girls and boys[7].

– Solidarités International comes to the aid of people affected by conflict and violence, epidemics, natural and climatic disasters and economic collapse[8]. It has been acting at the request of populations and in accord with local partners to help those whose safety, health and lives are threatened by covering their basic needs: drinking, eating, shelter and cleanliness, since 1980.

---

3 Available at: www.actioncontrelafaim.org/nous-decouvrir/.

4 Available at: www.carefrance.org/care/qui-sommes-nous/qui-sommes-nous.htm.

5 Available at: www.handicap-international.fr/fr/l-association.

6 Available at: www.medecinsdumonde.org/fr/qui-sommes-nous.

7 Available at: www.plan-international.fr/info/qui-sommes-nous.

8 Available at: www.solidarites.org/fr/depuis-1980/mandat-humanitaire/.

Association ALIMA

Founded in 2009, Alliance for International Medical Action is a medical humanitarian organization with a presence in 11 African countries, headquartered in Dakar, Senegal. It is an African medical alliance whose purpose is to liaise between national NGOs and international research institutes[9].

Figure 9.3. *Screenshot of the Covid-19 campaign website of the NGO ALIMA*

Fondation Caritas France

Fondation Caritas France[10] was created in June 2009 by Secours Catholique to complement its capacities for action. It is a sheltering foundation, recognized as being of public utility in France. Its purpose is to combat poverty and social exclusion in France and internationally.

As such, it regularly launches fundraising campaigns, targeting potential major donors who wish to donate and benefit from tax deduction schemes against property wealth tax, for example. It therefore initiated, from its official website, communication on Covid-19 fundraising.

9 Available at: www.alima.ngo/qui-sommes-nous/.

10 Available at: www.fondationcaritasfrance.org/qui-sommes-nous/.

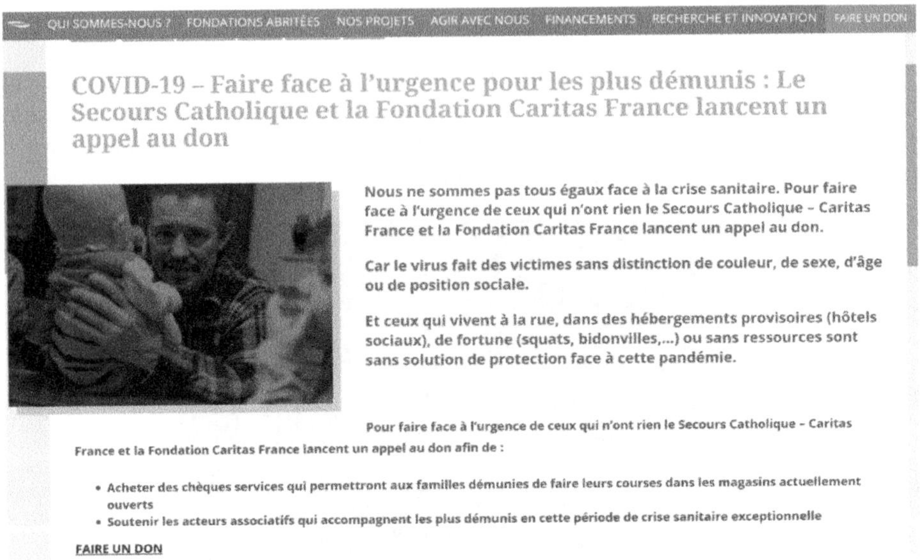

Figure 9.4. *Screenshot of the Covid-19 campaign website of the NGO Fondation Caritas France. For a color version of this figure, see www.iste.co.uk/pinede/digital.zip*

Fondation Entreprendre

Founded in 2008 and recognized as being of public utility in 2011, this is a sheltering foundation that works for the entrepreneurial cause in France[11]. Its chosen mission is to support and federate an ecosystem of actors in the general interest who take action on the ground to:

– develop entrepreneurial skills;

– promote equal entrepreneurial opportunities;

– support all entrepreneurial projects.

Its fundraising communication during Covid-19 was launched on its official website with a dedicated page. The communication focuses on the economic crisis and the difficulties being experienced by businesses.

11 Available at: www.fondation-entreprendre.org/la-fondation/.

Figure 9.5. *Screenshot of the Covid-19 campaign website of the NGO Fondation Entreprendre. For a color version of this figure, see www.iste.co.uk/pinede/digital.zip*

Fondation Hôpitaux de Paris

Fondation Hôpitaux de Paris[12] is a French foundation created in 1989 to improve the quality of daily life of children, adolescents and the elderly who are hospitalized in France. Its missions are as follows:

– family reunification;

– the development of activities;

– improved reception facilities and comfort;

– fight against pain;

– care facilities for adolescents in distress;

the transition from adolescence to young adulthood;

– the respite of loved ones.

12 Available at: www.fondationhopitaux.fr/fondation/.

Through its official website, it communicated on the efforts made in support of hospitals before appealing for donations. Its fundraising thus had the theme of support for the hospital system in difficulty because of the health crisis.

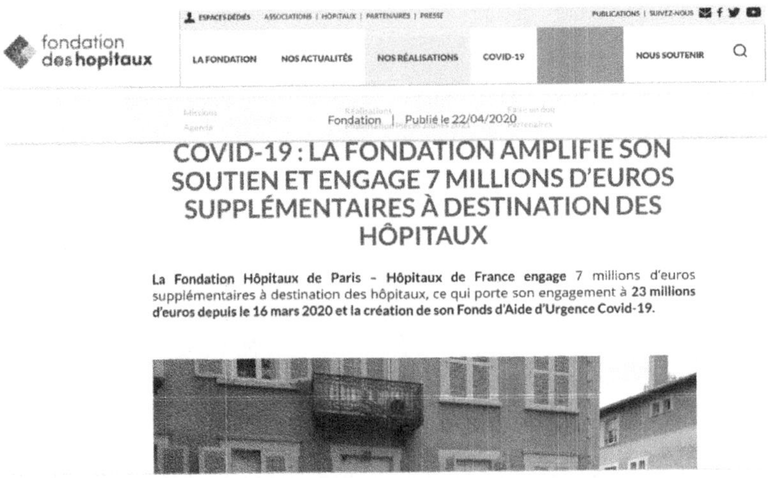

Figure 9.6. *Screenshot of the campaign website of the NGO Fondation Hôpitaux de Paris. For a color version of this figure, see www.iste.co.uk/pinede/digital.zip*

9.2.2.1.2. Materials and procedure

The corpus analyzed consists of the websites and dedicated Facebook pages for each of the organizations targeted. The corpus is summarized in Table 9.1.

An analysis grid showing the media and contents identified took into account the following criteria:

– editorial positioning;

– audience interaction;

– media strategy/strategies;

– content dissemination strategy/strategies;

– influencing and fundraising strategy/strategies.

	Web page	Facebook page
Alliance Urgence	allianceurgences.org	www.facebook.com/allianceurgences
Association ALIMA	oxygenforafrica.alima-ngo.org	www.facebook.com/ALIMAong
Fondation Caritas France	fondationcaritasfrance.org	www.facebook.com/Fondation CaritasFrance
Fondation Entreprendre	fondation-entreprendre.org	www.facebook.com/Fondation Entreprendre
Fondation Hôpitaux de Paris	fondationhopitaux.fr	www.facebook.com/Fondation Hopitaux

Table 9.1. *Corpus analyzed*

All this was linked together with the theoretical elements (cited above) seen on the one hand from the angle of the future donors being approached by the organizations that put in place discursive elements using levers aimed at generating counter donation, positive social action, factors of personal involvement and, on the other hand, the ability of the public – thus prospected – to seek value in the act of giving through the prism of self-representation and of the construction of a personal digital identity (Georges 2009), but also through the interactional approach of the physical relationship of complementarity and cooperation between the user and the digital object.

The digital channel was exclusively the space of proposal and media coverage of the offer, then of conversation and possibly of the act of conversion or transformation of the targeted prospects into donors. Thus, we were able to qualitatively assess the materiality of influential communication on tactically orchestrated digital media to take advantage of the strategic positioning of the Covid-19 cause with, in the background, a wide and diversified range of underlying communication themes that allowed the initiation of a timely fundraising strategy fostered by the Internet channel and the very nature of the social networking site (Facebook) because of its conversational universe.

The various Internet pages and also the Facebook pages dedicated to fundraising in the context relevant to this study were submitted to the analysis grid presented above. The content was then sorted and studied.

Through this analysis, we undertook to verify and synthesize the various parameters of involvement for individuals who were solicited by various organizations.

9.2.2.2. *The questionnaire*

Using a short questionnaire, we explored the perception of the African audience (in this case Beninese) of the fundraising appeals launched for their benefit. In formalizing this work, it seemed to us important and original to question the actual audience affiliation between donors and donation recipients.

In particular, we looked at how Africa perceived a fundraising appeal for its benefit in a context such as this. A short questionnaire was written in an exploratory rationale.

9.2.2.2.1. Population

The questionnaire was distributed to all close colleagues, work associates and personal acquaintances. A total of 44 participants responded to the survey. The average age is 44 years (SD = 10).

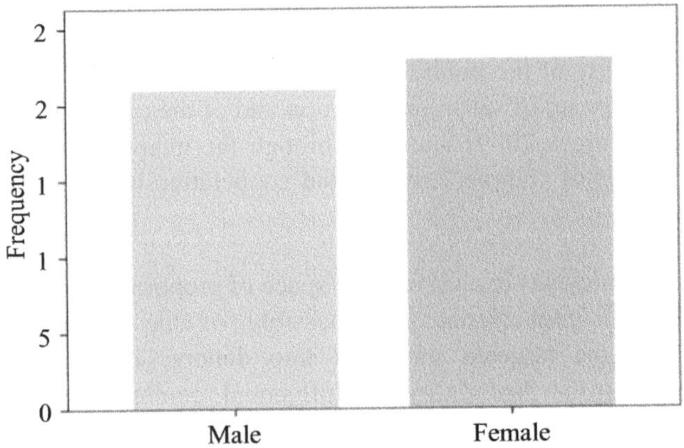

Figure 9.7. *Gender of respondents*

Forty-seven percent (21 individuals) of respondents are male, as opposed to 53% (23 individuals) female.

Individuals educated to at least university degree level are overrepresented, at 93%. This could be one of the main limitations of this investigation.

In fact, this percentage does not represent local reality, since in reality very few people have this level of education. It would be advisable to develop the results further by approaching more respondents.

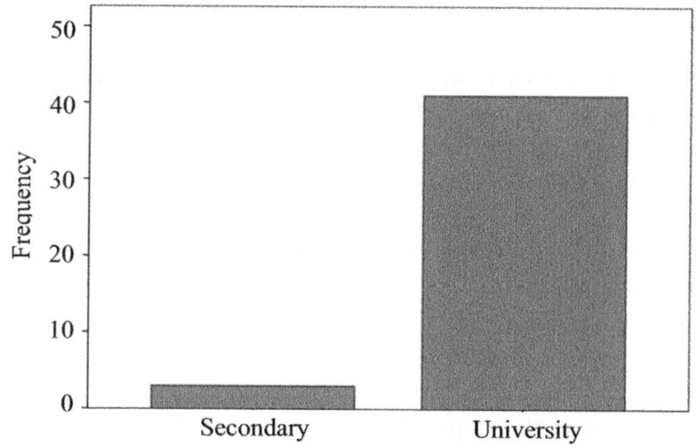

Figure 9.8. *Respondents' level of education*

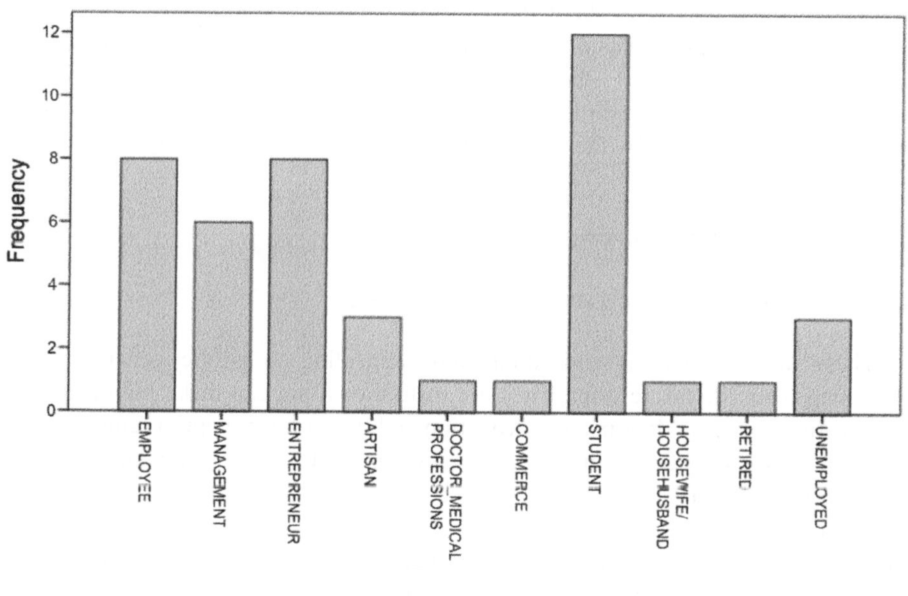

Figure 9.9. *Respondents' occupation*

All the social categories are represented, with a slight dominance of students (27%), followed by entrepreneurs and employees (18% for each category) and management (13%).

9.2.2.2.2. Materials and procedure

The materials consist of a short questionnaire for exploratory purposes, self-administered online. It is composed of a set of 13 questions designed to question respondents on what they think about international solidarity in the context of the pandemic related to the coronavirus crisis.

First, it allowed us to gather personal details (age, sex, occupation, level of education and marital status) of the individuals who were willing to respond. Then, closed questions were asked to establish whether the respondent or someone they know has contracted the virus or if someone in their circle of acquaintances has died from it. Two questions asked using the Likert scale (Likert 1932) made it possible to measure the degree of attachment the respondent may have toward victims, or the degree of severity that they attributed to the pandemic in Africa. This is a psychometric tool for measuring the attitude, the point of view and the position of an individual consists of a statement for which one must express a level of agreement or disagreement.

Finally, open questions about the donation were asked to gather participants' views on the appropriateness of the fundraising, the usefulness of the donation and their views on the nature of the donations that Africa should benefit from in this pandemic context. The questionnaire as described was disseminated online, and the responses were collected by the same channel during the month of May 2021.

9.3. Results and discussion

9.3.1. *Typology of actors and media coverage*

These are associations and foundations appealing to public generosity and benefiting from the tax rescript. They are institutions that can make public appeals for donations offering donors a tax deduction and thus a tax receipt in return. This is the result of the changes to professionalize the associative and humanitarian sector that began in the 1970s. This corresponds to a dual issue of seeking financial autonomy and the proliferation of actors involved, which has generated strong competition. Thus, in a context of State disengagement, NGOs have made a strategic issue of the source of the funds that support their social missions. They rely on the generosity of the public to ensure a sort of autonomy of action. It was simpler not to count on state aid or so-called institutional aid, which proves more restrictive and precarious because it is linked to current crises and was becoming increasingly scarce (Lefèvre 2007; Aferiat 2009).

From our analysis, it appears that these five charities made a conscious choice to focus their media positioning on a digital ecosystem based on three types of media channels: official website, landing page or microsite especially designed for the campaign. To this mechanism, they added pages on social media (Facebook in particular). This positioning seems to be well proven, established and designed to increase the number of points of contact with the audience and strengthen the visibility of the content created especially for Covid-19-related fundraising. This online mechanism is publicized by sending out marketing emails and purchasing online space, visible during the period on the Facebook, Google, Yahoo and Microsoft portals in the form of sponsored links or so-called native advertising. This visibility is complemented by statements made in the traditional media, with press releases and spot broadcasts. All the content broadcast in the media incorporates slogans and hooks that steer toward donation with hypertext links redirecting to donation pages. It should be borne in mind that we were in a context of heavy media coverage of the Covid-19 cause, compounded by a sense of inaction or collective lethargy kept up by the shock that may have been generated by the "house arrest" situation that the first lockdown decision seemed to create. It was legitimate for the associations in our study to deploy these online fundraising campaigns: legitimate in terms of the subthemes, legitimate in terms of previous actions already carried out and legitimate to use the digital channel. In correlation with the observation made by Lefèvre (2007), who makes a link between the direct marketing techniques of mail order sales and the fundraising marketing strategy adopted since 1980, the appropriation of digital tools in this context is also very close to e-commerce practices. The winning triptych in this kind of online fundraising operation comes from the urgency of the cause, the emotion in the message and the media coverage of the contents (Ahouandjinou et al. 2018). These ingredients are conveniently reunited here and seem to justify the campaign deployment strategy.

9.3.2. *Editorial positioning*

The general theme was the Covid-19 emergency, and the subthemes varied depending on the organizational positioning of the charities. We were able to identify two broad categories that correspond to the fields of intervention of the organizations studied.

As far as the international organizations are concerned (Alliance Urgence and ALIMA), the subthemes are emergency and international solidarity and mobilization to combat the COVID-19 emergency in Africa. Their content shows bias toward an iconographic and discursive choice focusing on Africa.

As for the associations operating in France, we were able to identify and categorize the following subthemes:

– the fight against poverty and precariousness in France for Fondation Caritas France;

– mobilization to save jobs and businesses for Fondation Entreprendre;

– support for hospitals for Fondation Hôpitaux de Paris.

The semantic universe, the discursive medium developed on the various digital platforms, is common for the five organizations. Included in it are mobilization, pandemic, support, emergency, vulnerability, engagement, solidarity, donation, Covid-19, coronavirus and so on.

The well-established argumentative tone is adopted, manifesting an expressive function that is very marked by the urgency of the economic and socio-sanitary crisis situation (choice of red and black colors for some) as well as the arousal of emotion with statements such as those reported in Box 9.1.

"Your donations make it possible to support fundraising for the purchase by Association ALIMA of respiratory equipment, 20 people give €50 = €1,000 = 1 oxygen concentrator."

"We are not all equal in the face of the health crisis. To address the emergency of those who have nothing, Secours Catholique Caritas France and Fondation Caritas France are launching a fundraising appeal."

"To enable the Fondation des Hôpitaux de Paris-Hôpitaux de France to continue its work and help patients, caregivers and their families."

"There is an unprecedented health catastrophe looming before our eyes, with mortality rates that will be much higher still than those we are currently experiencing in Europe, where we are already struggling to cope."

"Supporting entrepreneurs is at the heart of Fondation Entreprendre's concerns. With the Covid-19 health crisis, the foundation has strengthened its work to further support entrepreneurs in difficulty."

Box 9.1. *Hooks used by the organizations for the fundraising campaign*

The discourse of the five charities expresses narrative speech with an argumentative register that seeks to:

– convince (didactic register) with the use of key statistics to highlight the effort already made by the institution and to illustrate the value of a donation. The purpose here is to show the mobilization of the organization to address the situation and the intention to enlist the donor's participation or involvement to make them a stakeholder in the act of giving;

– persuade (between injunctive and oratorical register) to arouse emotion and urge the act of giving. While the primary intention is to make the cause known through a narrative objective with cognitive and promotional intent, the desire to persuade here has the purpose of urging the action (the conative objective) of an online donation. It is expressed in the complementary use of texts, images and videos, with the aim of mobilizing attention. These elements are sometimes supplemented by equivalences in materialized actions to the value of the donation and above all by the button that allows one to make this donation online. It is all these elements combined that characterize and create the mechanics of online narration to the advantage of the marketing objective of donating. The audience is made to feel valued and involved in becoming a donor-actor.

9.3.3. *Interaction with the donor audience*

Social media (especially Facebook) were the only channels of interaction with the solicited donors. In analyzing the organizations' various official Facebook pages, we noted that the discourse connected to this operation was heavily reposted.

The interest of the various communities who subscribe to the pages is essentially substantiated by clicks ("likes") to show approval, a lot of shares and a few comments. Table 9.2 provides a detailed and comprehensive report of the comments made by subscribers to each page on the specific occasion of this campaign.

	Facebook page	Comments noted
Alliance Urgence	www.facebook.com/ allianceurgences	Instead of criticism, rich countries must mobilize to help poor countries. Until all countries eradicate the virus, we will no longer be able to live as before. Help the poor, SOS, please help them. India is a very poor country, hygiene and barrier measures are still not being complied with. The population is short of masks due to lack of financial means, it is sad let us help them.

	Facebook page	Comments noted
Association ALIMA	www.facebook.com/ ALIMAong	Congratulations to you, ALIMA is the number one project to be proud of. As in the motto, patients are put first. Bravo ALIMA and keep up the good work. Thank you to all humanitarians, a phew of relief and let us hope that this equipment will be used effectively and efficiently. Wishing Covid-19 patients a swift recovery, but will humanitarians be working to vaccinate Africans against Covid-19?
Fondation Caritas France	www.facebook.com/ FondationCaritasFrance	Our integration and fabric recycling workshop has increased its mask production capacity as a result of new materials given to us thanks to the support of Caritas. Thank you for your support and guidance during this health crisis.
Fondation Entreprendre	www.facebook.com/ FondationEntreprendre	There is a lot to be done, and we are not alone in taking up the challenge. To valiant hearts nothing is impossible, congratulations to Fondation Entreprendre.
Fondation Hôpitaux de Paris	www.facebook.com/ FondationHopitaux	How can people who have no Internet access participate in the donation? I participated in the fundraising operation and I am proud to have contributed to the good cause of the Fondation des Hôpitaux. Bravo to the foundation for its investment in our nurses. I suggest that the funds from all offenses relating to non-compliance with Covid rules be donated to the foundation.

Table 9.2. *List of comments posted by users on Facebook*

These comments relay and amplify the original message of the institutions. Beyond simple "likes", comments constitute an act of engagement and audience positioning in relation to the communication. Likes, shares and comments are the indicators increasingly being sought by the organizations. In particular, commenting is an act that shows the establishment of a more advanced form of interaction and cooperation with the proposed digital object (Pignier 2012). It is testament to a degree of buy-in from the people targeted by the messages and advertisements. Comments also constitute an act of positioning, identity building and self-presentation (of the Internet user) in the natively conversational universe of

Facebook (Georges 2009; Cardon 2013). The arguments put forward by the institutions on their page to elicit audience reaction play on the latter's emotional register. In addition, the audience regards the messages appealing for donations as an absolute truth, proved by the legitimacy conferred on their authors.

However, the donor audience, the greater part of which is external to the beneficiary audience and its spaces, only has as reality the imagery conveyed on the cause and on the fields of intervention such as Africa. The funds raised are thus destined for an audience that is "foreign" to the donor, no longer exactly meeting the traditional characteristics of the donation (Mauss 2012) in archaic societies, namely donating, receiving and re-donating. Here, we see the emergence of other characteristics of the donation in modern societies (Caillé 1998). According to him, modern societies develop another form of donation, that is, destined for foreigners. As a result, the donation no longer engenders stable interpersonal bonds of closeness and inter-knowledge. Speaking about interaction here would be limited to the relationships between the fundraising institutions and the donor audience, in other words the Internet users. At this level, even virtual interaction generates just as much influence of one over the other, a rather primordial result in all the "rites of interaction". In this context, the interaction is of a positive nature, especially as it demonstrates cooperation and participation in support of a common cause.

9.3.4. *On the question of the perception of fundraising appeals for Africa*

The results, cursory as they are, point the way to a more comprehensive study. However, we will present them here because the survey was set up in order to try to base certain comments on field data. The collected data were processed using the statistical software SPSS. Simple descriptive analyses were carried out.

Fifteen respondents out of all those who took the survey reported knowing someone who had died of the disease. This figure may seem high, but it should be tempered by the fact that this survey was carried out with a non-representative sample. Therefore, the results cannot be generalized. It would not be surprising if these 15 people actually all knew two or three victims who are the same people. Indeed, Africa, whose population represents 17% of the world's population, was recording barely 5% of global cases due to the pandemic in August 2020 (Hardy and Flori 2021). In Benin, in February 2020, there were 5,039 diagnosed patients per 62 deaths (Flash Infos – Covid-19 2020)[13].

13 Available at: www.gouv.bj/coronavirus/flashinfos/.

	Number of respondents	Lowest estimate on a scale of 10	Highest estimate on a scale of 10	Average
Degree of proximity of respondents to the victims (having contracted the disease or having died)	15	1.00	6.00	2.00
Perceived degree of severity of the pandemic in Africa	44	1.00	10.00	4.00

Table 9.3. *Descriptive statistics on the degree of proximity of deceased victims of Covid-19 to respondents and their perception of the severity of the pandemic in Africa*

It must be noted that out of 10, the maximum degree of proximity to victims reported by respondents is 6. Moreover, on average, the degree of proximity is 2/10. These figures show that few people have been affected by the pandemic in their daily lives. Even if they know people who have contracted the disease or even died as a result of Covid-19, they are usually people outside their direct circle. Overall, few people were actually directly affected by the disease.

Furthermore, on average, it can be seen in Table 9.3 that the participants assign a score of 4/10 to the degree of severity of the pandemic on the African continent. This score is fairly average and a slight contradiction to the previous figures. This may be due to the non-health-related consequences of the disease. These consequences, whether social or economic, have certainly weighed on the entire population. Indeed, "the countries of sub-Saharan Africa affected by the Covid-19 pandemic are increasingly facing a decline in raw materials and a slump in international trade" (Tougan and Théwis 2020). This has a direct impact on the availability of raw materials, in particular foodstuffs and, in turn, prices which have soared. In addition, household productivity has fallen sharply because in Africa forms of activity stemming from the unofficial economy provide the bulk of jobs available to urban households (Maldonado and Gaufryau 2001). However, these unofficial activities have been greatly impacted by crisis management.

At the social level, the barrier measures (especially the banning of physical contact) recommended by the health authorities and the local arrangements put in place (setting up a *cordon sanitaire* around the worst affected cities, closing borders, obligatory quarantine for all arrivals at the international airport, etc.) had a definite impact on the quality of the social bond and forced the populations to reformulate customary habits. For example, gatherings of more than 50 people were banned for a long time, resulting in a restructuring of the rituals for births, marriages, deaths and so on.

The economic and social repercussions of the pandemic, since the health-related repercussions are scarcely noticeable to the population, could explain the reasons why our respondents consider that Africa is moderately affected by the pandemic. Even though the numbers of deaths and infections defy all forecasts, the pandemic has hit the continent hard.

9.3.5. *On the question of international solidarity*

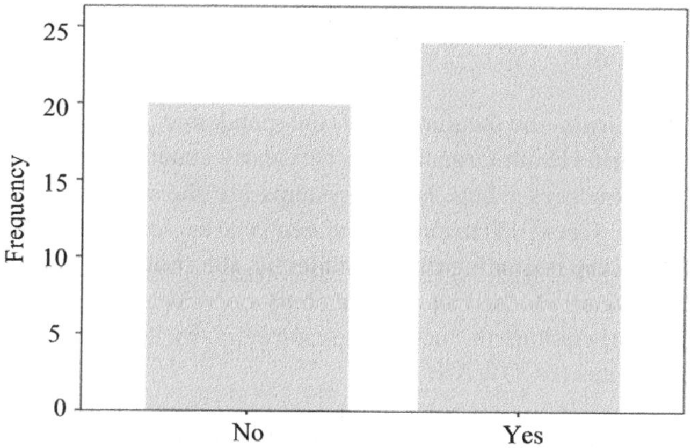

Figure 9.10. *Respondents' views on the need for international solidarity with Africa*

9.3.5.1. *The need for international aid for Africa*

A small majority of respondents (54%) believe that Africa does actually need international aid to manage the Covid-19 crisis (see Figure 9.10). People who support this view put forward a range of arguments.

9.3.5.1.1. Donation of the richest to the poorest: a "normal" action

> "It is normal that in times of crisis the richest help the poorest." (Comment taken from data from the online questionnaire)

Donation here is taken as law and no longer as a voluntary act, proof of generosity and benevolence. The idea here is that it is entirely normal, and even expected, for the richest countries (their governments but also their citizens) to have an ethical aim to redistribute wealth. The comments recorded clearly refer to the fact that "from now on it is solely a question of rights, rights for the most deprived, inferred from a principle of solidarity" (Chanial 2020), and we can extrapolate here by saying that it is exclusively a principle of north-south solidarity that seems to regard donation as the counter donation of the supposed or/proven dispossessions (agricultural, mining, human, etc.) of the pre-colonial, colonial and post-colonial periods.

9.3.5.1.2. The inability of African infrastructure to contain management of the pandemic without aid

> Africa does not have the medical infrastructure to manage the pandemic effectively. (Comment taken from data from the online questionnaire)

It is true that from the beginning of the pandemic and its spreading to all continents, the World Health Organization very early stated its concern about health management "in countries where health systems are the weakest"[14]. In Benin, for example, only one Covid-19 management center was set up (at the time of the survey) and at the very beginning of the pandemic, the shortage of respirators across the country raised fears for the worst. It was only on 9 August 2020 that the country was offered medical equipment, including respirators, by the Economic Community of West African States (ECOWAS)[15].

Current immunization management shows that without international solidarity, through the Covax program (a global collaboration aimed at accelerating development, production and equitable access to Covid-19 tests, treatments and vaccines)[16], vaccines would have taken longer to become available to the entire population in Benin. Regional and international solidarity has thus contributed greatly to the prevention, detection and management of the disease.

---

14 Available at: www.who.int/fr/news-room/detail/30-03-2020-who-releases-guidelines-to-help-countries-main-tain-essential-healthservices-during-the-covid-19-pandemic.

15 Available at: www.gouv.bj/actualite/803/coronavirus-cedeao-fait-plusieurs-equipements-benin/.

16 Available at: www.gavi.org/fr/facilite-covax#quoi.

9.3.5.1.3. Support to limit the economic consequences of the pandemic

> Africa has fewer patients but is suffering more drastically from the economic aftermath of the crisis. (Comment taken from data from the online questionnaire)

In the face of the pandemic, Africa has adapted, to everyone's surprise, by gearing up an exceptional resilience. However, in economic terms, it was already weakened through a fabric particularly affected by other diseases (malaria, HIV, cholera, etc.), and a structure based largely on the unofficial sector. Covid-19 "is threatening to push as many as 58 million people into extreme poverty. However, in addition to the poor Africans, the Covid pandemic is also affecting Africa's thriving middle class, about 170 million of the 1.3 billion Africans currently classed as middle class. Nearly 8 million of these could be plunged into poverty because of coronavirus and its economic consequences. This setback will be felt for decades" (Kohnert 2021). Everyone, in their daily lives, will have taken stock of the economic repercussions of Covid-19, as market prices have soared due to food items being less available.

9.3.5.2. *The absence of a need for international aid for Africa*

The interesting figure here is still the 46% who seem to think otherwise, namely that Africa does not need international aid, in the context of managing the pandemic. Among the reasons given to justify this point of view, we find the key arguments explained below.

9.3.5.2.1. Other continents more concerned

> France is more affected by the pandemic than Africa. (Comment taken from data from the online questionnaire)

In case it needs to be repeated, in terms of health, Africa is doing quite well. As of April 23, 2021, a total of 4,522,489 confirmed Covid-19 cases and 119,816 deaths were reported (Kohnert 2021). For comparison, in the same period (April 2021), France reported 4,827,920 cases for 96,678 deaths[17].

This argument is based on the realities on the ground, which lead some people to make conjectures about the sparing of Africa.

---

17 Available at: www.mesvaccins.net/web/news/17337-situation-hebdomadaire-de-la-pandemie-de-covid-19-n-15-26-avril-2021-partie-1-situation-monde-pacifique-occidental-europe.

9.3.5.2.2. Africa's own resources to fight the pandemic

> The local pharmacopoeia is rich in diverse remedies against the disease. (Comment taken from data from the online questionnaire)

When the pandemic reached its external borders, Africa quickly turned to its traditional medicine to support conventional prevention techniques (barrier measures). In fact, the healthcare system is precarious, as has been described, and no effective treatment against the disease is available. Rapidly, there began to circulate on social media recipes based on leaves, spices, tree-bark, and roots supposed to prevent and even cure Covid-19. Thus, "a total of 318 recipes from 145 plant species have been inventoried across various publications" (Haidara et al. 2020). Benin was no exception in this. While, to date, there are no studies to prove the effectiveness of these traditional recipes, it must be noted that the low rate of contamination and deaths, according to official statistics, strengthens people's confidence in their effectiveness.

9.3.6. *Typology of aid for Africa*

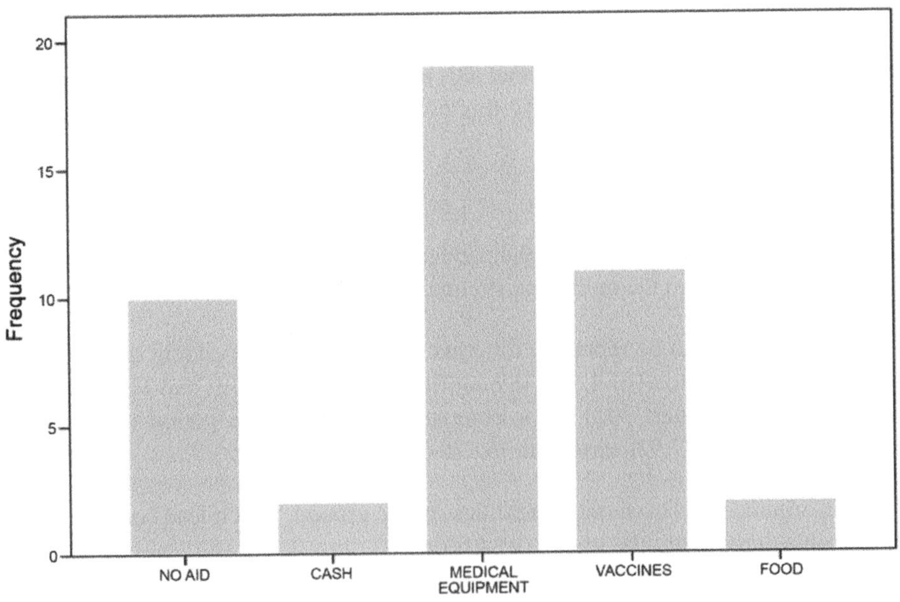

Figure 9.11. *Respondents' views on Africa's needs for international solidarity*

According to our respondents, the greatest need in terms of aid is medical equipment (43%) and vaccines (25%). These data suggest that the issue of health management of the pandemic remains a major concern for our respondents. It is important to mention, however, that the vast majority of Benin's inhabitants tend to be reluctant to be vaccinated. At the time of self-administration of the questionnaire in Benin, Sinovac and Astra Zeneca vaccines were available. Vaccination centers were empty, despite appeals from the government and awareness-raising messages disseminated on every channel.

9.4. Conclusion

In view of the global health crisis due to Covid-19, the responsiveness of the organizations whose fundraising campaigns are the subject of this study was immediate. This immediacy was greatly facilitated by the use of digital technology, with the creation of pages and special content on websites and pages on social media. The context of lockdown and physical and social distancing encouraged this. The accessibility and ergonomics offered by digital technology allow speed both in communication policies and the transmission of messages on a large scale. During this pandemic, the entire planet was kept informed of what was happening in the farthest lands. The pandemic had extensive media coverage on all possible channels, and populations were solicited through the same channels to mobilize the resources to tackle it. Foundations and charities did not hesitate to use it to reach the French public and urge donations. They thus developed narrative mechanisms and communication materials adapted to the context. To do this, they based their semantic choices on the main themes transmitted at the time on all the media channels, which were able to generate support for a globally shared cause. The urgency was particularly underlined by the adoption of an appropriate communication style. The compliance of the African populations with regard to fundraising appeals for Africa, in retrospect, remains the least uncorrelated to the reality at the time, difficult to measure. It would be interesting to look here at the effect that the media and their coverage of the pandemic have had on the populations' perception of the pandemic's risk. Indeed, "communication plays a predominant role in people's reading of the risk" (Joffe and Orfali 2005).

In addition, while the populations seem willing to receive aid relating to vaccine accessibility, it would be interesting to conduct a study on the real acceptability of vaccines against Covid-19 by the populations and also on the opportunity to appeal for charitable donations to fund the health system, preventive measures and people in need due to the economic crisis created by this situation.

9.5. References

Aferiat, Y. (2009). Yaële Aferiat (AFF): Le fundraising ? un petit plus dont on ne peut pas se passer... [Online]. Available at: https://www.letudiant.fr/educpros/entretiens/yaele-aferiat-aff-le-fundraising-un-petit-plus-dont-on-ne-peut-pas-se-passer.html [Accessed 8 October 2021].

Ahouandjinou, G., Affognon, P., Silva, C., Da Cruz, M. (2018). Charity e-business ou la collecte de fonds sur le numérique en France. *Revue des sciences du langage et de la communication (ReSciLaC)*, 8, 409–430.

Alberola-Ila, E., Arslan, Y., Cheng, G., Moessner, R. (2020). The fiscal response to the Covid-19 crisis in advanced and emerging market economies. Report, BIS Bulletins, Bank for International Settlements, 23 [Online]. Available at: https://ideas.repec.org/p/bis/bisblt/23.html [Accessed 8 October 2021].

Caillé, A. (1998). Don et association. *La Revue du M.A.U.S.S. Semestrielle*, 11 [Online]. Available at: http://www.journaldumauss.net/?Don-et-association [Accessed 15 October 2021].

Cardon, D. (2013). Liens faibles et liens forts sur les réseaux sociaux. *Les Cahiers français*, 372, 61–66.

Chanial, P. (2020). Ce que donner aux pauvres veut dire. Théorie du don et protection sociale. [Online]. Available at: https://www.cairn.info/aemo-aed-con-trole-social-des-pauvres--9782749255071-page-281.htm [Accessed 6 October 2021].

Dupont, S. (2002). Enjeux d'Internet dans la communication des associations. PhD Thesis, École de Journalisme et de Communication de Marseille, Marseille [Online]. Available at: https://wikimemoires.net/2013/08/les-enjeux-d-inter-net-dans-la-communication-des-associations/ [Accessed 10 October 2021].

Georges, F. (2009). Représentation de soi et identité numérique. *Réseaux*, 154(2), 165–193.

Gergen, K.J. and Gergen, M.M. (1986). *Altruism: Giving and Receiving Help*. Spinger, New York.

Guédeney, N. (2011). Les racines de l'estime de soi : apports de la théorie de l'attachement. *Devenir*, 23(2), 129–144.

Haidara, M., Diarra, M.L., Doumbia, S., Denou, A., Dembele, D., Diarra, B., Sanogo, R. (2020). Plantes médicinales de l'Afrique de l'Ouest pour la prise en charge des affections respiratoires pouvant se manifester au cours de la Covid-19. *International Journal of Biological and Chemical Sciences*, 14(8), 2941–2950.

Hardy, É.J.L. and Flori, P. (2021). Spécificités épidémiologiques de la COVID-19 en Afrique : préoccupation de santé publique actuelle ou future ? *Annales pharmaceutiques françaises*, 79(2), 216–226.

Joffe, H. and Orfali, B. (2005). De la perception à la représentation du risque : le rôle des médias. *Hermès*, 41(1), 121–129.

Kohnert, D. (2021). Sur l'impact socio-économique des pandémies en Afrique : leçons tirées du COVID-19, de la trypanosomiase, du VIH-SIDA, de la fièvre jaune, du choléra. Report, Social Science Research Network, Rochester [Online]. Available at: https://papers.ssrn.com/abstract=3840345 [Accessed 7 October 2021].

Lefevre, S. (2007). Le sale boulot et les bonnes causes. *Politix*, 79(3), 149–172.

Likert, R. (1932). A technique for the measurement of attitudes. *Archives of Psychology*, 140, 1–55.

Maldonado, C. and Gaufryau, B. (2001). *L'économie informelle en Afrique francophone : structure, dynamiques et politiques*. International Labour Organization, Geneva.

Mauss, M. (2012). *Essai sur le don. Forme et raison de l'échange dans les sociétés archaïques*. PUF, Paris.

Pignier, N. (2012). Le plaisir de l'interaction entre l'usager et les objets TIC numériques. *Interfaces numériques*, 1(1) [Online]. Avalaible at: https://www.unilim.fr/interfaces-numeriques/74.

Poels, G. and Lefort, V. (2021). Au second semestre 2020, les JT ont moins couvert la pandémie de Covid-19. *La Revue des médias* [Online]. Available at: http://larevuedesmedias.ina.fr/covid-19-un-an-jt-journal-televise-2020 [Accessed 4 October 2021].

Rouquette, M.-L. (1997). *La chasse à l'immigré : violence, mémoire et représentations*. Mardaga, Liège.

Thielmann, I., Spadaro, G., Balliet, D. (2020). Personality and prosocial behavior: A theoretical framework and meta-analysis. *Psychological Bulletin*, 146(1), 30–90.

Tougan, U.P. and Théwis, A. (2020). Covid-19 et sécurité alimentaire en Afrique Subsaharienne : implications et mesures proactives d'atténuation des risques de malnutrition et de famine. *International Journal of Progressive Sciences and Technologies*, 20(1), 172–193.

Vintila, A. (2012). L'implication personnelle, variable explicative majeure de la pensée sociale. Quelques rappels du modèle tridimensionnel proposé par M.-L. Rouquette. *Psihologia socială*, 30, 121–128.

PART 3

Communication of Organizations and Online Narrative

10

Communicating through Narrative: Organizations Facing the Challenge of their Collective Dimension?

Julien FALGAS
Crem, Université de Lorraine, Metz, France

10.1. Introduction

D'Almeida (2004) regards the communication of organizations as "the production of stories intended to give spatial, temporal and social unity to working groups threatened with implosion". However, organizations are giving increasing prominence to their digital presence in their communication strategies, whereas Christian Salmon – the emblematic author of the critique of *storytelling* – asserts that *storytelling* has been overtaken by new digital forms of communication: one could say the *clash* has taken over from the *story* (Salmon 2019).

What are the links between the communication of organizations, online digital systems and narrative production? How should organizational communication be situated in relation to the practices of scriptwriting one's own story that are common on digital social networking sites? On digital systems, could narration be a communication act more closely linked to the individual dimension? If so, would narration be an unnatural form of representation for organizations? Can non-human actors claim to be narrators? Or does the strength of the narrations produced within an organization lie in the collective nature of stories taken up in equal measure by

Digital Presences of Organizations,
coordinated by Nathalie PINÈDE, Luc MASSOU and Patrick MPONDO-DICKA.

both the human actors who constitute it and those who interact with the organization?

Driven by these questions, it seems necessary to propose a definitional and notional framework capable of providing an infocommunicational perspective. Behind the act of narrating, the notion of narration is associated with the notions of storytelling and story. We propose to clarify the contours of this triad, the terms of which are often used imprecisely.

Our proposal stems from an approach that borrows from the sociology of Howard S. Becker. The application of our proposal to content analysis is more a strategy for formulating hypotheses than a self-sufficient analytical method. This is the approach that we will apply here by testing our proposal against a series of Web publications from a banking organization.

Faced with the diversity of communicational forms and mechanisms imposed on organizations in the digital environment, we will question both the pertinence of approaching organizations' communication in narrative terms and the pertinence of doing so on the basis of a Web page analysis.

10.2. Defining the act of narrating by the storytelling, narration and story triad

We have made definitional choices in order to lay the foundations for a doctoral research project in information and communication sciences devoted to narrative innovation (Falgas 2014). This basis proved fertile for prefacing and introducing contributions to the proceedings of the symposium "Mettre en récit, Enjeux des formes contemporaines de narration" organized by the association of young researchers of the Center for Research on Mediations (AJC Crem) on 15 March 2018 in Metz (Falgas 2021). In this case, the focus was on guiding our reading of the contributions of young researchers at a colloquium that explicitly mobilized the notions of storytelling and narration, without however subscribing to a narratological approach. Here, we will consider the mobilization of our definitional choices for Web page analysis.

In a review of the Anglo-Saxon literature devoted to the narrative approach of organizations for *La Revue française de gestion*, Giroux and Marroquin (2005) point out that "the concrete definition of what a narrative text is varies considerably from one author to another and the narrative analysis sometimes seems to be somewhat unsystematic" (p. 30). According to their observations, the researchers give the following statuses to narration:

– a source of data collected through interviews;

– a process to be explained, based on the observation of individuals narrating stories;

– a method of analysis for the study of texts, discourses and media productions;

– a mode of presenting data, appropriate for showing the affective dimension[1];

– a means of intervention to bring about change, build a shared vision of the future, stimulate communication and share knowledge.

Ultimately, Giroux and Marroquin regret that the authors make little use of the French research in narratology. In her *Introduction à la narratologie*, the linguist Revaz (2009) does however note that it is impossible to provide an unambiguous definition of either storytelling or narration. As in many fields, the definition of their research topic is a hot topic of debate for narratologists. Commenting on the words of Baroni (2016), supporting an institutionalization of narratology, Saurier and Vallée (2017) point out that terms such as storytelling or "narration [...] contain an implied clarity on the subject, without being defined, thus presenting a troublingly approximate usage" (p. 280). In the introduction to a special issue of the periodical *Organization* devoted to *storytelling* and organizational change, Brown et al. (2009) go so far as to judge questions and definitional efforts as sterile.

Without entering the arena of the definitional debate, it was necessary for us to base the notion of narrative innovation on unambiguous operational definitions of the terms storytelling, story and, of course, narration.

Revaz identifies several properties that define the degree of narrativity. Thus, all narration consists of a representation of actions or events, whose cumulative properties determine the degree of narrativity:

– the chronicle is characterized by inscription in a chronology;

– the relation is characterized by the existence of causal links between successive actions or events;

1 We were able to record this dimension in an earlier work in which we used narration choosing to chronicle the highlights of our collaboration with the information platform The Conversation France (Appel and Falgas 2019). This narrative approach to academic writing promoted the highlighting of the affective dimension which, in a more traditional context, would have gone unmentioned, although it has been decisive in the action research we were reviewing.

– storytelling in the strict sense requires a plot, "that is, a mode of composition comprising a knot and an unknotting" (Revaz 2009, p. 128). Let us highlight here the lexical field of thread, which we will come back to at the end of this section.

The linguist Adam (1996) asserts that "in order to speak of 'storytelling' one must show at least one event" (p. 10). The singleness of the event for Adam may seem to contradict the idea of causal succession of actions and events identified by Revaz. However, Adam (1996) provides an example of minimal storytelling: "The child cried. Dad took him in his arms" (p. 12). According to him, this example constitutes one and the same event, but it does indeed mobilize two actions inscribed in a causal succession. It could also be considered that each of the two actions itself constitutes an event. This is just one of so many examples of the subtle definitional variances that are likely to take us away from a "practical" definition of narration, storytelling and story. Such a definition is necessary, however, if we are claiming to render the reflection effective in narrative terms.

In any case, Adam uses the notion of representation, which implies an interpretation of the real or fictional deeds that are narrated. The representation aims to stimulate and guide the production of meaning in the recipient. Adam (1996) explains that "to become a story, an event must be narrated in the form of at least two temporally ordered propositions, forming a story" (p. 12). This particular form of representation constitutes narration, in other words, a representation of the story. The term *story* refers to a succession of actions or events which, by being put into a plot, can be revealed in an order or at a pace that is different to their chronology.

How can the story be distinguished from the narration? Although wishing to confirm the legitimacy of social sciences in embracing narrative questions, Brown et al. (2009) accept that the authors they have supervised mobilize the terms *story* and *narrative* indiscriminately. Above all, they take the view that *storytelling* relates to events organized in sequence, with plots that are woven and intertwined into unified and complex constructs that reveal something meaningful (Brown et al. 2009). Let us emphasize once again the occurrence of the lexical field of thread in the notion of weaving.

In an infocommunicational perspective, beyond the plotting deemed necessary by Revaz, the term storytelling identifies for us the communication act through which the narrative is embodied. To interrogate the act of narrating, to study the story, is to focus on a particular type of communication: the narrative. In terms of discourse analysis, Adam (1996) speaks of "textual types" and identifies in particular "the descriptive, the explanatory, the argumentative, the narrative, the conversational, the injunctive-instructive types and the rhetorical-poetical type" (p. 10). Considering the narrative as a type of communication allows us to mobilize tools other than those of linguistics and to focus on other dimensions than that of text (be it constituted of an image, film or oral speech).

So, we can define the act of narrating as well as the terms story, narration and storytelling as summarized in Table 10.1.

Term	Definition
Story	A succession of actions or events (real or fictional)
Narrate	To represent a story
Narration	The representation of a story
Storytelling	A communication act of a narrative nature

Table 10.1. *Story, narration, storytelling: what it is covered by the word narrate*

Storytelling must be situated both in the plurality of media that it can use to embody narration (Barthes 1966) and in the plurality of discourse forms with which narrative discourse is in co-presence (not to say in competition) on digital screens (Falgas 2014). Thus, in everyday life, the idea of storytelling commonly refers to an aesthetic experience or entertainment. The cultural industries have made it a product for everyday consumption, distributed by platforms that "remain value capture instruments at the service of actors whose objective is always profit" (Dessinges and Perticoz 2019, p. 10) and who as such frame and sustain the consumption of stories through mechanisms that manage to shift user autonomy in the choice of programs into the background while preserving the illusion of their freedom. Storytelling as a means of transmitting values is instrumentalized under its Anglo-Saxon name, which describes a method of communication used to seduce or influence on the basis of the values of a brand or an organization (Salmon 2008; Citton 2010; Marti and Pélissier 2012). By using the notion of representation to define narration, we are able to move away from the analysis of narrative phenomena to question the ins and outs of narrative communication.

Looking at artifactual representations such as texts, shots, films or images, Becker (2009) divides the communication process into four stages that make up what he calls the "manufacturing of representations" (pp. 34–40).

The producer-manufacturer first makes a selection, necessarily partial, of data that will be represented. In our case, the selection focuses on the actions and events that constitute the story.

The producer-manufacturer then performs a transcription of the selected data, following standards specific to his/her medium, which must allow users to judge the resulting representation acceptable. In this case, we will focus on Web publications. Although website interface codes are not especially narrative, in a media environment marked by modularity (Manovitch 2010) and convergence (Jenkins 2006), they can borrow from the media repertoire with a strong narrative tradition such as literature or comic strips, or from that of video games, whose narrative potentialities are of particular interest to researchers (Genvo 2018).

The next step is the arrangement of the data, namely the tone, the aesthetic choices (typography, graphics, etc.) adopted by the representation. This step is central in narratological analyses. However, as is illustrated by the example produced by Baroni (2018) to argue for the need to continue work on narrative theorization, narratology focuses more particularly on the description and interpretation of the arrangement choices than on the elucidation of their human and material production conditions.

Finally, users make their interpretation based on the knowledge and skills they possess. The study of this stage in combination with the previous three enables us above all to establish the decisive role of reference frameworks common to producer-manufacturers and users in the implementation of the process of narrative innovation through which new narrative forms can emerge (Falgas 2014).

In short, considering storytelling as a communication act (narrating is a way of communicating) embodied in the narration as a representation, the story constitutes the selection of successive actions and events. It is transcribed according to the standards of a given medium and arranged through aesthetic and stylistic choices before being interpreted by its audiences. Table 10.2 summarizes the breaking down of the stages of manufacturing the representation in the specific case of the narrative representation.

1. Selection	Story	A succession of actions or events (real or fictional)
2. Arrangement	Narrate	To represent a story
3. Transcription	Narration	The representation of a story
4. Interpretation	Storytelling	A communication act of a narrative nature

Table 10.2. *The manufacturing of the narration, as a representation in the meaning of H.S. Becker*

For D'Almeida (2004), economic storytelling is a way for companies to address the event in its primacy to re-engage with a long timeframe. She divides the narrative production of organizations around two hubs: in-house storytelling and engagement storytelling (D'Almeida 2012). In-house storytelling showcases internal values and an imagined community in order to bind together the internal audience for whom it is primarily intended.

Engagement storytelling in its turn showcases universal values and seeks to position the organization as an actor in quest of the common good. D'Almeida (2004) notes the failure of in-house storytelling whose "we" clashes with multiple other "we's" (unions, location, profession, etc.), and the "I" of the actors, employees, and especially the young, who demand their authenticity. The heroic storytelling of the entrepreneurial adventure of the founder is shown to be flawed by the realities on the ground, often in contradiction with the values asserted by the story.

The engagement storytelling that historically follows the in-house storytelling seeks to overcome its shortcomings by asserting the organization's mission in terms of universal values and issues external to itself. The objective is to be associated with a universal "we". Paradoxically, this leads private companies to present themselves as providing a public service of general interest. Such a form of narrative communication seems less problematic, even natural, for companies of a cooperative nature or those having adopted the status of mission-oriented companies.

This is why we chose to analyze Web publications of Crédit Coopératif, a French cooperative bank that initially served cooperative and participatory societies (SCOPs) and social and solidarity financial institutions, such as associations and mutual companies. The analysis will be deployed in line with the framework of the manufacturing of the narration, in order to judge its scope in terms of Web page analysis. The sociological origins of our analysis framework may raise fears that it will show itself to be ineffective or not precise enough for strict content analysis. We will question to what extent the framework of the manufacturing of the narration can contribute to the founding of hypotheses liable to escape narratological approaches or more broadly approaches through content analysis alone.

10.3. Application to the Web page analysis: the analysis framework of the manufacturing of representations

In 2020, Crédit Coopératif published a website entitled "Le pouvoir de nous engager" (The power to engage us), intended to demonstrate that "wherever it goes, your money does good"[2] (Figure 10.1). This website makes particular use of an infographic about the traceability of the sums deposited in the current accounts of

2 Available at: www.lepouvoirdenousengager.fr.

the bank's customers (Figure 10.2)[3] and an "immersive 3D experience" which features the cooperative bank's 2019 data (Figure 10.3)[4].

Figure 10.1. *Screenshot of the section visible to the visitor landing on the home page of the website "Le Pouvoir de nous engager". For a color version of this figure, see www.iste.co.uk/pinede/digital.zip*

Figure 10.2. *Screenshot of the first item displayed under the title screen of the home page of "Le Pouvoir de nous engager". This is a link to an infographic dedicated to the traceability of the sums deposited in the current accounts of the bank's customers. For a color version of this figure, see www.iste.co.uk/pinede/digital.zip*

3 Available at: www.lepouvoirdenousengager.fr/comprendre#infographie [Accessed 9 March 2021].

4 Available at: www.lepouvoirdenousengager.fr/circuitdelargent/ [Accessed 9 March 2021].

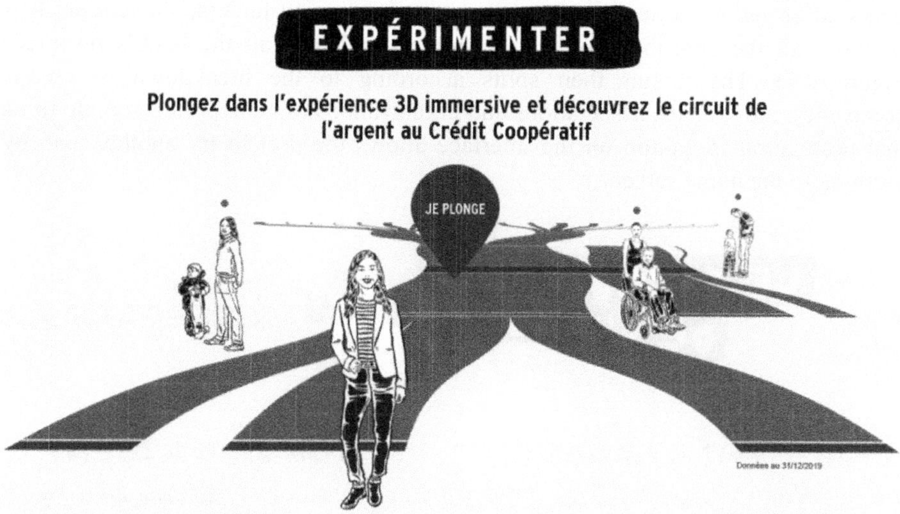

Figure 10.3. *Screenshot, bottom of home page of the website "Le Pouvoir de nous engager", the link to the "immersive 3D experience" featuring the bank's 2019 data. For a color version of this figure, see www.iste.co.uk/pinede/digital.zip*

The home screen of the immersive 3D experience, "Le Circuit de l'argent" (The money circuit) (Figure 10.4), invites the user to assume the identity of their choice from a drop-down menu entitled "I am" (a company, an association, an organization of general interest and an individual). The message is also addressed to the bank's employees, since it is possible to take on that role through their bond holdings or their equity. The user must also opt for an objective by choosing from a second drop-down menu entitled "I want to see the impact of my money on"[5].

By confirming their choices by clicking on the "discover" button, the user accesses a 3D circuit in subjective view whose width is proportional to the financial sums involved (Figure 10.5). The user navigates the circuit by means of the up and down arrows on the keyboard or the arrow buttons on the interface. At the various stages on the circuit, illustrations represent scenarios and people that are clickable to

5 The choices offered are as follows: distribution cooperatives, agricultural cooperatives, SCOPs, other cooperatives, eco-activities, SMEs/SMIs, construction sector, other actors in the real economy, individuals, social housing, disability, the local public sector, the elderly and health, social associations, children and integration, training, education and research, the environment, culture, tourism and sport, mutual societies, other institutions in the social and institutional economy and other jobs in banking and fixed banking assets.

access information or testimonies (Figure 10.6). For customers, the circuit first combines all the contributions from customers and then all the bank's resources (Figure 10.7). The circuit then splits according to the breakdown of credits (companies, individuals, associations and organizations of general interest), up to its final destination. A button on the interface allows the user to try another path by returning to the home screen.

Figure 10.4. *Screenshot of the "immersive 3D experience" home page featuring the bank's 2019 data. For a color version of this figure, see www.iste.co.uk/pinede/digital.zip*

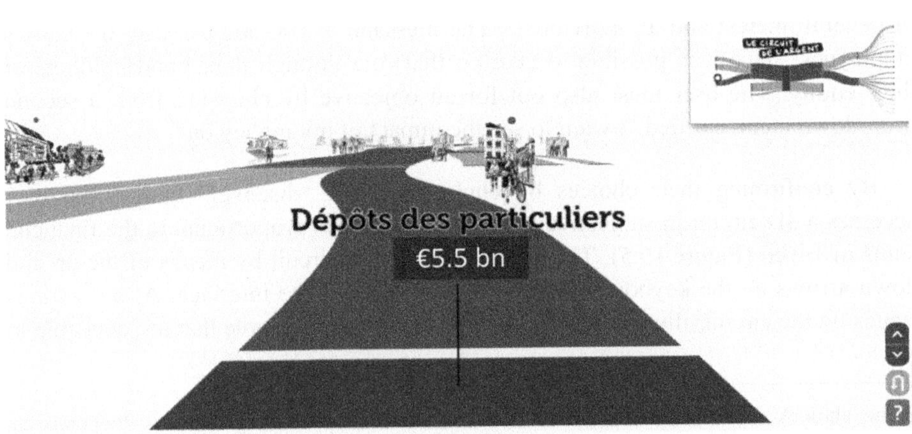

Figure 10.5. *Screenshot of the first stage of the "immersive 3D experience" with the choice of "an individual" in the "you are" drop-down menu on the home screen. For a color version of this figure, see www.iste.co.uk/pinede/digital.zip*

Figure 10.6. *Screenshot on clicking one of the scenarios arranged along the route of the "immersive 3D experience". For a color version of this figure, see www.iste.co.uk/pinede/digital.zip*

Figure 10.7. *Successive screenshots of the "immersive 3D experience" with the choices "an individual" and "eco-businesses" in the drop-down menus on the home screen. For a color version of this figure, see www.iste.co.uk/pinede/digital.zip*

Our analysis of this succession of screens will follow the four stages of production of the representation as we have defined them. Two other examples will follow, treated more synthetically.

The selection has to do with the main components of the storytelling: roles, objectives and key moments in the financial flow path. These various components contribute to framing the message in order to ensure full control of the meaning of the storytelling by its producers. Did the designers deliberately exclude certain aspects? If so, which ones and for what reasons? How were the numerous objectives proposed for "seeing the impact of [their] money" identified?

One might have expected the sustainable development goals set by the United Nations to be translated[6], rather than categories differentiating the type of structure that benefit from investments. This selection suggests that the instructions were to do with showcasing information from the bank's annual report.

The transcription borrows from the codes of customization of a Web browser, but also from those of the adventure game "in which you are the hero". Was the challenge for the designers to assert a fun or innovative organizational identity? Or simply to show some originality in the publication of the bank's financial report? Is the fun, interactive transcription intended to mask the selection of information? As we have been able to argue in the past, the "multimedia storyteller" gets the audience to play games in order to better draw them into the storytelling (Falgas 2004).

The arrangement is based on a chronological succession and choices of colors and typography inspired by revolutionary aesthetics, consistent with the bank's graphic charter, which associates red and black with handwritten inscriptions and line drawings in a style more "thumbnail sketch" than "clear design". While the arrangement is initially based on the second-person ("your money") and the first-person plural ("we engage") at the personalization options stage, the immersive experience itself makes use of impersonal forms to provide descriptions and explanations, using the "we" to designate the actor bank. This choice of a more institutional arrangement tends to objectify the message and the data that the Internet visitor navigates in subjective immersion.

Because of these various representational choices, the bank seems to seek the interpretation according to which it shows itself to be transparent, since it offers everyone the opportunity to slip into the shoes of the other actors. Emphasis is placed on the empowerment and responsibility of customers in supporting the

6 Available at: www.un.org/sustainabledevelopment/ [Accessed 1 July 2021].

collective action led by the bank. Everything combines to suggest that one's individual engagement (as a customer) makes the bank's customer an actor in a collective engagement that is beneficial to the common good. To what extent is such an interpretation made by the bank's customers and staff?

The infographic "Tracé, traçable" (Traced, traceable) focuses on the "Agir" account, a current account where sums can be allocated as the client chooses to finance ecological projects, social utility projects and/or economic solidarity activities (integration, fair trade, cooperatives) (Figure 10.8). In order to highlight the traceability of sums entrusted to the bank, footprints are used to track the reading (Figure 10.9). The footsteps ostensibly avoid a massive gray cloud showing the activities that the bank undertakes not to finance (pesticides, nuclear energy, fossil fuels and biofuel production to the detriment of food production) (Figure 10.10).

Figure 10.8. *Screenshot of the first stage of the infographic "Tracé, traçable". For a color version of this figure, see www.iste.co.uk/pinede/digital.zip*

Beyond the selected events (choice over allocation of one's money, taken into account by the bank, concrete impact), the storytelling aims here to show what we are avoiding by being a customer of Crédit Coopératif. The transcription adopts the codes of didactic computer graphics and mobilizes a schematic and illustrative iconography. The arrangement through the footprints metaphor embodies the promise of telling where the money goes. The use of the first-person singular and a path that forks puts the stress on the customer's responsibility while at the same time reveals to them the impact of their choices through explanations in the third person.

The "we" here refers to the bank, establishing a dialogue with its future client who is called upon to become a co-operant.

Figure 10.9. *Screenshot of the second stage of the infographic "Tracé, traçable", which displays as the Web page gradually scrolls. For a color version of this figure, see www.iste.co.uk/pinede/digital.zip*

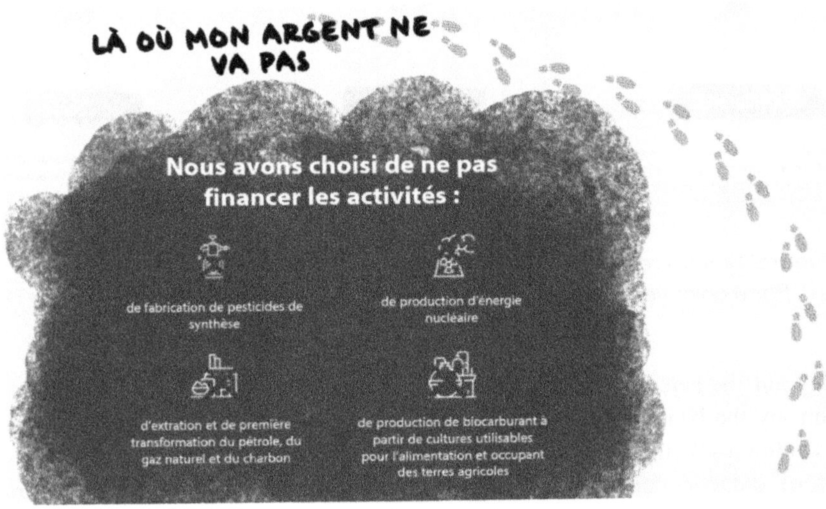

Figure 10.10. *Screenshot of the stage dedicated to activities associated with the competition in the infographic "Tracé, traçable". For a color version of this figure, see www.iste.co.uk/pinede/digital.zip*

As with the immersive experience, the emphasis is on transparency. But the interpretation relies implicitly on demonstrating that the traditional banking sector helps finance intensive agriculture and the production of polluting energies.

Therefore, the responsibility for change lies with the future customer, called upon to buy into Crédit Coopératif's values and project. How is this allusion-based strategy actually interpreted? What is its impact compared to the more polished discourse used by the immersive experience?

The narrative approach is even more explicit on the part of Crédit Coopératif if we consider the "Il était une fois" (Once upon a time) page of its institutional website (Figure 10.11)[7].

Here, press cartoonist Camille Basse narrates 125 years of the bank's history in comic strip form (Figure 10.12).

Figure 10.11. *Screenshot of the Web page devoted to the history of the bank on Crédit Coopératif's institutional website. For a color version of this figure, see www.iste.co.uk/pinede/digital.zip*

7 Available at: www.credit-cooperatif.coop/Institutionnel/Banque-et-fiere-de-l-etre/Il-etait-une-fois [Accessed 3 March 2021].

Figure 10.12. *Excerpts from the website devoted to the history of the bank on Crédit Coopératif institutional website. For a color version of this figure, see www.iste.co.uk/pinede/digital.zip*

The selection of events is given legitimacy by the reference at the end of the Web page to the book *Financer les utopies, une histoire du Crédit Coopératif (1893–2013)* signed by the historian Michel Dreyfus of Editions Actes Sud in 2013 (Dreyfus 2013). This time, the transcription codes are those of the comic strip and borrow from the comic-strip blog. The arrangement is chronological and tinged with humor, divided into chapters that are introduced with a "recap of previous episodes". The interpretation sought focuses on the bank's pioneering role in terms of taking account of social and environmental responsibility.

By way of comparison, the page devoted to the history of Société Générale[8] selects information that highlights its quantitative development and growth, emphasizing its ability to create innovative banking products whose purpose is to make a profit and its commitment to "supporting growth of the consumer society" (Figure 10.13). HSBC Bank presents itself through a commented slide show[9] that borrows from the transcription codes of travel photographs as much as of the historical timeline in order to assert the bank's international character and legitimacy (Dreyfus 2013).

8 Available at: www.societegenerale.com/fr/le-groupe-societe-generale/identite/histoire [Accessed 11 March 2021].

9 Available at: www.about.hsbc.fr/fr-fr/our-company/company-history [Accessed 11 March 2021].

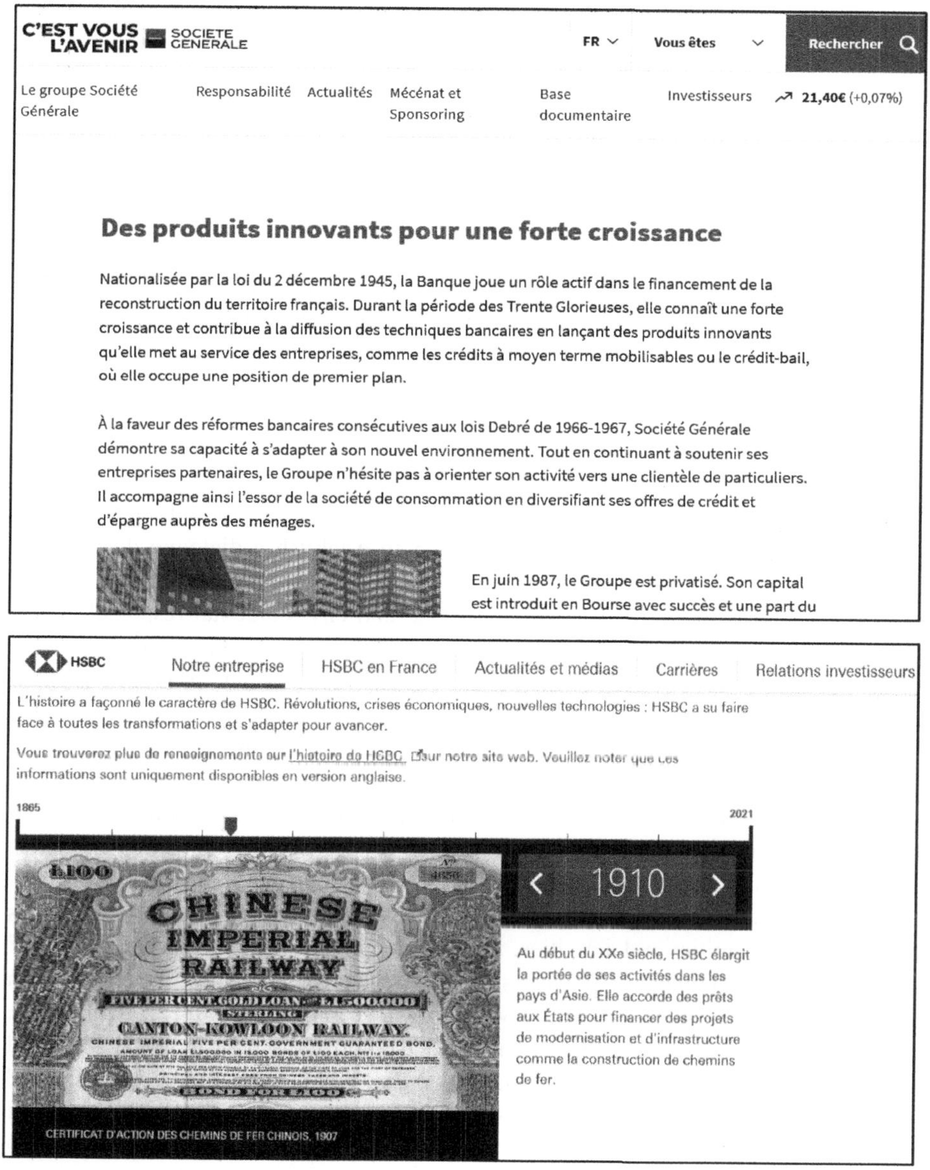

Figure 10.13. *Screenshots of the Web pages devoted to their history from two other banks chosen for their media exposure in the context of the civil disobedience acts of the "chair thieves", organized as a protest against tax evasion. For a color version of this figure, see www.iste.co.uk/pinede/digital.zip*

10.4. From the manufacturing of the narration to a critique of the narrative communication of organizations on digital social networking sites

Our observations confirm the narrative nature of the publications analyzed. D'Almeida (2012) reminds us that for the organization, "the challenge is not the representation but the configuration of the action and the construction of its meaning. These discourses and texts are storytelling in the sense that they possess a narrative structure and a goal that is both explanatory and unifying" (p. 9). Becker (2009) is saying the same when he points out that the representation of social reality is derived from the activity of an interpretive community of producers, aimed at users: for him, the subject of the investigation is the collective activity and not the artifacts.

We have seen the importance of the "we" in Crédit Coopératif's communication. We have also seen that this communication personalized the storytelling according to the individual "I" of its recipients in order to establish a dialogue designed to engage the individual in collective action. Cooperative banking uses values such as engagement and transparency. For them, social and environmental responsibility is presented as consubstantial: it is not a specific section of their institutional website as is the case for Société Générale or HSBC. The stories produced by the organization give structure and are used to produce meaning for its community of "co-operant" clients and also staff, to which the individual is invited to affiliate. The use of a cartoonist or a historian overcomes the difficulty of telling the stories as an organization: these are human and legitimate narrators expressing themselves. To borrow terms from the sociology of translation (Akrich et al. 2006), this choice of communication makes the non-human actor more transparent, since they assert themself as a network-actor by giving visibility to the way in which human actors translate their identities and activities. A similar approach can be observed for MAIF mutual insurance company in its institutional magazine for its members[10]: each edition includes an interview with a well-known member (top athlete, intellectual, etc.) who links their choice of mutual insurance company to their personal story and the values they support. Beyond its representational function, as Giroux and Marroquin (2016) suggest, narration is a vector of the process of the production of meaning (Weick 1995), and the narrative act has a collective and co-constructional dimension. Brown et al. (2009) stress the fact that stories and narratives help to give meaning to change, to explain it, tame it and sometimes celebrate it, but also to propel or hinder it.

10 Available at: www.satellites.maif.fr/maif/maif-mag/ [Accessed 11 March 2021].

With regard to digital publications, D'Almeida (2008) notes that the narratives published on the Web undermine the traditional form of storytelling because everyone and anyone can be an author or a subject, since the electronic media no longer restricts storytelling to the powerful few: "The knot of storytelling and of the threads of life are constructed with greater difficulty, signs of an ambient disunity and a very contemporary problem in giving meaning to the multiplicity and discontinuity of the subject" (p. 98). The terms "knot" and "threads of life", and more generally the authors' use of the lexical field of threads and weaving, refer us to the work that the Anglo-Saxon anthropologist Tim Ingold devoted to "lines" (Ingold 2014). His interpretation of the notions of network and meshwork illuminates the sense of mismatch between storytelling and the contemporary digital environment, conceived in the terms of the network:

> Where the network contains nodes, meshwork is made up of nodes. Nodes are not reservoirs; they have neither an inside nor an outside. […] In the case of a network, the lines are connected at their extremity, whereas with a meshwork they are knotted in the middle; their extremities, still free, seek to attach other lines to themselves. What is life, indeed, but a proliferation of unresolved threads! (Ingold 2014, p. 224)

Nodal networked content could therefore not help in knotting the threads of life necessary for storytelling and the production of meaning. As reservoirs, the content of the nodal points may appear rich and full of promise for analysis. However, this analysis says nothing about the life that animates the social meshwork that the networking of digital content cannot accurately account for. And this is in line with our observations arising from the analysis of a few of Crédit Coopératif's Web publications: analysis seems like a relevant method of formulating questions and hypotheses, but not as a way of answering them when it comes to illuminating the collective activity of which Web publications are the artifacts. Can the analysis of traces on socio-digital media contribute to this? After all, each of the publications we have analyzed is intended to be shared on socio-digital media, mentioned in the form of clickable logos or even by explicit encouragement to "share".

More than 30 years ago, Perriault (1989) was suggesting that communication machines act as putty for an increasingly alveolar society and that filling imbalances with it could contribute to increasing them. In fact, the ease of accurately sharing content on socio-digital media and the development of employee advocacy tools to amplify this quantitative dissemination tend to sanitize the narrative scope of communication. On socio-digital media, storytelling is not retold in an editorial context; the "retellers" themselves have not often assimilated the storytelling they are sharing by mimicry[11]. Jammet (2018) notes the preponderant role of the algorithmic architecture of platforms in the weakening of the community and conversational promises of the role of community manager. One can therefore doubt the sincerity of the traces and data on which an analysis based on the circulation of content within social-digital media would be based. Just like the nodal points constituted by Web publications, the connections that social networking website establish with them do not seem to be able to give us any information about the production of meaning that the actors are striving to achieve.

Cooren (2010) has used the metaphor of ventriloquism in the context of the theory of the network actor (or more properly, the sociology of translation) because it "makes it possible not only to identify the beings that the interlocutors animate in their conversations, but also to show that, in doing so, these same speakers position themselves as being animated by the beings that they animate. In other words, the ventriloquist is not necessarily who we think, which is taking us towards the decentralization proposed by the theory of the network actor" (p. 11). In this case, the promise to turn social media users into puppets committed to the interests of the organizations that employ them is at the heart of the value proposition of employee advocacy services such as Smarp[12] or Sharee[13]. These mechanisms are indeed designed to feed the organization's employees with content whose dissemination on digital media would be beneficial to it. Content, whether produced by the employees or not, is selected and moderated by those in charge of communication or of community management. Everyone has to echo the communication of their organization on their own personal profiles. Indicators and metrics demonstrate the effectiveness of the system, while badges, rankings and rewards mark out the best-performing members of staff. It has been forgotten rather too quickly that – as François Cooren points out – all the vibrancy of the ventriloquist resides in the communication between the ventriloquist and his puppet. However, as its name suggests, the purpose of the employee advocacy department is to promote the interests of its organization, not to develop its relationship with it. A professional handbook for communicators gives the following definition (Van Laethem 2019, p. 290):

> Employee advocacy is an approach that aims to mobilize employees to become ambassadors for their company, or a brand, as part of their professional activity, and sometimes even in their daily lives.

---

11 This is why Twitter experimented with and then in 2020 rolled out the display of an alert message to encourage its users to read the article they are about to share.

12 Available at: www.smarp.com/ [Accessed 8 July 2021].

13 Available at: www.sharee.fr/ [Accessed 8 July 2021].

> By taking on this role, employees communicate on behalf of the company and give credibility to brand discourse supported by the telling of their own user experiences. Words that are welcome in a context of digital transformation that makes it necessary for companies to stand out on the Web and to bring internal teams onboard in their digital development.

This tendency to favor strategies whose results are measured in terms of audience measurement and scope of influence is detrimental not only to the cohesion of the organization, but more generally to the cohesion of our societies. This intense content production is proving to be more of a source of infobesity and difficulties in distinguishing fake news (Badouard 2017) than a source of meaning and cohesion. While we can look upon the ability of individuals to use this as a source of entertaining and – sometimes – satirical or critical memes, it has to be said that this activity is above all in the best interests of the "duopoly" of Google and Facebook (Smyrnaios 2017), whose economics are based on the access and sharing of free online content most likely to generate advertising and the collection of data that are useful for this activity (Ertzscheid 2017). This situation is fostering a crisis of inspiration and – consequently – imagination (Falgas 2018): faced with a mass of content with diverse and often unclear origins, sometimes misleading and often slanted by particular interests, audiences are tending to lose confidence in organizations, traditional media and institutions and prefer information exchanged by their social circle and available as a result of a query on a search engine. However, the information available from search engines, just like that accessible through social media, is heavily filtered (Simonnot 2009), and so is not conducive to nurturing the inspiration of new, stimulating ideas for imagination and creativity. The situation would not be so worrying if we were not facing deep crises in our societies and our development model, requiring unprecedented capacities for inventiveness (Citton and Rasmi 2020).

Considerations such as these appear far removed from the concerns that lead organizations to communicate on digital social media and to claim to produce meaning through narrative strategies. However, they are engaging their social and environmental responsibility just as they are engaging the responsibility of the academic world in the choice of data on which it bases its analyses (Appel and Falgas 2018).

10.5. Conclusion

The paradigm shift from network to meshwork feeds into ongoing action research, which aims to experiment with other ways of inhabiting the digital environment and to overcome the impercipience to which it is subject (Falgas 2020). Digital impercipience (Robert 2020) describes the communication practices of organizations, which use systems for accessing and sharing content that however provide them with neither the means to cultivate their relationship with their staff nor the means to serve the values they claim to support. The dominance of social networking websites as we know them is seen as inexorable. Since a Web publication is designed to generate "engagement" as measured by platforms, and thereby justify the activity of communication professionals, to what extent is the engagement that is measured the result of buy-in by Internet users to the values conveyed by the publication concerned?

As this questioning illustrates, by basing the analysis of Web publications on the four stages of the manufacturing of representations, we have detected in them narrative components. This approach proves fruitful in formulating interpretative hypotheses that go beyond the purely narratological framework and question the conditions of creation and reception of these narratives. Content analysis using an approach such as this is in fact an invitation to observe or speak with the content producers and the content users in order to question the blind spots of the selection, the arrangement or transcription choices and also the interpretation made of the contents.

For example, since the historical page appears as a must for any institutional banking website, how did its designers approach it in the case of Crédit Coopératif? Did they make a comparison of other competing pages, or did they rely on other frames of reference? How did the collaboration with the comic book author and the historian come about? Are they customers of the bank? What is the extent of their buy-in to the values it advocates? Elucidation of the benchmark meshwork that played a part in the publication of this content would allow us to question how well it aligns with the frames of reference used by its visitors.

Our approach makes it possible to establish a number of questions and hypotheses that could enrich a sociological survey. Further extensions could also be added by a semiotic analysis of the interface or by a semio-pragmatic analysis of the interface, in relation to its production context.

We can question the routine or conscious nature of the elements identified over the course of the analysis. Indeed, the precepts of storytelling are held up as standards for communication professionals and are framed by a relatively stable set of good practices in handbooks with strong normative pretensions (Dufour 2021). We should add that the design of Web interfaces is also very signposted by training and handbooks that help standardize the design of features expected and recognized by Internet users, or even features popularized by the GAFA interfaces, for which we struggle to imagine alternatives (Berners-Lee 2018).

We have highlighted the fact that some transcription frameworks such as fun interaction or Web personalization may tend to make the selection of actions and events invisible. On the other hand, we cannot say that these are conscious choices on the part of the designers of the Web pages analyzed. There is also nothing to suggest that this occultation is in response to the wishes of the sponsor.

In terms of further work mobilizing the analytical framework we have used here, we suggest considering the hypothesis that the result observed in the context of a content analysis stems from the frames of reference shared by the actors involved in the communication process using these contents.

As such, it seems promising to consider the analysis of Web publications as a preliminary to semi-structured interviews for the purpose of mobilizing an indexical analysis designed to identify the signs of the existence of decisive frames of reference for the production of meaning between actors (Falgas 2014).

10.6. References

Adam, J.-M. (1996). *Le Récit. Que sais-je ?* Presses Universitaires de France, Paris [Online]. Available at: https://doi.org/10.3917/puf.adam.1996.01

Akrich, M., Callon, M., Latour, B. (2006). *Sociologie de la traduction : textes fondateurs*. Les Presses des Mines, Paris.

Appel, V. and Falgas, J. (2018). Responsabilité sociétale des universités et environnement numérique : la notion d'empreinte, un enjeu de réflexivité. *Communication – Information, médias, théories, pratiques*, 35(2) [Online]. Available at: https://dx.doi.org/10.4000/communication.8018.

Appel, V. and Falgas, J. (2019). The conversation France. *Communication*, 36(2) [Online]. Available at: http://dx.doi.org/10.4000/communication.10498.

Baroni, R. (2016). L'empire de la narratologie, ses défis et ses faiblesses. *Questions de communication*, 30, 219–238 [Online]. Available at: https://doi.org/10.4000/questionsdecommunication.10766.

Baroni, R. (2018). Face à l'horreur du Bataclan : récit informatif, récit immersif et récit immergé. *Questions de communication*, 2(2), 107–132 [Online]. Available at: https://doi.org/10.4000/questionsdecommunication.15659.

Becker, H.S. (2009). *Comment parler de la société : artistes, écrivains, chercheurs et représentations sociales*. La Découverte, Paris.

Berners-Lee, T. (2018). The web is under threat. Join us and fight for it [Online]. Available at: https://webfoundation.org/2018/03/web-birthday-29/ [Accessed 27 January 2020].

Brown, A.D., Gabriel, Y., Gherardi, S. (2009). Storytelling and change: An unfolding story. *Organization*, 16(3), 323–333 [Online]. Available at: https://doi.org/10.1177/1350508409102298.

Citton, Y. (2010). *Mythocratie. Storytelling et imaginaire de gauche*. Éditions Amsterdam, Paris.

Citton, Y. and Rasmi, J. (2020). *Générations collapsonautes. Naviguer par temps d'effondrements*. Le Seuil, Paris.

Cooren, F. (2010). Ventriloquie, performativité et communication : ou comment fait-on parler les choses. *Réseaux*, 5(5), 33–54 [Online]. Available at: https://doi.org/10.3917/res.163.0033.

D'Almeida, N. (2004). Les organisations entre récits et médias. *Canadian Journal of Communication*, 29(1), 25–46 [Online]. Available at: https://doi.org/10.22230/cjc.2004v29n1a1402.

D'Almeida, N. (2008). Des comptes aux contes. Communication, organisation, symboles. *Revue Mei*, 29, 85–98.

D'Almeida, N. (2012). *Les promesses de la communication*. Presses Universitaires de France, Paris [Online]. Available at: https://doi.org/10.3917/puf.almei.2012.01.

Dessinges, C. and Perticoz, L. (2019). Les consommations de séries télévisées des publics étudiants face à Netflix : une autonomie en question. *Les Enjeux de l'information et de la communication*, 1(1), 5–23 [Online]. Available at: https://doi.org/10.3917/enic.026.0005.

Dreyfus, M. (2013). *Financer les utopies : une histoire du Crédit coopératif (1893–2013)*. Fondation du Crédit coopératif-Actes Sud, Paris.

Dufour, S. (2021). La narratologie est-elle soluble dans le storytelling ? *Communication & management*, 18, 15–29 [Online]. Available at: https://doi.org/10.3917/comma.181.0015.

Falgas, J. (2004). Toile Ludique, vers un Conte Multimédia | v1.0. Master's Thesis in Plastic Arts, University of Metz, Metz [Online]. Available at: https://hal.univ-lorraine.fr/hal-01689410.

Falgas, J. (2014). Raconter à l'ère numérique : auteurs et lecteurs héritiers de la bande dessinée face aux nouveaux dispositifs de publication. PhD Thesis, Université de Lorraine, Metz [Online]. Available at: https://hal.univ-lorraine.fr/tel-01750894.

Falgas, J. (2018). Needle, une innovation issue des SIC face à la crise de l'inspiration. In *Congrès de la SFSIC. Création, créativité et médiations*. LabSIC (Université Paris 13), Société française des sciences de l'information et de la communication (SFSIC), La Plaine Saint-Denis [Online]. Available at: https://hal.univ-lorraine.fr/hal-01818969.

Falgas, J. (2020). De la critique à l'action, relier le pensé et l'imaginé. In *Numérique – Vol. 2. Interprétations critiques et logiques pragmatiques de l'impensé*, Robert, P. (ed.). Edition des archives contemporaines, Paris [Online]. Available at: https://dx.doi.org/10.17184/eac.2649.

Falgas, J. (2021). Introductory preface. In *Mettre en récit. Enjeux des formes contemporaines de narration*, Kouassi Kouassi, O. (ed.). L'Harmattan, Paris.

Genvo, S. (2018). Présentation. *Sciences du jeu*, 9 [Online]. Available at: https://doi.org/10.4000/sdj.896.

Giroux, N. and Marroquin L. (2005). L'approche narrative des organisations. *Revue française de gestion*, 31(159), 1544 [Online]. Available at: https://doi.org/10.3166/rfg.159.

Ingold, T. (2014). *Une brève histoire des lignes*. Zones Sensibles, Pactum Serva.

Jammet, T. (2018). L'activité de community management à l'épreuve de l'architecture algorithmique du web social. *Réseaux*, 212, 149–178 [Online]. Available at: https://doi.org/10.3917/res.212.0149.

Jenkins, H. (2006). *Convergence Culture: Where Old and New Media Collide*. New York University Press, New York.

Manovitch, L. (2010). *Le langage des nouveaux médias*. Les Presses du réel, Dijon.

Marti, M. and Pélissier, N. (2012). *Storytelling. Succès des histoires, histoire d'un succès*. L'Harmattan, Paris.

Perriault, J. (1989). *La logique de l'usage : essai sur les machines à communiquer*. L'Harmattan, Paris.

Revaz, F. (2009). *Introduction à la narratologie action et narration*. De Boeck, Brussels.

Robert, P. (ed.) (2020). *L'impensé numérique – Vol. 2 – Interprétations critiques et logiques pragmatiques de l'impensé*. Editions des archives contemporaines, Paris.

Salmon, C. (2007). *Storytelling : la machine à fabriquer des histoires et à formater les esprits*. La Découverte, Paris.

Salmon, C. (2019). *L'ère du clash*. Fayard, Paris.

Saurier, D. and Vallée, O. (2017). Récits, figures et chemins de traverse. *Questions de communication*, 31, 279–290 [Online]. Available at: https://doi.org/10.4000/questionsdecommunication.11152.

Simonnot, B. and Gallezot, G. (ed.) (2009). *L'entonnoir : Google sous la loupe des sciences de l'information et de la communication*. C&F, Caen.

Van Laethem, N. (2019). Outil 96. L'employee advocacy. In *La méga boîte à outils de l'agilité*, Van Laethem, N. (ed.). Dunod, Paris.

Weick, K.E. (1995). *Sensemaking in Organizations*. SAGE, Paris.

11

Transmedia and Online Storytelling: From Ephemeral Universes to Archives

Mélanie BOURDAA
MICA, Université Bordeaux Montaigne, Pessac, France

11.1. Introduction

Transmedia storytelling, defined by Jenkins (2006) in his book *Convergence Culture*, puts forward a production strategy that aims to increase the storytelling of a cultural work by disseminating it across a number of media platforms digital or non-digital. We have called this "augmented storytelling" (Bourdaa 2012) to indicate the importance of creating a narrative, which will then be exploded and amplified on other media platforms, whose affordances will be fundamental for its writing. The term is indeed quite recent but the practices are not new and make it possible to understand the evolutions of the cultural industries and the creation of a new media ecosystem. As Freeman (2018) points out, transmedia storytelling is always based on changes within the industry, with storytelling adapting to the synergies and evolutions of the (new) media to create engaging, coherent and sometimes playful narrative worlds.

Producers of TV series, like the American showrunners, are increasingly keen to develop narrative universes on new media platforms in order to target new audiences and give fans food for thought while at the same time rewarding them for their

Digital Presences of Organizations,
coordinated by Nathalie PINÈDE, Luc MASSOU and Patrick MPONDO-DICKA.

intellectual and emotional investment. Secondary and satellite content sometimes takes the form of novelization or comic strips, underlining the fact that transmedia storytelling strategies can be deployed on non-digital platforms while at the same time developing the narrative aspects of the series. For example, *Twin Peaks* (ABC, 1990–1991) offered *The Diary of Laura Palmer*, a diary written by the character Laura Palmer that gave an insight into her life and details about her relationships with other characters before she was murdered at the beginning of the series. *How I Met Your Mother* published *The BroCode*, first seen in the episode "The Goat" (Season 3, episode 17) and *The Playbook*, first seen in an episode called "The Playbook" (Season 5, episode 8). These are books written by the character Barney Stinson containing rules or tips for seducing women. For example, The BroCode contains 150 articles, a glossary of terms, the code history, amendments, violations and approved punishments, all invented by Barney, some of which have been mentioned in the series, others being original additions for the book.

But what interests us here is seeing how online storytelling, through websites, blogs or social media content, can enrich a narrative world or give fictional characters a life beyond the screen. From a methodological point of view, we looked at the analyzed works in their entirety in order to fully understand the narrative universes as well as the characters and their development. We then looked for digital traces and online storytelling collected and archived by the fan communities. This naturally involved knowing the fan communities and their organization, codes, rules, and language. Their efforts in archiving and collecting allowed us to take into account all of the multiplatform universes deployed for each work. The approach was then diachronic and descriptive in order to better understand the communicative, narrative and sometimes economic issues of the use of the Internet and social media in transmedia strategies. This diachronic approach will make it possible to highlight in particular the technological and cultural evolutions of websites and social media sites in the narrative content deployed but also in the affordances developed.

We will take case studies (movies and television series) that seem to us emblematic of a use of online devices, emblematic in their innovative nature, in their narrative nature and in their target audiences. We chose to analyze one movie, *The Hunger Games*, which includes serial markers (opuses, presence of cliffhangers) in its storytelling and three American series, *Westworld*, *13 Reasons Why* and *Mr. Robot*, broadcast on channels other than network channels. Their transmedia strategy had interesting biases: for *The Hunger Games* and *Westworld*, the online sites evolved as the diegetic storytelling developed. But with *13 Reasons Why* and *Mr. Robot*, the strategy was centered on social media to seek out audiences in their daily routine and give an account of the psychology of the characters. Finally, we will see how fans play a vital role in making these strategies available and in preserving and documenting them. The research question will be: Given the ephemeral nature of online media strategies (websites and social media), what archiving are fans able to do?

11.2. New term, old creations: a quick historical overview

Freeman (2018) wrote in his book *Historicising Transmedia Storytelling* that transmedia practices have a history and existed long before the introduction of the term and the new technologies into production strategies and reception tactics. Comic strips often used to be an option back then to enrich plots and develop characters on newspaper pages or in various magazines. For example, L. Frank Baum created a narrative world around *The Wizard of Oz* consisting of mock newspapers, conferences, billboards, novels, musicals and comic strips in order to please a migratory audience and to give more depth to the characters, introduce new ones and explore the land of Oz as if it were a real place. The author used advertising techniques to promote and above all to expand his universe. The comic strip series entitled *Queer Visitor from the Marvelous Land of Oz* picks up, in a story that takes place just after the end of the book, a new temporality and a new life for the characters. As Freeman (2014) notes, this choice is apt and follows certain economic rationales:

> The era's newspaper comic strips and their institutional tendency to prioritize recurring characters as successful advertising mechanisms (as witnessed in the cross-media dispersion of Buster Brown) had in fact influenced Baum to return to the series' more familiar faces of Dorothy, the Scarecrow, and the Tin Woodman. (p. 371)

Here, favorite characters shift from one medium to another, giving new perspectives on their lives after the end of the book and enriching their stories beyond the pages.

Of course, this experimentation dates from the early 20th century and used only a non-digital format. The advent of new digital technologies and their appropriation by users, producers and broadcasters of audiovisual content have introduced a new media ecosystem that Jenkins has named cultural convergence. Rose (2012) underlined the importance of new technologies in the creation and development of interactive and immersive processes, praising the adaptability of the creative and cultural industries in a changing media ecosystem.

Not surprisingly, the first large-scale experimentation took place around productions in the cinematographic genre, whose complex narrative universes can expand and stretch to form engaging storytelling. In addition, the film industry has developed marketing strategies showcasing spin-off productions: theme parks (Disney), merchandising (figurines and goodies) and games (video games and board games). The first attempt to bring together new and old media to develop a transmedia marketing campaign was created for the promotion of the independent horror film *The Blair Witch Project* in 1999. As Atkinson (2018) recalls, "The movie release of *The Blair Witch Project* was accompanied by an extensive narrative campaign that, at the time, had been labeled viral marketing" (p. 15). Interestingly, as an independent film, the movie enabled the implementation of a natively transmedia strategy, in a movement that Jason Mittell called "centripetal": the objective was to deepen audience engagement with the film's narrative mythology and the characters. To do this, the creators put a website online a year before the release of the film, containing elements about the film's dead protagonists: crime scenes, photographs showing clues and Donahue's private journal, artifacts legitimizing the story and blurring the boundaries between reality and fiction (a border already blurred by the genre itself, a found-footage movie), and audio recordings of the investigators. This website was supplemented by posters of missing persons presenting the movie characters, a documentary on the disappearance and the label "deceased" for the characters on their IMDb records[1]. For Onebring (2017), the multiplatform storytelling of the film permitted a hierarchical meaning, with one dominant work (the movie) and a number of complementary works (p. 445). As a transmedia marketing object, it offered the opportunity to develop characters and a narrative mythology in advance of the movie's release, to immerse future viewers in the atmosphere and the story, and to allow them to navigate around the universe by gradually discovering the story as they click.

In terms of television series, the first examples took place on the American network channels, which then experimented with the link between Internet and television and how the Internet could offer complementary, interactive narrative elements to audiences. In fact, in the wake of NBC, which created the first complete interactive platform, NBC 360, in 2006, American television channels set up companion websites for the programs they broadcast. Jennifer Gillan calls this process "must-click TV". For her, this form of interactivity "starts from the premise that the content available across the various media must be interconnected to be part of a global experience (for example *Heroes Evolution*), an experience built to

1 IMDb: Internet Movie Database. Available at: www.imdb.com.

encourage TV viewers to engage at the emotional level, that would ideally lead to economic profit" (Gillan 2010, p. 4). The dedicated platform for *Heroes*, for example, offered additional content on the characters in the form of satellite websites, a webcomic focusing on the supporting characters in the series and an interactive game in which players created for themselves a Heroes character with special abilities, which allowed them to evolve in the universe of the series. This experience was both engaging, because it facilitated the active reception of fans, and augmented, because it offered complementary narrative content, and so enabled viewers of the series to discover additional information about the characters and the universe. For Gillan, in addition to the strong marketing and economic aspect of the device for television channels, it also highlighted the close link between television and the Internet, while creating a continuous to-and-fro between online and offline media, with the viewing experience complemented with hypertext navigation to discover new narrative elements.

11.3. Evolutionary transmedia websites: a progression of and in storytelling

An interesting and engaging way to use websites for a transmedia strategy based on a franchise or TV series is to develop them as the narrative unfolds. To better understand the challenges in terms of complementary online storytelling and transmedia deployment, we will focus on two case studies: the tetralogy *The Hunger Games*, produced by Lionsgate, and the television series *Westworld*, broadcast on HBO.

11.3.1. *Case study: The Hunger Games*

Lionsgate implemented a marketing strategy for the release of *The Hunger Games* movies with the creation of an interactive website focused on exploring the Capitol and its dictatorship, which then served as the main platform for the strategy, bringing together all the additional narrative elements. This choice can be explained by the fact that *The Hunger Games* is told from the point of view of the heroine Katniss Everdeen, and that she only visits the Capitol for a day and a night, going to the tributes' training center in the first book and the first movie. Lionsgate wanted to give a new perspective on an element that audiences were not really familiar with. As Kohnen (2012) explains:

> In order to create this investment, official transmedia has to offer material about the world of *THG* that appears new and exciting to

> fans; at the same time, this material cannot give away too many details about the film itself. This is particularly crucial for a book adaptation because many fans are familiar with the story and are most interested in seeing how this story has been translated to the screen. In addition, official transmedia cannot stray too far from 'canon'.

When fans entered the interactive website (capitol.pn) for the first time, they had to create an account, which allowed them to receive a virtual ID card along with their district number, virtually becoming an official citizen of Panem, with direct access to the Capitol's information service. Fans could explore the website and discover information about the various districts and about the Capitol via Facebook accounts and descriptions. These accounts gave official news of the 12 districts, their culture and their inhabitants in order to immerse fans and potential viewers in the *Hunger Games* world. A 360° view from the train station where Katniss and Peeta first arrive at the Capitol allowed fans to discover the richness of the place. In addition, they could access an online magazine, *Capitol Couture*, written by Capitol fashion journalists. This glamor magazine, in the form of a Tumblr, gave a glimpse of the city's inhabitants, their fashion habits and their tastes. This first part of the strategy constituted an entrance into the universe through a place as yet little exploited. In the period between *The Hunger Games* and *Catching Fire*, the second movie in the saga, Lionsgate continued to develop its strategy, keeping fans in the narrative universe while putting in place a marketing strategy. This strategy followed the storytelling of the movies, but still used the same interactive platform, the same social media accounts and the same Tumblr. The plot of *Catching Fire* focuses on the 75th Hunger Games, called the Quarter Quells. For these special games, the Capitol's dictator, President Snow, has changed the rules and decreed that competing tributes from each district be chosen from the previous winners of the games, leaving Peeta and Katniss with no choice other than to return to the arena to defend their lives once more. *Capital Couture* on Tumblr was still active and was used as a propaganda tool to support the oppressive Capitol regime. Lionsgate then revealed portraits of the contestants at the Quarter Quells, inviting fans to discover the new characters in the movie. The glamour displayed in the images reflected the luxury of the Capitol and the control that President Snow sought to retain over the masses.

To promote the third movie, *Mockingjay – Part 1*, Lionsgate took advantage of this momentum and launched a new phase of the transmedia campaign. This third part of the strategy put the emphasis on interactivity, participation and immersion in the universe by focusing on Capitol propaganda and the growing strength of the rebellion. At the Quarter Quells, competitors from certain districts helped

Katniss escape death to make her a symbol of resistance. In the process, Peeta was captured by President Snow, tortured and subjected to brainwashing to turn him into a symbol of dictatorship and oppression. The third movie is about the struggle against President Snow, the rise of rebellion in the districts and the rebirth of District 13, where all the rebels and their leader Katniss are hiding. The interactive website capitol.pn was once again the main propaganda platform of the dictatorship. On the home page, President Snow broadcast information via *Capitol TV*, dressed in white (to show not so subtly the purity of his intentions) and sitting on a throne with Peeta and Johanna, the tributes captured at the end of the second film, by his side. Fans who had signed up for the first game and received a citizen ID card could find the messages directly in their mailbox. However, just like in the movie, this time the marketing campaign reflected the increasingly organized rebellion.

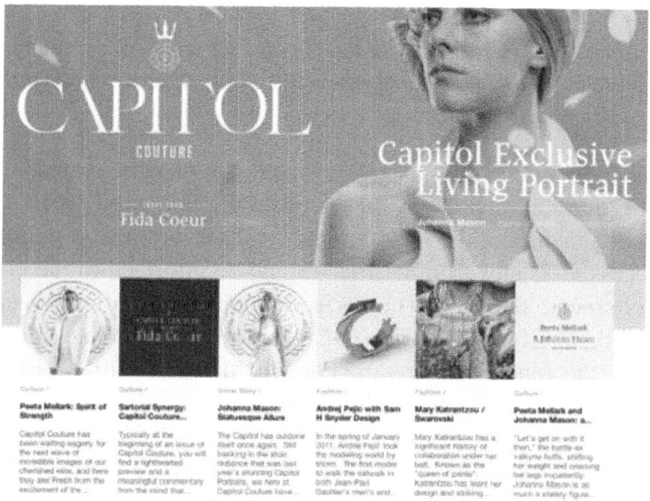

Figure 11.1. *Screenshot of the Capitol Couture website. For a color version of this figure, see www.iste.co.uk/pinede/digital.zip*

In September 2014, Mockingjay symbols began to appear in various cities around the world. For example, in France, symbols were tagged in the Metro, in farmers' fields and on the Normandy beaches. In the United States, they were posted on giant billboards in Washington, DC, declaring that the rebellion was ready to fight President Snow.

Figure 11.2. *Screenshot of the Capitol TV website. For a color version of this figure, see www.iste.co.uk/pinede/digital.zip*

Additionally, to invite fans to get involved, Lionsgate created a mobile app, called "Our Leader the Mockingjay". Fans could digitally tag District 13's logo and symbol on walls, then post the result online to share with the community. Finally, they could access messages from District 13 and be informed of the progress of the rebellion. To immerse fans in the universe, the application offered a virtual tour of District 13, with a room plan, schematic cutaways of places and finally a 3D visualization of the rebels' hovercraft. For the fourth and final movie, Lionsgate launched a new feature in its transmedia campaign.

The publicity for *Mockingjay – Part 2* focuses purely on the rebellion. For this part of the campaign, the rebels have managed to hack the Capitol's website, changing the name of the URL to resistance.pn. The propaganda switches round here, following the storytelling of the movies, and the rebels broadcast video messages of Katniss in her new outfit at the head of an army of soldiers dressed in white. They also introduced the "Pillars of Panem", heroes ready to fight the Capitol and lead the rebellion. They encouraged fans to join the resistance and help Katniss and her friends by sharing the news on social media.

This transmedia strategy, which follows the narrative universe that unfolds over the course of the cinematographical opuses, shows a strong digital anchorage since Lionsgate gambled on online storytelling and digital appropriations by fans. Digital technology permitted the strategy to be developed as and when the movies were released, keeping the same online interface so as not to spread audiences across several media platforms. However, the fans rejected this strategy, which they deemed too glamorous in comparison with the political messages presented in the literary saga. They then decided to "reclaim the storytelling" to organize cultural and social actions that were better aligned with the values of the characters developed by the author of the saga.

11.3.2. *Case study: Westworld*

Looking now at television series, HBO, with its futuristic series *Westworld* (first aired 2016), adapted from a 1973 cinematographic work, uses the same evolutionary transmedia device by using numerous websites spun off from the storytelling. In an apparently not-too-distant future, the Delos company has created theme parks containing reconstructions of historical periods[2]. Visitors to these parks are greeted by Hosts, robots with a perfect resemblance to humans, right down to the feelings they can express. However, these robot hosts revolt at the end of Season 1 and kill park visitors, administrators and security personnel, causing chaos and a shift in the balance of power between humans and robots, developed in Seasons 2 and 3. As Bréda (2017) points out, "*Westworld* is a work of fiction that talks about fiction", a kind of "metastorytelling" that builds a narrative universe (the park and its false pretences) inside a narrative universe (the series). Diegesis then fabricates a complete narrative universe, and the characters travel between reality and fiction (storytelling linked to the amusement park) within the fiction itself (the series).

In order to enrich and augment the narrative universe of its series, HBO developed a number of websites, breaking down the fourth wall and presenting companies and characters. The website delosdestinations.com presents itself as a travel website where fans can discover the various theme parks available for booking. The themes are revealed to coincide with the seasons and their appearance in the series; at the moment, as we wait for Season 4, scheduled for 2022, Park 5 is closed and Park 4 is blurred, inviting fans to discover the next theme in the series. Each park has its own website, accessible by clicking on the corresponding image on the main website. The ambiance of each park is then revealed. Interestingly, and to fit with the storytelling of the series, Westworld Park and its western ambiance is offline and thus inaccessible, since the robots destroyed it at the end of Season 1. In addition, to blur the line between reality and fiction, the website credits are attributed to Delos and Incite (revealed in Season 3), the series' two flagship companies that were behind the creation of the Parks and the Hosts. Finally, the fans/website visitors have the opportunity to chat with a chatbot called Haiden that provides narrative details about the parks and the various Hosts, as well as the

2 As we write this chapter, we know of four: The Western, which focuses on the main narrative, Shogun in feudal Japan, The Raj in India and Nazi Germany.

booking options. These websites have of course evolved following the launch of the seasons on HBO: the parks' themes were unveiled before each season, as teasers, the website was hacked by the robots-hosts who had taken control at the end of Season 1 before being put back online by Delos Incorporated at the end of Season 3.

Incite's website followed the same trajectory, that is, a reveal to promote Season 3 with an exploration of the company and its functions together with the characters, to be hacked again at the end of the season, since Dolores, one of the rebel robots, manages to block the website and its communications. To align with the storytelling of the series, it thus remains offline and its information is currently inaccessible. Here again, the website credits are interesting since they are attributed to Incite for the year 2058, confirming that the story is set in the not too distant future. Finally, the Delos Incorporated website has been constantly enriched over the series to reveal all the information necessary to understand the innovations offered by the company. It presents itself as an innovative artificial intelligence company based on the San Francisco campus and offers three robots with specific functionalities: agriculture, surveillance and construction.

Figure 11.3. *Screenshot of the Delos Destinations website before it was hacked. For a color version of this figure, see www.iste.co.uk/pinede/digital.zip*

This constellation of satellite websites constitutes the online storytelling strategy based on *Westworld* that, just as for *The Hunger Games*, made it possible to roll out an evolution following the storytelling of the series. This strategy was complemented by ephemeral events such as an immersive virtual reality experience in the park and the construction of a park in Austin during the SXSW technology event, offering visitors a living theater experience.

These two case studies show the extent to which websites and online storytelling can be adapted to transmedia strategies, particularly in accessibility of information for audiences and in a narrative evolution that follows the diegetic development of cinematographical works or multi-season serials. The website is then regarded as the central platform of the strategy that is enriched, changed, scaled up and hacked for transmedia storytelling needs. In addition, it is a favorite place for discovery for audiences acculturated to new technologies, navigating from hypertext link to hypertext link to reveal a digital cartography of the complementary narrative universe. This is all the more relevant for *Westworld*, where the mapping and topography of places is an important narrative element found in the transmedia strategy through interactive maps on the various websites of the parks.

11.4. Apps and social media: an engaging transmedia strategy

Mobile apps and social media are favored platforms for augmenting storytelling and a narrative universe and giving substance to the characters, beyond the cinematic or television screen. The aim is to make the boundary between reality and fiction even more porous by inviting audiences to play with everyday devices.

11.4.1. *Case study: Mr. Robot*

The video games company TellTale was developed for the *Mr. Robot* series, broadcast on the American cable channel USA from 2015 to 2019, a transmedia strategy based on a website (which we will not analyze here) and a mobile app designed to intrude into the everyday lives of players. As Blake (2017) reminds us, transmedia strategies "are created to foster an active role for audiences using multiple forms of interaction and participation. Others are more focused on creating an affective experience for audiences" (p. 532). *Mr. Robot* centers on Elliot, a hacker suffering from paranoia and schizophrenia, who launches a collective, F Society to fight against the world as we know it and capitalist corporations, including the company E Corp. Launched in an advertising spot for this company (thus present in the diegesis), which is suddenly interrupted by a masked character calling to "hack our democracy", the mobile app presents itself as an internal communication device of E Corp for which players must accept the conditions of use, blurring the boundaries between reality and fiction. When players are connected to the app's interface, they can chat with each other or with characters created for the needs of the game or characters from the series. One of these characters, Darlene, then asks the players, harassing them with text messages that merge with more mundane text messages, to help her fight the company. The players are then recruited by the hackers' collective in the series, they converse with Darlene and an anonymous character reminiscent of Elliot and unknowingly take on the role of amateur hacker. The players then enter the story and become actors through using an everyday object, their mobile phone. They thus access the fictional space and enter the narrative universe of the series in which they become actors. The objective of the game was to immerse players in the paranoia inherent in the series, which manifests itself through the character of Elliot, while developing the narrative universe through the dialogues in the text messages and notifications. In the app, this paranoia was there in the actual role assigned to the players, but also in the missions and assignments offered (whether the player was able to accept or not). The game was therefore presented as a role-play in which the players were actors in their own adventures and were immersed in the storytelling through their missions but also real-time conversations with the characters in the series, who thus infiltrated the daily lives of the players.

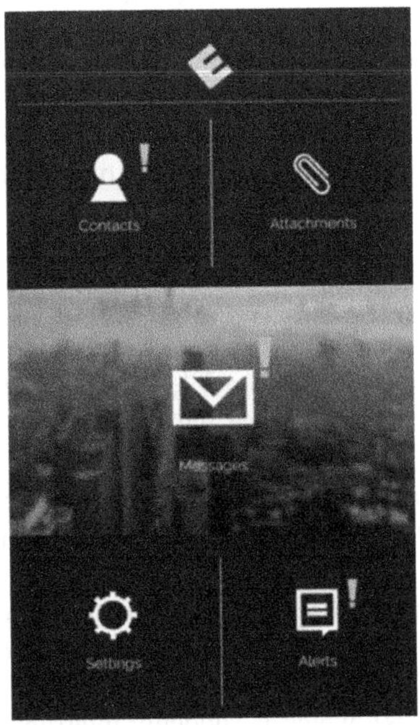

Figure 11.4. *E Corp mobile app interface. For a color version of this figure, see www.iste.co.uk/pinede/digital.zip*

11.4.2. *Case study: 13 Reasons Why*

The *13 Reasons Why* series, adapted from the eponymous book written by Jay Asher, was produced and aired on the Netflix streaming platform. The storytelling centers around the character of Hannah, a teenager who commits suicide at the beginning of the first episode, leaving audio tapes to her classmates explaining how they are the cause of her unhappiness and her choice to end her life. The 13 episodes correspond to the 13 sides of audio cassettes and the 13 reasons that lead to the girl's suicide, each episode being focused on one particular character, as announced by the now famous "Welcome to Your Tape" at the beginning of the episode.

Netflix based its transmedia device on social media, in total consistency with the series' storytelling and the media practices of the target audience of the fiction, namely teenagers and young adults. The deployment of the strategy was staggered over time, being positioned as advertising before the episodes were broadcast on the platform and ongoing from the time of broadcast.

Since Hannah's character was dead from the start of the series, audiences discover her in the diegetic world through flashbacks and the voice-over storytelling on the tapes that explain the facts and give the character's subjective point of view. The storytelling offered is thus nonlinear. The transmedia strategy also makes incursions into the character's past to better reveal her private life and highlight her psychological characteristics. Scolari (2009) calls this kind of device interstitial microstories that fill negative spaces in the main story, in this case elements of the girl's past and indirectly other characters who gravitate around her. Thus, in the French strategy, audiences can discover Hannah's smartphone in its entirety. For example, her Instagram account @itsmehannahbaker contains key moments from the character's past life as well as reblogs of photos of other characters, whose accounts can also be explored. Users can also discover conversations on FaceTime or in text messages between Hannah and the other characters in the series, including Clay and the person she thought of as her best friend, Jessica. In one conversation between the two friends, the audience thus learns of the existence of the famous list that is going to be one of the reasons why Hannah commits suicide, and the cascade of stalker messages that follows.

This immersion into the private lives of the character and her teenage friends is a way of learning about the relationships that united them, glimpsing the beginnings of the stalking of which Hannah will be the victim, and their daily life. It is interesting to note that the profiles of the two main characters, Hannah and Clay, are public while the other characters' profiles are private and can only be viewed after subscribing, thus reinforcing the mysterious nature of their lives. The use of social media (Instagram, Snapchat, Facebook) as well as a technological interface such as a smartphone is totally consistent with the media practices of the characters in the series. The stalking of Hannah in the series begins with the posting of a photo on social media channels, which the high school teens use for sharing. The strategy of

13 Reasons Why, developed around Hannah's character, aims once again to break down the fourth wall and shows the girl's daily life before the start of the series through her social media activity. It is all the more relevant because it is inspired by the media practices of the target audience, the teenage audience, to give them a chance to see, experience and understand a life that has reached tipping point. As Bölin (2010) reminds us, "in transmedia storytelling, designers develop texts across several technological platforms, thus taking advantage of the qualities and capabilities of each platform" (p. 75). The affordances of the platforms open so many opportunities to exploit content in a transmedia strategy. Conscious of immersing audiences in the horror of the main character, Netflix decided to offer concrete support and psychological help to show that Hannah did not have what the audiences can have in real life.

Transmedia narratives are seen here as "entertainment experiences that are built from multiple encounters with the storytelling" (Dowd et al. 2013, p. 4) or else "as a storytelling and an interactive world apprehended on a number of media platforms" (Zeiser 2015, p. 9). In the case studies we have analyzed during this chapter, this augmented storytelling was deployed on websites and social media, while ensuring consistency with the narrative universe and the characters. The affordance of websites and social media fostered a rapid and immersive engagement in the universe by the audience: not only are these platforms part of the audience's daily routine but in addition, diegetic details (such as the website credits or the sending of text messages on smartphones) kept the audience in the storytelling, which infiltrated and intruded upon their daily life and their private life. Moreover, these transmedia strategies, in keeping with the coherence of the universe, gave body and life to the characters outside of the broadcast of episodes or cinematographic opuses and constructed a media ecosystem for diegetic companies that thus tipped into the real world.

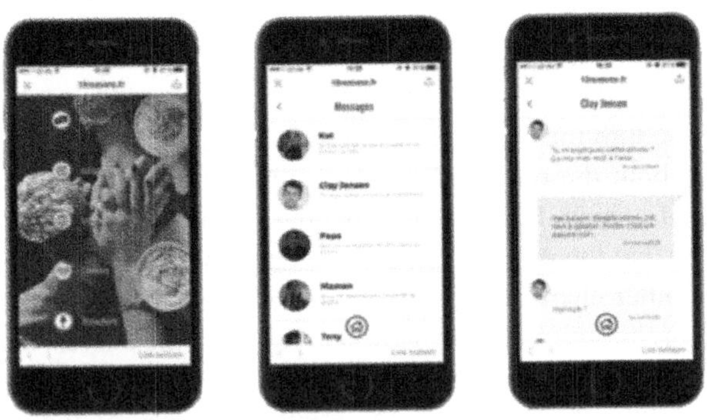

Figure 11.5. *Hannah Baker's phone Interface. For a color version of this figure, see www.iste.co.uk/pinede/digital.zip*

In this context, audiences have an active role to play, in their hypertextual navigation to discover the scattered clues of the fictional world but also in their actions to take the storytelling forward. They thus take on two important missions in this transmedia ecosystem: an archaeologist "digging" on the platforms in search of clues and information to share, and a cartographer reconstructing the narrative universe exploded by the production.

11.5. Fans' archives: preserving ephemeral devices

Most of these transmedia strategies are ephemeral, in the sense that they are put online only for the duration of the showing of the films or series. This ephemeral nature forces audiences to discover the strategy at a time T, or they will see the content vanish after the life of the movie or TV series. To overcome this evanescence of digital transmedia strategies, fans will implement archiving tactics allowing them to both centralize the information discovered and preserve the memory of the complete narrative universe. This activity of gathering information on the narrative universe that is then made available to other audiences does not strictly speaking have the same transformative effect as other fan activities (writing fan fiction, video editing, fan art). Whatever form it takes (wiki, Redux, website), fans play a very specific role in this activity, that of archivists but also that of curators, who will use their skills to recruit other people into the community (Kompare 2018). These curators will have as their objective to make known the transmedia fictional universe, to give it visibility and to preserve it. In order to bring together all the elements of the storytelling scattered across various media platforms, fans create wikis, real encyclopedias reconstructing the serial universes. The wiki system is mainly participatory and collaborative by definition, as evidenced by the functioning of the best known of them, Wikipedia. The way fan-created wikis work is similar, since fans update, edit and link together the scattered information they have collected to recreate the coherence of the narrative universe. These encyclopedias actually constitute real databases but also real archives of serial storytelling of the narrative universe developed.

Bachimont (2000–2001) highlights two properties of archives that seem to us to correspond to the constitution of encyclopedias: the preservation of the material trace of the expression of the contents and the preservation of the readability of these traces. When creating wikis and encyclopedias of serials, fans primarily seek to preserve the information related to the series in one place accessible to all, while building an ergonomics of reading and a simple informational architecture. Just like archives, these encyclopedias evolve, are classified and categorized in a specific, original way by fans, are public and easily accessible and carry within them both the story and the factual memory of the narrative universe and its evolution in time, and sometimes in space.

In the case of storytelling and transmedia universes, the fans' work of archiving and preserving the memory of the production is all the more relevant in an ephemeral process of websites and spin-off social media. Their collective work aims to gather information on the narrative universe, create collaborative spaces to aggregate content and editorialize it. Another way to keep transmedia storytelling alive while at the same time offering the experience to audiences is to create redux, mirror websites of the spin-off sites online. For example, to promote Christopher Nolan's second installment of the *Batman* trilogy, *The Dark Knight*, Warner Bros. had offered an alternate reality game that plunged audiences into the dark universe of the superhero. Audiences engaged in this cross-platform storytelling would learn about the film's two protagonists, the Joker and Harvey Dent, and, after picking their side, would carry out missions to help the two characters prepare the bank heist at the beginning of the film and his election to the post of Attorney General of Gotham City. But above all, 42 Entertainment, the communication agency commissioned by Warner Bros., had recreated the entire digital narrative ecosystem of Gotham City by offering a multitude of websites (city taxis, municipal police website, ferries website, a pizzeria, numerous media websites including Gotham TV and the *Gotham News*) containing valuable clues to pursue the adventure. Thus, a real user experience and a user journey had been designed to move audiences from one website to another for the duration of the advertising campaign (6 months before the release of the film). To preserve the digital traces of this transmedia digital game, ephemeral by its nature, the fan audiences redeveloped all the websites in the advertising campaign, as a mirror effect of the strategy, searchable after the end of the promotional part of the film. The website that compiles all the data is called WhysoseriousRedux, named after the promotional campaign, and presents itself as "a complete archive compiled by fans".

Anita Cheng, the initiator of this redux, explains that she wanted to relive the experience of the game and let other audiences relive it and, to do this, she created her archive as if the Gotham police investigation had been hacked by the Joker. So she developed a website using the same graphic design as 42 Entertainment, comprising 450 pages of clues, traces and documents used in the game. Krystin Wells, experiential designer at 42 Entertainment, praised the archival and curatorial work done: "You were able to piece together the puzzle of real-time storytelling in a relevant way."[3] This titanic work required technical skills as a Web designer and archivist in order to know how to classify the recreated documents but also skills as

3 Available at: www.anitacheng.com/work/wssr (Accessed June 9 2021).

a player to reinject into this project the real-time game dynamics put in place in the initial project.

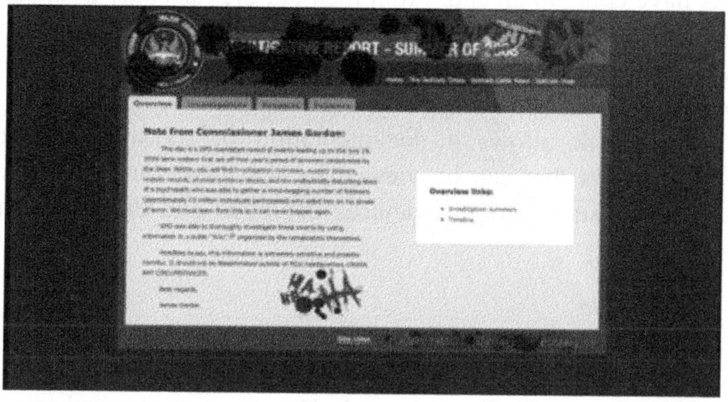

Figure 11.6. *Screenshot from WhysoseriousRedux. For a color version of this figure, see www.iste.co.uk/pinede/digital.zip*

Given the ephemeral nature of these transmedia marketing campaigns, the archiving work of fans is more than necessary to permit data preservation and accessibility for players who would like to discover the complete narrative universe after the official timeframe of the campaign.

11.6. Conclusion

Online websites and storytelling via social media have contributed to making multiplatform narrative universes visible and accessible to the audiences of the cultural and creative industries, in particular audiovisual serial productions and works. These devices have also fostered forms of interaction and participation by audiences, who can gather in one digital place to discover additional elements of the universe. Finally, the integration of websites and online storytelling allows a narrative evolution in the strategy, which can thus follow that implemented in the opus and its seasons. This evolution reveals, as the storytelling unfolds, new characters and new places. The diachronic nature of our approach enabled us to note the evolutions from *The Blair Witch Project* to *Westworld*. The affordances of online platforms are actually much better exploited and make it possible to build a progressive, engaging storytelling for audiences. The acculturation of audiences to transmedia strategies also allows the implementation of hidden devices, found down rabbit holes that audiences must look for, and a reinforcement of fun and gamification elements.

However, this reinforces the ephemeral nature of these strategies, which are deactivated as soon as the marketing campaign ends or when showings of the opus or the seasons have come to an end. From then on, the fans play a fundamental role in archiving and preserving these strategies and digital traces left by the production. Through their skills and their work, they allow other fans to relive a multiplatform narrative experience that was originally conceived as being fixed in a specific temporality. This work allows a documentation of transmedia strategies, the availability of a corpus that can be viewed by the public and researchers, which testifies both to the richness of the devices deployed and the engagement of the audiences.

11.7. References

Atkinson, S. (2018). Transmedia film. From embedded engagement to embodied experience. In *The Routledge Companion to Transmedia Studies*, Freeman M., Rampazzo Gambaroto, R. (eds). Routledge, London/New York.

Bachimont, B. (2000–2001). L'archive numérique : entre authenticité et interprétabilité. *Archives*, 32(1), 3–15.

Blake, J. (2017). Second screen interactions in the cinema: Experimenting with trans-media narratives and commercializing user participation. *Participations. The Journal of Audience and Reception Studies*, 14(2), 526–544.

Bolin, G. (2010). Digitization, multiplatform texts and audience reception. *Popular Communication*, 8(1), 72–83.

Bourdaa, M. (2012). Le Transmédia : entre narration augmentée et logiques immersives [Online]. Available at: https://larevuedesmedias.ina.fr/le-transmédia-entre-narration-augmentee-et-logiques-immersives [Accessed June 18, 2021].

Breda, H. (2017). Les "mondes possibles" de Westworld : du "méta-storytelling" à l'immersion transmédia. *Synergies Italy*, 13, 107–118.

Dowd, T., Niederman, M., Fry, M., Steiff, J. (2013). *Storytelling Across Media: Trans-media for Creatives and Producers*. Routledge, London/New York.

Freeman, M. (2018). *Historicising Transmedia Storytelling. Early Twentieth-Century Transmedia Story Worlds*. Routledge, London/New York.

Gillan, J. (2010). *Television and New Media. Must-Click TV*. Routledge, London/New York.

Jenkins, H. (2006). *Convergence Culture. Where Old and New Media Collide*. NYU Press, New York.

Kohnen, M. (2012). Creating a spark: Official and fan-produced transmedia for *The Hunger Games* [Online]. Available at: http://blog.commarts.wisc.edu/2012/05/11/creating-a-spark-official-and-fan-produced-transmédia-for-the-hunger-games/ [Accessed June 18, 2021].

Kompare, D. (2018). Fan curators and the gateways into fandom. In *The Routledge Companion to Media Fandom*, Click, M.A., Scott, S. (eds). Routledge, London/New York.

Rose, F. (2012). *The Art of Immersion. How the Digital Generation is Remaking Hollywood, Madison Avenue, and the Way We Tell Stories.* W.W. Norton Company, New York.

Scolari, C. (2009). Transmedia storytelling. Implicit consumers, narrative worlds and branding in contemporary media production. *International Journal of Communication*, 3, 586–606 [Online]. Available at: http://ijoc.org/index.php/ijoc/article/view/477.

Zeiser, A. (2015). *Transmedia Marketing: From Film and TV to Games and Digital Media.* Focal Press, London.

12

Augmented Storytelling and Netflix Series Promotion Strategy

Frédéric AUBRUN[1] and Thomas BIHAY[2]

[1] *Omnes Education, INSEEC, Lyon, France*

[2] *GERiiCO, Université de Lille, France*

12.1. Introduction

The continuous dissemination of digital technology, in a context of the attention economy (Citton 2014; Boullier 2019), generates new cultural and commercial mediations, which manifest themselves through original communication and media channels designed to capture the attention of the widest possible audience. In the field of advertising, consumer distrust of traditional advertising (Semprini 2005) has led companies to review their marketing strategies in order to build a new relationship of trust and differentiate themselves from their competitors. As Lehu (2006, p. 40) explains, "the traditional advertising model may not be dead, but it has not worked properly for a few years now. The most disturbing thing for marketers is that it is having great difficulty in reinventing itself, because it is not changing to another model, but to other models". This is evidenced by the strategies of brand content (Bô and Guével 2009), transmedia storytelling (Jenkins 2006) or inbound marketing (Oliveri et al. 2017).

The market for subscription video on demand (SVOD) platforms is part of this profound transformation linked to the hyperesthetization of the economy, within which the industrial and cultural spheres should no longer be considered

Digital Presences of Organizations,
coordinated by Nathalie PINÈDE, Luc MASSOU and Patrick MPONDO-DICKA.

dichotomously but interdependently: "We are at the point where the systems of production, distribution and consumption are impregnated, penetrated, reshaped by operations of a fundamentally aesthetic nature", explain Lipovetsky and Serroy (2013, pp. 11–12). This is reflected in particular by a harmonization of creative and commercial logics in semiodiscursive devices: by placing (narrative) content at the center of its marketing strategy, the Netflix platform would then seem to meet the new challenges of audiovisual media. In this context, Perticoz (2019) suggests regarding audiovisual media as the future of digital cultural platforms, and not the other way around, by leveraging the symbolic social capital that constitutes their catalogs.

In an extension of this hypothesis, it may be interesting to study the narrative logics implemented by Netflix to promote its original series through a content analysis. The study focuses on two cases: *Stranger Things*, a science fiction series released in 2016, and *13 Reasons Why,* which deals with a number of issues related to adolescence, including suicide, broadcast from 2017 to 2020. In other words, we are examining how Netflix promotes its series through *transmedia storytelling* strategies. Jenkins (2006) defines transmedia storytelling as "a process where integral elements of a fiction get dispersed systematically across multiple delivery channels for the purpose of creating a unified and coordinated entertainment experience". The main hypothesis guiding this research is as follows: Netflix's original series are fictional universes, in other words, imaginary worlds based on real potentialities (Dolezel 1998). They are therefore reserves of stories from which the platform draws its marketing sources. Each fictional universe thus serves as a pretext to extend or prolong the storytelling in transmedia promotion strategies based on one central story, which Jenkins (2006) calls "mothership".

These transmedia strategies are apprehended through a socio-semiotic approach that Andréa Semprini distinguishes from the traditional semiotic approach "by its vocation to extend analysis to issues of the sociocultural type" (2007, p. 16). It consists of taking into account the way in which an object with a particular meaning, in this case the series, is taken up by a system of discursivity in which the fictional universe constitutes a semiotic resource. The enunciation theory takes on paramount importance in this shift from a semiotic view to a socio-semiotic view, identifying it as a "pivotal element of the textual conversation in discourse, a principle that allows consideration of the text's production and reception bodies while retaining a semiotic perspective" (Semprini 2007, p. 21). From this perspective, the series studied here are regarded as social discourses, namely occurrences of a discursive and social nature.

> They derive their discursive character from their intrinsically semiotic nature and from their presence, as enunciated occurrences, in a flow of exchange where multiple bodies of production and reception engage with each other. Their social character comes from the specificity of the space within which these discourses circulate: a public social space, where groups or collective actors constitute the bodies of production and reception which we have just mentioned. (Semprini 1996, p. 15)

Applying this definitional principle to our object of study, Netflix's original series could be said to function as social discourses, taking on real meaning only in this metaserial space, evolving alongside other mediation bodies, having their own codes and representations.

The series studied, *13 Reasons Why* and *Stranger Things*, are representative of the creation of immersive narrative transmedia extensions around a mothership content that allow fans to discover from other media a coherent and enriched universe. This research therefore belongs to the field of information and communication sciences by virtue of its subject of study and the semionarratological slant adopted.

For the first case being studied, *13 Reasons Why*, the analysis focuses on the first two seasons. These are strongly linked since various transmedia content has been created on the issue of suicide to which has been added supplementary online content relating to other teenage issues, such as drugs and rape. This is particularly the case for the mobile website created for the launch of the series, which testifies to the narrative stretching capacity of the promotional device based on the central diegetic theme of the series, suicide. The first season of the series led to a controversy about suicide that fueled the transmedia strategy developed to promote the second season. The lack of discussion on the subject and solutions mentioned in the series aroused a lot of criticism and this narrative void seems to have been taken into account in the promotion of the second season. Three other digital devices are studied for this purpose: a wiki, an information website and a discussion guide. They are linked to the promotion strategy, which consisted of blurring the purely promotional aspect by adopting a pedagogical discourse within the media space, and in this way responding to the controversy aroused by the first season. They link back to a strategy of unadvertization (Patrin-Leclère et al. 2014) promotional discourse, which is presented as aiming to raise audience awareness on the issue of suicide. Unadvertization refers to the "tactics of advertisers who aim to dissociate themselves from the most recognizable forms of advertising and to replace them with forms of communication that are supposed to be more discreet, free from the markers of advertising" (Patrin-Leclère et al. 2014, p. 18).

The second case selected is *Stranger Things*. The study focuses on the transmedia storytelling device developed to promote the second season. This device is rich, because it is based on plural and heterogeneous content, platforms and actions. It refers back to "transmediageny" (Marion 1997), namely the ability to diffuse a story from various media configurations, but also to the central place given to "gamification" (Laurichesse 2016) in such strategies. The content examined comprises: the Portal World Lens linked to the Snapchat app, which allows immersion in the fictional universe through visiting a key location of the plot, the living room of the series' protagonists, Feed Dart, a website dedicated to a central creature in the second season, Google Home, which allows interaction with a key character, Dustin, to carry out an investigation related to the season's plot and, finally, a video game, *Stranger Things: The Game*, inspired by 1980s arcade games, accessible on Android.

It is therefore a question of how the central diegetic elements of these series are reused to extend their narrative universes coherently across a number of media channels for promotional purposes.

12.2. Augmented storytelling from explicit, implicit and zero textures

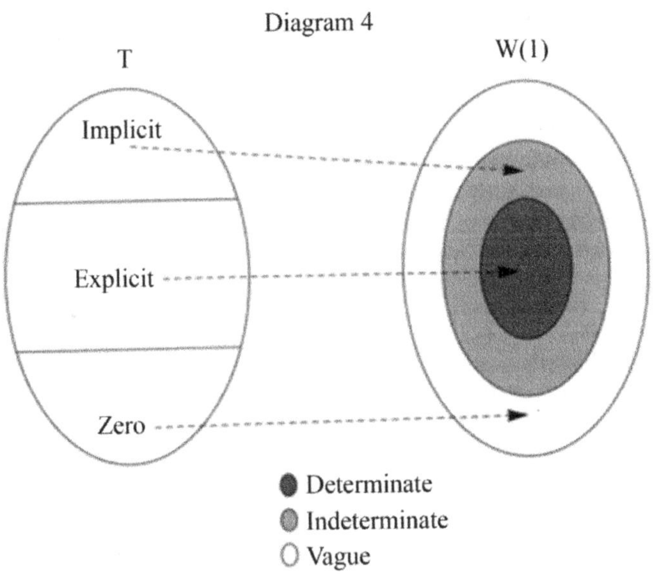

Figure 12.1. *Lubomir Dolezel's diagram, "The intentional saturation function"*

One practice used by Netflix to promote its series is to tap into the explicit, implicit and zero textures of their fictional universes. According to Lubomir Dolezel (1998), fictional worlds are artificial and therefore present an incompleteness that can be fed by an infinity of stories. He distinguishes three types of textures: "The explicit texture constructs the determinate domain, the implicit texture constructs the indeterminate domain, and the zero texture constructs the vague domain" (Dolezel 1998, p. 182). In other words, the explicit texture is that which appears directly in the narrative, while the implicit texture designates that which could contribute to it, but which is not clearly mentioned. The last texture, which we call the zero or vague texture, is more complex. It has to do with the infinity of possibilities, which were not conceived of by the original authors but that are able to contribute to the narrative without affecting its authenticity. Based on "augmented storytelling" (Bourdaa 2012), Netflix gives access to complementary narrative elements that feed on the textures of its series.

12.2.1. *The implicit texture in the promotion of 13 Reasons Why*

To support the release of the first season of *13 Reasons Why*, the platform launched a digital operation connected to the narrative universe of the series, only accessible on smartphone. The aim was to create an immersive experience in the heroine's world through the creation of a mobile website: www.13reasons.fr. In this season, the audience witnessed Hannah Baker's suicide, an event forming an integral part of the explicit texture, that was to be featured in many other promotional narrative extensions. The mobile website is part of this logic, since it draws its originality from the implicit texture related to this suicide, inviting discovery of an unexplored facet of the reasons that lead this character to suicide. In fact, by connecting on their mobile, viewers can discover the content of the heroine's phone, which is mentioned but not shown in the series. This allows them to investigate in parallel the reasons for the main character's suicide. This device plunges fans into her social environment, which relates back to the implicit texture of the story. It gives them access to additional information that helps them understand the scenario, but without revealing the plot. The text messages exchanged between the heroine and her friends are often mentioned, without being read out or shown in the episodes of the series, in most cases. Here, the online content extends the fictional universe by adding new narrative elements that allow viewers to better project themselves into the season being promoted, but without changing the plot or the meaning of the series. To use the terminology of Barthes (1964), they play a "relay function", since the additional content adds information that the series does not give (or not much). The promotion takes over the relay from the series, so to speak, ensuring a certain narrative complementarity of the series.

Indirectly, this dedicated site is a way of pointing the finger at school bullying, a theme of the explicit texture. On 13reasons.fr, viewers have access to Hannah's messages and contacts, her Instagram account, her browser history and so on. They can read the last text messages she and her classmates exchanged before her death and scroll through her Instagram feed. Similarly, in her browser history, they find links to websites related to the themes mentioned in the series, including a Facebook help page showing how to block someone on the network in the event of harassment.

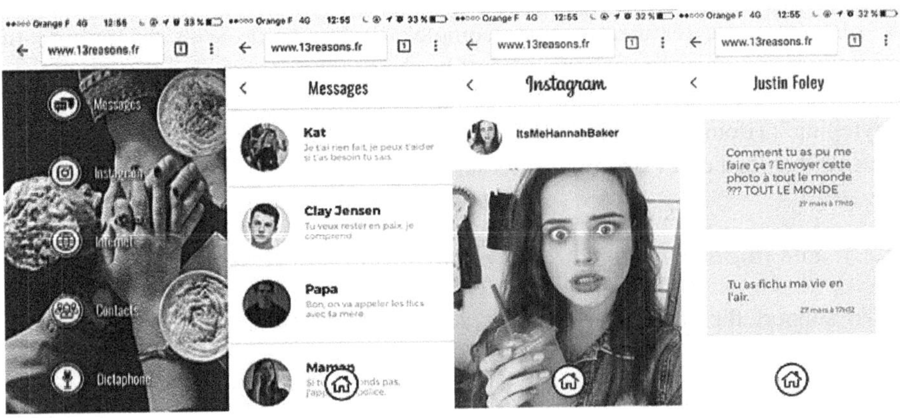

Figure 12.2. *Extracts from the mobile website dedicated to Hannah's phone content. For a color version of this figure, see www.iste.co.uk/pinede/digital.zip*

The transmedia storytelling strategy developed to promote the second season of *Stranger Things* is based more on the explicit texture, making the fantastic fictional universe of the series the center of its device.

12.2.2. *The upside down, or the epicenter of the* Stranger Things *story*

Netflix's transmedia storytelling strategies are based on immersive interactive experiences designed to plunge the audience into the fictional universe. The Portal World Lens, developed by the platform as an extension of the second season of *Stranger Things*, is representative of this. This portal is accessible via the Snapchat app and allows the viewer, who has become an "interactor" (Guéneau 2006), to visit a central room of the diegetic universe, namely the living room in the protagonists' house, where creatures emerge from a parallel universe in the first season. Here, Netflix is drawing upon the explicit texture of the fictional universe of the series for this promotional material, since viewers recognize this key location from the plot.

This is an augmented reality experience. By activating the lens, they can "enter another world", in this case the "Upside Down" version of this room.

There are a number of Easter eggs in the app when viewers visit this room and the next ones, that is, hidden functions that they can activate, either by interacting with each of them or via the Shazam app, since the closing credits of the series trigger them all. These hidden functions link back to specific scenes from the first season (explicit texture), and this helps to immerse viewers in the diegetic universe, while at the same time reminding them of these scenes from the first season. So, for example, if viewers click on the living room wall at a specific place, a creature's arm breaks the wall and thrusts through it. This app is based on a central principle of transmedia storytelling strategies and, more broadly, of *interactive storytelling* to which this app links back in part, namely that of "ludicization" (Bénézech and Lavigne 2016; Gantier 2016), also termed "gamification" (Laurichesse 2016). Indeed, there does develop a game, or a complicity, between the series and the audience, the latter experiencing pleasure in finding and activating the various functions, making good use of their knowledge of the plot in the first season. Thus, the device here appeals to the "mediacy" (Esquenazi 2010) of the audience, namely to all the knowledge that viewers have acquired about the series' universe. Finally, these Easter eggs also seem to refer more inclusively to the series' universe, which has strong links to the 1980s and the geek culture, omnipresent throughout the episodes.

12.2.3. *Co-creation as a process of immersion in the fiction*

The transmedia storytelling strategy deployed by Netflix also relies on audience involvement in promoting the series, including co-creation processes. The Feed Dart website for Season 2 of *Stranger Things* testifies to this. Dart is a young creature belonging to the upside down world, taken in by Dustin, who makes a pet of him. Dart has the particularity of eating everything he finds, which leads the protagonists into adventures, with the creature's appetite increasing as he grows. The Feed Dart website allows the viewer to feed Dart by uploading a photo of an object or even of a loved one. A video of the creature devouring the photo is then generated on the website for sharing on social media, which thus gives visibility to Netflix and its series. It thus refers back to what Frank Rose calls "deep media" (Bourdaa 2012), namely the use of an immersive process designed to ensure that the audience is active in the storytelling; in other words, in our case, in the strategy of transmedia storytelling. However, it should be noted that, more in the order of co-production and co-creation relating to digital uses, it is more about transforming all and sundry into a relay valorizing Netflix and its series, rather than a partner engaged in a real co-production. But the fact remains that this communication operation for Season 2 continues to draw on the explicit texture of its narrative by playing on social media's viral ability to showcase a new creature from the fantastic bestiary of *Stranger Things*.

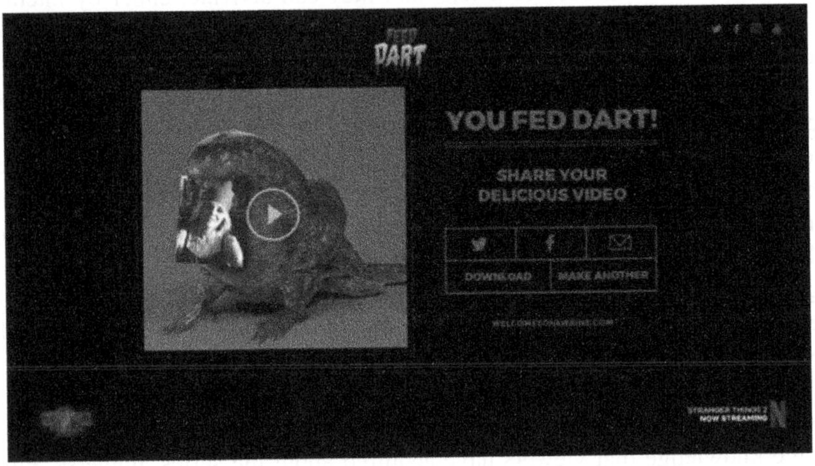

Figure 12.3. *Screenshot from feeddart.com. For a color version of this figure, see www.iste.co.uk/pinede/digital.zip*

12.3. Unadvertization of promotional discourse of series

Through this development of narrative universes across different media, the promotional and advertising natures of Netflix's discourse tend to efface themselves – in both form and content – in favor of a media and cultural showcase in the case of *Stranger Things*, or a discourse with an educational purpose in the case of *13 Reasons Why*. This strategy of unadvertization (Patrin-Leclère et al. 2014; Bihay and Aubrun 2015) of promotional discourse often supports the launch of original Netflix series but also their subsequent seasons in order to extend the discourse of the series beyond the screen. "The hybridization of communication is crossed by enhancement of the media and cultural reach of brand messages and the apparent discretion of the advertising discourse, relegated to the background. However, the whole is indeed intended to promote the issuing brand", explains Caroline Marti (Patrin-Leclère et al. 2014, pp. 100–101). This media incursion into promotional discourse allows Netflix to put itself in the background to further enhance the narrative universe of its series through immersive interactive experiences, and through content that draws on the explicit, implicit or zero textures of these universes. Hidden behind this unadvertization, in reality, is hyperadvertization (Patrin-Leclère et al. 2014) that extends the discursive space beyond the “primary frame” (Goffman 1991) of the series.

12.3.1. *Gamification as a media and cultural showcase*

To promote the second season of *Stranger Things*, in addition to the Portal World Lens, Netflix developed another immersive interactive experience. This aims, for its part, to enhance and extend the narrative universe of the series by means of a game that uses a voice recognition device. In fact, as part of a partnership with Google, those having a Google Home speaker were able to voice-activate an interactive game based on their interaction with Dustin, one of the protagonists in the series. This interaction mimics the interactions cultivated by the teenage protagonists on their walkie-talkies all through the episodes. Viewers are then invited to help Dustin conduct an investigation to understand the events that are happening in Hawkins, the city where the story takes place. In the course of conversations with Dustin, and also other characters, they discover some of the elements of the new season’s plot, but without it being revealed to them in full. The objective therefore is to offer viewers a fun gateway into the narrative universe of *Stranger Things* with experiences that are complementary to it.

This interactive device, like those of the Portal World Lens and the dedicated website that gives access to the smartphone of the heroine in *13 Reasons Why*, relates back to “advergaming”, in other words, the way in which “gamification” is regularly used to advantage within transmedia storytelling strategies, with the aim of promoting products or cultural content, as highlighted by Laurichesse (2016) in a study on promotional Web documentaries. According to her, in addition to a promotional objective, this storytelling process helps to capture audiences’ attention and engage them by making extensive use of the fun, immersive model of video games. This narrative process can also have a role in blending reality with fiction, the “true” with the “false”, to reinforce the viewer’s immersion in the narrative universe. The use of gamification thus contributes in part to strengthening the fictional world and giving it credibility, although no one is deceived: there is no scam or cheating. Netflix’s strategy here is based on what Marion (1997) calls the “two sides of being under an illusion”, namely the fact that every viewer’s attitude to narrative reception is based on their implicit acceptance of the rules specific to the narrative system and the choice they make to subject themselves to those rules. In other words, for this strategy to work, the viewer must agree to:

> Play the game with the story and with the genre to which one thinks it belongs. For narrative interaction to thrive, the [viewer] must enter a hermeneutical game: where do they want to take me, what do they

> want me to imagine or to reconstruct about the world, what position must I take to take to enter into this narrative "gameplay"? [...] To enter into a fiction, you have to agree to be duped, knowing that you are being. To feel more "inside", a piece of us must remain "outside". (Marion 1997, p. 65)

The platform's strategy is therefore based on the premise of (willing) participation by the viewer, so that they can get full enjoyment from this fun device. It also refers back to unadvertization, since it contributes to promoting the series using an interactive experience offered to its audience. In this sense, gamification thus acts as a media and cultural showcase that overlays Netflix's discourse, like a palimpsest. This strategy allows the platform to form a single semiotic entity with the promotional discourse that supports the series.

12.3.2. *"Media recycling" at the heart of the promotional process*

This game also testifies to another narrative logic at work at the heart of the *Stranger Things* series along with the transmedia storytelling strategies developed for its promotion. This logic is closely connected to what Marion (1992, pp. 71–72) calls media "recycling", which is the fact that contemporary media culture constantly reuses outdated elements and/or elements from other genres and media. In the light of this study, however, this recycling should be understood in a broader sense. Indeed, as far as this series is concerned, the plot and the diegetic universe in many ways have their roots in the context of the 1980s. In addition to implicit references to the context of the Cold War, the diegesis largely refers to the geek culture and teenage practices of that era, which are also referred back to by the *Dungeons & Dragons* game, arcade game rooms and even the brand of the bicycles that occupy a central place in the plot, as well as the walkie-talkies used by the protagonists, which are reused as part of the partnership formed with Google. The aesthetics of the series, whether it is the settings in which the protagonists evolve or even the grain of the image, also testifies to this widespread recycling of the 1980s, since the reflection is developed right through to the actual plastic of the series. Numerous references are also made to other cultural and media productions of the 1980s, including the film *Ghostbusters*, released in 1984.

Stranger Things: The Game, released on Android to promote the second season, is also part of this logic of media recycling, but also of *advergaming*. It picks up on the aesthetics of the arcade games of the time and the viewers who play it are invited to relive the challenges experienced by the characters in six cult places of the plot such as the city of Hawkins, a research laboratory or the forest of the upside down world. There, they discover several facets of the season, including new characters, which however do not spoil the pleasure experienced in watching it.

This strategy also extends beyond traditional media forms, as it aims to anchor aesthetic and diegetic elements of the series in reality. So, for example, in 2017, at New York Comic-Con, a convention devoted to comics, video games and other cultural and media productions, bicycle taxis of the 1980s bicycle brand featured in the series were used as transport for the audience. The drivers were disguised as Dustin. A similar strategy was also implemented in the Paris metro, for instance at Saint-Lazare station, where posters of the series were placed in the hall, along with cathode ray TV sets, bicycles and arcade machines similar to those in the series. As part of this immersive experience, travelers had the opportunity to discover *Stranger Things: The Game*. This narrative logic seems common to the two series studied, although the strategy adopted for *13 Reasons Why* seems to be based on a recycling of various contemporary controversies, to be put into the specific socio-cultural context of the United States. It contributes to confirming the hypothesis that Netflix draws on the fictional universes of the two series to reuse them in plural media forms.

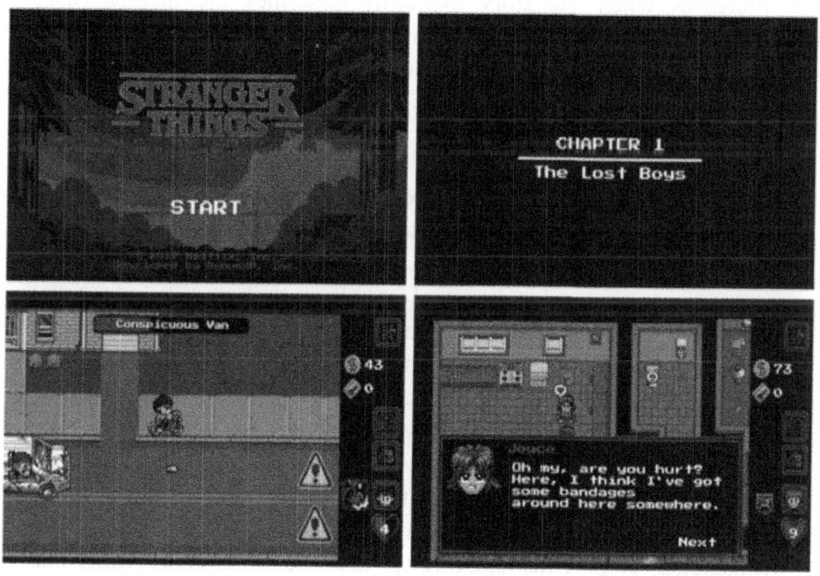

Figure 12.4. *Extracts from* Stranger Things: The Game. *For a color version of this figure, see www.iste.co.uk/pinede/digital.zip*

12.3.3. *Beyond the reasons: a device in pedagogical form*

Finally, Netflix also uses criticism and societal context to build an appropriate promotional communication by extending the discursive space beyond its "primary analytical framework" (Goffman 1991). Through this notion, Goffman (1991) refers to "a framework that allows us, in a given situation, to give meaning to one or another of its aspects, which would otherwise be devoid of meaning" (p. 30). Indeed, it was precisely by the unadvertization of its promotional discourse through a range of pedagogical content that Netflix responded to the controversy generated around suicide after the broadcasting of the first season – the platform having been accused of glorifying suicide in the eyes of high school students. During a scene broadcast at the end of the first season, we were able to see on the screen that the main character, Hannah Baker, took her life by slitting her veins in her bathtub. In the United States, many organizations pointed the finger at the fact that Netflix was giving publicity to the theme of suicide without providing a clear answer in terms of prevention and awareness among adolescents based specifically on various scientific studies. By way of example, the Foundation for Suicide Prevention used Madelyn S. Gould's article "Suicide and the Media" (2006) to declare that "the number of suicides increases when the story explicitly describes the method, uses harsh dramatic images […] or makes death attractive". One of the writers of the series, Nic Sheff, had responded openly to these criticisms by publishing a letter in *Vanity Fair*[1].

> This response was actually quite surprising to me. From the very beginning, I agreed that we should depict the suicide with as much detail and accuracy as possible. I even argued for it – relating the story of my own suicide attempt. […] It seemed to me the perfect opportunity to show what an actual suicide really looks like – to dispel the myth of the quiet drifting off, and to make viewers face the reality of what happens when you jump from a burning building into something much, much worse. […] It overwhelmingly seems to me that the most irresponsible thing we could've done would have been not to show the death at all. In AA, they call it playing the tape: encouraging alcoholics to really think through in detail the exact sequence of events that will occur after relapse. It's the same thing with suicide. To play the tape through is to see the ultimate reality that suicide is not a relief at all – it's a screaming, agonizing, horror. […] And so I stand behind what we did 100 percent.

1 [Online]. Available at: www.vanityfair.com/hollywood/2017/04/13-reasons-why-suicide-controversy-nic-sheff-writer.

However, despite these scriptwriting choices taken by the creators, it would seem that Netflix decided to take more notice of the negative reactions stirred up by the "interpretation community" (Fish 1980), making numerous changes in the editing of the series and adopting a pedagogical discourse in the promotional strategy for the second season. This new direction led by the producers is a way of anticipating possible future criticisms from the "interpretation communities", which "are made up of those who share the same interpretation strategies not to read the texts but to write them, establish their properties, attribute intentions to them" (Fish 1980, p. 171).

Thus, in the broadcast of the very first episode, viewers can now see a warning card informing them of the sensitive topics addressed by the series in that episode. In addition, the warnings that were already present for episodes 9 (which contains a rape scene) and 13 (which contains the famous suicide scene) have been changed by the Netflix producers, making them more explicit by adding a reference to the website 13ReasonsWhy.info. This website lists, on a country-by-country basis, the official organizations responsible for combating bullying in schools. The suicide scene was also redacted by Netflix 2 years later with public justification on Twitter in a post dated July 16, 2019:

> We've heard from many young people that '13 Reasons Why' encouraged them to start conversations about difficult issues like depression and suicide and get help. As we prepare to launch season three later this summer, we've been mindful about the ongoing debate around the show. So on the advice of medical experts, including Dr. Christine Moutier, chief medical officer at the American Foundation for Suicide Prevention, we've decided with creator Brian Yorkey and the producers to edit the scene in which Hannah takes her own life from Season 1.

Thus, Netflix's promotional strategy consists of tapping into the implicit and zero textures (Dolezel 1998) of the serial narrative in order to generate debate and discussion around the series' central diegetic themes (suicide, online harassment, rape, firearms, etc.) through pedagogical content: a discussion guide, a wiki based on the series and the documentary series, *Beyond the Reasons*, developed as an add-on to the series *13 Reasons Why*. This includes input from actors and other members of the production teams of the series alongside mental health professionals on themes such as suicide, drugs, alcohol and firearms. These diegetic universes are a way of serving Netflix's commercial strategy in a pedagogical form and filling the narrative void in the series. The series in fact explains the reasons that lead to suicide but not how to prevent it.

Figure 12.5. *Netflix's tweet about the redaction of the suicide scene. For a color version of this figure, see www.iste.co.uk/pinede/digital.zip*

The promotional content developed by Netflix therefore tries to fill this narrative void, and this time fulfills an anchoring function at the connotative level (Barthes 1964) by doing more than taking over from the series: it guides the interpretation of recipients to show them the proper aim to be ascribed to the series. In other words, a story with the pedagogical intention of making young viewers aware of the issues of suicide and harassment. This semiotic slippage from sales pitch to societal discourse is characteristic of unadvertization (Patrin-Leclère et al. 2014) but also, more generally, brand dissemination within society. As Semprini observes (2005, p. 249), "brand dissemination beyond the commercial sphere shows above all the ability of brand logic to transform, adapt, transcend itself to support a virtually infinite variety of content and discourse". Netflix thus seems to position itself as a social influencer through this promotional strategy.

12.4. Conclusion

Ultimately, it appears that Netflix series are indeed reserves of stories from which the company draws its promotional sources. Each fictional universe serves as a pretext to extend the narrative in strategies of transmedia promotion stemming from a "mothership" (Jenkins 2006). For the promotion of *Stranger Things*, the focus is on creating "augmented storytelling" (Bourdaa 2012) from each key diegetic element in the season by playing with 1980s aesthetics, the geek culture and the cultural and media productions that are representative of those things, while for *13 Reasons Why*, the platform draws on the implicit and zero textures of the narrative in order to disguise the promotional discourse as pedagogical discourse, beyond the series, as illustrated in Figure 12.6.

More generally, this comparative study reveals the narrative potential of Netflix series or, to put it another way, the ability to diffuse their fictional universes, which here refers back in part to the concept of transmediageny as proposed by Philippe Marion, namely storytelling's ability to adapt to various media configurations.

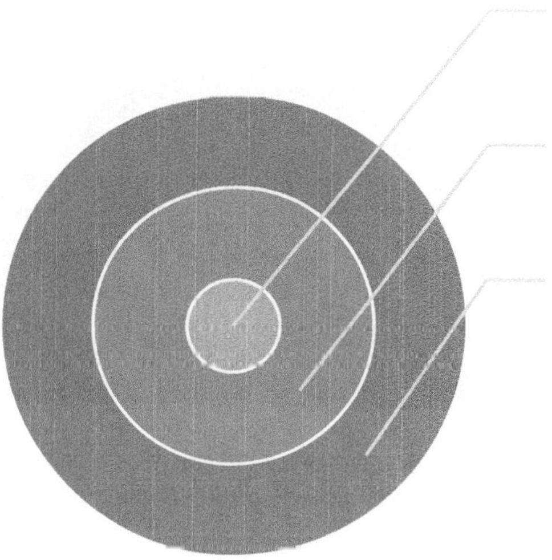

Figure 12.6. *The "intentional saturation function" (Lubomir Dolezel) in the promotional device of the* Stranger Things *and* 13 Reasons Why *series. For a color version of this figure, see www.iste.co.uk/pinede/digital.zip*

The two cases studied illustrate two types of *transmedia storytelling* strategies that Netflix uses to promote its original series: on the one hand, *media recycling* that results in the reuse of the esthetic and diegetic elements of the 1980s in *Stranger Things* and by the recycling of various contemporary polemics in *13 Reasons Why*; on the other hand, the strategy of unadvertization of the promotional discourse through a media and cultural showcase for *Stranger Things* and a pedagogical discourse to raise awareness among young people on adolescent themes (online harassment, suicide, rape, etc.) for *13 Reasons Why.*

These strategies help to confirm the hypothesis according to which Netflix taps into the fictional universes of both series to reuse them in plural media forms. They are also representative of those set up by the platform to promote its other series. Thus, for the release of Season 2 of *Sex Education* (aired on January 17, 2020), Netflix released *Le petit manuel Sex Education* in 12 chapters in collaboration with photographer Charlotte Abramow[2]. "In this fun, visual little guide, which is neither a scientific work nor an exhaustive work, you will find tips for a fulfilling sex life", the artist explains in the introduction. Once again, immersion into the series' fictional universe is being invited by this unadvertization of content in pedagogical form, with chapters such as sexuality, contraception, consent, sexual orientations, etc., which are all themes addressed in the series. Similarly, to launch the third season of its series *La Casa del Papel*, Netflix used piracy as a promotional strategy to stay with the theme of *hacking*, at the center of the fictional universe of the series.

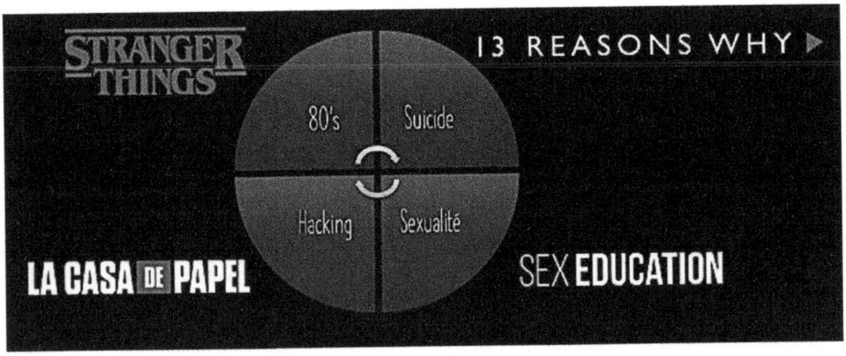

Figure 12.7. *Transmediagenic promotional narratives. For a color version of this figure, see www.iste.co.uk/pinede/digital.zip*

Ultimately, this unadvertization does indeed tend to consolidate Netflix's societal positioning by investing the public space in a logic of hyperadvertization, "that is to say at the confluence of the combined waves of advertization and unadvertization, [which] goes beyond the professional field of media and marketing and takes a political turn" (Patrin-Leclère et al. 2014, p. 192). Moreover, this reflection is in line with the thoughts of Soulages (2013), when he apprehends advertising discourse as "a space of beliefs concerning the identities, roles and social practices of a given community" (p. 39).

2 Downloadable from www.sexeducation.fr.

Indeed, this researcher points out that, behind the curtains of the advertising spectacle, what is being acted out is not a reflection of reality, but a plethora of advertising avatars, places of inscription of imaginations. Imagination being understood in the sense of Charaudeau (2005), namely as "an image of reality, but as this image interprets reality, brings it into a universe of meanings" (p. 158). By studying these possible worlds through "augmented storytelling" (Bourdaa 2012) and the promotion strategy of the Netflix original series, the platform appears as a new guarantor of the hypermodern individual, supplanting the role of the government by taking on its role as a social influencer. With the decline of the large traditional structures of meaning, Netflix clearly demonstrates the entry of its brand – as an autonomous semiotic entity – into a hypermodern phase, leaning toward a political positioning as media guide.

12.5. References

Barthes, R. (1964). Rhétorique de l'image. *Communication*, 4(1), 40–51.

Bénézech, M. and Lavigne, M. (2016). Jouer le documentaire. *Entrelacs*, 12(1) [Online]. Available at: http://journals.openedition.org/entrelacs/1841 [Accessed 31 May 2021].

Bihay, T. and Aubrun, F. (2015). L'écrin médiatique comme prétexte publicitaire : l'exemple des webséries de marque. In *Colloque doctoral international. Le scénario comme prétexte*. Leuven and Louvain-la-Neuve, 24–25 October.

Bô, D. and Guével, M. (2009). *Brand content : comment les marques se transforment en médias*. Dunod, Paris.

Boullier, D. (2019). *Sociologie du numérique*. Armand Colin, Paris.

Bourdaa, M. (2012). Le transmédia : entre narration augmentée et logiques immersives [Online]. Available at: https://larevuedesmedias.ina.fr/le-transmedia-entre-narration-augmentee-et-logiques-immersives [Accessed 31 May 2021].

Charaudeau, P. (2005). *Le discours politique : les masques du pouvoir*. Vuibert, Paris.

Citton, Y. (2014). *Pour une écologie de l'attention*. Le Seuil, Paris.

Dolezel, L. (1998). *Heterocosmica: Fiction and Possible Worlds*. The Johns Hopkins University Press, Baltimore.

Esquenazi, J.-P. (2010). *Les séries télévisées : l'avenir du cinéma ?* Armand Colin, Paris.

Fish, S. (1980). *Is There a Text in This Class?* Harvard University Press, Cambridge.

Glove, S. (2016). Scénariser le rôle et le pouvoir d'agir de l'utilisateur : vers une typologie interactionnelle du documentaire interactif. *Entrelacs*, 12(1) [Online]. Available at: http://journals.openedition.org/entrelacs/1840 [Accessed 31 May 2021].

Goffman, E. (1991). *Les cadres de l'expérience*. Éditions de Minuit, Paris.

Guéneau, C. (2006). Du spectateur à l'interacteur ? *Médiamorphoses*, 18, 68–73.

Jenkins, H. (2006). *Convergence Culture. Where Old and New Media Collide*. NYU Press, New York.

Laurichesse, H. (2016). Le versant promotionnel du webdocumentaire dans les univers fictionnels transmédiatiques. *Entrelacs*, 12(1) [Online]. Available at: http://journals.openedition.org/entrelacs/1876 [Accessed 31 May 2021].

Lehu, J.-M. (2006). *La publicité est dans le film*. Éditions d'Organisation, Paris.

Lipovetsky, G. and Serroy, J. (2013). *L'Esthétisation du monde : vivre à l'âge du capitalisme artiste*. Gallimard, Paris.

Marion, P. (1997). Narratologie médiatique et médiagénie des récits. *Recherches en communication*, 7, 61–88.

Oliveri, N., Espinosa, M., Waty-Viarouge, C. (2017). *La création de contenus au cœur de la stratégie de communication : storytelling, brand content, inbound marketing*. L'Harmattan, Paris.

Patrin-Leclère, V., Marti de Montety, C., Berthelot-Guiet, K. (2014). *La fin de la publicité ? Tours et contours de la dépublicitarisation*. Le Bord de L'eau, Lormont.

Perticoz, L. (2019). Filière de l'audiovisuel et plateformes SVOD : une analyse croisée des stratégies de Disney et Netflix. *tic&société*, 13(1–2) [Online]. Available at: https://journals.openedition.org/ticetsociete/3470 [Accessed 25 August 2021].

Semprini, A. (1996). *Analyser la communication : comment analyser les images, les médias, la publicité*. L'Harmattan, Paris.

Semprini, A. (2005). *La marque : une puissance fragile*. Vuibert, Paris.

Semprini, A. (2007). *Analyser la communication 2 : regards sociosémiotiques*. L'Harmattan, Paris.

Soulages, J.-C. (2013). L'ordre du discours publicitaire. *Semen*, 36, 39–52.

List of Authors

Géraud AHOUANDJINOU
Université d'Abomey-Calavi
Cotonou
Benin

Frédéric AUBRUN
Omnes Education
INSEEC
Lyon
France

Agnès BADOU
Université d'Abomey-Calavi
Cotonou
Benin

Thomas BIHAY
GERiiCO
Université de Lille
France

Mélanie BOURDAA
MICA
Université Bordeaux Montaigne
Pessac
France

Christelle CHAUZAL-LARGUIER
Communication et Sociétés
Université Clermont Auvergne
Clermont-Ferrand
France

Thierry CÔME
LAREQUOI
Université de Paris-Saclay
Guyancourt
France

Julien FALGAS
Crem
Université de Lorraine
Metz
France

Alexander FRAME
TIL
Université de Bourgogne
Dijon
France

Anh Ngoc HOANG
CHUS
Université Catholique de l'Ouest
Angers
France

Ismène KPÉDJO
Université d'Abomey-Calavi
Cotonou
Benin

Mariannig LE BÉCHEC
ELICO
Université Claude-Bernard Lyon 1
France

Cécile-Marie MARTIN
Université des Antilles
Pointe-à-Pitre
France

Luc MASSOU
Crem
Université de Lorraine
Metz
France

Sandra MELLOT
ESMA
CinéCréatis Nantes
France

Patrick MPONDO-DICKA
LERASS
Université Toulouse 2 – Jean-Jaurès
France

Will NOONAN
TIL
Université de Bourgogne
Dijon
France

Marcy Delsione OVOUNDAGA
GRESEC
Université Grenoble Alpes
Échirolles
France

Nathalie PINÈDE
MICA
Université Bordeaux Montaigne
Pessac
France

Magali PRODHOMME
CHUS
Université Catholique de l'Ouest
Angers
France

Stela RAYTCHEVA
LAREQUOI
Université de Paris-Saclay
Guyancourt
France

Marion ROLLANDIN
Communication et Sociétés
Université Clermont Auvergne
Clermont-Ferrand
France

Gilles ROUET
LAREQUOI
Université de Paris-Saclay
Guyancourt
France

Sébastien ROUQUETTE
Communication et Sociétés
Université Clermont Auvergne
Clermont-Ferrand
France

Peter STOCKINGER
INALCO
Plidam
Paris
France

Anaïs THEVIOT
CHUS
Université Catholique de l'Ouest
Angers
France

Ornheilia ZOUNON
Université d'Abomey-Calavi
Cotonou
Benin

Index

F, G, I

L, M, N

P, S

T, U, V, W

Printed and bound by CPI Group (UK) Ltd, Croydon, CR0 4YY

13/09/2026

14960998-0007